The Original Teachings of Jesus

THE ORIGINAL TEACHINGS OF JESUS

Everything you always wanted to know, now revealed.
An absolute must read for lovers of Jesus

HAJEE MAHBOOB KASSIM

© Hajee Mahboob Kassim 1971
This revised edition 2018

All rights reserved. No part of this publication may be reproduced, stored in a retrieval system, or transmitted, in any form or by any means, electronic, mechanical, photocopying, recording or otherwise without the prior permission of the author.

Perpustakaan Negara Malaysia   Cataloguing-in-Publication Data

Hajee Mahboob Kassim, 1920-2000
   The Original Teachings of Jesus/ Hajee Mahboob Kassim.
   ISBN 978-967-0729-30-5
   1. Jesus Christ--Teachings. 2. Jesus Christ--Islamic interpretations. 3. Christianity and other religions--Islam. I. Title.
   236.9

This revised edition published in 2018 by

DAR AL WAHI PUBLICATION
House of Revelation (Co. No. 001592307-T)
P.O. Box 12909, 50792 Kuala Lumpur, Malaysia
Email: daralwahi@yahoo.com ▪ Website: www.daralwahi.com

Malaysian distributor
A. S. NOORDEEN (Co. No. 000271801-D)
P.O. BOX 42 – Gombak, 53800 Kuala Lumpur, Malaysia
Tel: (603) 4023 6003
www.asnislamicbooks.com

Cover design, layout & typesetting by
DAR AL WAHI PUBLICATION, Graphics Department

Contents

The Author's Note vii

Acknowledgment xi

PART 1
The cause of disunity amongst mankind

1. The origin of religion 3
2. Nimrod—the genius mastermind 9
3. Abraham—the friend of God—sent to destroy Nimrod, the evil genius 57
4. The life of Abraham 99
5. Important events connected with prophets 161
6. Buddhism 185

PART 2
The Religions of the Advanced Western Civilisation

7. The miraculous conception and birth of Holy Jesus 191
8. The day and date of the birth of Holy Jesus 203
9. The teachings of Holy Jesus 209
10. The mission of Holy Jesus 359
11. The fruits of disobedience to Holy Jesus 443

The Author's Note

This treatise is based on extracts from works of learned scholars, researchers, scientists and several rare manuscripts—among which some are the only copies known to be in existence.

Readers of this book may be surprised at the disclosures made herein and wonder why such vital facts have been suppressed and concealed!

Those unfamiliar with the Qur'an will be delighted to pursue the detailed and venerated accounts of the *dedication* of the Virgin Mary by her mother *from even before her birth!* As also the descriptions of the miraculous conception and birth of the Holy Jesus, which occur in numerous surahs (Chapters), some of which have been presented in this volume. They include how *baby Jesus from his cradle, miraculously defended the virginity of his mother,* when she was accused by Jewish ladies of an illicit relationship and that the *date of his birth is a blessed day, which however is not Christmas day!* These bring out the many wonderful aspects of this momentous event not even known to the readers of the New Testament.

The excerpts reproduced in this research are based amongst other sources on the "*Gospel of Barnabas*". So a few lines are given hereunder as to who is the author of this Gospel.

Saint Barnabas

Saint Barnabas was a Levite Jew from Cyprus. His name was Joses. Barnabas was not his name nor his family title. He met Holy Jesus, son of Virgin Mary (peace of God be on them). He was so much influenced by Jesus that he sold all his properties. He donated the entire proceeds for the propagation of the teachings of Jesus (Acts 4:36-37). He became a very ardent follower of Jesus. Under the personal dictations of Jesus he recorded the Evangel of Jesus in Hebrew Language, the mother-tongue of Jesus. These dictations of Jesus were written down in the presence of Jesus before his departure from earthly life.

For his devotion to Jesus he was given in Hebrew the title of "'Bar Nabuha". "Bar" means "Son of", whilst "Nabuha" means "of the Nabi *i.e.*, Prophet". This title of Barnabuha or "Son of the Prophet" was given by all the Jewish Prophets to their religious heir or successor. For example the Barnabuha of Moses was Joshua, of Samuel was David, of David was Solomon, of Elijah was Elisha, of Elisha was Jehu, of Zakariah was his son John, of John the Baptist was Jesus when he anointed Jesus. Hence the title of Barnabas the Greek form of Barnabuha means that the Levite Jew Joses was made the Barnabuha or the spiritual heir by Holy Jesus. Thus by this appointment it was the duty of St. Barnabas to carry on the real teachings of Jesus after he was lifted to heaven.

The copy of a Gospel written in Hebrew in the personal handwriting of St. Barnabas was found in 382 A.D. lying upon his chest, during an excavation in Cyprus when the grave of St. Barnabas was disclosed. The said Gospel was intact. As if it had just been placed inside the grave. So also was the body of St. Barnabas. Both of these are no doubt miracles. Otherwise both the Gospel and the body of St. Barnabas could not have remained intact for over 300 years in the damp Mediterranean climate.

Often I sit in amazement and wonder as to how the several thousands of quotations have come into my hands out of the many hundreds of books which have gone into the compilation of this treatise. I well realise that single handed I could never have collected so many references even in fifty years, working ten hours per day. Then comes the question of the numerous subjects delved into. I think that it is necessary frankly to disclose this secret.

When I was ordained a Khalifa, *i.e.*, spiritual head, of Chishty Musharafi Sufi School in 1958, I was ordered to write a book in English that would be beneficial to mankind by His Holiness Khwaja Diwan Syed Enayat Hussain Ali Khan Moini Chishty of Ajmer (a descendant of His Holiness Khwaja Syed Moinuddin Hasan Chishty of Ajmer, the Patron Saint of the Indian subcontinent).

For five years *i.e.* until 1963, I groped in the dark during which I noted numerous quotations in a subject-wise index from the Qur'an. But *still I did not have any topic upon which to write.* What was I to do? His Holiness Khwaja Diwan Syed Enayat Hussain had already departed from earthly life in 1959.

It was in this state of perplexity that I prayed in 1963 to my Patron Saint His Holiness Khwaja Syed Moinuddin Hasan Chishty of Ajmer (peace of Allah be upon him) for spiritual guidance. As if by a miracle, I became an instrument in his hands. People unknown to me started coming to me from all walks of life between 1963 and 1970, as if drawn by some magnetic force, with various books on numerous topics. I gave them a patient hearing and copied down the passages they referred to or made extracts from the books they loaned to me for a week or so. Many of them never came back to meet me again. In this extremely mysterious and unexplainable manner I got not only the materials but also the various topics and headings to be included—Truth is sometimes more fantastic than fiction!

So I humbly surrendered myself, and did exactly according to the spiritual guidance of this saint, who has left this earth about seven and a half centuries ago! As such all credit for this wonderful book must go to my Patron Saint His Holiness Khwaja Syed Moinuddin Hasan Chishty of Ajmer (d. 6th Rajab 630 A.H. / 1233 A.D.).

The result of this spiritual guidance is such that not only each chapter but even every heading and sub-heading is a wonderful masterpiece, with something highly logical or scientific or novel or interesting from which people of goodwill all over the world can derive knowledge.

**The Good Lord, Almighty and Kind,
Let this be a Guidance to Humankind.**

Hajee Mahboob Kassim
Calcutta, 6th August 1971

Acknowledgment

The author takes this opportunity of expressing his gratitude to Ameerali A. Gangjee, Asgarali A. Gangjee and Faiyaz Ahmed for the loan of numerous books and to Sk. Enayatullah of the National Library, Calcutta for procuring numerous books which have assisted in compiling this research and to Aga Afzal Mirza and Pratap Chunder Bonnerjee for editing and Mr Bonnerjee for also reading the proofs of this treatise.

The author also wishes to thank the authors, publishers and authors' representatives for permission to use excerpts from their books, articles, *etc.*

Part 1
THE CAUSE OF DISUNITY AMONGST MANKIND

Chapter 1

The Origin of Religion

A. The beginning

As mankind multiplied from the children of Adam, people started becoming wicked and disobedient to the Creator. The people renounced the Almighty and his Divine Laws sent through Adam, who thus became the first prophet or messenger of God. He guided his descendants—mankind—until his death at the ripe old age of 930 years (Genesis 5:5).

Time and again Prophet after Prophet was sent by the Lord to show the right path and to correct the wicked by means of more laws to be observed.

As all the efforts of these Prophets could not stem the tide of wickedness, so a very great Prophet was sent in the Seventh Century of man's existence. He was Prophet Enoch (called "Idris" in Arabic) who was born when Adam was 622 years old. He was the most learned man during the pre-deluge period and introduced the spinning of cotton into yarn and its weaving into cloth. He also invented writing upon parchments. At the age of 365 years he was bodily lifted up to heaven alive (Genesis 5:23-24)

B. The early calculation of day, week and months

In that period a day ended when the Sun set. The new month

began when the new moon was visible to the naked eye. A week consisted of seven days. The days of the week did not have any separate names as at present. Except for the first day which was called "*Shamba*" and the seventh day which was called "*Jumma*" or the "Day of Gathering" together for prayers or "Sabbath day", the other days were numbered as follows:

a. Shamba was the day of commencement of the week. This is equivalent to our Saturday.

b. One day after Shamba equals Sunday

c. Two days after Shamba equals Monday

d. Three days after Shamba equals Tuesday

e. Four days after Shamba equals Wednesday

f. Five days after Shamba or night before Jumma equals Thursday

g. Jumma or the gathering day for prayers equals Friday, the day when everybody gathered to observe prayers. No work was allowed on this day. Hence it became the "Sabbath" day.

This ancient system of the day, week and month calculation from the time of Adam is still prevalent throughout the Muslim world.

At that prehistoric time the first six days of the week were spent in looking after worldly affairs and the seventh or last day of the week or Jumma, was reserved wholly for prayers as will be evident from:

"And God blessed the seventh day of the week and sanctified it ..." (Genesis 2: 3).

The rules for the observance of the Sabbath were very strict as will appear from the Fourth Commandment. Those breaking them were to be stoned to death. That no relaxation was to be allowed under any circumstances is evident from the fact that the Israelites were obliged to observe the Sabbath even during their forty years' wanderings in the wilderness.

C. The two Fallen Angels

During the period of Enoch two angels named Horus and Marduk or Merodach approached God Almighty and placed before Him their complaint that:

> "O Lord! see how wicked the people of the earth are becoming, yet You have made them the Viceroy over all Your creations whilst we the Angels only hymn Thy praise day and night" (Qur'an 2: 30).

> "If we are sent on earth we shall be able to prove that we are superior to them and deserve the higher position".

These two angels were amongst the cleverest of the heavenly host. God warned them that because they had full knowledge of the rewards in heaven and they had studied *"Lauhae Mahfooz"* (*i.e.* the preserved table containing all the laws of God in heaven in which all kinds of knowledge and power are recorded) they would be severely punished if they broke any orders of God during their stay on earth. They agreed. God gave them the *"Nafs Ammara"* or the animal instinct in man which tempts man to commit sins in addition to *"Nafs Lauama"* or the "Conscience" which they as angels already possessed and which draws man towards goodness and perfection (for greater details please refer to the book *Destruction or Peace,* chapter 17: B-4).

Horus and Marduk led perfect lives for a while trying to teach goodness to mankind and set themselves up as models. But soon a very beautiful married Persian woman named "Bedhas" enticed them with her charms and got them to take wine, murder her husband and worship an idol before she would permit them to commit adultery with her. They fell for her charms and after taking wine they murdered her husband and committed idolatry before she permitted them to commit adultery (pages 133-134, Vol. I, *Tafrihul Askia Fil Ahwal Ul Ambia*).

Now they realised that they were doomed. So they went running to Prophet Enoch requesting him to plead for them before God. Enoch told them that he would pray for them on the coming Jumma or Sabbath Friday. But his prayers went unanswered. So he told the angels that he would pray for them again during the next Jumma or Sabbath Friday. On the second Sabbath Friday he was informed that a choice was given to the two fallen angels of either receiving punishment on earth or on the Day of Judgment. They preferred to be punished on earth because the punishment on earth would eventually have an end to it, whilst the punishment on the Day of Judgment would be eternal.

So their punishment was that they were hung upside down in an underground well tied with chains and are to be whipped continuously until this earth is totally destroyed by some catastrophe into fragments and ashes. They would remain alive till the destruction of this earth. This underground chamber is in a concealed cave with a shaft or passage with numerous steps leading deep into the bowels of the earth at a place called "Babel" (Pages 134-136, Vol. I, *ibid*).

Human beings will only be able to contact them very occasionally *i.e.* say once in hundreds of years and that also with a great amount of troubles, obstacles and dangers to life. Whenever contacted the fallen angels could teach them Magic and all sciences they wanted to know after warning them that they would lose their souls and be severely punished (pages 137-139, Vol. I, *ibid*).

D. The Deluge

Eventually mankind became so wicked that instead of worshipping God they took to idolatry. They completely violated the sanctity of sexual morals and marriage and prided themselves on their broadmindedness and freedom. Every man and woman indulged in any sexual abuse that gave pleasure. The present world conditions are similar.

So angry was God at all this that He destroyed every living thing on the face of the earth by drowning them in a great deluge during 2370 B.C. save and except Noah, his wife, his three believing sons and their three wives and a few pairs of animals *i.e.* those who went into the Ark were saved (Genesis 7: 7-9).

Thus mankind started afresh to inhabit the earth through the three sons of Noah (Genesis 9: 1, 7, 18-19). Everybody in the new generations were warned of the terrible devastation that God Almighty had perpetrated upon them for their disobedience, sexual indulgence and idolatry.

God promised that He would never again destroy the whole of mankind by water (Genesis 9: 9-17). This time the warning is that the wicked disobedient mankind will be destroyed by Fire—a clear indication towards a Nuclear Holocaust!

Chapter 2

Nimrod—The Genius Mastermind

A. The curse of Noah

After the great deluge it so happened that one day Noah had got drunk, and his clothes fell off his body (Genesis 9: 21). His son Ham, seeing the nakedness of his father made fun of it before his two elder brothers (Genesis 9: 22). When Noah came to know of it, he cursed Ham and his children (Genesis 9: 24-26).

The cursed Ham gave birth to a number of sons. One of them was Cush (Genesis 10: 6). Just before his death Cush took a beautiful young virgin named Semiramis for a wife. He died on the very next day after he had consummated his marriage with Semiramis, who thus became pregnant. Approximately nine months later in or about 2275 B.C. Semiramis gave birth to a posthumous son, now famous under the title of Nimrod. She claimed that she was a virgin and that Nimrod was a divine child born without any human contact. The Holy Bible refutes this false claim as follows:

"And Cush, begat Nimrod: he began to be a mighty one in the earth" (Genesis 10: 8).

Thus it is observed that Nimrod was the great-grandson of Noah through his cursed son Ham!

In all his three hundred and fifty years after the deluge, Noah did not make himself king over his human family, even though he was the family head of the whole human race (Genesis 9: 28). The reason apparently was that he looked upon the true God as his Ruler and King. Therefore, so long as Noah was alive, no question arose of any one being made a king over the human race.

Noah died in 2020 B.C. But Nimrod forcibly made himself the first king of mankind after the deluge from about 2250 B.C. or about 230 years before the death of Noah. This is confirmed by the extensive research carried out by the Watch Tower Bible and Tract Society of Pennsylvania under the title of *"Babylon the Great Has Fallen God's Kingdom Rules"*.

The first edition of 1963 records as follows on page 23:

"Nimrod, the first king reported among mankind, was not 'king by the grace of God'. We can see this from the purpose for which his capital city (Babylon) was built and from the attitude God took towards it".

B. The meaning of Nimrod

Nimrod (or in Hebrew "Na-marood") has been derived from the Hebrew verb "Marad" which means "To rebel".

In this case the name "Namarood" would be actually the first person, plural number of the verb "Marad" in the jussive mood and would mean "We will rebel" or "Let us rebel" (page 21, *Babylon the Great Has Fallen! God's Kingdom Rules*).

On page 22 of *ibid* is the following:

"If the name Nimrod is thus taken from the verb meaning to rebel, then this name must have been given to this man after he had started out on his rebellious course; it was not the name given to him at birth. But regardless of the exact meanings of his name, Nimrod displayed rebellion against Jehovah God in starting world politics and setting himself up as king. Babylon, his capital, thus was a kingdom in rebellion against God, the Universal Sovereign. So from her very start she was no part of the Universal organisation of Jehovah God, and Babylon never became part of it later on. She was never a kingdom of God. She never departed from her opposition to God".

True to his title of "Nimrod", this grandson of the cursed Ham, has become the source and origin of wickedness, rebellion and blasphemy throughout the earth.

C. The popularity of Nimrod

The Encyclopedia Britannica, Volume 24, edition of 1911, page 617, under Semiramis gives the following information:

> "Of this we already have evidence in (the ancient Greek historian) Herodotus, who ascribes to her the banks that confined the Euphrates (i. 184) and knows her name as borne by a gate of Babylon (iii. 155) ... according to the legends, in her birth as well as in her disappearance from earth, Semiramis appears as a goddess, the daughter of the fish-goddess Atargatis, and herself connected with the doves of Ishtar or Astarte" (see also Hislop's *"The Two Babylons"*, pages 86 and 270).

Nimrod was brought up by Semiramis, an exceptionally clever woman, as a spoilt son, a mother's darling. He was himself very intelligent, a great leader of men, a fearless hunter, a mighty fighter in rebellion against the One True God (Genesis 10: 8-10).

Later as he grew up into a fine specimen of the radiance of youth, his jealous mother, the beautiful queen Semiramis made him her husband also. Thus Semiramis was both mother and wife of Nimrod! On page 356 of *"The Golden Bough"* by Sir James George Frazer—Abridged Edition published in 1950 by Macmillan & Co. Ltd., London, it is recorded as follows:

"The worship of the Great Mother of gods and her lover or son was very popular under the Roman Empire. Inscriptions prove that the two received divine honours ... not only in Italy and especially at Rome, but also in the provinces, particularly in Africa, Spain, Portugal, France, Germany and Bulgaria. *Their worship survived the establishment of Christianity by Constantine*; for Symachus records the recurrence of the festival of the Great Mother and in the days of Augustine her effeminate priests still paraded the streets and squares of Carthage ..."

It was the mother and son who discovered the manufacture of burnt clay bricks and cuneiform clay tablets which were burnt after being written on to make permanent records and established the first empire in the world with several other important and beautiful cities (Genesis 10: 10-11). Nimrod's popularity as the first King of Mankind, his clever administration at the guidance of his mother-wife, and his novel ideas (such as even shooting and killing God Almighty) knew no bounds as will be seen later.

On page 22 of the research *"Babylon the Great has Fallen!"* one reads that ancient Jewish historians have come to the finding that it was Nimrod who excited mankind to affront and condemn God. He persuaded them that their success in building Babel (*"Bab"* means gate or gateway whilst *"El"* means "the perfection". Therefore Babel stands for the gateway to success, progress, and perfection) with its bridge across the Euphrates, its palaces, temples and its hanging gardens were not the work of God but that these achievements were the work of mankind by their intelligence, under his guidance and leadership.

> Hence God was something to be ignored and for whom no necessity existed. The people should rely only upon the strength of their arms and their skill if they wanted success in life. It was defeatism and cowardice to put the blame for ones shortcomings on God who did not come into the picture.

This has become the genesis on which all atheistic religions have since been based!

Anybody who refused to accept Nimrod was tortured and if he still dissented then he was put to death. Accordingly a reign of tyranny was started against the believers in the God of Noah. Nimrod thus wiped out all opposition to his Anti-God teachings.

D. Source of Nimrod's dynamic Power and knowledge

Christian Churches and the learned European Scholars have carried out extensive researches, a few of which are listed below:

1. "*Babylon The Great Has Fallen!—God's Kingdom Rules*," by Watch Tower Bible & Tract Society of Pennsylvania published in 1963.

2. "*The Two Babylons*" by The Rev. Alexander Hislop, published in 1953.

3. "*The Golden Bough*" by Sir James George Frazer— published 1950 by Macmillan & Co. Ltd., London.

From these it appears that throughout the universe Nimrod is the source of mischief and wickedness, which did not die with him but is still continuing to influence many millions all over the world although over four thousand years have passed since. One does feel dumbfounded and puzzled as to how this could have been possible!

Nimrod was born in 2275 B.C. about 95 years after the deluge. This was certainly a very short period for mankind *i.e.* members of Noah's family to acquire the vast knowledge that the genius Nimrod has displayed *viz*:

1. The first use of irrigation in the valleys of the Tigris and Euphrates for agriculture (This knowledge, of building dams and digging canals was carried to Egypt from here).

2. The first extraction of copper.

3. The invention of manufacture of bronze.

4. Invention of sexagesimal system which divides a circle into 360 degrees, a degree into 60 minutes and a minute into 60 seconds.

5. The division of the day into 24 hours, each hour to consist of 60 minutes divided into 60 seconds. The new date commences from midnight instead of "Sun Set" as the time of Sun Set varied from day to day, hence this was not a scientific method according to Nimrod.

6. Astronomy.

7. The twelve constellations of the Zodiac.

8. The calculation of the solar year comprising 365 days, 5 hours, 49 minutes and 30 seconds. (These ideas were taken to Egypt from here).

9. The division of the solar year into twelve months according to the twelve constellations of the Zodiac.

10. The calculation of the Horoscope based upon the Zodiac.

11. Astrology, palmistry and forecasting.

12. Making burnt clay bricks for buildings.

13. Mathematical calculations for large buildings, bridges, temples, palaces, and dams.

14. Cuneiform Tablets.

15. Magic, the art of Witchcraft *i.e.* how to influence people without their realising this fact.

16. The alteration of the commencement of the week from Saturday to "Dies Solis" or Sun-god's day and the naming of the days after the various deities *i.e.* Sun's day, Moon's

day *etc.*

These and so many other notions and the prowess, which he displayed during his life, fill one with wonder and amazement as to how he could possibly have acquired so much knowledge, out of practically nothing. The high degree of perfection is evident from the fact that in these 4,000 years we have not advanced much further on many aspects of these subjects beyond what he has disclosed—especially in the calculation of the Solar Year, the method of computing and dividing days, hours, minutes, the twelve Zodiacal constellations, Astrology, Palmistry, and the Horoscope for forecasting.

It was Nimrod, who calculated and showed the "Precession of Equinox" with the same accuracy as done by astronomers of today, at "fifty second nine thirds and three fourths of a third of a degree" in a year, and by such calculation it can be computed that it takes the sun 2,150 years to retrograde out of one sign, of the Zodiac into another. Hence he calculated the precession of equinox during his period was in the constellation of Aries *i.e.* from 2537 B.C. to 388 B.C. The people who went to Egypt from the Tower of Babel carried this knowledge with them and the old records of Egypt show this calculation by their priests.

Whilst on such subjects as "Magic", "Witchcraft" and how to influence other people to his ways of thought without their being aware of it or being able to get out of the spell cast, we the human race are still today far, far behind the powers he had attained and displayed.

Although four thousand years have gone by yet the research by the Christian Church and European Scholars show that many millions of people are still under his magical spell and influence due to which they are following mechanically his religious teachings without even realising what they are doing!

This is very vividly brought out in the Holy Bible as:

"Babylon ... made *all The Earth* drunken: the nations have drunken her wine; therefore the nations are *Mad*" (Jeremiah 51: 7).

The question is how he acquired such wondrous knowledge. The answer is found in the following books of research:

1. "*Tafrihul Askia Fil Ahwal Ul Ambia*" written between 1261 and 1300 A.H. by Abul Mohsin Hasan Alvi Kakori, son of Abul Hasan Hussain Alvi. The Fourth Edition was published in two volumes by Munshi Navalkishore, Lucknow in Urdu in 1342 A.H. / March 1924.

2. "*Ashan ul Muwaiz*" written by Abdul Wahed, son of Muhammad Mogni, assisted by Khan Bahadur Hakim Md. Ahsanullah. The original was written in Persian and completed in the year 1265 A.H. / 1848 A.D. Translated into Urdu by Syed Bakr Hussain Khan, son of Syed Ali Naqi Khan. Seventh Edition published by Munshi Navalkishore, Lucknow in 1926 in two volumes.

There are several such researches. They all give the same basic information although derived independently from different sources.

Semiramis and Nimrod acquired their vast and intricate knowledge in so short a time from Horus and Marduk, the two fallen angels, who are hanging suspended in the underground well at Babel (pages 134-139, Vol. I, *Tafrihul Askia Fil Ahwal Ul Ambia*).

That is the reason why his "Magical" influence has been so very great that even though four thousand years have passed, yet the Hypnotic "Spell" cast by him on mankind, which he had learnt from these two fallen angels, is still so very powerful and long-lasting that once a person entered Nimrodism by "Baptism" which is a ceremony of bathing in the waters (for greater details please refer to book *Destruction or Peace*, chapter 5: F-4), even if belonging to a Godly faith would soon find themselves ensnared into it. Their children, generation after generation, would automatically continue to follow and observe Nimrod's teachings and adore him as "The only begotten son of god born of the great virgin mother". In spite of all efforts mankind still finds it extremely difficult to divest itself of the religion of Nimrod. Once they have been "Baptised" they thus come so much under the influence of his magical spell on the "Baptised" even after all these four thousand years that they still feel helpless to break away from it. Therefore, they refuse to listen to reason as if enchanted. It is quite apparent to an outside observer that they are under some kind of spell which mars their free thinking. The millions of pagans, who came under the influence of this religion, have carried with them Nimrodism, all over the world, ever since God Almighty broke up the unity of mankind at the tower of Babel, and scattered them all over the earth. Due to the change of languages, the names of this religion have altered from place to place. But the religion of Nimrod and his principles have remained constant for thousands of years even where there was no contact between one group of people and another for thousands of years *e.g.* the natives of Central America and Peru. When the European discoverers first landed in Central America they found that their religion was being already followed by the natives.

The Pagan Europeans had been converted from Baalism to Mithraism with the spread of the Roman Empire from Asia Minor to England. Both these religions had their origin in Nimrod, hence in principle they were identical. The Roman Emperor Constantine has continued "Nimrodism" but under a new name coined by him. This religion has spread throughout Europe according to the research of the Church and the European Scholars.

The last of the religious books briefly refers to the source of Nimrod's vast knowledge and magical powers as follows:

> "... but the devils (this is a reference to King Nimrod, Queen Semiramis and their priests of the temple tower of Babel) disbelieved (in God's teachings), teaching mankind magic and that which was revealed (*i.e.* Astrology, Zodiac, Horoscope, Forecasting *etc.*) to the two angels *In Babel*, Horus (in Arabic Harut) and Marduk or Merodach (in Arabic Marut). Nor did they (the two angels) teach it to anyone till they had said: Beware we (*i.e.* our knowledge) are a temptation, therefore disbelieve not (in the guidance of Allah). And from these two (fallen angels, certain) people learnt that (black magic) by which they cause division between man and wife (or equally between mankind in general and the right path of Allah); but they injure thereby no-one save to that extent as Allah tolerates. And they thereby learn that (*i.e.* magic and the religious principles of Nimrod) which harmeth them and profiteth them not. And surely they do know that he who trafficketh therein will have no (happy) portion in the Hereafter: and surely evil is the price for which they sell their souls, if they but knew" (Qur'an 2: 102).

This brief quotation from the Qur'an makes it apparent that:

1. Nimrod chose this site for his capital and named it Babel (or The Gateway to progress, success and perfection) because it was here that he acquired from the two fallen angels his vastly superior knowledge which has remained more or less the same for the past 4,000 years defying further developments in many fields of scientific knowledge. As far as the art of "Black Magic" is concerned it is almost dead and very little of it is left because the more important and very powerful "charm" practised by Nimrod was not disclosed by him to mankind. This was his most powerful secret weapon. It has disappeared with him. This is better appreciated when it is realised that in

all other fields, scientists have acquired further knowledge hundreds of times more in the last two centuries but their learning and advancement have not been able to improve much upon what was disclosed by Nimrod especially as far as it concerns the calculations of a Day, Hours, Minutes, Solar Year, a circle, Astrology, Zodiacal calculations, Horoscope, Forecasting and Black Magic. These seem to be complete in themselves. They defy further new theories to outdate what Nimrod taught as far back as four millennia ago.

2. In honour of these two angels, his tutors, Nimrod built in Babylon, the temple to Marduk a little to the south of the tower of Babel whilst the group that went to Egypt built temples in honour of Horus, whom they called the "only begotten son of God".

As these angels Marduk and Horus could only be contacted once in hundreds of years and that also after undergoing great trials, dangers and difficulties, so they could not be encountered by most people, hence their names have been identified with that of Nimrod, resulting in further deification of this master-mind.

(a) The principles relating to the birth of a Divine Son

Legends relating to Nimrod's miraculous birth are based upon Zodiacal calculations. In the last week of December on a clear night one sees above his head the three bright stars (called the three kings) of the belt of Orion pointing to the East. Soon rises the star Sirus (called the Herald of the sun-god or the Messianic star) the brightest of all the host of heaven. It is followed by the rising of the constellation of Virgo or "virgin" at about midnight, which announces the birth of the son of sun-god by the virgin queen of the heavens. Daylight hours in the Northern hemisphere reach their minimum on the 24th December, which was taken to indicate that the rule of the power of "Sun god" had reached its minimum. Hence if a "son" is born at midnight of 24th/25th December then each day as he will grow bigger little by little so also would he cause the daylight to increase each day little by little from this date.

This is interpreted by the Pagans to mean that as the son of sun-god starts growing bigger from this moment, so also he is chasing away bit by bit the evil darkness from the wicked world, which he has come to save by the sacrifice of his precious and sacred life.

(b) The celebration of the birth of the Divine Son

These are the bases of the belief that Nimrod or Baal or Mithra *etc.* was accordingly born of a virgin mother at midnight on 24th/25th December in a cave. His birth is celebrated at midnight and as soon as midnight of 24th/25th December was reached, a Light used to be lighted and bells of joy rung and music commenced and everybody would exclaim with joy:

"The Virgin has brought forth, the light is waxing" and start singing hymns in praise of "Sun-god" for the favour of "This only begotten and beloved son come to redeem the sinners".

The Messianic star (*i.e.* Sirus) announced the birth of "son of god" and the three kings from afar (the three stars in Orion's belt) paid homage to him (by pointing towards the East).

From this origin has spread all over the earth the theory of the birth of "the only begotten son of the "Sun-god".

(c) The Holy Communion and sacramental food and drink

On this day everyone would fast for the whole day and many would even take a purgative so that all impurity (food) in the body would come out and the body could thus be cleansed and emptied.

Anyone coming to this great annual feast of the "Nativity of the Sun" would bring some food or drink to drop into this well before sitting down to pray.

Nimrod would appear on the magical well of "Eternal Life" with a light in his hand, dressed in the red-hooded robes of "Santa Claus" as soon as the constellation of "Virgo" arose at midnight. The bells would ring and the music commenced. Everyone would stand up and exclaim joyously:

> "The virgin has brought forth the only begotten son of god, now the light and power of the sun has commenced to increase".

A dry piece of log known as the "Yule log" would be placed there. Nimrod by the power of magic would cause a green tree to sprout out laden with gifts for those present. The dead Yule log indicated that goodness and piety had died amongst mankind. The sprouting of a fresh green tree signified the birth of a saviour, who would infuse new life into mankind. The gifts on the tree indicated that Nimrod was a gift from God to save the wicked. This is the origin of the Santa Claus, Xmas gifts and the Christmas tree.

Nimrod would announce: "I am the oblation, I am the sacrifice, I am the ancestral offering". Thus saying he would bless the consecrated food and drink from the well of Eternal Life which would mainly consist of Yule cakes, pork, goose flesh and wine and distribute it saying "Take this food, it is my flesh and take this wine, it is my blood and become the pure flesh and blood of the sinless deity, the only begotten son of God born of the great virgin mother, the queen of the heavens".

With this toast of *"Waes Haeil"* (meaning "become well" or

"become pure") they would start drinking. From it has come the word *"Wassail"* which has become equivalent with "to drink liquor". Toasting good wishes over drinks has come from this origin.

The holly wreath with its red and green colours and even the Mistletoe are sex symbols representing propagation of life. To kiss members of the opposite sex under them meant that the people were placing themselves under the spell of the deity of love *i.e.* "Cupid". This honour was bestowed upon Nimrod because of his ever-readiness to make love to any and every beautiful girl, he set his eyes upon. Thus he became the sweet-heart of all of them including his own mother who became his wife. St. Valentine is none other than the mighty hunter, Nimrod! Valentine's Day is celebrated on the 14th February to send tidings of love to one's sweet-heart.

As many as received Nimrod or believed in his teachings to such he taught magic and gave them powers to become "sons of god" whereby they believed they would attain eternal bliss and happiness.

Everyone would then go to this magical well of "Eternal Life" and ask for whatever extra helping of food or drink they liked. This food and drink would magically be served on plates and in glasses to them. Those eating and drinking them were filled with the magical feeling of rejuvenation and good health. Hence the "Well of Eternal Life".

After enjoying themselves the whole night, at the time of leaving they would ask the magical well to return the food or drinks they had dropped when they had come in. The well would return the very same food and drinks, not anything else! This was the sacred food which they preserved and gave to the sick or dying during the year which they believed would make them the pure and sinless deity, the only begotten son of god, thereby attaining *eternal happiness in the next life in the son of god.*

That this teaching of Nimrod has spread all over the world will be seen from the following studies:

"The Golden Bough" by James G. Frazer reads:

On page 488:

> "Of all the modes of purification adopted on these occasions none perhaps brings out the sacramental virtue of the rite so clearly as the Creek and Seminole practice of taking a purgative before swallowing the new corn. The intention is thereby to prevent the sacred food from being polluted by contact with common food in the stomach of the eater. For the same reasons Catholics partake of the Eucharist fasting".

> "The custom of eating bread sacramentally as the body of god was practised by the Aztecs before the discovery and conquest of Mexico by the Spaniards".

On page 490:

> "The doctrine of transubstantiation, or the magical conversion of bread into flesh, was also familiar to the Aryans of ancient India long before the spread and even the rise of Christianity. The Brahmans taught that the rice-cakes offered in sacrifice were substitutes for human beings, and that they were actually converted into the real bodies of men by the manipulation of the priests. We read that "when it (the rice-cake) still consists of rice-meal, it is the hair. When he pours water on it, it becomes skin. When he mixes it, it becomes flesh: for then it becomes consistent; and consistent also is the flesh. When it is baked, it becomes the bones: for then it becomes somewhat hard; and hard is the bone. And when he is about to take it off (the fire) and sprinkles it with butter, he changes it into marrow. This is the completeness which they call the, five-fold animal sacrifice".

> "Now, too, we can perfectly understand why on the day of

their solemn communion with the deity the Mexicans refused to eat any other food than the consecrated bread which they revered as the very flesh and bones of their god, and why up till noon they might drink nothing at all, not even water. They feared no doubt to defile the portion of god in their stomachs by contact with common things. A similar pious fear led the Creek and Seminole Indians, as we saw, to adopt the more thoroughgoing expedient of rinsing out their bodies by a strong purgative before they dared to partake of the sacrament of first fruits".

In Chapter 6 of *"Primitive Folk"* by Elie Reculus one reads:

"In the truly orthodox conception of sacrifice, the consecrated offering be it man, woman or virgin, lamb or heifer, cock or dove, represents the deity himself".

In the *"Bhagwat Gita,"* Lord Krishna says:

"I am the oblation, I am the sacrifice, I am the ancestral offering".

Thus the "Holy Communion" or the ancient "Eucharistic Ceremony" which was taught by Nimrod at the tower of "Babel" was being observed by his worshippers' right from India and China in the East to Mexico and Peru in the West from thousands of years before the birth of Jesus.

The most important question before the human race today is:|
Was Babylon's religion destroyed with it?
Or
Has the religion survived to this day in the form of Greater Babylonia?
If so:
In what form is it?
Who are its adherents?
By what names do they call themselves?

Because it naturally follows that as completely and

thoroughly as Babylon was destroyed in spite of all its advancements and achievements so also will the religion of Nimrod be destroyed and banished one day as thoroughly and completely from the face of the earth leaving behind perhaps a few minute and silent items of evidence of what disaster can also befall a scientifically advanced mankind for having incurred the wrath of the Almighty God.

The object of this research is to bring home to the world those significant facts which are not commonly known to the public at large. But nevertheless they are frightfully important for the safety of mankind in general. It was due to Nimrod's religion that disaster after disaster have haunted mankind from time to time. On a number of such occasions a section of the human race has been wiped out in some sudden manner. Some of such examples are Sodom, Gomorrah, Pompeii, the destruction of the Egyptian Army by drowning in the Red Sea, the destruction of Jerusalem twice, Babylon, the Jews in Nazi Germany and so many other cases. With all our scientific weapons of mass destruction very nearly the whole of the human race can easily be wiped out. Hence the intelligent are forced seriously to meditate upon:

Scientific World—Whither Bound?

To

Self Destruction!

or

Is Universal Peace Possible?

If so-By what means?

F. Nimrodism—Atheistic Paganism

Nimrod's exalted position of the infallible Pontifex Maximus encouraged the already proud and arrogant monarch completely to spite God and originate a rebellious religion; a challenge in which he could make a complete distortion of the True God, and

His laws.

Nimrod was an absolute atheist. He could not reconcile himself to the existence of a Supreme Divine Being, Who could not be seen or contacted. Therefore for him such a "God" was not a necessity and could well be done away with. He based all his successes upon his knowledge, strength and ability. All failures were put down to inefficiency or improper calculation or insufficient experimentation or wrong concepts. Thus it was shirking of responsibility and cowardice for anyone to put the blame for failures on the Supreme God who did not even exist according to him. Many scientists of today have the same conviction.

1. The only begotten divine son born of the great virgin queen of the heavens

Nimrod was fully aware of the fact that the advanced consciousness of the primitive mankind created in individuals "*Hope*" and "*Fear*" to such an extent as is unknown to other animals. These two passions would make them bow, if not rightly guided, even to false deities created out of man's mental conjecture.

The Sun plays a most important role in human lives. It is something which can be seen, its heat felt, its rays light the universe by day. Besides it is-

   a. The giver of life, the vivifier and resurrector of the dead earth, the upbringer of vegetations.

   b. Its light drives away darkness (which is interpreted as the destroyer of the dark, unknown evil forces which cause fear) and destroys germs which are harmful to mankind.

   c. It gives universal benefit all over the earth without any distinction between man and beast, between good and evil, hence it is the just and logical ruler.

Taking advantage of this situation Nimrod, who was well versed in the different phases or aspects of the Sun in the Zodiac and the cause of seasons, started Sun-worship and based its ceremonies on asterical calculation representing the Sun as a triad or a three-faced god or three gods in one—*viz*:

a. The Giver of life or The Creator.

b. The Destroyer.

c. The Just Ruler of the Universe.

This more or less fulfilled all the needs of the primitive intelligence of man.

When Nimrod and his mother Semiramis could display such knowledge and magical powers described above, quite naturally his mother and he became the source of deity worship. Their claim that Semiramis was a virgin and had given birth to a divine son without any human contact gained so very much credence and popularity on account of the impossible feats performed by their magical powers that every house in his empire contained the pictures and images of their Great Virgin Queen Mother Semiramis with the divine child Nimrod in her arms (page 20, "*The Two Babylons*" by Hislop).

Thus started for the first time on the face of the earth the idol worship of the great "Virgin Queen of the Heavens, the Mother of god" with her "only begotten divine son of god" in her arms.

Therefore whatsoever Nimrod did, even when it was wrong or unjust, was acclaimed and praised by his courtiers as a great and wondrous deed.

He became the first living person on earth to be publicly acknowledged as "Infallible" *i.e.* the one who could do no wrong whatsoever his deeds might be. If he raped a young woman, she had to consider herself the luckiest girl on earth because she had had an association with the only begotten son of god. If he murdered anybody, the family were to think themselves blessed because the murdered man had been sacrificed on the altar for the appeasement of the angry god for the sins of the family, and now they had as a result of this sacrifice become blessed. Thus Nimrod was free to do whatever he pleased without any qualms, whether he committed crimes against man or beast.

Therefore, he was the first Sovereign Pontiff or Pontifex Maximus. The subsequent emperors and thereafter the heads of his religion have assumed this title and role.

When God's curse fell at the tower of Babel breaking up the unity of mankind and changing their language, the result was that the name of Nimrod, the only begotten son of Sun-god and Semiramis the virgin queen of the heavens became changed from place to place as this religion spread from Babylon to the far corners of the earth as will be seen from the following chart:

NAME OF COUNTRY	ALLEGED VIRGIN MOTHER'S NAME	NAME OF ALLEGED SON OF GOD	SOME OF NIMROD'S UNIVERSALLY POPULAR TITLES
Babylon	Semiramis or Rhea or Astarte or Ishtar	Baal or Bacchus or Merodach or Tammuz or Nimrod	The only Begotten Son; The only Mediator (between god and man); The Good Shepherd; The Redeemer;
Persia	Mother of god	Mithra	
Greece	Leto or Ceres or Irene	Apollo or Plutus	
Italy	Alcemne	Hercules	

Rome	Fortuna	Jupiter-puer	The Sin Bearer;
Syria and Phrygia	Cybele	Adonis or Attis	Well Beloved Son;
Egypt	Neith or Isis	Osiris or Horus	The Healer; The Saviour; (and figured as a lamb) The Light Bringer; The Lamented One; The Deliverer; The Liberator; The Slain;
Scandinavia	Frigga	Balder	
Mexico, Peru and Central America	Chimalman	Quetzalcoatl	
India	Isi	Iswar	
Asia Minor	Cybele	Deoius	

It will, therefore, be observed from the above that the concept of a god incarnate, the son of a virgin mother which originated at the tower of Babel through Nimrod and Semiramis is common in all the above cases.

On pages 20 and 21, of *"The Two Babylons"* by the Rev. Alexander Hislop we find the undermentioned passages:

> "The Babylonians in their popular religion, supremely worshipped a goddess mother and a son, who were represented in picture and in images as infant or child in his Mother's arms. From Babylon, this worship of the mother and the child spread to the ends of the earth. In Egypt, the Mother and the child were worshipped under the names of Isis and Osiris. In India, even to this day as Isi and Iswara; in Asia, as Cybele and Deoius; in Pagan Rome as Fortuna and Jupiter-puer or Jupiter, the boy; in Greece as Ceres, the Great Mother, with the babe at her breast, or as Irene, the goddess of peace, with the boy Plutus in her arms; and even in Tibet, in China and Japan, the Jesuit missionaries were astonished to find the

counterpart of the Madonna and her child as devoutly worshipped as in Papal Rome itself; Shing Moo, the Holy Mother in China being represented with a child in her arms, and a glory around her, exactly as if a Roman Catholic artist had been employed to set her up.

"The original of that mother, so widely worshipped, there is reason to believe, was Semiramis, already referred to, who, it is known, was worshipped by the Babylonians, and other eastern nations under the name of Rhea, the great goddess Mother".

Certain feasts were celebrated connected with the only begotten divine son born of the virgin mother *viz*:

a. The feast of the Nativity of the only begotten divine son born of the virgin mother on 25th December has already been covered earlier under the heading of "the Magical Well of Deification and Eternal Life".

b. The feast of Astarte or Ishtar; the queen of the heavens or the virgin goddess of spring and fruitfulness, was observed with the following objectives on the first Sunday after the full moon following the "Spring Equinox" *viz*:

   a) Because the daylight in the northern hemisphere became greater day by day over the period of night it was considered that the virgin became pregnant at the Spring Equinox with the divine child who was to be born nine months later on the 25th December. Hence the "Easter Eggs" to denote the immaculate conception for the birth of the only begotten divine son in the womb of the virgin Ishtar or queen Semiramis.

   b) Nimrod had foretold :-

      i) He would meet with a violent death to save the

wicked world.

ii) His death would be in an act of defence of his religion.

iii) By this sacrifice of his life he would become the lamented, the saviour for the sinners, the liberator, the deliverer, the sin bearer, the one mediator, the good shepherd, the lamb of the heavens who has come to be slain.

iv) He would be killed, *by the evil forces of darkness and illiteracy.*

c) The Vernal Equinox occurred at that time when the sun in its elliptical revolution, as it passed the Equator, made the shape of a cross in the constellation of Aries or the "Lamb". This was taken as the triumph of the sun-god, whose virgin queen had succeeded in rescuing her only begotten divine son, who had sacrificed his life to the powers of darkness to save humanity and to send him to heaven to look after his believers. Therefore, he became Aries or *the lamb of the Heavens.* This event is celebrated with hot cross buns; the round bun represents the sun and the cross on it as the magical sign made by the sun, which saved the saviour from the imprisonment of the forces of darkness.

To express his hate against this person who would be the cause of his death by violence, Nimrod used to abuse him as "a swine". Accordingly to express his revenge in advance against this "would-be killer" he and his followers enjoyed swine flesh at all their feasts.

(a) The Babylonian Passion Play

The legend of this great sacrifice of Nimrod is to be found in the cuneiform tablets dug up by the German excavators in 1903-1904 at Kalah Shargat, the site of the ancient Asshur, which was one of the ancient cities built and controlled by Nimrod.

"The Quest" of London dated January, 1922 has given the translation of these cuneiform tablets under the heading of *"The Babylonian Passion Play"* as follows:-

"Baal is taken prisoner.

"Baal is tried in the House on the Mount (the Hall of Justice).

"Baal is led away to the Mount.

"Together with Baal, a malefactor is led away and put to death. Another, who is also charged as a malefactor, is let go, thus not taken away with Baal.

"After Baal had gone to the Mount, the city breaks out into tumult, and fighting takes place in it.

"Baal's clothes are carried away.

"A woman wipes away the heart's blood of Baal flowing from a drawn-out weapon (spear?)

"Baal goes down into the Mount away from sun and light, disappears from life, and is held fast in the Mount as in a prison.

"Guards watch Baal imprisoned in the stronghold of the Mount.

"A goddess sits with Baal: she comes to tend to him.

"They seek for Baal where he is held fast. In particular a weeping woman seeks for him at the 'Gate of Burial'. When he is being carried away she lamented: "O, my brother! O, my brother!

"Baal is again brought back to life (as the sun of spring), he comes again out of the Mount.

"His chief feast, the Babylonian New Year's festival in March at the time of the spring equinox, is celebrated also as his triumph over the *Powers of Darkness* (*cp.* the creation hymn 'Once when on high' as the New Year's festival hymn)".

For the "*Powers of Darkness*" for greater details please refer to book *Destruction or Peace*, chapter 12: H, 1-11. This will give the reader a clearer idea on these theories.

2. The Sign of the Cross

Nimrod won the title of "Tam-Muz" which means "Fire, the Perfector" (for details on this incident please refer to Chapter. 6: F, of *Destruction or Peace*). He threw the "Idol Breaker" into the fire for trying to teach that God is one and alone who has no form or equals. Thereby Nimrod presented to his followers that he was "Fire, the Perfector" or Tam-Muz. The initial letter of "Tam-Muz" was written in Hebrew script as an upright sign of the Cross and was pronounced as "Tau". So the sign of the cross was the initial letter of the name of the Babylonian god "Tammuz" or Bacchus or Nimrod. Hence, the worship of the cross was the worship of "Tammuz" or Bacchus or Nimrod.

The Persian variety of Nimrodism was known as Mithraism. With the conquest of Babylon by the Persians and Medes in 539 B.C., Mithraism spread throughout the Middle East and Europe reaching the British Isles by 70 B.C. During this century a cross has been discovered in Ireland (page 90 of the "*Sources of Christianity*" by Khwaja Kamal-ud-din, published in 1924, printed by Unwin Brothers Ltd., London & Woking). On this cross is the effigy of Mithra with a Parthian Crown of a Persian prince on his head. From this relic it is clear that in Mithraism it was already preached that the divine son born of the virgin mother who had come to save sinners had been killed on a cross.

The death on the cross was thus a symbolic way of giving expression to the idea that the only begotten son of the sun-god would meet with a violent death in the defence of his religion to become the saviour of his followers. Hence the sign of the cross was a symbol of their saviour, who would protect them from all harm.

The sign of the cross was, therefore, used as a sacred magical symbol to ward off evil, especially because Nimrod preached that after his divine sacrifice to save wicked humanity, he would be raised from the dead to the position of "The lamb of heaven" when the Sun crossed the Equator making the sign of the cross at the Spring Equinox.

On page 62 of the *"Sources of Christianity"* is the following statement:

> "St. Jerome admits that Mithra and Baal were the same, and called the sons of the Lord".

The upright sign of the cross thus became the symbol of safety and protection for the followers of Nimrod.

This worship of the sign of the cross which spread from Babylon is noted in *"New Light on the Most Ancient East"*, by Archaeologist V. Gordon Childe, pages 184-185 (edition of 1953), in Chapter IX entitled "Indian Civilization in the Third Millennium B.C.". There you will read:

> "The swastika and the cross, common on stamps and plaques, were religious or magical symbols as in Babylonia and Elam in the earliest prehistoric period, but preserve that character also in modern India as elsewhere".

Says *"The Two Babylons"* (Hislop), on page 199 regarding the cross:

"It was worshipped in Mexico for ages before the Roman Catholic missionaries set foot there, large stone crosses being erected ..."

"The cross thus widely worshipped, or regarded as a sacred emblem, was the unique vocal symbol of Bacchus, the Babylonian Messiah, for he was represented with a head-band covered with crosses ..."

"This symbol of the Babylonian god is revered at this day in all the wide wastes of Tartary (Asian and European location of Tatars), where Buddhism prevails, and the way in which it is represented among them forms a striking commentary on the language applied by Rome to the Cross".

"The Cross", says Colonel Wilford, in the *Asiatic Researches*,

"... though not an object of worship among the Bud'has or Buddhists is a favourite emblem and device among them".

On page 146 of *"Babylon the Great"* is a quotation from page 204 of *"The Two Babylons"*:

"... (in Christendom) the Tau, the sign of the Cross, the indisputable sign of Tammuz, the false Messiah, was everywhere substituted in its stead (instead of the Greek letter Chi or X as in Christos) ..."

The *Encyclopedia Americana* edition of 1929 Volume 8, page 238; under "Crosses and Crucifixes", says:

"The Cross as a symbol dates back to an unknown antiquity. It was recognized in all countries throughout the world at all times. Before the present era the Buddhists, Brahmans, and Druids utilized the device. Seymour tells us: 'The Druids considered that the long arm of the cross symbolized the way of life, the short arms the three conditions of the spirit world, equivalent to heaven, purgatory and hell'. With the ancient Egyptians the cross was a reverenced symbol. Their *ankh* (*crux ansata* or handled cross) represented life, and a perpendicular shaft with several arms at right angles (Nile cross) appears to have had some reference to fertility of crops. Five of their planet symbols were represented by a cross attached to a circle or part of a circle. Prescott says that when the first Europeans arrived in Mexico, to their surprise, they found 'the cross', the sacred emblem of their own faith, raised as an object of worship in the temples of Anahuac".

In *Wilkinson*, Vol. I, page 376 we read:

".... Men as well as women wore earrings and they frequently had a small cross suspended to a necklace … showing that it was largely in use as early as the fifteenth century before the Christian era".

In *Crabb's Mythology*, page 163 you find:

"There is hardly a pagan tribe where the cross has not been found. The cross was worshipped by Pagan Celts long before the incarnation and death of Christ".

In *"Indian Antiquities"* by Maurice, Vol. Vl, page 49:

"It is a fact not less remarkable than well attested, that the Druids in their groves were accustomed to select the most stately and beautiful tree as an emblem of the Deity they adored, and having cut the side branches, they affixed two of the largest of them … in such a manner that those branches extended on each like the arms of a man, and together with the body, presented the appearance of a HUGE CROSS, and on the bark, in several places, was also inscribed the letter Tau".

The origin of the upright sign of the cross is therefore traced back to the Hebrew letter "Tau" which is the initial letter of "Tammuz" the title of Nimrod.

3. Trinity in unity

Nimrod based his religion on the following anti-God principles with the sun, himself and his mother as the three principal actors.

Thus the Babylonian god consisted of a triad of:

a. Shamash (the Sun-god)

b. Sin (the Moon-god or Nimrod or Baal or Tammuz)

c. and Ishtar (goddess queen of the Zodiac or Semiramis or Rhea or the Great Virgin Mother).

For further proof see page 324 of *"Israel and Babylon"* by W. Landsdell Wordle.

In India in the ancient cave temples, the supreme Deity is represented by three heads on one body under the title of *"Eko Devah Trimurthi"* which means god the one with three faces or three gods in one god or trinity in unity.

This supreme deity is still worshipped. His name in India is Siva and he is:

a. god of life or creator

b. god of death or destroyer and

c. god of administration or ruler of the universe *i.e.*, He is the Sun-god.

On pages 184-185 of *"New Light on the Most Ancient East"* (1953 edition) by Archaeologist V. Gordon Childe in Chapter IX entitled "Indian Civilisation in the Third Millennium B.C." you will read:

"A 'Seal' from Mohenjodaro depicts a horned deity with three faces ... Siva".

It will thus be seen that god consisting of a trinity in unity or three gods in one god has been in existence all over the known world from the third millennium B.C. and this strange theory had its origin in Nimrod of Babylon, as observed in the following quotation from pages 16-17 of *"The Two Babylons"* by the Rev. Hislop:

> "So utterly idolatrous was the Babylonian recognition of the Divine Unity, that Jehovah, the Living God, severely condemned His own people for giving any countenance to it: 'They that sanctify themselves, and purify themselves in the gardens behind one tree in the midst, eating swine's flesh, and the abomination, and the mouse, shall be consumed together, saith the LORD' (Isaiah 66: 17). In the unity of that one and only god of the Babylonians, there were three persons, and to symbolise that doctrine of the Trinity, they employed, as the discoveries of Layard prove, the equilateral triangle just as it is well known, the Church of Rome does to this day. In both cases such a comparison is most degrading to the King Eternal, and is fitted utterly to pervert the minds of those who contemplate it, as if there was or could be any similitude between such a figure and Him who hath said, 'To whom will ye liken God, and what likeness will ye compare unto Him ?' ..." (Isaiah 40:18; and Isaiah 40:25)

4. Baptism

Nimrod preached that the son of the Sun-god was initiated into the religion by:

1. Facing the West (the point of sinking of the sun) and cursing the *Prince of Darkness* the evil.

2. To face the East (rising point of Sun or light) and to be baptised from the sacred fount of Alpheus and Peneus (*i.e.* Euphrates and Tigris) which according to mythology had the powers of cleaning the Augean Stables in one day for Hercules (King Augeas of Elis had stabled 3,000 oxen in these stables without their being cleaned for 30 years). Thus these sacred waters according to the teachings of Nimrod had the powers of removing instantly all the dirty

black sins of mankind. The example that he set before his public to accept this theory was that dirty clothes become clean when washed with water and soap.

It, therefore, did not matter how heinous or atrocious the sins were, for they all would be washed away as soon as one was "Baptised" and the person immediately would become pure and clean. Thus started the system of Baptism by standing in waist-deep waters usually of a flowing river or a tank and pouring water on the head of the person from a receptacle. This form of purification has been prevalent amongst millions of Hindus in India and others throughout the world since more than 2,000 years before the birth of Jesus.

Mythology informs us that immediately this son of the Sun-god was baptised, the god of the heavens (Jupiter or the Sun-god) descended in a great light and announced to the whole world as under:

"This is my only begotten son in whom I am well pleased."

Tertullian in his *"Our Sun-god"* has written on page 179 as follows:

> "The Devil, whose business is to prevent the truth, mimics the exact circumstances of the Divine Sacraments in the Mysteries of Idols. He himself baptises some, that is to say, his believers and followers; he promises forgiveness of sins from the sacred fount and thereby initiates them into the religion of Mithra. Thus he marks the forehead of his own soldiers, thus he celebrates the oblation of bread, he brings in the symbol of resurrection: and wins the Crown with the sword".

5. The twelve divine guides or apostles of the sun

Nimrod, the great astronomer, and astrologer, traced the circular path followed by the Sun in the sky during the various seasons to complete the annual solar cycle. This is called the Zodiac, which he divided into twelve more or less regular portions or months, to be able to forecast more accurately what could best be grown in that particular period, what influence it would have upon plants, animals and even human beings. He claimed that each of these constellations of the Zodiac controlled and guided the lives, career, health, character, behaviour, marriage and destiny of that person, who was born during its corresponding period of influence.

He gave to each of these twelve guides or satellites of the Sun an appropriate name, sign and period of influence. The names have changed with the changes of languages but the principles have remained the same throughout these 4,000 years.

1. *Aries* symbolises the ram possessing formidable horns and guides the lives of those born between about 21st March and 19th April. The Babylonian New Year starts from this period.

2. *Taurus* is symbolised by a mighty bull and guides the lives of those born between about 20th April and 20th May.

3. *Gemini* is symbolised by a pair of twin children and guides the lives of those born between about 21st May and 21st June.

4. *Cancer* is symbolised by a crab and guides the lives of those born between about 22nd June and 22nd July.

5. *Leo* as the name implies is symbolised by a lion and guides the lives of those born between about 23rd July and 22nd August.

6. *Virgo* as the name implies is symbolised by a virgin and guides the lives of those born between about 23rd August and 22nd September.

7. *Libra* is symbolised by a pair of scales or a balance and guides the lives of those born between about 23rd September and 23rd October.

8. *Scorpio* as the name implies is symbolised by a scorpion or serpent with a poisoned tail and guides the lives of those born between about 24th October and 22nd November.

9. *Sagittarius* is symbolised by a centaur—a creature, whose upper half is that of a man and lower half that of a horse and who is shooting an arrow from his bow. It guides the lives of those born between about 23rd November and 21st December.

10. *Capricorn* is symbolised by a goat having the tail of a fish and guides the lives of those born between 22nd December and 20th January.

11. *Aquarius* is symbolised by a man pouring out a stream of water from a pitcher and guides the lives of those born between about 21st January and 19th February.

12. *Pisces* is symbolised by a pair of fishes and guides the lives of those born between about 20th February and 20th March.

The "Horoscope" had been developed from this basis with the exact position of the Sun, the Moon and the planets at the time of birth of an individual in relation to the Zodiacal sign under which he or she is born.

The system of the twelve months in the solar calendar year therefore has its origin in these ancient theories.

This also is the origin of the twelve guides or apostles of the Sun worshippers.

Hence according to the mythology of Sun worshippers twelve guides or apostles or experts were a *sine qua non* for them.

All men cannot be the same, some have to be bad also. Hence the theory that one of these twelve guides or Apostles would be the source of traitors and betrayers of the faith and trust of others. Therefore, the killer of the only begotten son of Sun-god, the enemy of the Sun should be one of the twelve heavenly guides. This is the constellation of "Scorpio" or the serpent. The entry of the sun into this sign of the Zodiac causes its declination, hence this must be the traitor amongst the heavenly apostles who will betray the saviour.

From this has developed the mythological story of the betrayal of the only begotten son by one of the twelve divine heavenly guides.

It was for this reason that the serpent was treated as the Satan in the Zodiac or amongst the Apostles of the Sun-god.

The serpent and Satan have been identified as the same in many of the olden scriptures. Perhaps this even explains the reference of Satan coming in the form of a serpent to tempt Adam and Eve and to make them commit their first sin. Thus it was the serpent or Satan who robbed them of the bliss of the Garden of Eden (for greater details please refer to book *Destruction or Peace*, chapter 20: B, C and D).

6. The principles of Nimrodism

1. The laws (of God) are a curse for mankind.

2. The laws (of goodness) are not the faith.

3. As the laws of God are very restrictive for the wicked, the man who undertakes upon himself the grave risks of upholding them, is like the cursed one, who has hanged himself from a tree for his mistakes and failures by the very rules of the law he has been trying to observe.

4. Accordingly he taught: Do not tempt God by following His laws; otherwise He would judge and punish you for having broken His laws, which the people are unable to fulfil.

5. Hence it was safer and better not to acknowledge the laws of God and not to recognize even His existence at all so that there could be no question of God judging man by the laws that man has refused to recognise or abide by. Thus in his claim of infallibility, Nimrod considers himself even superior to God and thinks he is entitled to dictate to God on how man is to be treated and not judged by God in any manner because he has been declared "Infallible" by all mankind, who were still united and spoke one common language until this time as confirmed in Genesis 11: 1.

6. It was Nimrod, who taught that it was no longer necessary to follow any laws of goodness or to do any good deeds. Under such circumstances the world must of necessity become a place for doing only wicked and evil deeds.

7. About the spring equinox a heavenly messenger came and gave glad tidings to a virgin woman that without any human contact she was going to conceive a male child who was the "*Word*" or the son of the god of gods (*i.e.* Sun-god).

8. This "only beloved begotten son" was to be born during the winter solstice—*i.e.* about 25th December, in a cave or in an underground chamber.

9. This son of god was to spend a life of toil and was to sacrifice his life for the saving of mankind from the anger of god for their sins.

10. He was the Light-bringer, the Healer, the Sin-bearer, the

Mediator, the Saviour and the Deliverer *etc.*

11. He would be vanquished by the "*Power of Darkness*" and descend into the captivity of the underground world or Hell. (for greater details please refer to the book *Destruction or Peace*, chapter 6: I, J and K for who destroyed Nimrod).

12. He would rise again from the dead and become the Saviour of mankind.

13. He founded the communion of saints and temples or churches dedicated to the name of these sages.

14. His disciples had to be baptised to enter his religion.

15. One's sins would be wiped out if one ate the sacramental meals of "Bread and Wine" which were the flesh and the blood of this "only begotten son of god" and hence when you eat the holy sacraments you become in flesh and blood the pure "son of god", *i.e.* you become sinless.

Hence Nimrodism has no basis for the attainment of eternal life by doing good deeds according to the laws of God!

Since this genius had achieved all his successes through contemplation, meditation, magical powers and applied knowledge to produce inventions and results, he wanted to have groups of thinkers and meditators, the genius of humanity to assist him in furthering man's material progress. He had them grouped according to their particular skills and knowledge *e.g.* the astronomers, the astrologers, the agricultural experts, the architects, the engineers, the chemists, the metallurgists *etc.* They were the elite of his society. He grouped them according to their special skills or knowledge. Both men and women were drafted. In order that they may be free all the time to concentrate upon further developments, they were prohibited from marrying or having any worldly connections. Their hair was shaved off from the scalps of their heads in a circular disc form leaving a fringe of hair all round. It was a replica of the round circular sun with its flames shooting out from its edge and is known as the clerical tonsure. This is the origin of the various monastic orders of the priests of "The Flaming Sun-god", each group being under a separate "temple" which became famous after the name of its sage or expert, who was thus raised to the status of a saint. This is the origin of the priest-class which is called Brahman in India.

From this has originated the use of temples dedicated to the particular sages or saints, which are ornamented on occasions with fruits, flowers, branches of trees, incense, lamps, and candles; votive offerings on recovery from illness; holy water; asylums; holy days and seasons, use of the calendars, blessings on the fields, sacerdotal vestments, the clerical tonsure, the praying before images, the wearing of the "Cross" in chains, round the neck as a charm to ward off evil and the ring given to a woman when she either marries or enters a nunnery is to indicate to her that she is willingly submitting herself to be chained henceforth in lifelong bondage and slavery either to her husband or to the deity as the case may be. Thus she reduces her status to that of a helpless slave for life and acknowledges herself an inferior creature who is deprived of the right of equality with her husband *i.e.* man. Prayers are to be said facing the East, the rising place of the Sun.

The following are quotations from pages 210 and 220 of "*The Two Babylons*" by the Rev. Hislop:

> "Now, while Semiramis, the real original of the Chaldean Queen of Heaven, to whom the 'unbloody sacrifice' of the mass was first offered, was in her own person, as we have already seen, the very paragon of impurity, she at the same time affected the greatest fervour for that kind of sanctity which looks down with contempt on God's holy ordinance of marriage. The Mysteries over which she presided were scenes

of the rankest pollution, and yet the higher orders of the priesthood were bound to a life of celibacy as a life of peculiar and pre-eminent holiness. Strange though it may seem, yet the voice of antiquity assigns to that abandoned queen the invention of clerical celibacy, and that in the most stringent form. In some countries, as in Egypt, human nature asserted its rights, and though the general system, of Babylon was retained, the yoke of celibacy was abolished, and the priesthood were permitted to marry. But every scholar knows that when the worship of Cybele, the Babylonian goddess, was introduced into Pagan Rome, it was introduced in its primitive form, with its celibate clergy".

"The effects of its introduction were most disastrous. The records of all nations where priestly celibacy has been introduced have proved that instead of ministering to the purity of those condemned to it, it has only plunged them in the deepest pollution. The history of Tibet, and China, and Japan, where the Babylonian institute of priesthood has prevailed from time immemorial, bears testimony to the abominations that have flowed from it. The excesses committed by the celibate priests of Bacchus in Pagan Rome in their secret Mysteries, were such that the senate felt called upon to expel them from the bounds of the Roman Republic. In Papal Rome the same abominations have flowed from priestly celibacy, in connection with the corrupt and corrupting systems of the confessional, insomuch that all men who have examined the subject have been compelled to admire the amazing significance of the same divinely bestowed on it, both in a literal and figurative sense, 'Babylon the Great, *The Mother of Harlots and Abominations of the earth*'."

"These celibate priests have all a certain mark set upon them at their ordination; and that is the clerical tonsure".

Monasteries have been in existence amongst the Sun-worshippers all over the world from times unknown. As seen above, these had their origin in Babylon. These included virgins in service of female deities and male ascetics. They never married and thus did not attach themselves to worldly ties. Hence they lived contrary to the rules of natural laws. Numerous books of reference can be quoted here, the most popular and well known being "*Our Sun god*" by Tertullian, page 179.

The distinction for a Sun-worshipper ascetic was that he would shave his hair from the scalp of his head in a circular disc to denote that he was carrying the regard and respect of the Sun on top of his head, the highest and most reverential place in the human body. This practice was followed in Babylon, Arabia, Egypt, Pagan Rome, Persia, India, China and wherever Sun worship was practised.

A quotation from Herodotus lib. III, Chapter 8; p.115C is as follows:

> "The Arabians acknowledge no other gods than Bacchus and Urania (*i.e.* Semiramis or Astarte or Ishtar, the Queen of Heaven), and they say that their hair was cut in the same manner as Bacchus's is cut, now they cut it in a circular form, saving it round the temples".

In the *"Two Babylons"* by the Rev. Hislop on pages 221-224 we find the following passages:

> "Over all the world, where the traces of the Chaldean system are found, this tonsure or shaving of the head is always found along with it. The priests of Osiris, the Egyptian Bacchus, were always distinguished by the shaving of their heads. In Pagan Rome, in India, and even in China, the distinguishing mark of the Babylonian priesthood was the shaven head".

> "In the religion of the Babylonian Messiah this institution was in vogue from the earliest times. In that system there were monks and nuns in abundance. In Tibet and Japan, where the Chaldean system was early introduced, monasteries are still to

be found, and with the same disastrous results to morals as in Papal Europe. In Scandinavia, the priestesses of Freya, who were generally kings' daughters, whose duty it was to watch the sacred fire, and who were to perpetual virginity, were just an order of nuns. In Athens there were virgins maintained at the public expense, who were strictly bound to single life. In Pagan Rome, the Vestal who had the same duty to perform as the priestesses of Freya, occupy a similar position. Even in Peru, during the reign of the Incas, the same system prevailed and showed so remarkable an analogy, as to indicate that the Vestals of Rome, the nuns of the Papacy, and Holy Virgins of Peru, must have sprung from a common origin. Thus does Prescott refer to the Peruvian nunneries: 'Another singular analogy with Roman Catholic institutions is presented by the Virgins of the sun, the elect, as they are called. These were young maidens dedicated to the service of the deity, who at a tender age were taken from their homes, and introduced into convents, they were placed under the care of certain elderly matrons, mamaconas, who had grown grey within their walls. It was their duty to watch over the sacred fire obtained at the Festival Raymi. From the moment they entered the establishment they were cut off from communication with the world, even with their own family and friends ... Woe to the unhappy maiden who was detected in an intrigue: by the stern law of the Incas she was to be buried alive.' This was precisely the fate of the Roman Vestal who was proved to have violated her vow. Neither in Peru, however, nor in Pagan Rome was the obligation to virginity so stringent as in the papacy. It was not perpetual, and therefore not so exceedingly demoralising. After a time, the nuns might be delivered from their confinement, and marry: from all hopes of which they are absolutely cut off in the Church of Rome. In all these cases, however, it is plain that the principles on which these institutions were founded were originally the same. 'One is astonished', adds Prescott, "to find so close a resemblance between the institutions of the American Indian, the ancient

Roman, and the modern Catholic.'

Prescott finds it difficult to account for this resemblance: but the one little sentence from the prophet Jeremiah which was quoted at the commencement of this inquiry, accounts for it completely:

> 'Babylon hath been a golden cup in the *Lord's* hand, that hath made *All The Earth Drunken* ..." (Jeremiah 51: 7).

Under these Nimrodic teachings the doers of good deeds were to be looked down upon and shunned as people who were living in a wrong age and were thus out of date and had no place in this society. Sacramental feasts of the first fruit, corn, swine-flesh, goose, yule cakes and drinks would wipe away all sins, *i.e.* merriment, enjoyment, feastings, dancing and drunkenness were the means of wiping out the pin-pricks from one's conscience for sins committed thus making one immune even from feeling guilty for the heinous sins and reprehensible crimes committed!

Accordingly it was Nimrod, who invented the doctrine that by partaking of such foods and strong drinks which were the flesh and the blood of deity, one became the pure and sinless deity himself. Therefore all sins committed before are completely wiped away just as chalk writings on a slate are wiped away when rubbed with a wet piece of cloth. What could be more tempting to a person? Indeed, how very alluring these were for sinners, who wanted some kind of an excuse to believe in and have faith, thereon that their sins were forgiven and they were now safe from God's punishment for their sins by feastings, merriment, dancing and drunkenness? At least it killed their conscience and relieved them as long as they carried on with it night after night—it was great fun indeed! Hence millions have flocked to this religion for the past four thousand years!

7. Nimrod's ambitions

Nimrod's ambitions knew no bounds. Not only did he make himself the first king of mankind after the deluge but he also deified himself into the only begotten son of god, born at the winter solstice or the Nativity of the Sun, through the great virgin mother. He was thus the innocent lamb of the heavens—the god come in human form to save sinners.

As if this were not honour enough, he got himself deified into "god Himself" by calling himself "Trinity in Unity". He got his subjects also to accept this theory.

Still not satisfied with even so much, he strove to set himself up as superior to God Himself, Whom he reduced in his teachings to:

- a. A secondary position and rank of having the dishonour to sit on the left hand of Nimrod on the day of judgment in front of the Universe. Hence God is in a lower position to Nimrod according to his teachings.

- b. The reason for his being honoured by sitting in the superior position to God Himself, *i.e.* on His right hand is that Nimrod took on human bodily form and went through the tortures and trials of earthly life, which God Himself did not go through. Hence Nimrod's claim to superiority over God Himself!

- c. Because he had the actual experience of living an earthly life it follows that he had the necessary "knowledge" of how to conduct "Judgment" on human beings—he himself having been once a human being also!

- d. In these circumstances God Himself, being the inexperienced one, would helplessly as a mere puppet witness the "experienced and superior" Nimrod conducting the affairs of the Day of Judgment!

e. When God, according to Nimrod, was something inferior, the question of the "Necessity of God being in existence" or His laws being followed did not even arise.

f. Accordingly all followers of the laws of God and the doers of good deeds would be condemned by Nimrod the "Only begotten son" to hell for their small mistakes. Thus Nimrod converted God into the Merciless, the Unjust and the Cruel.

g. Whilst the "baptised" sinners would all go straight to heaven for their faith alone.

h. Good deeds were the curse with which the followers of God's laws were tempting God to punish them!

One would have thought that Nimrod had thus reached the limit of blasphemy and mockery of God, that human intelligence could ever conjecture, but no! Certainly not so, with Nimrod! He even raised himself to the "Infallible Pontifex Maximus" by trying to kill the Almighty God Himself to win the Biblical title of "A mighty hunter in rebellion against the Lord" (Genesis 10: 9). (For details of Nimrod trying to kill God, please refer to Chapter 6: G of the book *Destruction or Peace*).

Nimrod thus set himself up as superior to God in every conceivable way!

Is not all this the highest and the most wicked form of blasphemy that the human mind can ever conjecture against God Almighty, Who is All Love, All Justice and All Perfection? It is also an insult to His Majesty's Dignity, the Creator of all that is in the Heavens and all in the Earth and all in between them!

G. The curse of God on Nimrod according to the Holy Bible

Having thus established his Pagan-atheistic religion with a

wonderful empire of beautiful cities and palaces and stupendous feats, Nimrod built the most gorgeous temple called "Bab-el" which means "the Gate Way" to perfection and success.

He reached the height of his glory when this wonderful temple was successfully completed with numerous floors and several meditation rooms and prayer halls on each floor. This first skyscraper in the history of mankind was completed in 2239 B.C. God's curse fell upon mankind when this magnificent temple was put to anti-God worship. The curse broke up the unity of the entire human race. The people went to sleep speaking one common language but awoke the next morning speaking different languages! They did not understand one another. There was complete confusion and chaos. Disputes and misunderstanding arose as to what was being said by one group to the other. The natural result was separation and disunity. Groups speaking the same language gathered together. Nimrod and his group being the most powerful stayed on at Babylon. Each of the other language groups went in different directions and settled down in new countries.

The teachings of Nimrod accordingly spread all over the face of the earth. Only the names of the begotten son and his virgin mother became changed due to the changes in the language. But the principles of Sun-worship and its dates remained unaltered as it was based upon the different phases of the Sun in the Northern Hemisphere.

This incident finds mention in the Holy Bible as:

"AND the whole earth was of one language, and of one speech.

"And it came to pass, as they journeyed from the east, that they found a plain in the land of Shinar (the site where Babylon was built on the plains between the rivers Euphrates and Tigris); and they dwelt there.

"And they said one to another, Go to, let us make brick, and burn them thoroughly. And they had brick for stone, and lime had they for mortar.

"And they said, Go to, let us build us; city and a tower whose top *may reach* unto heaven; and let us make us a name, lest we be scattered abroad upon the face of the whole earth.

"And the LORD came down to see the city and the tower, which the children of men builded.

"And the LORD said, Behold the people is one, they have all one language; and this they begin to do: and now nothing will be restrained from them, which they have imagined to do.

"Go to, let us (*i.e.* God Almighty) go down, and there confound their language, that they may not understand one another's speech.

"So the LORD scattered them abroad from thence upon the face of all the earth: and they left off to build the city.

"Therefore is the name of it called Babel; because the LORD did there confound the LANGUAGE of all the earth" and from thence did the LORD scatter them abroad upon the face of all the earth" (Genesis 11: 1-9).

As a matter of fact almost all the pagan religions in existence today on the face of the earth have their origin directly or indirectly in the teachings of King Nimrod.

As long as this group of religions flourishes with millions of adherents the curse of God from the tower of Babel will be upon mankind, and there can be no unity or peace amongst the people of the world.

H. Nimrod's attempt to reunite mankind through marriage

Everything Nimrod did was calculated to do something against God Almighty's decrees.

Nimrod planned to reunite the different groups by putting the following scheme into operation:

1. Nobody should be permitted to marry a relative.

2. Marriage should always be contracted with someone belonging to some other family group so that unity and friendship might grow amongst the different groups of mankind and thus they could reunite and undo what God Almighty had done to destroy the unity of mankind at the tower of Babel.

3. If a person had more than one wife there was every possibility of jealousy between the two or more wives belonging to the two or more different groups of people. It would mean that such disputes between the wives were likely to result in disputes between the husband's family group and the two or more family groups from where the different wives came. Thus this was a possible source of disunity amongst different groups of the human race. Hence only one wife was the order of the day.

4. To support this theory he preached that marriage in the same family meant the same blood. This, Nimrod declared, was harmful to the health of the children.

5. Nimrod's followers, till this day, follow this principle of one marriage and that also with a non-relative.

The Pharaohs of Egypt used to marry their own sisters. Historical records show that this did not leave any ill effects upon the health and intellectual powers of their children. In fact, such children of the rulers of Egypt were all the more exceptionally clever, healthy and beautiful.

From the time of Abraham about 4,000 years ago his children, both the Jews and the Arabs, have intermarried amongst cousins without any ill effects. Thus the four millennia prove the fallacy of Nimrod's theory of ill effects due to intermarriages. It was nothing but eyewash and bluff to bring about the reuniting of mankind which was split by God's curse.

How far Nimrod has succeeded and / or failed in his attempts at reuniting mankind into one people with one government is quite apparent from the numerous worldwide disputes and troubles between one group of nations and another. So much so that a stage has now come about that if man does not reconcile himself with his fellow beings there is every danger of man destroying himself with the increasingly deadly weapons of mass destruction that he is daily developing and inventing.

Chapter 3

Abraham—The Friend of God sent to destroy Nimrod the evil genius

A. The dream of King Nimrod

On page 188 of Vol. I of *"Tafrihul Askia Fil Ahwal Ul Ambia"* is described the dream which King Nimrod had in 2019 B.C. He saw a star rising from the Western Horizon instead of the East. As this star rose slowly higher into the sky it became brighter and brighter. When it reached the zenith it became the brightest and stopped over there. Then the bright light started slowly to spread over the face of the earth. Finally this light lit up the whole earth.

King Nimrod found out the interpretation of this dream as follows:

1. A child was going to be born within a year who would break idols.

2. This child would be responsible for establishing on a permanent footing on this earth: *"God is one and alone, Who has no equals and none comparable with Him."*

3. He would prove to the world that it was blasphemy to follow the religion taught by Nimrod of: *The Only Begotten son of god born of the great virgin queen mother* (see *Destruction or Peace,* Chapter 5: F-1) *the lamb of the heavens who has come to sacrifice himself to save the*

sinners (see *Destruction or Peace*, Chapter 6: J), *the first to claim a seat on the right hand of God, hence in a position even superior to God Himself, and exercising God's power of forgiving Nimrod's baptised sinners and condemning to hell the believers in the true and one God—the doers of good deeds—for their small mistakes* (see *Destruction or Peace*, Chapter 5: F-7).

4. He would prove before the world that Nimrod's claims were false and absurd in all respects especially:

    a. *Trinity in unity* (see *Destruction or Peace*, Chapter 5: F-3 and 6: H)

    b. *Only begotten son of god* (see *Destruction or Peace*, Chapter 5: E-7 a, b and c; F-1).

    God incarnate come on earth (see *Destruction or Peace*, Chapter 16: D 1, 2, 3, 4, 5, 6 and 7).

    And divinity (see *Destruction or Peace*, Chapter 6: G; 16: A and C)

    c. *Infallible Pontifex Maximus* (see *Destruction or Peace*, Chapter 6: H)

5. By Divine aid this child would be responsible for not only the destruction of the mighty army and power of Nimrod but would also be instrumental in his eventual death by violence (see *Destruction or Peace*, Chapter 6: J) because of his refusal to believe in the absolute Oneness of God as taught by this child.

6. This child would be a very important prophet. From his descendants would come several lines of prophets and saints for the guidance of mankind. This is the interpretation of the star becoming brighter as it continued to rise.

7. This star reaching its zenith and stopping there, then after sometime shining its brightest indicated two things *viz*:

   1. The last prophet would be the greatest of all the earlier prophets because it had reached the Zenith.

   2. After some time shining at its brightest and lighting up the world indicated that a child would be born from this greatest prophet who would bring the world to one universal religion for all mankind after destroying Nimrodism by whatever name it might be known at that point of time.

8. Thus would end the curse of God Almighty which broke up the unity of mankind at the temple of Babylon on which Nimrod had built for his deification (see *Destruction or Peace*, Chapter 5: G). Then the entire world would be reunited into a single brotherhood (see *Destruction or Peace*, Chapters 25, 26, 29 and 30) under this saint's banner of '*Surrender to the Will of God*'. Gone would be the differences of caste, colour, nationality, richness or poverty (see *Destruction or Peace*, Chapter 7: I). Everyone would be on the same equal footing. Wars would become a thing of the past, (see *Destruction or Peace*, Chapter 24: B and C; 25: W; 29: C-8a to d). Weapons of war would be converted into instruments for prosperity and progress *e.g.* atomic energy for peace *etc.* (see *Destruction or Peace*, Chapters 29: C-8a to d; 30: C). Peace and brotherhood would prevail once again after a lapse of about 4,000 years from the birth of this child.

9. This child would be born in a city named "UR", which was situated about 50 miles from the Persian Gulf, near the confluence of the Euphrates and Tigris rivers.

10. That the sperm had not as yet left the father's body to

enter the mother's womb to start the creation of this child.

These interpretations of his dream quite naturally upset Nimrod very much. He, thinking himself to be the "Be All and End All" and having sway over all mankind, therefore resolved to prevent the conception and birth of this child at all costs and thus defeat God and bring His plans to naught!

Even today many think in the same way, that "Might is Right" and God can do nothing against worldly scientific progress. Do not realise that our birth and death which are the commencement and the end of our individual existence on this earth are solely in His hands? Has the scientific world of today yet been able to break this control of God and keep thousands alive eternally by scientific robot lungs, hearts, organs, limbs *etc*? Have we succeeded eternally even in a single case so far in spite of all our scientific progress and discoveries? Can we tell, by our scientific knowledge positively the correct date, day, hour, minute and second when any individual is going to die? How very weak and incomplete are all our scientific achievements of today in the face of God's will and powers (see *Destruction or Peace*, Chapter 16: B).

B. Steps to prevent the birth of Abraham

Ur about this time was a powerful, prosperous and busy city with at least a quarter million inhabitants according to Keller in "*The Bible as History*".

On page 189, Vol. I, of "*Tafrihul Askia Fil Ahwal Ul Ambia*" one can read about the determination with which King Nimrod with his armies occupied Ur to stop the birth of Abraham. He thought that by sheer force he could prevent the birth of all children. Nimrod never hesitated to order anything that his fanciful imagination could conceive.

Accordingly a royal proclamation was announced at Ur as follows:

1. With immediate effect no man may have any sexual relations with his wife under pain of death.
2. And no woman may have any sexual relations with her husband under pain of death.
3. Also, guards were to be mounted on female quarters to prevent men from entering therein.
4. That all males must leave the city immediately and stay in the camp with Nimrod's soldiers, until further orders.
5. Soldiers were to be placed around the city sealing the women inside it.
6. That men were not permitted to enter the city and women were not allowed to come out of the city of Ur during any part of the day or night.
7. Every pregnant woman was to be kept separate if she gave birth to a male child it was to be killed on the spot.

By these arrangements which he personally supervised, King Nimrod now felt confident he could prevent the birth of Abraham or kill him upon his birth.

These arrangements were continued for a period of nearly two years until about 2017 B.C.

C. Nimrod's anti-marriage teachings at this juncture.

In order that the people may not become restive at these severe restrictions on their liberties and in order to justify his action, King Nimrod's clever brain invented some ingenious theories, *viz:*

That these orders which he had issued were for the purification of the human soul in general and for the pious religious-minded people of Ur in particular in order that they may get an opportunity to live a period of their lives in a state of perfection without any worldly attachment to wealth, wife, or children, thus enabling them to attain self-control and nearness to immortality, death being the greatest fear in the minds of the primitive, whilst attainment of immortality was the goal they always sought after.

For this purpose he organised daily prayer meetings, fastings and simple food so that he could train his chosen people to lead a life of renunciation to worldly attachments in order to attain immortality.

For the married he developed the following theory which finds its expression in the form of a dialogue between a husband and his wife quoted in an "*aranyaka*" to explain Nimrod's path to immortality. This teaching of Nimrod has become one of the authoritative ways of renunciation to attain immortality (pages 34-37, "*The Teachings of the Mystics*" by Walter T. Stace, published by The New American Library of New York under Mentor Book series):

Husband: My dearest wife, I have resolved to give up the world and all its charms and comforts and to begin a life of renunciation. I wish, therefore, to divide my properties between you and my children.

Wife: My lord, if the whole earth belonged to me, with all its wealth, should I through its possession attain immortality?

Husband: No my dear. Your life would be like that of the rich. None can possibly hope to attain immortality through attachment to worldly things like husband, wife, children, and properties. Immortality cannot be purchased by wealth.

Wife: Then what is the use of the wealth that you are leaving to me? If you have decided to enter the path to immortality, then I too wish to embark upon it, renouncing the world and all its attachments. Therefore, kindly be so good as to educate me, that I too may take to that path and attain eternal success and immortality.

Husband: Near to me you have always been, my dear wife. But now you wish to learn about the truth which is nearest to my heart. Come my dear, sit by me. I will explain it to you. Meditate carefully on what I say.

It is not for the sake of the husband, my beloved, that the husband is dear but it is due to love instilled in us by the Immortal Creator.

It is not for the sake of the wife, my beloved, that the wife is dear, but it is due to love instilled in us by the Immortal Creator.

It is not for the sake of the children, my beloved, that the children are dear, but it is due to love instilled in us by the Immortal Creator.

It is not for the sake of creatures, my beloved, that the creatures are prized, but for the sake of love instilled in us by the Immortal Creator.

It is not for the sake of wealth, my beloved, that worldly possessions are dear but it is due to love instilled in us by the Immortal Creator.

It is not for the sake of the higher worlds, my beloved, that the higher order of life is desired, but out of love for perfection instilled in us by the Immortal Creator.

It is not for the sake of the gods, my beloved, that the gods are worshipped but out of love for the Immortal Creator instilled in us.

It is not for the sake of itself my beloved, that anything whatsoever it might be, is esteemed but out of love instilled in us by the Immortal Creator.

Thus to attain immortality, you have to divorce all worldly attachments and leave in your heart no place for anything whatsoever but the pure love of the one and only Creator. That is the pure undivided love for the Immortal Creator. Hear about Him, reflect upon Him and meditate upon him. Only by knowing Him, can one achieve success. To know Him, my beloved, you have to hear about Him. After that meditate upon Him. Then only can you realise and know him.

Think on:

As for touch the medium is the skin.

As for smell the medium is the nose.

As for taste the medium is the tongue,

As for sound the medium is the ears.

As for sight the medium is the eyes.

As for thought the medium is the mind.

As for divine wisdom the medium is the heart.

Oh my beloved, know well that a pure heart free from all worldly attachment is the path to immortality. Having said this they both renounced the world to lead a separate life of seclusion in search of the Divine Light and Immortality. That is the way to the highest form of success according to the teachings of this genius.

King Nimrod's counsels to women were:

A virgin dedicates herself to God, so that she may be holy in body, mind and spirit. Accordingly she has in her heart a place for only one absolute and complete love and that is the love of her Creator. She has no room for any other loves or worldly attractions. She can thus easily attain the highest form of success which is immortality. But the married woman has no option because she has to take care of worldly things such as house management, the welfare of the children and how she may please her husband. A married woman thus loses all opportunity of achieving immortality, which can only be acquired by a heart which is free from worldly attachment.

The teachings of this master-mind for unmarried men were:

A wise man wishing to attain immortality and perfection should therefore avoid married life as if it were a pit of live coals; realise that there is no passion more violent than voluptuousness. Fortunately there is only one such passion. If there were two, not a single man in the whole universe could follow the truth, so beware of fixing your eyes upon woman. (If you find yourself in their company, let it be as though you were not present). If you speak to them, guard well your hearts lest you succumb to the temptation of their charms and lose the chance of immortality.

King Nimrod by his magical powers of influencing the minds of people, with over one year of preaching and the separation of the men from the women folk, effectively turned the city of Ur into a holy city. The entire northwest quarter was converted into monasteries, ziggurat, and temples with thousands of celibate monks and nuns. Chapels for the purpose of worship were also scattered throughout the city, and every home, except those of the poorest people, had its own chapel.

1. Man Born Sinful

King Nimrod thus preached that the soul was immortal. It was imprisoned in the body of man. The soul is pure but the body is contaminated. The goal of life should be to soar above the sordid demands of the body, and to achieve the liberation of the soul through contemplation of the eternal, thereby attaining immortality. Such an objective can be achieved only by taking the harsh and narrow path of asceticism.

Under these theories of Nimrod the act of production of children was "a call of the sinful flesh" therefore every child born was out of a "sinful" act between the parents, hence everyone has been born "sinful"! See *Destruction or Peace,* Chapter 20: B, C and D for Adam's Immortal Sin!

The only exception being Nimrod, the only begotten son of god, because he was born of a virgin, without any human contact, thus he was not only born free of any sin, but also he could commit no sin irrespective of whatever might be his deeds. So he was infallible and sinless.

This teaching of Nimrod was a part and parcel of the ancient Babylonian mysteries which regarded sex as something low and degrading. From here this teaching spread to Mesopotamia, Persia, India and China in the East, and Egypt, Greece, and the Roman Empire including Europe in the West. It gained such a strong foothold all over that many people disregarded completely such divine laws as:

> "And God blessed them (*i.e.* Adam and Eve), and God said unto them, Be fruitful, and multiply, and replenish the earth, ..." (Genesis 1: 28).
>
> "And God blessed Noah and his sons, and said unto them, Be fruitful, and multiply, and replenish the earth" (Genesis 9: 1).
>
> "And God saw everything that he had made, and, behold, it was *Very Good*" (Genesis 1: 31).

This would naturally include sex for production of the children which God has blessed.

Divine laws, however, expressly forbid adultery, fornication and illicit sex relationships as something very rotten and evil but not the sanctity of marriage, which is regarded as *"Very Good"* and *"Blessed"* as quoted above.

2. The Title of "The Sacred Heart"—Baal

This teaching of Nimrod about keeping the heart pure from worldly attachment of marriage and observing celibacy won for him the title of "The sacred heart". In the Chaldean tongue "Bal" meant "heart". Hence "Baal" with a double 'a' meant the "Special Heart" or "The Sacred Heart". Accordingly pictures were drawn of Nimrod for the purposes of worship, depicting him with a heart on top of which was drawn "Tau" of Tammuz, *i.e.* the upright sign of the cross. This is how he acquired the title of "Baal" which means "The Sacred Heart".

D. The Birth of Abraham

On page 189, Vol. I, *"Tafrihul Askia Fil Ahwal Ul Ambia"* it is recorded that a few months after celibacy had been imposed on the town of Ur, it became necessary for Nimrod to procure something from the city which he required urgently.

Accordingly Nimrod summoned his most trusted governor of Ur. This man's name was "Terah" (or Azar). He made Terah promise under pain of death that he would not go near his wife whilst he was permitted inside the town. Terah was given a time limit to find the required article from the official treasury in the town and return. When Terah arrived at the treasury or the place where this article was, he found it within a very short time and started his return journey towards the city gates. He still had about half an hour to spare. His house was situated on the path out of the city and he had a sudden urge to see the members of his family. He thought no harm would be done if he were to see them for a few moments especially as he was ahead of schedule and could return in good time to the gate. Terah also knew very well that if he did not take advantage of this opportune moment he would not have another chance to see his family until Nimrod returned from Ur to Babylon which might not be for another year or more. So he entered his house secretly. Terah's wife was at home, and was delighted at her husband's sudden appearance. This encounter resulted in the the conception of Abraham. Alarmed at this Terah warned his wife not to admit that they had even seen each other, otherwise both would be killed by King Nimrod. Thereupon he rushed out secretly and returned to Nimrod's camp-headquarters outside the city in good time, still ahead of schedule.

The very next morning Nimrod found out by his magical powers that this child, who was to destroy him, was now in the mother's womb. Naturally he was furious. He interrogated Terah for a long time. But Terah pleaded his innocence pointing out that he had returned well ahead of schedule, so could not have had the time to visit his wife. His wife was also questioned but she too denied having seen her husband for the past several months:

Nevertheless a soldier was appointed to watch over Terah's wife. At the first sign of pregnancy she was to be killed along with Terah.

Nimrod promptly ordered every pregnant woman in Ur to be kept under military watch and all new-born male babies were to be put to death during the following year and a half.

Thus a reign of terror and bloodshed prevailed until Nimrod was satisfied that this child, who was to cause his death must have been completely destroyed.

For nine months Terah's wife showed no signs of pregnancy. Therefore the soldier appointed to watch over her was withdrawn. The men-folk were eventually allowed to return. But all pregnant women were kept separately under surveillance. All new-born male children were killed. The very next day after the withdrawal of the guard, Terah's wife, although showing no outward signs of pregnancy, felt the movement of a child in her womb. She was frightened because if found out all three, Terah, herself and the child, would be put to death. So for her own and her husband's safety she secretly selected a cave outside the town and kept some torn clothes in it. When the child came she, out of fear, left the babe in the cave wrapped in torn clothes and sealed its mouth with a piece of rock.

Terah somehow found out that his wife had been out of the town for a period of several hours. So he asked her where she had been for such a long time. She replied that she had given birth to a male child whom she had buried in the hills. Terah warned her to keep this news secret otherwise both of them would be killed by Nimrod's soldiers who were still in the town slaughtering new-born male children. To make sure that this male child was dead, even if his wife might have lied, he did not permit his wife out of his sight for seven days. After seven days, when she got a chance she, visited the cave expecting to see the child dead but she was extremely surprised to find that the child was looking not only healthy but also as big as a one-month-old babe and that out of the four fingers and the thumb of his right hand were oozing milk, water, fruit-juice, honey and oil which this child was sucking. The child kept on growing alarmingly (Page 190, Vol. I, *Tafrihul Askia Fil Ahwal Ul Ambia*).

Abraham was born at Ur under these trying circumstances about 352 years after the Deluge or around 2018 B.C. His original name was Abram which means "Lofty father" (Genesis 11: 26-27). It was subsequently changed by God to Abraham, which means "A father of many nations" (Genesis 17: 5), when the Covenant was made that every male child shall be circumcised. From him sprang the Ishmaelites or the Meccans, Israelities or the Jews as also the Edomites, Medanites and Midianites.

When Abraham was 15 months old, he looked like a fifteen year old boy. It was only at this stage that Terah met the boy and allowed him to come to his house from the cave in which he was born. (page 190, Vol. I, *Tafrihul Askia Fil Ahwal Ul Ambia*). This happened a few months after Nimrod's soldiers were completely withdrawn from Ur.

This incident reminds one of the massacre of new-born male Jewish children by the Pharaoh of Egypt at the time of the birth of Moses (Exodus 1: 15-22).

E. How Abraham Acquired Knowledge of God and His Teachings

The undermentioned verses recount briefly but very vividly how Abraham acquired knowledge of God in a logical and systematic manner and taught these to the members of his family and relatives:

> "Thus did We[1] (Allah) show Abraham the kingdom of the heavens and the earth that he might be of those possessing certainty.
>
> "When the night grew dark upon him, he beheld a star. (He thought to himself that the bright star represented Astarte the queen of Heavens as worshipped by his father). Accordingly he said: Is this my Lord? But when it set, he said: I love not things that set.
>
> "And when he saw the moon uprising (he thought to himself

---

[1] In many oriental languages, including Arabic, when a king or a great personage addresses somebody he usually uses "We" or "Us" which is a proud form of saying "I" or "me" in the singular number: Similarly "We" and "Us" have been used very often in the Qur'an by Allah and represent the singular number and not the plural.

it represented Nimrod the only begotten son of God as had been taught to him by his father), he therefore said: Is this my Lord? But when it (the moon) set, (in the west) he said: If my Lord does not guide me, I surely shall become one of the folks who are astray.

"And when he saw the sun rising (as was taught to him by his father Terah representing the god of the gods), he cried: Is this my Lord? This is (indeed) greater! And when it set he exclaimed: Oh my people! I am free from all that ye associate (with Allah like Nimrod's teachings of Trinity in unity, *etc*).

"Lo! I have turned my face towards Him, Who created the heavens and the earth: as one by nature upright, and I am not of the idolaters.

"(Remember) when Abraham said unto his father Azar (this is the title or call name of Terah): Takest thou idols for gods? Lo! I see thee and thy (household) folk in error manifest.

"His people (members of the family and relatives) argued with him. He said: Dispute ye with me concerning Allah when He hath guided me? I fear not at all of that which ye set beside Him (and no harm will come to me) unless my Lord willeth. My Lord includeth all things in His knowledge. Will ye not then remember (what happened a few hundred years earlier—the Great Deluge which destroyed the entire mankind except the family of Noah and his three sons and their wives and a few pairs of animals)?

"How should I fear which ye (yourselves create out of imagination and in ignorance have) set up besides Him, when ye fear not to set up (rivals like Nimrod) beside Allah, things for which He hath revealed unto you no warrant? Which of the two factions hath more right to safety? (Answer me that)" if ye have knowledge.

"Those who believe and obscure not their belief by wrong doings, theirs is safety; and they are rightly guided.

"That is Our (Allah's) argument. We (Allah) gave it to Abraham against his folk. We (Allah) raise unto degrees of wisdom whom We (Allah) will. Lo! Thy Lord is Wise, Aware" (Qur'an 6: 76-80, 75, 81-84).

"And (I, Allah) make mention (O Muhammad) in this Scripture of Abraham. Lo! He was a saint, a Prophet.

"When he said unto his father: O my father! Why worshippest thou that which heareth not nor seeth, nor can in aught avail thee?

"O my father! Lo! there hath come unto me of knowledge that which came not unto thee. So follow me, and I will lead thee on a right path.

"O my father! Serve not the devil. Lo! The devil (this is a reference to Nimrod, who is described in the Holy Bible as the mighty hunter in rebellion against God) is a rebel unto the Beneficent.

"O my father! Lo! I fear lest a punishment from the Beneficent overtake thee so that thou become a comrade of the devil (*i.e.* Nimrod the cursed, due to whom the unity of mankind was destroyed at the Tower of Babel).

"He (Terah or Azar, *i.e.* the father of Abraham) said: Rejectest thou my gods, O Abraham? If thou cease not, I shall surely stone thee (to death). Depart from me a long while!

"He (Abraham) said: Peace be unto thee! I shall ask forgiveness of my Lord for thee. Lo! He was ever gracious unto me.

"I shall withdraw from you and that unto which ye pray beside Allah, and I shall pray unto my Lord. It may be that, in prayer unto my Lord, I shall not be unblest" (Qur'an 19: 41-48).

From the above passages it is clear that Abraham was gifted with the knowledge of God together with an understanding of His Teachings.

F. Abraham, the idol breaker, thrown into the fire by Nimrod or Tammuz—Fire the perfector

When Abraham, in spite of repeated attempts, found that it was useless to preach to Terah, his father, and to the other members of the family and his relatives, he decided upon preaching to the public. According to the historical records on the lives of the earlier prophets to be found on pages 203 and 204, Vol. I, "*Tafrihul Askia Fil Ahwal Ul Ambia*", Abraham was about 16 years old at this point of time.

The Qur'an shows that Abraham preached to the people of Ur as follows:

What are these images unto which ye pay devotion?

"They replied: We found our fathers worshippers of them.

"He said: Verily ye and your fathers were in plain error, (for believing in Nimrod as the only begotten son of the Sun-god, the moon or the lamb (Aries) of the heavens, the trinity in unity, who has come to save sinners by the sacrifice of his life, who was born of Semiramis, the virgin queen of the heavens, thus committing blasphemy because God has no equals nor trinities in unities, neither any father nor mother, nor husband nor virgin wife nor any begotten son nor any daughter nor a brother nor a sister. And that standing before idols and praying was idolatry. Further, Nimrod was the son of Cush, the son of Ham, the son of Noah. Semiramis was not a virgin but the wife of Cush. Idols had no power to hear prayers nor any power to move nor give any help to their worshippers. Idols were the creation of man therefore inferior to man, whilst God is the Creator of the entire Universe therefore superior to all that is in it, hence the only one who deserves to be worshipped. It was He, who destroyed humanity by the great Deluge for their disobedience and disbelief in Him).

They asked: Bringest thou into us the truth, or art thou some jester?

"He explained: Nay, but your Lord is the Lord of the heavens and the earth, Who created them; and I am of those who testify unto that" (Qur'an 21: 52-56).

In his arguments with the public Abraham repeatedly pointed out that "idols" were nothing but their own creation. The idols could not even talk nor walk nor hear prayers nor be of any assistance to others. The logic of Abraham caused great confusion amongst the people of Ur. Since they were so much under the magical spell cast by Nimrod, they still used to threaten to kill Abraham just as his own father had done (Qur'an 19: 46) as read earlier.

During one of his arguments Abraham had threatened that he would destroy their idols only for the purpose of bringing home the point that idols had no power whatsoever. Further, to prove that when idols were even unable to defend themselves from being broken by some ordinary human being then how could the idols defend others *viz*: their worshippers. Hence to pray before idols was absolutely meaningless and a waste of time and energy. This is referred to in the Qur'an as follows:

"And, by Allah, I shall circumvent your idols after ye have gone away and turned your backs" (Qur'an 21: 57).

One day, for celebrating some pagan feast, all the people of the town of Ur went out, possibly for bathing in the river to wash their sins away. Abraham seized this opportunity and destroyed all the idols excepting the biggest one. When the people returned and saw all the idols shattered except the biggest one, they were enraged. This incident is briefly recorded in the Qur'an as:

"Then he (Abraham) reduced them (idols) to fragments, all save the chief of them, that haply they (the people of Ur) might have recourse to it.

"They said: Who hath done this to our gods? Surely it must be some evil-doer.

"They said: We heard a youth make mention of them, who is called Abraham.

"They said: Then bring him (hither) before the people's eyes that they may testify.

"They said: Is it thou who hast done this to our gods, O Abraham?

"He (Abraham) replied: But this, their chief hath done it. So question him, if he can speak (and tell you who has done it).

"Then gathered they apart and (Abraham) said: Lo! Ye yourselves are the wrong-doers.

"And they were utterly confounded (by Abraham), and (after they had gathered their wits) they said: Well thou knowest that these speak not.

"He said: Then (are) ye (so very foolish as to) worship instead of Allah that which cannot profit you at all, nor harm you?

"Fie on you and all that ye worship instead of Allah. Have ye then no sense?" (Qur'an 21: 58-67).

The people of Ur, were so much upset by Abraham's deeds and arguments that they reported the matter to their king the famous Nimrod of Babylon, who realised very well that this was the youth who would cause his downfall. He was able to corroborate this fact by means of his magical powers. He thus came to know how Abraham was born and escaped the massacre 15/17 years earlier at Ur.

His teachings of celibacy and keeping the men-folk away from the women of Ur for over a year had failed completely. He also knew by now that Abraham was the son of Terah born out of the incident of his sending Terah into the town to fetch something important for him, and Terah had broken his oath of not seeing his wife while inside Ur to fetch the important article. Thus Abraham had been conceived as had been foretold in his dream.

King Nimrod came immediately to Ur and publicly questioned Abraham. Abraham was then 16/17 years old. This incident took place about 237 years after the Tower of Babel or early in the year 2001 B.C. Their discussion is briefly narrated in the following passages:

> "Then turned he (Abraham) to their gods and said: Will ye not eat?
>
> "What aileth you that ye speak not?
>
> "He said: (Are ye so very foolish and ignorant) that ye worship that, which ye yourselves have carved out" (Qur'an 37: 91-92, 95).
>
> "He said: You have chosen idols instead of Allah. The love between you (*i.e.* between idolaters and their idols) is only in this life on earth. On the Day of Resurrection ye will deny each other, and curse each other, and your abode will be the Fire (of Hell), and ye will have no helpers.
>
> "Do they not realise how Allah produceth creation (*i.e.* prehistoric men then destroyed them completely, then created a new mankind from Adam, then He destroyed it by the great Deluge except the family of Noah and his three sons and their wives and the few pairs of animals that were saved in the ark), then reproduceth it? Lo! For Allah that is easy.
>
> "But if they deny, then (remember) nations have denied before you (and have refused to follow God's laws according to the teachings of the earlier prophets for which reason they were destroyed by the great Deluge). The messenger is only to convey (the Divine message) plainly" (Qur'an 29: 25, 19, 18).
>
> "They (Nimrod and his priests and followers) cried: Burn him (Abraham) and stand by your gods" (Qur'an 21: 68).

It was the practice of proud and arrogant Nimrod that

whenever anybody opposed his teachings, he used to have the person publicly burnt at the stake, so that his cries could be heard by the public and everybody was thus frightened to oppose this imperious king.

Whenever this used to happen Nimrod would exclaim that he had purified the earth of an evil. Thus he won, the title of "TAM MUZ" or "Fire, the Perfecter".

The initial "T" or "Tau" of Tammuz was written in old Hebrew as an upright Cross (see *Destruction or Peace,* Chapter 5: F-2). Since this was the method adopted by King Nimrod to burn Abraham, "The Sign of the Cross" is a sign which is hated by all the descendants of Abraham and his followers, because the "upright cross" reminded them of the stakes at which the followers of the True God used to be burnt by Nimrod for their refusal to accept Trintity of "the only begotten son of god born of the virgin queen of the heavens".

This system of burning people alive at the stake has become a well-recognised feature amongst the followers of Nimrodism.

On pages 203-204, Vol. I, "*Tafrihul Askia Fil Ahwal Ul Ambia*" it is recorded that timber for the fire was collected and piled up for thirty days at a place called Amwala Bani-ana, where the signs of the great fire were still to be found. It took seven days to light this huge pile of wood.

So intense was the heat of this fire that it was impossible for anyone to approach it. A problem arose as to how Abraham was to be thrown into this fire. A catapult was invented for this purpose. This was the first man-made machine that came into existence through the ingenuity of Nimrod, the evil genius.

As Abraham was brought, a man named Paijama was ordered to undress him and place him on the catapult. As soon as he touched the clothes covering the lower half of the body of

Abraham he was paralysed and that was his end.

Then Abraham was placed on the catapult, with his clothes on and flung into the fire.

Whilst all this was going on, the angels in Heaven pleaded with God Almighty for permission to save Abraham. The Angel of Wind said, 'Give me authority and I will blow away the entire pile of burning wood before Abraham can be thrown into it'. The Angel of Rains said, 'Give me authority and I will put out the fire before Abraham can fall into it'. The entire Heavenly dwellers pleaded for the safety of Abraham. To this Allah replied, "Go and ask My Khalil (*i.e.* Friend) and see what he has to say".

Thereupon all the Angels flashed into view and pleaded with Abraham for his authority. But Abraham's reply was:

> "If God wants His friend (Khalil) to die then it is wrong for the Khalil or friend to try and save himself against the wishes of his beloved. That is the essence of true love. Therefore let God do whatsoever pleases Him and in the fulfilment of that I am happy and satisfied. I am of those who joyfully submit themselves to the Will of God".

God was gratified with this wonderful reply of Abraham. This retort of Abraham is further supported by the following divine passages:

> "O People (*i.e.* believers in) the (divine) Scriptures! Why do you argue about Abraham, when the Torah and the Evangel were not revealed until (long) after Him? Have ye then no sense?
>
> "Abraham was not a Jew, nor a Nazarene, but he was an upright man who was a "Muslim" (*i.e.* one who had surrendered himself to the Will of Allah) and he was not an idolater.
>
> "Lo! those of mankind, who have the best claim to Abraham,

are those who follow his principles (*i.e.* are Muslims *i.e.*, surrender to the Will of Allah) and this Prophet (*i.e.*, Muhammad) and those who believe (in Islam *i.e.*, the religion of surrender to the Will of God); and Allah is the Protecting Friend of the believers" (Qur'an 3: 65, 67-68).

"And who forsakes the religion of Abraham, save he who makes a fool of himself? And most certainly We (Allah) made him pure (literally "chose" him) in this world and lo! in the Hereafter he is among the righteous.

"When his Lord said unto him: "*Aslim*" (surrender)! be said: "*Aslamto*" (I have surrendered) to the Lord of the entire creation" (Qur'an 2: 130-131).

Thus Abraham proved not only to mankind but also before the spiritual forces *i.e.*, the whole universe that he was one who had absolutely surrendered himself to the Will of his Creator and that he was happy in God's pleasures. This was his trend of thought when he was flung by Nimrod from the catapult into the blazing inferno!

God issued an order directly on the fire as Abraham was falling into the pyre as follows:

> We (Allah) said: O fire! Be a coolness and a (place of) peace for Abraham" (Qur'an 21: 69).

After Abraham had fallen into the fire everybody was surprised to hear clearly the voice of Abraham coming from the fire speaking to someone (who was Angel Gabriel). The latter stated that by Allah's orders he was freeing Abraham from the chains in which he had been bound by King Nimrod's followers and that the fire had been ordered by God to become a place of comfort for Abraham and that no harm was going to come to him and thus Nimrod's efforts to destroy him would be a complete failure.

When everybody miraculously heard all this talk between

Abraham and the Angel Gabriel coming from the pyre, naturally a heated debate arose as to what should now be done.

Princess Razia, the sixteen-year-old daughter of King Nimrod, had accompanied her father from Babylon for this occasion. Upon hearing this talk which was taking place in the fire and the discussions between her father and his advisers, she pointed out to them that it was an unbelievable miracle that such a big fire was not harming Abraham in any way. Also the statement of Angel Gabriel to Abraham that he would safely escape clearly showed that the God of Abraham was indeed the one and only True God. Therefore the idols broken by Abraham were nothing but worthless creations of ignorant people, and could not be of any assistance to anybody. Hence she declared to her father: "Behold! The God of Abraham is the True God. Therefore, everyone should forthwith accept Abraham's teachings".

Nimrod was so furious at this that he and his advisers thought it best to kill the princess and make her an example of what happens to believers in Abraham. No sooner than did Razia see their faces full of fury, raging with anger and on the verge of pouncing upon her like hungry lions upon a defenceless victim than she realised she had no alternative but to accept the red high flames. Immediately she leapt down from the royal dais and blindly rushed into the raging inferno exclaiming:

"Oh God of Abraham, be my safety!"

Princess Razia, however, safely reached the centre of the blazing inferno to find Abraham unharmed and that neither her own clothes nor her hair nor her body were singed. This all the more convinced her about the absolute powers of the God of Abraham. She immediately became a disciple of the faith of Abraham.

King Nimrod in his rage thundered like lightning and commanded his courtiers who were standing on the ground near the platform to catch her. One Haroon ran after her but was immediately burnt to death. No one else could do anything.

When the wicked king realised that he was powerless to stop his daughter from accepting the religion of Abraham he cursed and abused her bitterly. His courtiers followed suit.

Abraham educated Razia that to call anyone the only begotten son of god, the lamb of the heavens come to save sinners was blasphemy. To pray before idols was idolatry and to deserve Heaven in the life hereafter one had to do good deeds. God alone would arbitrate on the Day of Judgement. Nimrod's theory that he would be sitting on the right hand of God as the only begotten son, the saviour, the sin-bearer forgiving the baptised sinners was nothing but blasphemy and fantasy. One's sins are not forgiven for one's partaking of sacramental meals and drinks. It was the height of absurdity to think that by partaking of the sacramental foods one could become the pure sinless flesh and blood of the deity himself.

Everybody watching the pyre miraculously heard these teachings of Abraham and Razia's acceptance of the religion of Abraham. This all the more infuriated Nimrod.

After acquiring knowledge of the true religion of Abraham, Princess Razia walked out of the fire on the opposite side to where her father and his courtiers were and went into the surrounding forest. As she was escaping into the forest she was sighted. King Nimrod and his men gave her chase. (pages 203-204, Vol. I, *"Tafrihul Askia Fil Ahwal Ul Ambia"*).

As soon as Nimrod and his men disappeared from view in the chase, Abraham received instructions to flee immediately from the kingdoms of Nimrod to Haran with the believing members of his family.

Abraham walked out of the fire unharmed. His sister Sarah (who was then six years old) and his nephew Lot, both believed in Abraham's religion. They decided to escape with him before Nimrod returned from his hunt.

Terah the father of Abraham, was afraid he would be killed now that Nimrod knew fully the truth about the birth of Abraham and how he had lied about not going near his wife when he had been sent into the city of Ur. So he also decided to escape from the wrath of his king and joined Abraham and the two believers. They all fled away together.

Thus the divine message to Abraham quoted hereunder was fulfilled:

> "And they (*i.e.* Nimrod and his followers) wished to set a snare for him (*i.e.* when Abraham came out alive from the fire they would surround and kill him on the spot), but We (Allah) made them the great losers (by getting Princess Razia to be converted to the faith of Abraham and escape into the forest, with her father and his men hunting for her, whilst Abraham made good his escape).
>
> "And We (Allah) rescued him (Abraham) and Lot (and eventually brought them), to the land, which We (Allah) have blessed (*i.e.* from Mecca for Ishmael to Palestine for Isaac with Madinah and Beersheba in between) for the peoples" (Qur'an 21: 70-71).

In spite of a search everywhere for Princess Razia in the forest she was not found and nothing more is known about her after this incredible episode.

When King Nimrod returned tired and disappointed from the unsuccessful chase after his daughter Razia, he was shocked to learn that Abraham and those who believed in him together with

Terah had all eluded him. He was naturally inflamed and he kept on plotting how to do away with Abraham, because he knew very well from his dream that Abraham would not only bring about his downfall but would also cause his death by violence.

From page 245 of *"The Two Babylons,"* by the Rev. A. Hislop we observe the following:

> "The name Tammuz as applied to Nimrod or Osiris, was equivalent to Alorus or the 'god of fire', and seems to have been given to him as the great purifier by fire. Tammuz is derived from TAM, 'to make perfect', and MUZ, 'fire' and signifies 'Fire, the perfecter', or the 'perfecting fire'. To this meaning of the name, as well as to the character of Nimrod as the Father of the gods, the Zoroastrian verse alludes when it says: 'All things are the progeny of ONE FIRE. THE FATHER perfected all things, and delivered them to second mind, whom all nations call the first' ... And hence, too no doubt the necessity of the fire of purgatory to 'perfect' men's souls and to purge away all the sins that they have carried with them into the unseen world".

Further, in the appendix of *"The Two Babylons"*, The Rev. Hislop points out that "Zoroaster" means "fire the perfecter".

G. How Nimrod won the Title of "A Mighty Hunter in Rebellion against God"

Nimrod now realised how he had failed to prevent the birth of Abraham and also to kill him upon his birth, or to burn him when he was 16 years old. Therefore Nimrod decided to hunt and kill the God of Abraham, Who had so cleverly contrived Abraham's escape from his clutches by sending him on a futile chase into the forest after his own daughter Princess Razia.

Accordingly he built a tower in about three years which was stated to be 5,000 yards high with the object of shooting and killing God with his arrows. When this tall tower was ready, Nimrod climbed on to it. But to his great chagrin he found the heavens, the supposed abode of God, as far away from the ground as from this high tower. He came down rather thwarted. The next day a great storm came and blew away the top of this tower. (Page 209, Vol. I, "*Tafrihul Askia Fil Ahwal Ul Ambia*" and page 140, Vol. I, *Ajaibul Kasas*).

He therefore captured four large birds, having speed and great stamina for long distance flights. He fed them well over a period and strengthened them. Next he constructed a light but sturdy two-storied box with one window in each of the two compartments, the window of the upper floor opening upwards and the lower looking downwards. He occupied the upper chamber armed with bows and arrows and a companion of his got into the lower floor. He tied four large pieces of meat to four long poles at the four corners out of the reach of the four birds, who were chained to the four corners of this contraption. Thus the birds flew up after the tempting meat just over their heads but out of their reach, drawing up the casket with Nimrod and his accomplice. After flying upward for a full day he asked his companion to open the lower window and report upon what he could see. He replied that he saw only a vast blue expanse like an ocean below him. Then Nimrod opened the upper window only to find that the sky was as far away from there as it was from the earth below. He flew upwards for another day. Then he asked his friend to open the lower window once again and report upon what he saw. The answer was that they had flown so far away from the earth that no part of the earth, not even the blue expanse of the Ocean, was visible to the naked eye. A vast expanse of a layer of light smoke far below was all that could be seen. Nimrod now thought that he had flown up high enough as he was experiencing difficulty in breathing due to the rarefied atmosphere at this height.

The haughty king then shot several arrows straight upwards into the sky through his upper window in his attempt to shoot and kill the God of Abraham and Noah. According to the orders of God Almighty, these arrows were caught by the Angels and dipped in the blood of fish and then allowed to fall back upon the casket by the natural force of gravity. When the blood stained arrows fell back and struck the casket in which the two were flying, Nimrod, seeing the blood-stained arrows, happily lowered the meats by swinging the poles downward, but still out of reach of the eagles to commence their journey earthward.

When he returned with the blood-stained arrows in proof of his hunting and killing God, he was proudly acclaimed "The mighty hunter in rebellion against God". Thus he won the great title of the "Mighty hunter" which is attached to his name in the Holy Bible (Genesis 10: 9). This not only made Nimrod, the Pontifex Maximus, the supreme and infallible being who had not even failed in killing and destroying the God of Abraham and Noah, but it also made his believers imagine that their religion was now without doubt far superior to the religion of God taught by Noah and Abraham. Thus spread throughout the world the religion of the mighty hunter, the "Super-religion" of "the only begotten son of god through the great virgin mother, the lamb of the heavens come to save sinners" claiming ascendancy over all other religions.

H. Excommunication

When Abraham was about 77 years old, he was ordered at Beersheba by God to go back to King Nimrod in Babylon and once again to try and bring him back to the belief in the true God. Abraham accordingly went to Nimrod. When Nimrod saw Abraham he boasted that he had killed the God of Abraham and Noah by shooting arrows into the heavens and proudly related his hunting expedition in the flying casket. After hearing everything Abraham, asked Nimrod whether the sky was as far away from the great height reached after two days of upward flight as it was from earth. Nimrod had to admit that even at that great height which he had attained after two days of upward flight, the sky was still apparently as far away from him as it was from the ground. Then Abraham asked him if it was possible for him to shoot his arrows from the ground so that they may reach and get stuck in heaven without falling back to the ground? Nimrod had to admit that his arrows if shot from the ground could never reach anywhere near heaven. At this Abraham pointed out that since heaven was as far away from the great height reached by Nimrod as it was from the ground it was equally inconceivable for his arrows to have reached heaven as it was impossible from the ground. Nimrod had to concede to this logic of Abraham's argument. Yet Nimrod insisted he must have been successful because his arrows were tipped with blood when they fell back. Abraham smiled and said that Angel Gabriel had already informed him that when Nimrod had shot his arrows from his flying casket, the arrows had been caught by the Angels and under God's orders they were returned dipped in the blood of fish. Nimrod was naturally very angry when he realised how he had been duped by God Almighty (page 141, Vol. 1, *Ajaibul Kasas*).

Therefore, with a view to securing his supreme position further as the Pontifex Maximus, Nimrod boasted to Abraham that he had all the powers of God, such as even to take life at his sweet will and to grant life when he wanted. To prove his powers to Abraham he ordered a criminal sentenced to death to be released, thus giving life to one who had lost the right to live. He then ordered an innocent man to be taken from his house and killed, thus taking life when he wanted. This incident is quoted briefly in the last divine scripture as follows:

"Do you remember of him (King Nimrod), who had an argument with Abraham about his Lord, because Allah had given him the (first human) Kingdom (for the Kingdom of Nimrod please refer to Genesis 10: 9-19); how when Abraham said: My Lord is He Who giveth life and causeth death, he (King Nimrod) answered: I give life and cause death. Abraham said: Lo! Allah causeth the sun to rise in the East, so do thou cause it to come up from the West (if you are a god or the trinity in unity with God or the only begotten son of God). Thus was the disbeliever (the Infallible Pontifex Maximus) abashed (for the first time in his life), and Allah guideth not wrong doing folk" (Qur'an 2: 258).

Nimrod was very justifiably worried that if the truth of what Abraham had asserted became known to his followers, namely, that Nimrod was not god, nor the only begotten son of god, nor born of a virgin mother but the son of Cush, the grandson of Noah, nor trinity in unity but an inferior being who was certainly unable to make the sun rise from the West then he would not only lose his great title of "Mighty hunter in rebellion against God", but all his religious teachings also about the only begotten son of god come to save sinners would become discredited. He would also be ridiculed.

Nimrod therefore ordered that anybody listening to any other religious teachings henceforth, except those taught by him, would be excommunicated from the society and burnt at the stake. This order thus became a permanent feature of all religions originating from Nimrod to prevent the proliferation of other doctrines to the followers of his religion. This prohibition is still in force amongst the followers of Nimrodism.

I. Death of King Nimrod by violence

Nimrod decided he must do something drastic to demolish the Almighty God of Abraham and Noah. He challenged Abraham that he was going to prepare a huge army to fight and kill God once and for all. Accordingly this arrogant and mighty hunter in rebellion against God, this Pontifex Maximus—the Infallible sent a challenge to God through Abraham. Abraham therefore had to return to Beersheba without achieving any success.

After about seven years when Abraham was about 83 years old, he was again ordered by God Almighty to pay yet another visit to King Nimrod of Babylon and to try to bring him to the true faith. When Abraham arrived, he found Nimrod had gathered a huge army taking men from almost all countries and communities who followed his religion. He had armed them fully and trained them thoroughly. Nimrod, on seeing Abraham, challenged him to ask God to come and oppose him in an open confrontation on the battlefield, Abraham was very much upset but he prayed to God for an answer. The Angel Gabriel communicated that God was fully prepared to meet Nimrod and his huge army on a nominated field on a particular day and at a specific time. Nimrod accordingly went to the selected site which was quite close to Babylon. At the appointed day and time a cloud of small flying creatures appeared. The army of Nimrod could not destroy them. These tiny flying creatures simply fell upon the army and ate into the flesh and bones and drank their blood, killing each and every soldier. Nimrod alone fled from the battlefield to his queen in Babylon and narrated all that had happened. His queen asked him for a description of these flying creatures. Just then he saw one such creature approaching and he pointed it out. This creature flew into Nimrod's nose and bored its way into his brain and started biting. (According to E. Arnold's study this, creature bored its way into Nimrod's brain through his ear). It was so painful that Nimrod began beating his head with his hand. When he beat his head he felt relieved for a few minutes. Then again the biting started and he again beat his head and got solace for a few minutes. When the biting became very painful and the relief by beating his head with his hands became ineffective, Nimrod ordered an iron rod to be taken and his head to be hit with it every time the biting started. Thus he gained succour for a few minutes each time. This continued for forty days and nights without any peace or rest for the so-called Infallible Pontifex Maximus. Abraham came daily during this period and pleaded with Nimrod to give up his blasphemous claims to divinity, trinity in unity and the only begotten son born of the great virgin mother. Abraham preached to Nimrod to stop his rebellion against God Almighty and to seek his forgiveness. Nimrod proudly taunted him on the first day after his army had been destroyed, "Oh Abraham! Your God has indeed very foolishly killed a very large portion of the male population of the whole world, now who are left to accept your God?" Next day Abraham came back and replied that he had been informed by God, that there were plenty of things even besides human beings who believe in the True God. Nimrod haughtily insinuated that Abraham was now talking nonsense. Thereupon his personal household animals one by one spoke miraculously and gave evidence that the God of Abraham and Noah is the one and only true God. The furious Nimrod ordered them to be killed one by one as each gave evidence.

After each animal was killed Nimrod would mockingly ask, who was still left to give evidence God Almighty. Abraham would point to the next animal and it would speak miraculously and give evidence. This procedure continued for several days until not a single horse or cow or other pet, fowl or bird was left alive at the palace of Nimrod in Babylon because each one of them had given evidence of the true God of Abraham and Noah. After each killing Nimrod would ask Abraham, who remained to give evidence about God Almighty. Then Abraham said, "The trees in your garden will give evidence". Thus one by one each tree in his garden spoke miraculously and bore witness "*La Ilaaha Illal-*

Laahu Ibrahim Khalilullah" (There is no God but Allah and Abraham is the Friend of Allah). One by one the so-called only begotten son of the virgin had all his beautiful trees cut down and his wonderful Hanging Gardens of Babylon spoilt. Whenever each item was destroyed he would boastfully ask Abraham, who was left to give evidence. In this manner several days passed until not a fruit or flower tree was left.

Then Abraham said, the beautiful gate of your palace will give evidence of God Almighty. When the gate miraculously spoke, the blasphemer had it destroyed. Then the pillars of his palace and eventually the walls of his castle gave testimony and these too he destroyed systematically.

It was by now the fortieth day of the attack of the flying creature biting into the brains of the so-called Infallible Pontifex Maximus, when Abraham again came for the last time and pleaded with the haughty king to accept God Almighty and ask for His forgiveness but Nimrod, the claimant to the seat on the right hand of God, dispensing justice on the day of Judgment, proudly taunted, "Oh Abraham if there is anything else left to give evidence about the True God, bring it before me and I will destroy it, and thus show to you whose power is greater—Your God's power or mine?"

Abraham replied, "The royal robes you have on your body will give evidence". Thereupon his clothes miraculously spoke and testified that Allah is the One and Only and that none are comparable to Him. The rebel angrily threw off his royal robes and burnt them proudly boasting: "Now is there anything left to give evidence that there is only one true God, who has no equal and who is alone the Master and Creator of the entire universe and can challenge my claim of being the divine god, the trinity in unity?" Nimrod further said: "Have I not destroyed everything that gave evidence due to your magical powers against me, the lamb of the heavens who has come to save sinners. Now tell me indeed who is greater—your God or me, the Infallible Pontifex Maximus?"

Abraham indeed felt most disappointed. The Angel Gabriel thereupon appeared and informed Abraham that Nimrod and all those who followed his teaching of the only begotten son of god, *etc*, had been condemned to everlasting Hell by God and that he now had only a few breaths of life left; hence there was no cause for disappointment. Just as Nimrod was destroyed, so shall not only Babylon be devastated but also these blasphemous teachings shall one day be obliterated in some terrible disasters of such great magnitudes that very large sections of humanity will also be effaced. It is this prediction of the destruction of a large part of humanity as a result of the curse of God from the Tower of Babel which is haunting mankind today: It will end in the battle of Armageddon when Nimrodism will be annihilated and a new civilisation started.

Just then the insect which had got into Nimrod's brain started biting once more. The mighty rebel ordered a hard blow to be struck on his head. In obedience the king's servant struck a blow with the iron rod. Nimrod's skull was fractured and he fell down dead at the age of about 341 years *i.e.* in or about 1934 B.C. A few minutes later the insect crept out of his body and flew away. (Pages 209-212, Vol. I, *Tafrihul Askia Fil Ahwal Ul Ambia* and pages 141-143, Vol. I, *Ajaibul Kasas*).

Thus ended violently the life of Nimrod. However, this religion of Babylon did not come to an end upon his death. Its believers have and will continue to suffer many a disaster until it is totally effaced at the Battle of Armageddon.

J. The Great Sacrifice by which The Only Begotten Son is to Save Sinners

We have read how Nimrod experienced a period of forty days of agony ending in his turbulent death, the so-called sacrifice of his pure soul, with which he would save the "Baptised" sinners of the world—the death with a broken skull due to his refusal to accept Abraham's teachings that God is only one and not a Trinity in unity.

Thus at the hands of Abraham this rebellious blasphemer of Babylon as well as his followers have been condemned to hell. Can such a condemned Nimrod, the so-called saviour, redeemer, sin-bearer, son of God, trinity in unity *etc.*, save anybody from among his Baptised followers and sinners? Can sacramental food and wine make one the "Sinless" pure deity, who himself is full of sins and condemned to everlasting hell? Even if sacramental food were able to convert one into the deity who is damned, then are not his followers automatically condemning themselves to hell by eating and drinking such sacramental food and drink? Or is it the magical net dragging into its meshes the many millions, who have absolute faith in these principles, condemnation in hell? What is the correct position? Let everyone think for himself. Can the laws of God ever be a curse for mankind by any stretch of the imagination? Or is the magical hypnotic spell of Nimrod's baptism and the sign of the Cross so very strong as to blind the millions and intoxicate them so that they can no longer distinguish between blasphemy and the plain truth? Let them ponder over the warning of the Angel Gabriel to Abraham so to be found in the Holy Bible as:

> "Babylon, hath been a golden cup ... that made all the earth drunken the nations have drunken of her wine (by being "Baptised" and thus initiated into this religion on which the curse of God fell at the Tower of Babel—the religion of the

only begotten son of god born of the great virgin mother, the trinity in unity, the lamb of heavens come to save sinners by the sacrifice of his life to a violent death in maintaining his religion, sacramental food, idolatry, the signs of the cross, laws of God are a curse for mankind, sitting on the right hand of God on the day of Judgment to save baptized sinners and condemn doers of good deeds for small mistakes, *etc.*), *Therefore The Nations Are Mad."* (Jeremiah 51: 7).

Thus according to the Holy Bible the greatest obstacle to world unity is the magical and intoxicating religious influence of Nimrod of Babylon. This religion as seen earlier affirms:

1. Abraham as the betrayer of their saviour.
2. Abraham's teachings of God being One and Alone as the "forces of darkness".
3. The death of Nimrod at the instance of Abraham as the great sacrifice by the only begotten son of god by which he would save the baptised sinners *etc.*

K. Expressions of Hate by Nimrod's Followers

The man who single-handedly not only braved the wrath and might of King Nimrod, the proud hunter in rebellion against God but also destroyed his vaunted infallibility and brought about his downfall ending in his violent death was Prophet Abraham, the friend of Allah. Thus he terminated the Anti-God reign of the first Blasphemer who claimed divinity as son of God, Godhood in trinity and superiority over God on the Day of Judgment, the killer of God, the infallible Pontifex Maximus. After him his followers have continued to maintain these fantastic blasphemous claims.

In the East, the worst form of abuse is to call someone a pig or a swine. Therefore this enemy, who caused the violent death of the saviour, is abused in the pagan religious beliefs all over as the "wild boar" or the most ferocious type of a pig.

In revenge against Abraham, the instrument which caused the death of "the lamb of the heavens come to save sinners by the sacrifice of his life", his pagan followers ate swine-flesh in expression of their hatred and as an abuse towards this enemy of their sin-bearer, *i.e.* the Prophet Abraham, the Friend of Allah.

In *"The Two Babylons"* by the Rev. A. Hislop, pages 99-102, we read as under:

> "In many countries the boar was sacrificed to the god, for the injury a boar was fabled to have done him. According to one version of the story of the death of Adonis, or Tammuz, it was, as we have seen, in consequence of a wound from the tusk of a boar that he died. The Phrygian Attis, the beloved of Cybele, whose story was identified with that of Adonis, was fabled to have perished in like manner, by the tusk of a boar. Therefore, Diana, who though commonly represented in popular myths only as huntress Diana, was in reality the great mother of the gods, has frequently the boar's head as her accompaniment, in token not of any mere success in the chase, but of her triumph over, the grand enemy of the idolatrous system, in which she occupied so conspicuous a place. According to Theocritus, Venus was reconciled to the boar that killed Adonis, because when brought in chains before her it pleaded so pathetically that it had not killed her husband of *malice prepense*, but only through accident. But yet, in memory of the deed that mystic boar had done, many a boar lost its head or was offered in sacrifice to the offended goddess. In Smith, Diana is represented with a boar's head lying beside her, on the top of a heap of stones, and in the accompanying woodcut, in which the Roman Emperor Trajan is represented burning incense to the same goddess, the boar's head forms a very prominent figure. On Christmas day the Continental Saxons offered a boar in sacrifice to the Sun, to

propitiate her for the loss of her beloved Adonis. In Rome a similar observance had evidently existed, for a boar formed the great article at the feast of Saturn, as appears from the following words of Martial:

"That boar will make you a good Saturnalia".

"Hence the boar's head is still a standing dish in England at the Christmas dinner, while the reason of it is long since forgotten.

"There can be no doubt, then, that the Pagan festival at the winter solstice—in other words Christmas—was held in honour of the birth of the Babylonian Messiah".

The Watch Tower Bible and Tract Society on page 144 of their research *"Babylon the Great Has Fallen"* have similarly referred to eating of swine-flesh by the Babylonians.

Under these circumstances the eater of swine flesh is without doubt a hater and an abuser of Abraham, the friend of Allah and a follower of Nimrod!

Therefore the institution or origin of the eating of swine-flesh throughout the world was nothing but an expression of abuse, hate and revenge against the so-called "Force of darkness", who caused the violent death of their saviour. Who was this enemy whose flesh was being eaten in this abusive and hateful revenge? It was certainly that of "Abraham, the friend of Allah". Therefore the eating of swine-flesh is tantamount to the eating of the flesh of the Prophet Abraham in an offensive and bitter revenge.

It was for this reason that not only the eating of swine-flesh has been forbidden by God from the time of Abraham but even the touching of the carcass of a pig is also strictly prohibited. This will be clear from the following laws recorded in the Holy Bible:

"And the Lord spake unto Moses and to Aaron, saying unto them,

"And the swine, though he divide the hoof, and be cloven-footed, yet he cheweth not cud; he is unclean to you.

"Of their flesh shall Ye not eat, and their carcase shall Ye not touch, they are unclean unto you.

"And for these Ye shall be unclean: whosoever toucheth the carcase of them shall be unclean (for the whole of that day) until the (next day which starts at) even (i.e., sunset).

"And whosoever beareth ought of the carcase of them shall wash his clothes and be unclean (for the whole of that day) until the (next day which starts at) even (i.e., sunset)" (Leviticus 11: 1, 7-8, 24-25).

"Thou shall not eat any abominable thing.

"And the swine ... it is unclean unto you: ye shall not eat of their flesh, nor touch their dead carcase" (Deuteronomy 14: 3 and 8)

L. Peculiarities about Nimrod's Followers

Unfortunately, it has been a peculiar feature of the followers of Nimrod that in spite of it being proved to them beyond any doubt that what they are following is absurd and blasphemous, yet they persist in his false religion. They deliberately try to take a wrong interpretation of any proof given or if that is not possible then call the truth a falsehood. Thereby they stubbornly refuse to follow the plain truth. They still have the audacity to boast that theirs is the ideal religion on the face of the earth. As a matter of fact this religion of Nimrod has been the source of all disunity amongst mankind, since the time of the curse of God Almighty at the Tower of Babel. This curse is still plaguing mankind and has been for the past 4,000 years, causing disunity, wars and destruction, each time greater than the previous occasion. If man does not take heed he will surely destroy a very large part of mankind due to this curse God, on account of following the blasphemous teachings of Nimrod.

Unfortunately, the theories of "We are the superior" have developed from this source. The Aryan group of Nations have always claimed that they are the superior class as compared to all other nations.

Today we see the same attitude in a far more intense form in South Africa and Rhodesia and in a milder form in the Southern States of the U.S.A.—All this is nothing but "Nimrodism".

Such expressions were found in the scientifically advanced Germany and led to the Second World War with all its horror and destruction including the genocide of millions of Jews in Nazi Germany's Horror Camps and gas chambers.

Are not these the results of the curse of God at the Tower of Babel on the followers of Nimrod? Are we so blind that we still fail to realise this?

"Scientific World—Whither Bound?
To Self Destruction!

M. Punishment to Chosen People of God for Following Nimrod's Religion

The first king of the Jews ruling over Israel to come under the magical spell cast upon mankind by Nimrod and introduce his worship of Baal—"The Sacred Heart" come to save sinners by the sacrifice of his life—was Ahab, son of Omri, who came under this magical charm against Jewish Laws. He married the pagan Princess Jezebel, the daughter of Ethbaal, king of the Zidonians who was already under this spell of Nimrod (1 Kings 16: 20-33).

The Prophet Elijah challenged and forced King Ahab and the Jews to get their 450 priests of Nimrodism to make a sacrifice of any one of two bullocks brought for this purpose. If fire from heaven came and lit it up then they were right, but if fire from heaven lit up Elijah's offerings, then God Almighty was the true God and not Nimrod—Baal. The priests of Baal failed whilst Elijah was successful. Hence all 450 priests of Nimrodism were put to death and this cursed pagan worship of Nimrod was destroyed (1 Kings 18: 20-41).

In 759 B.C. Ahaz, son of King Jotham, became the king of the Jews in Judah at the age of 20 years. He ruled from Jerusalem. He again came under the spell of Nimrod on mankind and followed Nimrod's religion of Sun worship. He built temples to Baal (*i.e.* Nimrod) the only begotten son of the Sun-god and made his children walk over the fire and sacrificed his sons to Baal. Thus the Jews were drunk and immersed in this magical spell of Nimrod for the second time in the space of a few years (2 Kings 16: 1-4).

Thereafter came several Jewish kings who married pagans and followed Nimrodism in spite of repeated warnings from God (2 King 17: 2-17; 21: 1-22.) Eventually Jerusalem was destroyed in 607 B.C. for the sake of Nimrodism and the Jewish race, the chosen people of God, were put to the sword or made captives and slaves (2 Kings 25: 1-21 and Jeremiah 52: 8-15), the irony of the whole thing being that the Jews were destroyed by Babylon itself!

Chapter 4

The Life of Abraham

A. Abraham's First Marriage

Haran[2] in those days was a separate but powerful kingdom over which King Nimrod had no control. This city was also devoted to Nimrod's religion, which spread as we have seen from God's curse at the Tower of Babel. The citizens worshipped Nanna, the moon god, the only begotten son of the Sun god through Astarte, the virgin queen of the Heavens.

The Holy Bible confirms the escape of Abraham by informing us in Genesis 11: 31 that Terah left Ur with Abraham, Lot and Sarah and "they came unto Haran and dwelt there".

> "And the days of Terah were two hundred and five years: and Terah died in Haran" (Genesis 11: 32).

Just because Terah, an idolater, had accompanied his son Abraham and the two believers, all were stopped from reaching the Promised lands.

Abraham was about 17 years old when he reached Haran. Terah died in Haran at the age of 205 years. Abraham was 75 years old when his father died. Accordingly Abraham spent 58

---

[2] In the Old Testament the name is "*Haran*". In the New Testament it is spelt "*Charran*".

years in Haran.

A Nazarene martyr named Stephen, when in the witness box before the Jewish supreme Court in Jerusalem, where he was sworn in, confirmed this to the Judges:

"... The God of glory appeared unto our (fore)father Abraham, when he was in Mesopotamia before he dwelt in Charran.

"And said unto him, Get thee out of thy country, and from thy kindred; and come unto the land which I shall shew thee.

"Then came he out of the land of the Chaldaeans and dwelt in Charran: and from thence when his father was dead he removed himself unto this land, wherein ye now dwell" (Acts 7: 2-4).

It was not the custom for a brother to marry his own sister or step-sister. In fact Nimrod had been teaching that marriage should be only between people who had no blood relationship. Nevertheless marriage amongst cousins was common but certainly not between brothers and sisters.

One is therefore puzzled and intrigued as to why Abraham married his step-sister Sarah—a most unusual course! What was the compelling reason which forced him into such a strange and unusual marriage alliance!

When they came to the city of Haran, Abraham was 17 years old. When he left he was 75 years old (Genesis 12: 4). Sarah was 7 years old on arrival and 65 years old when she departed.

When Nimrod found out that Abraham and his party had escaped to Haran from the fire into which he had thrown Abraham, he immediately decided to send to Haran his storytellers as propagandists were known in those days. These spread the story of how Abraham had broken their idol-gods and thus committed sacrilege and warned the people to have nothing to do with Abraham. Therefore the people of Haran would have nothing to do with Abraham and the two believers, whom they would have put to death, but for Terah, who was one of the finest sculptors and makers of idols besides being an authority on paganism. Hence Terah was a highly respected person amongst the idolaters.

Hence Abraham, Sarah and Lot patiently spent their 58 years sojourn in Haran ostracized by the populace. The results were as follows:

1. Lot grew up from a little boy to the ripe old age of almost 70 years but nobody was prepared to give his daughter in marriage to him, so he was forced to remain unmarried all the time that they were in Haran.

2. Sarah grew up from the age of 7 years till she neared the age when she would soon become too old to bear children, yet nobody in Haran was prepared to marry her in spite of her great beauty.

3. Abraham was also not offered a single girl by the local populace in marriage, during his entire stay of 58 years in Haran.

4. Under such desperate conditions what were they to do? They had to do something at least about Sarah's marriage. Abraham being the eldest of the three had to be married first. Hence there was no option left but for Sarah to be married to her step-brother Abraham. That is the only logical explanation about the compelling circumstances under which Abraham was forced to marry his step-sister Sarah—a most unusual feature, even in those early days of human history.

The Torah confirms that Sarah was the step-sister of Abraham in the following passage:

"And yet indeed she (Sarah) is my sister; she is the daughter of my father, but not the daughter of my mother (but of my step-mother); and she became my wife" (Genesis 20: 12).

It will be observed from this Biblical quotation that under certain abnormal and unavoidable circumstances certain types of marriages, which were normally forbidden did take place even with Prophets! The fact that Abraham and the two believers patiently spent 58 years in Haran with daily humiliations and deprivations, without allowing their faith in God Almighty, to be shaken, indeed deserves the highest praise.

B. Abraham's Second Marriage

On the death of Terah in Haran, Abraham, who was then 75 years old, was ordered to leave for the Promised Land. Sarah, who was married at about the age of 35 was now about 65 years old. She had by this time passed the age of child-bearing. Sarah remained without child. This is related in the Torah in the following passages:

"But Sarai[3] was barren: she had no child" (Genesis 11: 30).

1. "Now the Lord had said unto Abram, (this is the original name of Abraham— see *Destruction or Peace,* Chapter 6: D) Get thee out of thy country, and from thy kindred, and from thy father's house, unto a land that I will shew thee:

2. "And I will make of thee a great nation and I will bless thee, and make thy name great; and thou shalt be a blessing:

3. "And I will bless them that bless thee, and curse him that curseth thee: and in thee shall all families of the earth be

---

[3] Sarai is the original name. It was changed to Sarah when she was going to give birth to Isaac (Genesis 17: 15-16).

blessed (This is the interpretation of the dream of Nimrod. Also Nimrod and his followers would be cursed for cursing Abraham by observing the sign of the Cross, Baptism, Easter and Winter Solstice festivals and eating swine-flesh).

4. "So Abram departed, as the LORD had spoken unto him; and Lot went with him: and Abram was seventy and five years old when he departed out of Haran.

5. "And Abram took Sarai his wife, and Lot his brother's son and all their substance that they had gathered, and the souls (servants) that they had gotten in Haran; and they went forth to go into the land of Canaan; and into the land of Canaan they came.

6. "And the LORD appeared unto Abram, and said, Unto thy seed will I give this land: and there builded he an altar unto the LORD, who appeared unto him.

7. "And Abram journeyed, going on still toward the south.

8. "And there was a famine in the land: and Abram went down into Egypt to sojourn there; for the famine was grievous in the land.

9. "And it came to pass, when he was come near to enter into Egypt, that he said unto Sarai his wife, Behold now, I know that thou art a fair woman to look upon:

10. "Therefore it shall come to pass; when the Egyptians shall see thee, that they shall say, this is his wife: and they will kill me, but they will save thee alive.

11. "Say, I pray thee, thou art my sister: that it may be well with me for thy sake; and my soul shall live because of thee.

12. "And it came to pass, that, when Abram was come into

Egypt, the Egyptians beheld the woman that she was very fair.

13. "The princes also of Pharaoh saw her and commended her before Pharaoh: and the woman was taken into Pharaoh's house.

14. "And he entreated Abram well for her sake: and he had sheep, and oxen, and he asses, and menservants, and maidservants, and she asses, and camels.

15. "And the LORD plagued Pharaoh and his house with great plagues because of Sarai Abram's wife" (Genesis 12).

The Prophet Abraham came into Egypt in 1943/1942 B.C. during the reign of King Senusrit I. This Pharaoh ruled from 1971 to 1928 B.C. His wife was Queen Nufrit, daughter of Pharaoh Amenemhait I. Princess Hagar was their elder child. Their second child was Pharaoh Amenemhait II, who was born in 1942 B.C. when Abraham was about to leave Egypt after one year's stay.

On pages 208-209, Vol. I, of *"Tafrihul Askia Fil Ahwal Ul Ambia"* we read about this incident.

When Pharaoh Senusrit I saw Sarah and thought her to be the unmarried sister of Abraham, he wanted to take this beauty and make her his handmaid. So immediately upon their arrival in Egypt, he separated Abraham from his wife Sarah. That night he had Sarah sent alone into his private chamber. He accordingly approached her but before he could touch her he was totally paralysed. He asked Sarah to pray for his recovery. She prayed and the Pharaoh immediately got back the power of movement of his limbs. He was so impressed with this miraculous power of Sarah that he approached her a second time, but once more he was paralysed but this time his male courtiers were also affected. He requested Sarah to pray. As Sarah prayed they were all cured. Again a third time, Senusrit I approached Sarah and for the third time he was afflicted, but this time all the members of the royal family were plagued as mentioned in Genesis 12: 17 quoted hereinbefore.

Pharaoh Senusrit I sent Sarah to a separate apartment and went to sleep in a very disturbed state of mind. That night God ordered the Pharaoh in a dream to return Sarah to Abraham as she was his wife, and said that Abraham was one of the great prophets of God. Further, God threatened to destroy him together with his kingdom if this was not done. In the Torah we find this historical incident has also been recorded:

> "And Abraham said of Sarah his wife, she is my sister: and (King) Abimelech (the name given in the Bible of this Pharaoh) took Sarah.
>
> "But God came to Abimelech in a dream by night, and said to him, Behold, thou art but a dead man, for the woman which thou hast taken for she is a man's wife.
>
> "But Abimelech had not come near her: and he said Lord, wilt thou slay also a righteous nation?
>
> "Said he not unto me, She is my sister? and she, even she herself said, He is my brother: in the integrity of my heart and innocence of my hands have I done this.
>
> "And God said unto him in a dream, Yea, I know that thou didst this in the integrity of thy heart; *for I also withheld thee from sinning against me: therefore suffered I thee not to touch her.*
>
> "Now therefore restore the man his wife: for he is a prophet, and he shall pray for thee and thou shalt live: and if thou restore her not, know thou that thou shalt surely die, thou, and all that are thine.
>
> "Therefore Abimelech rose early in the morning, and called all his servants, and told all these things in their ears: and the men were sore afraid.

"Then Abimelech called Abraham, and said unto him, What hast thou done unto us? and in what have I offended thee, that thou hast brought on me and on my kingdom a great sin? thou hast done deeds unto me that ought not to be done" (Genesis 20: 2-9).

"And Pharaoh called Abram, and said, what is this that thou hast done unto me? Why didst thou not tell me that she was thy wife?

"Why saidst thou, she is my sister? So I might have taken her to me to wife: now therefore behold thy wife, take her, and go thy way" (Genesis 12: 18-19).

"And Abraham said, Because I thought, surely the fear of God is not in this place: and they will slay me for my wife's sake.

"And yet indeed she is my sister; she is the daughter of my father, but not the daughter of my (own) mother (but daughter of my step mother); and she became my wife.

"And it came to pass, when God caused me to wander from my father's house, that I said unto her, This is thy kindness which thou shalt shew unto me; at every place whither we shall come, say of me, he is my brother.

"And Abimelech took sheep, and oxen, and menservants, and gave them unto Abraham and restored him Sarah his wife.

"And Abimelech said, Behold, my land is before thee: dwell where it pleaseth thee.

"And unto Sarah he said, Behold, I have given thy brother a thousand pieces of silver; behold he is to thee a covering of thy eyes, unto all that are with thee, and with all other: thus she was reproved.

"So Abraham prayed unto God; and God healed Abimelech and his wife, and his maidservants; and they bore children.

"For the LORD had fast closed up all the wombs of the house of Abimelech, because of Sarah Abraham's wife" (Genesis 20:

11-18).

The prophet Abraham sojourned in Egypt for almost a year until there was rain in the promised lands and the drought was over.

Now this Pharaoh had only one daughter and no male heir to his throne. He asked Sarah to pray for a son, when he returned her to Abraham. Most of his courtiers also had only daughters. As a result of the blessings when Sarah was returned by the Pharaoh, his queen and her ladies in attendance became not only pregnant but all were blessed with male children. There was therefore great joy and celebration throughout the land. This Pharaoh with all his courtiers with their families converted to the religion of Abraham. He was the first Egyptian ruler who totally gave up idolatry and sun-worship and accepted the One and True God. Several rulers came thereafter following the correct religion of Abraham.

When Abraham and Sarah went to bid farewell to King Senusrit I and Queen Nufrit, after about one year's stay in Egypt, the Pharaoh and his queen said to them, "You are an old man over of 76 years and your wife is barren and 66 years old now so past child-bearing age. We know very well you are thirsting for a child whom you can call your own. We throughout Egypt have received great blessings and male heirs through your prayers. In fact, we have been blessed with a son and heir a few days back. Therefore as a token of our goodwill and friendship, we offer our own only daughter Princess Hagar of Egypt (who was then about eight years old) as a gift to you so that you may have a child whom you can call your own" (Rabbi Shalomo Issac, a very authoritative Jewish Rabbi in his explanation of chapter 16 of Genesis has written down in Hebrew that Hagar was the daughter of the Pharaoh of Egypt). So saying they handed over their eldest child, their one and only daughter Princess Hagar (in Arabic "Hazra") of Egypt to their spiritual guide and religious teacher Prophet

Abraham and Sarah and gave advice to their little daughter, that they considered it better for her to go with the prophet of God than to be married to some prince, when she grew up (page 209, Vol. I, *Tafrihul Askia Fil Ahwal Ul Ambia* and page 37, Vol. II, *Rahmatul Aalamin* by Kazi Md. Sulaiman Munsoorpuri).

When Abraham returned from Babylon to Beersheba after the death of King Nimrod and settled down there, he was about 84 years old. By this time Princess Hagar was 16 years of age. He thought of marrying her to some good youth, but Sarah did not agree since she loved Princess Hagar as her own child and did not want to part with her.

After another year or so Sarah realised that Princess Hagar had to be married. How could it be done without parting with her? So she suggested to Abraham that he marry Princess Hagar, and if she bore any children they would be their own children.

Abraham pointed out that once Princess Hagar was married to him then Sarah's love would soon be replaced by jealousy and hatred, and that would cause trouble. But Sarah remained firm and forced Abraham to agree (page 212, Vol. I, *Tafrihul Askia Fil Ahwal Ul Ambia*).

Thereupon Abraham aged about 85 years married Princess Hagar of Egypt who was then about seventeen. This is mentioned in the Torah:

> "And Sarai Abram's wife took Hagar ... the Egyptian, after Abram had dwelt ten years in the land of Canaan, and gave her to her husband Abram to be his wife" (Genesis 16: 3).

The Logos or the Holy Spirit was placed on the forehead of Prophet Adam, the original father of our present human race, at the time the immortal soul was ordered to enter his body. (For further details see *Destruction or Peace,*Chapter 17: A 1-8, B 1-6).

This Spirit or Logos went into the forehead of Eve when she

THE LIFE OF ABRAHAM

conceived Seth and on his birth, it had gone into the forehead of Seth. From Seth the Holy Spirit had come down step by step to Noah and from him step by step to Terah, his wife when she became pregnant with Abraham and then into Abraham's forehead. Now this Holy Spirit left Abraham and entered the forehead of Princess Hagar on the very first night of her marriage to Abraham as she conceived.

The Holy Spirit shining upon her forehead made Princess Hagar look very elegant and mature with womanly grace. Sarah was indeed filled with jealousy at the beauty of Princess Hagar of Egypt. The very next day after her marriage, Sarah out of hatred punctured both the ear lobes of Princess Hagar to make her ugly.

Princess Hagar plucked some flowers and stuck them in these holes which Sarah had punctured. Instead it made her look still more exquisite and Abraham was full of praise for this enhanced beauty. It is from this incident that Muslim women have their ear-lobes pierced to wear ear-rings (page 213, Vol. I, *Tafrihul Askia Fil Ahwal Ul Ambia*).

Quite understandably this filled Sarah with much greater jealousy for the beauty of Princess Hagar. So she waited for an opportunity and as soon as Abraham's back was turned when he had gone out on some work, she wreaked her vengeance on the innocent princess by mercilessly beating her for no rhyme or reason.

This treatment meted out by Sarah during the very first few days of her marriage completely alarmed Princess Hagar. She was already fully aware from her stay with this family for the past ten years how Sarah had dominated Abraham. Therefore she knew very well that the henpecked Abraham would not be able to give her any protection against the jealousies of Sarah. As a last resort she decided to flee to Egypt, her father's kingdom, from the unwarranted persecution by Sarah.

Because of this unjustified persecution by Sarah, God Almighty decided to reward Princess Hagar with an honour which no other woman had been blessed with so far, thus proving to the whole world that Princess Hagar was innocent and in the right, otherwise she could not have been blessed with such an honour. Hence she became the first woman from the time of creation of this world to receive a direct message of God through the Angel Gabriel, the divine messenger to the Prophets. Only two other women received such an honour later on. They were the Virgin Mary, the mother of Jesus of Nazareth and Amena, the mother of Prophet Muhammad.

The divine messenger Angel Gabriel appeared before Princess Hagar, when she was fleeing from Sarah and was on her way to her father's kingdom of Egypt. He informed her that Allah had heard her heart's prayers because of the unjust afflictions of piercing of her ear-lobes by Sarah and the beatings given by Sarah out of spite. So as a compensation as well as a reward Almighty God had decided to bless her with a noble and gentle son, as a result of her marriage to Abraham a few days earlier, and that she was already pregnant with this son in her womb. Until this child was born she was to return to the house of Abraham and that God would protect her from further molestations by Sarah. The Torah confirms this in the following passages:

> "And the Angel of the Lord said unto her (Princess Hagar), Behold, thou art with child, and thou shalt bear a son, and shall call his name Ishmael; (This honour of being the first woman to receive directly the divine messenger Angel Gabriel has been given to you) because the Lord hath heard thy affliction (from the unjust persecution of Sarah out of her jealousy at your beauty).
>
> "And the Angel of the Lord said unto her: Return (to the house of Abraham and God will protect you from the unjust persecution of Sarah up till child birth) ... (Genesis 16: 11, 9).

The Biblical records thus prove to the world not only the honour given to Princess Hagar of being the first woman to receive a direct visit of Angel Gabriel, the messenger of God to the prophets, but also the information that the Almighty "Hath heard thy affliction" thereby proving for all time that Hagar was the aggrieved and afflicted party.

C. Prophet Prince Ishmael—the First Born of Abraham

Princess Hagar returned to the house of Abraham and conveyed the divine message foretelling the birth of Ishmael as advised by Angel Gabriel. The Qur'an refers briefly to it thus:

> "My Lord: grant me (out) of the doers of good deeds.
>
> "So We (Allah) gave him (Abraham) good tidings (through Princess Hagar) of a gentle son Ishmael" (Qur'an 37: 100-101).

Sarah who had no child of her own, was overjoyed at this good news—the divine foretelling of the birth of a son and heir to Abraham meant that at last they were going to have a child all their own. She accordingly stopped further persecution until the first-born son and heir of the family was given birth to by Princess Hagar in 1932 B.C.

The Torah records:

> "And Hagar bare Abram a son: and Abram called his son's name, which Hagar bare, Ishmael.
>
> "And Abram was fourscore and six years old, when Hagar bare Ishmael to Abram" (Genesis 16: 15-16).

The Holy Spirit or Logos which had entered the forehead of Hagar from the forehead of Abraham on the night she conceived Ishmael, now left the forehead of his mother Princess Hagar and came into the forehead of Ishmael upon his birth (page 213, Vol. I, *Tafrihul Askia Fil Ahwal Ul Ambia*). Thus God Almighty by this fact of placing the Logos on the forehead of Ishmael made it explicit that God had selected this first born child of Abraham through his legally married wife Hagar to be the heir of Abraham.

So beautiful was Ishmael at birth due to the Holy Spirit shining on his forehead that Sarah took away the babe and played with him all day long. Only at times of breast feeding could Princess Hagar have her child. Abraham was so dominated by Sarah that he dared not interfere. This state of affairs continued for a few months (page 213, Vol. I, *ibid*).

It so happened one day whilst Princess Hagar was feeding the babe, Abraham came into the room. Seeing his younger wife feeding the child he started playing with them out of love. Sarah, when she realised that Princess Hagar was taking an unusually long time to feed Ishmael came to investigate. She was shocked to see the love play between Abraham, the mother and child. This filled Sarah with rage once more and she decided to take her revenge on the innocent Princess Hagar and the few-months-old Ishmael. She resolved to get rid of both of them from her life (page 213, Vol. I, *ibid*).

Sarah therefore waited for her opportunity and when Abraham came to her, she asked him to promise in the name of God that he would carry out faithfully whatever request she was going to make so as to render her happy. Abraham pointed out that he was doing all in his power to make her happy. But Sarah would have nothing less, so he faithfully promised in the name of God to carry out Sarah's request.

Sarah having thus extracted the "Oath on God" from the hen-pecked Abraham now insisted that Abraham should fulfil his promise in the name of God and to do as follows to please her:

1. To take Hagar and the babe Ishmael and to leave them in some far-off place.

2. That Abraham may not live as man and wife with Hagar any more.

So shocked was Abraham at these unjust demands into which Sarah had trapped him by his oath that he wept bitterly and prayed to God for guidance.

The Angel Gabriel appeared and informed Abraham that Allah had heard his prayers of distress for the innocent Princess Hagar and the babe Prince Ishmael. Since Sarah was so very dangerous in her hatred and jealousy, if she got any opportunity she could murder the innocent mother and child. Therefore for their safety Allah desired that they should be removed to such a far-off place where Sarah would no longer be a source of danger to these innocents. Accordingly Allah had decided to honour them by making them the first caretakers of His house of worship (*i.e.* Bait-Ullah or Kaabah at Mecca) which the angels had built on earth even before the creation of Adam. And that Allah would look after them and protect them from all harm at Mecca.

Thus assured, Abraham carried out Sarah's request by taking Princess Hagar and the babe Prince Ishmael on his camel which he loaded with food and a leather-pouch containing water. He then set off for "Bait-Ullah" or "Kaabah" at Mecca. In those days it was known as the wilderness of Paran, according to the Biblical name given in Genesis 21: 21. Having reached his destination he asked Princess Hagar to get down with the babe Ishmael. He unloaded the food and water and turned to go back. At this Princess Hagar asked her husband in whose care he was leaving her alone in the middle of the desert. Abraham replied by, Allah's orders and in His care. This satisfied Princess Hagar, who was one of those who had surrendered herself to live according to the will of Allah, irrespective of whether it meant trouble or comfort for her. It was for this reason that she did not decide upon going back to the Palace of her father in Egypt to live in comfort. As soon as

Abraham was out of sight he stopped his camel and turning his face towards Kaabah or Bait-Ullah or the House of Allah prayed for a long time for the safety and welfare of his second wife Hagar and his first born child Ishmael (page 215, Vol. I, *ibid*).

After some days the water left by Abraham ran out. The Princess's breast also became dry after a few days due to no water being available. As a result she had nothing with which to feed her babe. There were two hills nearby—Safa a hundred feet away and Marwah a hundred yards or so away.

As they were steep it was not possible for her to climb with the baby Ishmael in her arms. She was all alone with no habitation nearby. She thought that if she climbed up these hills she might see some animal or birds. By watching their direction of travel she might come to know where water may be available or perhaps see some passing caravan and ask for water for her child, who was dying of thirst and was now putting out his tongue for water. So she placed the child under the shade of a shrub and climbed the nearer hill, Safa. Not having found any signs by which she could procure some water, she climbed down from Safa and ran through the valley between the two hills and climbed up the other hill, Marwah. On seeing nothing which could help her she descended from Marwah and climbed up Safa. In this manner, she made seven trips between the hills Safa and Marwah. She would walk as long as she was on the higher slopes from where she could see her child. She would run through the valley in between the two hills from where she could not see the babe for fear that some wild animal might carry away Ishmael. By the seventh climb she was completely exhausted whereupon she sat down and prayed fervently to God for her child. Her prayers were immediately answered and Angel Gabriel appeared before her and asked her: "O Princess Hagar of Egypt, how is it that you are alone in this wilderness?" She replied: "I am here by the Will of the Almighty in whom I have complete faith and trust". Then the angel asked her: "What aileth thee that thou art crying?" She replied: "My baby Ishmael is dying out of thirst". The angel replied: "Fear not for God has heard your prayers and solved the difficulties of the babe. Look at where your child is laying and see, wherever he is throwing his little arms and legs, there water is spouting out in little streams".

Delightedly she ran to her baby and found that this water, which was coming out of the ground where baby Ishmael lay, was refreshing like honey and absolutely crystal clear. (Page 215 Vol. I, *ibid*).

Thus both were saved. She immediately built a mud well around it to preserve the water. This is the most sacred water in the world. Its name "Zam Zam" originated from the joyous gurgling sound made by the little baby, Ishmael, when given to drink the water by his mother in a water bottle as he was still too small, (only a few months old) to be able to drink the water by himself.

Thus Princess Hagar was again honoured with a second direct visit from the Angel Gabriel, a status which as we have read earlier no other women ever enjoyed except the Virgin Mary and Amena, mother of Muhammad. Thus these exalted women enjoy a high status amongst the noble and pious ladies of the world. But Hagar was honoured with one more blessing for the whole world and that was the Holy Well of "Zam Zam" which is even now in existence at Mecca.

For the Muslims it is obligatory to make these seven trips between the hills Safa and Marwah during their Hajj pilgrimage. Wherever Princess Hagar ran, the Muslims run and wherever she walked the Muslims walk. They drink the Holy sacred water of "Zam Zam" and pray just as the second wife of Abraham had done.

Thus the exact spots and incidents from the lives of Abraham, Princess Hagar and his first born son and heir Prince Ishmael, from whom has descended the Prophet Muhammad, have been not only carefully preserved and recorded but also meticulously repeated to inspire greater religious fervour during the sacred Pilgrimage to Mecca by millions of Muslims from all over the world.

The Holy Bible also briefly confirms these facts in the following passages:

> "Wherefore She (Sarah) said unto Abraham, cast out this ... woman and her son ...
>
> "And the thing (this injustice of Sarah out of her jealousy) was very grievous (and wrong) in Abraham's sight (especially) because of his (first born) son (and heir who was then only a few months old and was the first child he had in his 86 years of life).
>
> "And God said unto Abraham (through Angel Gabriel), Let it not be grievous in thy sight because of thy (first-born) son and because of thy (innocent wife as God would look after them) ... in all that Sarah hath said unto thee; hearken unto her voice (because if you do not do so she could murder them out of hatred and jealousy and that would be far more serious)" (Genesis 21: 10-12).

This incident took place when Abraham was 86 years old (Genesis 16: 16) and Ishmael only about 6 months. Isaac, the second son of Abraham was born 14 years after this incident when Abraham was 100 years old (Genesis 21: 5).

The Torah also confirms the incident of the child Ishmael almost dying of thirst. It also confirms the visit of Angel Gabriel and the Holy sacred water of "Zam Zam" at Mecca spouting out of the spot, where the baby Ishmael was lying dying of thirst. The Holy Bible also corroborates that at this point of time Ishmael was so very small that he was unable to drink water by himself and so he had to be fed water from a bottle as will be observed from the following passages:

> "And (when all) the water was spent from the bottle, and she cast (*i.e.* placed) the (baby) CHILD under one of the shrubs.
>
> "And she (Hagar) went, and sat her down over against him a good way off, as it were a bowshot (distance of a few hundred feet) for she said, Let me not see the death of the (baby) CHILD (Ishmael). And she sat over against him, and lifted up her voice, and wept.
>
> "And God heard the voice of the LAD (*i.e.* a child but not a young man of 19 years of age); and the Angel of God called to Hagar out of heaven, and said unto her, what aileth thee, Hagar? fear not; for God hath heard the voice of the LAD (*i.e.* the small child Ishmael) where he is (under the shrub and has caused springs of water to burst out of the ground and this would be a blessed spot for the future).
>
> "Arise, lift up the LAD, and hold him in thine hand ...
>
> "And God opened her eyes and she saw a well (*i.e.* a spring) of water (spouting out of the ground where the little hands and legs of baby Ishmael were hitting the ground because this spot where he was lying was blessed) and she went (running to the child and lifted him in her arms) and filled the bottle with water (as he was too small to drink even water by himself), and gave the LAD (*i.e.* a small child to) drink.
>
> "And God was with the LAD; and he grew up, and dwelt in the wilderness, and became an archer.
>
> "And he dwelt in the wilderness of Paran: ..." (Genesis 21: 15-21).

Thus it is clear that the place called Paran in the Holy Bible is the same as that which is called Mecca today.

Pharaoh Senusrit I could easily have taken his daughter

Princess Hagar and his grandson Prince Ishmael from Mecca or Paran to his palace in Egypt. But because he had surrendered himself, upon the teachings of Abraham, to live according to the will of Allah and since Hagar and Ishmael were at Mecca by the will of the one and true God, so he dared not take his daughter and grandchild to his palace in Egypt, but he let them live there. This only goes to show the religious fervour created by Prophet Abraham among his followers. This Pharaoh with all his courtiers had converted to the religion of Abraham as mentioned earlier. Instead of bringing Hagar and Ishmael over to Egypt, he spent a fortune and got a canal dug from the River Nile to the Red Sea, so that he could easily supply the needs of the two at Mecca.

On page 183, Vol. II, *"Tariq Umru Ibnil As"* by Hasan Ibrahim Misri, *Daktur Fil Adab*, published by Matbaatul Saadat Misri, it is recorded that when Pharaoh Senusrit I heard that his daughter Princess Hagar with his grand-child the baby Prince Ishmael had been left alone at Mecca, he built a special canal—a wonderful achievement of engineering for those early days—from the river Nile to the Red Sea. Now he could easily supply via Jeddah all the necessities of his daughter at Mecca. "Jed" means "Grandparents". The grave of "Eve" the mother of the human race, the wife of Adam is still in existence at Jeddah, Hence the name Jeddah or "place of our Grand Parent". Hagar and Ishmael lie buried beside the Kaabah at Mecca.

As there was easy communication between Egypt and Mecca on account of the canal from river Nile to the Red Sea, all the requirements of food and other supplies of these two in Mecca were being sent by two of the Pharaohs of Egypt—Hagar's father during his lifetime and later on by her brother, when he became the next ruler of Egypt. For this reason it was convenient for Princess Hagar to have a suitable princess from one of the royal families of Egypt sent to Mecca to be a wife to Prince-Prophet

Ishmael when he had grown up. This is mentioned in the Holy Scriptures:

> "And he (Prophet Prince Ishmael) dwelt in the wilderness of Paran: and his mother (Princess Hagar of Egypt) took him a wife out of the land of Egypt" (Genesis 21: 21).
>
> "And (Allah) makes mention in the scriptures (*i.e.* Torah and Evangel) of Ishmael, he was the keeper of promise, and he was a messenger (of Allah), a prophet.
>
> "He enjoined upon his people worship (of Allah, the Alone) and almsgiving and was acceptable in the sight of his Lord" (Qur'an 19: 54-55).

Thus Princess Hagar from the age of about 18 years and Prophet Prince Ishmael from the age of a few months lived their whole lives at Mecca, or Paran as it was then called. They never went into the presence of Sarah after this incident. This event took place fourteen years before the birth of Isaac, the second son of Abraham through Sarah.

D. Foretelling's of the Births of Prophets Isaac and Jacob

The last of the Heavenly Books gives the following interesting prophecies about the birth of Isaac, the second son of Abraham and his grandson Jacob and that both of them would be prophets of God. This revelation was made on Thursday the 9th day of the lunar month of Muharram in the solar year 1919 B.C.

> "Hath the story of Abraham's honoured guests (the three angels sent to destroy Sodom and Gomorrah) reached thee (O Muhammad)?
>
> "And when they came unto him and said: Peace! He answered: Peace (and thought) Folk unknown (to me).
>
> "Then he (Abraham) went apart unto his household so that they brought a fatted calf;

"And he set it before them, saying: Will ye not eat?" (Qur'an 51: 24-27).

"And Our (Allah's) messengers (*i.e.* the Angels) came unto Abraham with good news. They said: Peace! He answered: Peace! And delayed not to bring a roasted calf.

"And when he saw their hands reached not to it, he mistrusted them and conceived a fear of them. They said: Fear not! (we are the angels of Allah. Angels do not require human food for their sustenance. Hence we are unable to eat the human food you have placed before us); Lo! we are sent (for punishment) unto the folk of Lot" (Qur'an 11: 69-70).

"They said: Be not afraid! Lo! we bring thee good tidings of a boy possessing wisdom" (Qur'an 15: 53).

"Then his wife (Sarah, hearing these talks) came forward, making moan, and smote her face (before them), and cried: A barren old woman! (at this point of time Sarah was 89 years old and without any child" (Qur'an 51: 29).

"She (Sarah) said: Oh, woe is me! shall I bear a child when I am an old woman, and this my husband is an old man (of 99 years of age)? Lo! this (what you Angels of Allah say) is (indeed) a strange (unbelievable) thing!" (Qur'an 11: 72).

"He (Abraham) said: Bring ye me good tidings (of a son), when old age hath overtaken me? Of what (use is it now when I have no more power in me, to produce children and my wife Sarah has long since lost her capacity to bear children) then can ye bring good tidings ?" (Qur'an 15: 54).

"They the angels said: Disbelieveth thou at the commandment of Allah? (Then know very well that nothing whatsoever is impossible for Allah. He has only to command: Be and it is). The mercy of Allah and His blessings be upon you, O wives of the house (of Abraham): Lo! He (Allah) is the Owner of (All) Praise, the Owner of (All) Glory!" (Qur'an 11: 73).

"And his wife (Sarah), standing by, laughed when We (Allah)

gave her good tidings (through the Angel of the birth) of Isaac (as a son) and through Isaac, of (a grandson) Jacob" (Qur'an 11: 71)

"... We (Allah) gave him (Abraham a son) Isaac and (through him a grandson) Jacob. Each of them We (Allah) made a Prophet" (Qur'an 19: 49).

"And when the awe departed from Abraham, and the glad news (of a son Isaac and through him a grandson Jacob and that both would be prophets of Allah) was reached (*i.e.* fully appreciated by) him, he pleaded with Us (Allah) on behalf of the folk of Lot (*i.e.* the dwellers of Sodom and Gomorrah, *etc.*)

"Lo! Abraham was mild, imploring, penitent.

"(It was said) O Abraham! Forsake this; Lo! thy Lord's commandment hath gone forth, and Lo! there cometh unto them a doom which cannot be repelled" (Qur'an 11: 74-76).

"They said: Lo! we are sent unto a guilty folk,

"That we may send upon them stones of clay,

"A mark (for later generations) by the Lord for (the destruction of) the wicked.

"Then We (Allah) brought forth such believers as were there.

"But We (Allah) found there but only one house of Muslims (*i.e.* those surrendered to the Will of Allah).

"And We (Allah) left behind therein a warning for those who fear a painful doom" (Qur'an 51: 32-37)

Thus by the Will of God Almighty the wicked cities where Lot had settled down were destroyed on Friday, the tenth day of Muharram which corresponds to the tenth day of the Jewish Seventh Lunar month. Almost all important events affecting mankind have taken place on this day, date and month of the lunar calendar as we shall see later in see *Destruction or Peace*, Chapter 11.

These passages from the last of the heavenly books once again bring out the following:

1. That God Almighty can do whatever pleases Him whether it is logical and scientifically acceptable or not. For example, there is no coherent or scientific explanation to show how the disaster of Sodom and Gomorrah could have taken place by the natural forces of the laws of Nature. When human intelligence fails we have to admit the hand of God in it for after all human intellect is no doubt limited (see *Destruction or Peace*, Chapter 16: B).

2. The methods adopted by God Almighty are often beyond the ken of human imagination. Mankind must accept that every act of God has a purpose. To assume that we know what is good for us often leads us to work in a direction which is contrary to the Will of God.

3. It is for this reason that periodically God punishes and destroys the guilty, leaving behind mute evidence for disobedience to his Laws, in such a sudden, unique and startling way that man has no means to escape his destiny (see *Destruction or Peace*, Chapter 16: B).

4. For example, modern scientists have made stupendous equipment's and machines, which have been tested until they work to perfection. Yet these have often failed! Why? The answer is given in *Destruction or Peace*, Chapter 16: B and C—there is a Super Power, Who denies them success whenever He wishes without even explaining to them why they failed in spite of the fact that their scientific planning's and calculations were flawless! Modern scientists cannot therefore defy God in their attempts to achieve progress, however much they may try.

5. Do all these not bring home very vividly to us:

> "Scientific World—Whither Bound?
> To Self Destruction!
> or
> Universal Peace!
> By what means?

E. The Happiest Year In The Life Of Abraham

The happiest year in Abraham's life was undoubtedly the period between his 99th and 100th year of age (*i.e.* between 1919 B.C. and 1918 B.C.) for the following reasons amongst others as given in the Holy Bible *viz*:

1. When the three angels sent to destroy Sodom and Gomorrah had informed him that he was going to get his second son, Isaac, through Sarah, Abraham had pleaded with God that instead of getting any further children in his old age, it would be much better if Ishmael, his beloved son and first-born, be blessed with children:

    "Then Abraham fell on his face (in thanksgiving), and laughed, and said in his heart, shall a child be born unto him that is (about) a hundred years old? And shall Sarah, that is (about) ninety years old, bear?

    "And Abraham said unto God, O that (my beloved first born son and heir) Ishmael might live before thee (and be blessed with children rather than me in my old age)!

    "And as for Ishmael, I have heard thee: Behold I have blessed him, and will make him fruitful, and will multiply him exceedingly; *Twelve Princes shall he beget, and I will make him a Great Nation*" (Genesis 17: 17-18, 20).

2. Then Abraham offered thanksgiving to the Lord for the good news of one son Isaac through Sarah, and one grandson Jacob, through Isaac, and he was told that both of them would be prophets, and of twelve grandsons

through Ishmael. Naturally what more happiness could a 99-year-old man aspire for? But God Almighty decided to reward him for his thanksgiving as mentioned in the Torah:

"And when Abram was ninety years old and nine, the Lord appeared to Abram and said unto him, I am the Almighty God; walk before me, and be thou perfect.

"And I will make my covenant between me and thee, and will multiply thee exceedingly.

"And Abram fell on his face (in thanksgiving) and God talked with him saying,

"As for me, behold, my covenant is with thee, and thou shalt be a father of nations.

"Neither shall thy name any more be called Abram, but thy name shall be Abraham; for a father of many nations have I made thee" (Genesis 17: 1-5).

3. On this occasion God Almighty made A Permanent Covenant with Abraham to distinguish for all time to come between those who can claim to be the children and followers of Abraham and those that are not:-

"And I will make thee exceeding fruitful, and I will make nations of thee, and kings shall come out of thee.

"*And I will establish my covenant between me and thee and thy seed after thee in their generation for an everlasting covenant*, to be a God unto thee, and to thy seed after thee.

"And God said unto Abraham, thou shalt keep my covenant therefore, thou, and thy seed after thee in their generations.

"*This is my covenant, which ye shall keep, between me and you and thy seed after thee; Every man child among you shall be circumcised.*

THE LIFE OF ABRAHAM

"*And ye shall circumcise the flesh of your foreskin; and it shall be token of the covenant betwixt me and you.*

"And he that is eight days old shall be circumcised among you, every man child in your generation, he that is born in the house, or bought with money of (*i.e.* from) any stranger, which is not of thy seed.

"*He that is born in thy house, and he that is bought with thy money, must needs be circumcised: and my covenant shall be in your flesh for an everlasting covenant.*

"*And the uncircumcised man child whose flesh of his foreskin is not circumcised, that soul shall be cut off from his people; (and will thus be condemned because) he hath broken my covenant.*

"And Abraham took Ishmael his son, and all that were born in his house, and all that were bought with his money, every male among the men of Abraham's house; and circumcised the flesh of their foreskin in the self-same day, as God had said unto him.

"And Abraham was ninety years old and nine, when he was circumcised in the flesh of his foreskin.

"And Ishmael his son was thirteen years old, when he was circumcised in the flesh of his foreskin.

"In the self-same day was Abraham circumcised, and Ishmael his (only) son.

"And all the men of his house, born in the house, and bought with money of (*i.e.* from) stranger, were circumcised with him" (Genesis 17: 6-7, 9-14, 23-27).

4. The first part of the glad tidings given by the three angels sent to destroy Sodom and Gomorrah *etc.* was fulfilled about ten months later when Abraham was 100 years old. This is also quoted from the Old Testament:

"For Sarah conceived, and bare Abraham a son in his old

age, at the set time of which God had spoken to him.

"And Abraham called the name of his son that was born unto him, whom Sarah bare to him, Isaac.

"And Abraham circumcised his son Isaac being eight days old, as God had commanded him.

"And Abraham was an hundred years old, when his son Isaac was born unto him.

"And Sarah said, God hath made me to laugh, so that all that hear will laugh with me.

"And she said, who would have said unto Abraham, that Sarah should have given children suck? for I have born him a son in his old age.

"And the child grew, and was weaned: and Abraham made a great feast the same day that Isaac was weaned" (Genesis 21: 2-8).

The Holy Qur'an briefly gives Abraham's prayer of thanksgiving:

"Praise be to Allah, Who hath given me, in my old age, Ishmael and Isaac! Lo! my Lord is indeed the Hearer of Prayers" (Qur'an 14: 39).

5. As soon as any one part of the glad tidings given by the angels was fulfilled it became clear that the rest of the divine messages were also going to be realised in due time *viz*:

   a. His second son Isaac was going to have a son whose name would be Jacob and both of them would be prophets.

   b. His first born Ishmael was to be blessed with 12 sons or princes.

   c. The period of tribulation for Abraham, who had had

only one son for the past fourteen years and none up to the age of eighty-six, was now over.

d. Now he could spend his old age in happiness in a house to be filled with thirteen promised grandchildren.

e. He could now also visualise that as promised by God, he would in fact become the father of nations of

f. believers and a true "Abraham" *i.e.* "A true Father of Nations of circumcised believers".

What more happiness could one look forward to at the ripe old age of one hundred years? Hence undoubtedly the period 99-100 years of age was the most important and auspicious year in Abraham's life (1919 to 1918 B.C.) and was calculated to bring him unbounded joy as the years went by.

F. The Great Trial of Abraham

Abraham had no children up to the age of 85 years. He had promised in the course of one of his prayers in this period, when he was about to marry Princess Hagar, daughter of Pharaoh Senusrit I and Queen Nufrit of Egypt, that if he got a son and heir through his second marriage he would gladly sacrifice this boy in the way of Allah (page 217, Vol. I, *Tafrihul Askia Fil Ahwal Ul Ambia*).

A few days later the divine message of Angel Gabriel had come to Princess Hagar informing her that:

a. Though married to Abraham only a few days earlier, yet she was already pregnant with a son who was to be named Ishmael.

b. Instead of fleeing to Egypt at the persecution of Sarah through jealousy, she should return to Abraham.

c. God would protect her.

The love of Abraham for Ishmael was even greater because for reasons of safety both the few-months-old Ishmael and his mother had to be kept far away from Beersheba where Sarah lived. This love of Abraham for his first born Ishmael is evident as seen from the Biblical quotations from Genesis 17: 17-18 and 20 given in the previous section. When Abraham was informed that he was going to have a second son, Isaac, (but this time through Sarah), he had pleaded that his first born and heir Ishmael might be blessed with children instead of himself in his old age. In reply God informed Abraham that He had heard his prayer and:

a. Ishmael would be blessed with twelve princes, in addition to Isaac through Sarah,

b. Further, that Isaac would also be blessed with a son Jacob and that both of them would be prophets of Allah.

Thus it is clear that Abraham had very great affection for Ishmael, who was not only his first born son and heir but also his one and only child from the age of 86 years. At the age of 99 years Abraham was given the forecast by the angels on the 9th day of the lunar month of Muharram of his second son Isaac and thirteen grandsons of which Jacob would be from his second son Isaac and the rest from his first born Ishmael. Hence Ishmael was being blessed much more than Isaac in the matter of children.

The Arabic lunar month of "Zil Haj" is the month just preceding the Arabic lunar month of Muharram. Accordingly "Zil Haj" is the equivalent of the sixth Jewish lunar month.

On the eighth night of this lunar month of "Zil Haj" in the solar year 1919 B.C. when Abraham was about 99 years of age, he had a fantastic dream at Beersheba ordering him: "Take thy son, thine only son, whom thou lovest the most and sacrifice him to God Almighty" (page 217, Vol. I, *Tafrihul Askia Fil Ahwal Ul*

Ambia).

The one and only child that Abraham had at this moment was Ishmael. At this point, Abraham had no news whatsoever of any further children or grandchildren to console him or to carry on his name. The glad tidings of another son and thirteen grandchildren, including the change of his name from "Abram" to "Abraham" or "Father of Nations" and the order of circumcision were given to him one month later *i.e.* on the ninth day of the lunar month of Muharram.

Hence Abraham got up from his sleep in a very troubled state of mind and soul. He wondered what God could gain out of this sacrifice of Ishmael who was his one and only son, born at the age of 86 years. Now he was about 99 years old and well past child-producing capacity. After all, there should be someone to carry on his name. There were at this juncture no foretellings about any further child or children, not even a girl.

So Abraham thought that this dream must have been the work of Satan, for he could not bring himself to accept that this could be the order of God. On the very next night *i.e.* the ninth of "Zil Haj" he again had the same dream where he heard God Almighty ordering him: "Take thy son, thine only son, whom thou lovest the most and sacrifice him to God Almighty". Abraham still could not bring himself to believe that this was God's order.

On the third successive night he had the same dream: "Take thy son, thine only son, whom thou lovest the most and sacrifice him to God Almighty". Immediately he got up, convinced that it was indeed God's order and told Sarah about this dream. Just then he also remembered his own prayer to God at the time of his second marriage: "If You bless me with a son I will sacrifice him to You". He immediately took Sarah's permission and set out from Beersheba for Mecca on his fastest camel and reached there during the tenth day of "Zil Haj" (pages 217-218, Vol. I, *Tafrihul Askia Fil Ahwal Ul Ambia*).

Jesus has given the following information about the very great love that Abraham had for Ishmael:

> "Abraham loved his son Ishmael a little more than was right, wherefore God commanded, in order to kill that evil love out of the heart of Abraham, that he should slay his (one and only son whom he loved the most): which he would have done had the knife cut" (pages 229 and 231, Gospel of Barnabas by Lonsdale & Laura Ragg published by Clarendon Press, Oxford, 1907).

Abraham asked Princess Hagar to dress Ishmael in the best clothes he had. Hagar obeyed. He asked Ishmael to take a knife, a piece of rope and to accompany him. They proceeded towards the central Hill of Monah.

Satan realised that Abraham was determined to carry out God's order. So he came to Princess Hagar and asked her where Abraham had gone with Prince Ishmael and for what reason. She replied that he had gone to Monah Hills. Satan informed her that Abraham was going to sacrifice Ishmael in the name of Allah according to God's order. She replied courageously: "Whatever is the will of Allah let it be carried out. I am one of those who have surrendered herself for all these 13 years past to the Will of Allah".

Satan having failed to kindle the mother's love, came to Prince Ishmael and informed him that his father intended to sacrifice him according to God's orders. To his great surprise he was rebuffed by the boy Ishmael. "If it is the will of Allah, then I shall not be found lacking" was his forthright retort.

As Abraham neared Monah, Satan came to him and said: "Allah merely wanted to test you and you have proved your intentions. This son is the one and only child you have been blessed with in your old age to carry on your name. Let him go and return". Abraham realised that it was Satan who was testing him. Immediately he picked up seven pieces of stone and flung them at Satan. Satan was turned instantly into a stone column. This Satan is known as "Jamratul Ula".

After proceeding a little distance, he was again approached by another Satan, who advised Abraham not to commit the senseless murder of his one and only child Ishmael. Again Abraham pelted him with seven pieces of stone, and he too was transformed into a column of stone. This Satan is known as "Jamratul Wasta".

As he neared the central hill of Monah, a third Satan made a final attempt to dissuade him. Abraham again threw seven pieces of stone at him and immediately this Satan also became a stone column known as "Jamratul Uqba".

Muslims from all over the world pelt these three preserved stone monuments of the respective Satans with seven pieces of stone on each occasion. The first one for three days on the 10th, 11th and 12th of the lunar month of "Zil Haj" and the other two for two days each on the 11th and 12th "Zil Haj" in memory of Satan's temptations of the Holy Prophet Abraham when he was taking Ishmael, his one and only beloved child, to sacrifice him in accordance with God's orders.

When Abraham reached the top of the hill at Monah he told his son about his dream. Ishmael replied: "Then please fulfil Allah's will, you will not find me wanting in courage to face death for Allah's pleasure". Thus when father and son had come to a mutual agreement Abraham fastened his son with the rope, after which he tied his own eyes with a piece of cloth, so that he may not see his son, for fear that fatherly love may prevent him from sacrificing his one and only son. Abraham struck the first blow with his knife but it did not cut. So he hit a second blow but without any success. Thinking his fatherly love was interfering with his duty to his Lord, he struck a hard blow and the knife cut through the body. He opened his eyes to be surprised to see that Ishmael was standing smiling on one side and a ram had been cut with his last blow. (page 217, Vol I, *Tafrihul Askia Fil Ahwal Ul Ambia*).

Abraham was very perplexed at seeing Ishmael safe, and a ram killed by his blow. He did not know what to make of it. Thinking that he had not yet fulfilled the order of God he picked up the bloodstained knife to strike Ishmael with it. Immediately the Angel Gabriel called out from above him "Abraham, Abraham lay not your hands upon Ishmael, nor do any harm to Ishmael, for now you have already proved that you are a Muslim (*i.e.* one who surrendered himself to the Will of God) and to fulfil His orders and pleasures you have not even spared your one and only son Ishmael born to you at the old age of 86 years, without any news of any more sons or daughters. It was I who, under Allah's orders, prevented your knife from hurting Ishmael when you struck twice. It was I, who under Allah's orders; replaced Ishmael with a ram sent by Allah from heaven and which was sacrificed instead of Ishmael. Therefore, know that your sacrifice of your one and only beloved son Ishmael in the ways of Allah is complete and has been fully accepted by Allah with the greatest pleasure".

The Torah confirms these incidents as follows:

"And Abraham stretched forth his hand, and took the knife to slay his son.

"And the Angel of the Lord called unto him out of heaven, and said Abraham, Abraham: and he said, Here am I.

"And he (the Angel Gabriel) said, Lay not thine hand (any further) upon the lad, neither do thou anything (*i.e.* harm) unto him: for now I know that thou fearest God, seeing thou hast not witheld thy son, thine ONLY son from (being sacrificed to) ME" (Genesis 22: 10-12).

When Abraham heard all this he fell onto the ground in ecstasy and offered thanksgiving to his Creator.

Accordingly on the l0th day of the lunar month of "Zil Haj" every year all over the world Muslims celebrate "Eid-e-Abram" or "Feast of Abraham" by sacrificing rams on this day. Whilst those Muslims from all over the world, who have had the good fortune to go on the holy pilgrimage of Hajj to Mecca, perform this sacrifice of the ram also on the l0th of "Zil Haj" around the Hills at Monah and its surrounding plains at the very same spot where Abraham had performed this sacrifice of his one and only beloved son Ishmael. Thus the Muslims recall the "Great Sacrifice" of Abraham by repeating in the minutest detail—the performances of the great Prophet Abraham and his great son Prophet Prince Ishmael (peace of Allah be on them).

God Almighty was extremely pleased with Abraham's prayers of thanksgiving because his one and only beloved son Ishmael had been spared. So when Abraham finished his prayers, the Angel Gabriel again spoke to him for the second time and informed him:

You have willingly agreed to carry out God's orders even when it required of you to sacrifice your one and only beloved son Ishmael, especially when you had no news whatsoever of any further children or grandchildren, and all that at the ripe old age of about 99 years. Also your son Ishmael had willingly agreed to offer himself in sacrifice to appease God Almighty. Therefore Allah had decided to bless Ishmael with the Promised Prophet of the final period of the earth through whom the whole world would be blessed.

God had resolved to bless Abraham fully, so that he would not have to undergo any further great trials.

As a reward for this great sacrifice of his one and only beloved son Ishmael, Allah promised to disclose shortly to

Abraham how he proposed to multiply his seed, as the stars in heaven and as the grains of sand, on the sea shore. These details were revealed exactly one month after the incident of the sacrifice of Ishmael on the 10th of "Zil Haj". These revelations were made to Abraham on Thursday the 9th of Muharram by the three Angels, who destroyed Sodom and Gomorrah on Friday the 10th day of the lunar month of Muharram in 1919 B.C. as we have just read in the previous section.

Accordingly the most auspicious and fortunate year of Abraham's life would be the coming twelve months between 1919 and 1918 B.C. (*i.e.* from Ishmael being saved from the sacrifice till the birth and circumcision of Isaac) or the period when Abraham was between 99 and 100 years old.

Abraham then returned to Beersheba after handing over the charge of Ishmael to his mother.

This is confirmed in the Holy Bible as follows:

"And the angel of the Lord called unto Abraham out of heaven the second time (*i.e.* when he had finished his prayers of thanksgiving to the Lord after his one and only son had been saved from the sacrifice).

"And said, by myself have I sworn, saith the Lord, for because thou hast done this thing, and hast not withheld thy son, thine only son (who at that point of time was Ishmael and there was till then no news of any further children to carry on the name of Abraham):

"And in thy seed (through this one and only child *i.e.* Ishmael) shall all the nations of the earth be blessed; because thou hast obeyed My voice (and offered thy only son Ishmael in sacrifice to God's pleasures).

"That in blessing I will bless thee, and in multiplying I will multiply thy seed as the stars of heaven and as the sand which is upon the sea shore ...

"So Abraham returned unto his young men, and they rose up and went together to Beersheba; and Abraham dwelt at Beersheba" (Genesis 22: 15-19).

The last of the Heavenly Books also confirms briefly this incident of the sacrifice of Ishmael, and the conversations between father and son. As a recompense for this incident, Allah after a short time of one month, disclosed to Abraham the fact of his being blessed with Isaac; his second son in the following passages:

"My Lord! Grant me (out) of the doers of good deeds,

"So We (Allah) gave him tidings (through Princess Hagar of Egypt) of a gentle son (Ishmael).

"And when (Ishmael) was old enough to walk with him, (Abraham) said: O my dear son, I have seen in a dream that I must sacrifice thee. So look, what thinkest thou? He said O my father! Do thou which thou art commanded. Allah willing, thou shalt find me of the steadfast.

"Then, when they had both "Islama" (*i.e.* surrendered to the Will of Allah) and he (Abraham) had flung him (Ishmael) down upon his face.

"We (Allah) called unto him: O Abraham!

"Thou hast already fulfilled the vision. Lo! thus do We (Allah) reward the good.

"Lo! that verily was a clear test.

"Then We (Allah) ransomed him with a tremendous victim.

"And We (Allah) left for him among the later folk (the salutation):

"Peace be unto Abraham!

"Thus do We (Allah) reward the good.

"Lo! he is one of our believing slaves.

"Thereafter (*i.e.* after a month) We (Allah) gave him

(Abraham) tiding of the birth of Isaac, a Prophet of the righteous". (Qur'an 37: 100-112).

G. Some Forgeries in Relation to Abraham

It is indeed regrettable that certain people take great pains in forging or destroying the Holy Scriptures with the object of misguiding and deceiving the world. Let us consider a few such instances in relation to Abraham, the friend of Allah.

1. "And He (God) Said (To Abraham), Take Now Thy Son, Thine Only Son, Whom Thou Lovest"

> Abraham was blessed with his first son Ishmael when he was 86 years old (Genesis 16: 15-16).
>
> Isaac was Abraham's second son. Abraham was 100 years old when Isaac was born (Genesis 21: 5).
>
> Therefore Ishmael was 14 years of age when Isaac was born.
>
> Abraham died at the age of 175 years and was buried by Ishmael then aged 89 years and Isaac aged 75 years (Genesis 25: 7-9).
>
> Ishmael died at the age of 137 years (Genesis 25: 17).

The facts that emerge from these divine records are that Ishmael was the *one and only son* of Abraham for a period of fourteen years *i.e.* until the birth of Isaac. At no time after the birth of Isaac, was Abraham with *only one son*.

Hence it becomes self evident that some wicked mischief maker has distorted the Holy Bible, deleted the name of Ishmael and interpolated the name of Isaac, who was never the *one and only son* of Abraham at any stage of Abraham's life as shown above from the Holy Bible.

The falsified Bible therefore reads as follows:

"And He (God) said (to Abraham), Take now thy son; thine only son (Ishmael has been deleted and replaced with) Isaac, whom thou lovest, and get thee into the land of Moriah (in Arabic "Monah" a group of hills about 6 miles out of Mecca, the place to which Baby Ishmael and Hagar were exiled out of the jealousy of Sarah); and offer him there for a burnt offering upon one of the mountains which I will tell thee of" (Genesis 22: 2).

Thus it is clear that according to the Holy Bible the *one and only son* of Abraham for fourteen years before the birth of Isaac was Ishmael. Consequently it was Ishmael and none other, who must have been taken by Abraham to be sacrificed and that also at a place near Mecca and not a place near Beersheba, the residence of Abraham. This incident therefore took place not only before the birth of Isaac but also before the foretelling of the birth of Isaac had been revealed to Abraham. Otherwise, the very essence of the trial faced by Abraham in this respect would have been lost. Because Abraham could have very well consoled himself with the thought that even though God was taking away Ishmael, who was his first and naturally most loved son, yet instead He (Allah) was going to give him another son or Isaac as compensation. Then the very significance and importance of the trial faced by Abraham would no longer be valid. For this incident to be a real or a severe test for Abraham, it was obligatory that Abraham should face this ordeal when he had his *one and only son*, Ishmael, and no knowledge whatsoever of any further children. This is also substantiated from the Qur'an and the historical records of Abraham already quoted earlier from *"Tafrihul Askia Fil Ahwal Ul Ambia"*. Even *"Ehsan Ul Muwaiz"* and other historical studies confirm that it was Ishmael the *one and only son* of Abraham at that point of time, who was taken for the sacrifice which took place actually before the prediction of the birth of Isaac. This is further proved from the divine title blessed upon Ishmael by God.

He was the fourth prophet out of eight to be given such an honour *viz*:

"*La Illaha Illal-laahu Ismail Zabiullah*"

Translation: "There is none worthy of divine worship except Allah (and) Ishmael (is the one who willingly offered himself) is the sacrifice to Allah". The other divine titles are listed in *Destruction or Peace*, Chapter 8: I.

Hence the interpolation of the name of Isaac for Ishmael as the only son, who was taken for the sacrifice is a deliberate attempt to misguide the unsuspecting millions all over the world.

Here is a text from the New Testament:

"For it is written, that Abraham had two sons, the one by a bondmaid, the other by a free woman".

"But he who was of the bondwoman was born after the flesh; but he of the freewoman was by promise" (Galatians 4: 22-23).

Genesis 16: 3 tells us that the Egyptian Hagar, was married to Abraham. In Genesis 16: 7-12, is recorded the visit of the Angel Gabriel telling Princess Hagar that she was already pregnant even though just married to Abraham and that the child was a blessed one and his name would be Ishmael.

When Abraham was ninety nine years old, he was forewarned of the birth of Isaac.

Sarah died at the age of 127 years. Abraham was then 137 years (Genesis 23: I, 2).

After the death of Sarah (Princess Hagar having died even earlier), Abraham married Keturah (Genesis 25: I) and through her, he had six sons (Genesis 25: 2) till his death at the age of 175 years (Genesis 25: 8). The names of these six sons are:

1. Zimran

2. Jokshan
3. Medan
4. Midian
5. Ishbak
6. Shuah (Genesis 25: 2)

Abraham, therefore, had eight sons through three wives. Hence the statements made in Galatians 4: 22-23 that he had only two sons and only two wives are both false, misleading and contradictory to Genesis 25: 1-2.

Further, this statement mentions that only one of these two sons was born by a promise of God. But the Holy Bible proves that angels foretold the birth of two of these eight sons *viz*: Ishmael (Genesis 16: 6-11) and Isaac (Genesis 17: 16). Hence the remaining six through the third wife may be termed: "after the flesh". Thus the passages quoted above from Galatians 4: 22-23 are fabrications according to even the Holy Bible.

2. The Two Forgeries In Relation To Hagar and Ishmael

a. From Genesis 16: 7-11, we read that Hagar, who had been married to Abraham (Genesis 16: 3) hardly a week earlier, had been informed by the Angel Gabriel that she was already pregnant and should return to Abraham inspite of the unwarranted persecution of Sarah punching her earlobes and beating her out of envy. The exact phrase in the Holy Bible being:

"God had heard her (Princess Hagar's) affliction (by Sarah out of jealousy)" (Genesis 16: 11). A girl who was only 17 years of age and only just married for less than a week—could not by any stretch of the imagination have come to know that she was already pregnant, until God honoured her with the direct visit of Angel Gabriel thus raising her status to the honoured position of being the first woman to receive a visit of the Angel Gabriel since the creation of mankind. If Sarah was in the right she would surely not have been denied such a unique distinction by God!

When Hagar did not know and could not have known within one week of her marriage that she was already pregnant than the following passage of the Holy Bible MUST BE a definite fraud:

"And he (Abraham) went in unto Hagar, and she conceived: and when she saw that she has conceived (this is a forgery as a girl of 17 years of age could never have come to know that she had conceived in the very first night of her marriage), her mistress was despised in her eyes (How could this be possible?).

"And Sarai said unto Abraham, my wrong be upon thee: I have given my maid into thy bosom: and when she saw that she had conceived, I was despised in her eyes: The Lord judge between me and thee.

"But Abram said unto Sarai, Behold, thy maid is in thy hand; do to her as it pleaseth thee. And when Sarai dealt hardly with her, she fled from her face" (Genesis 16: 4-6).

Hagar came to know for the first time that she was pregnant, after she had already been tortured and beaten by Sarah and only after she had fled from the house of Abraham for Egypt. Whilst she was fleeing did the Angel Gabriel come before her and announced she was pregnant (Genesis 16: 11). Therefore, Hagar could not have despised Sarah even before she knew she was pregnant. Hence the passages Genesis 16: 4-6 are absolutely incorrect.

b. From Genesis 21: 19 it is clear that Ishmael was so very

small, when left in the wilderness, that he had to be fed water from a bottle by his mother. Isaac was born 14 years after this incident. Therefore, when Isaac was weaned, neither Ishmael nor his mother were present.

They had been sent away more than 14 years earlier and they were never brought back. Hence the under mentioned passages of the Holy Bible are certainly erroneous:

> "And Sarah saw the son of Hagar, the Egyptian, which she had born unto Abraham (who had not been there for 14 years before the birth of Isaac), mocking" (Genesis 21: 9).

Since Hagar and Ishmael had not been there for now more than 14 years, how could Ishmael have mocked Isaac?

Thus it is clear that both these forgeries have been inserted to cover up Sarah's jealousy on these two occasions. If Hagar was in the wrong and Sarah in the right as depicted by these forgeries, then the Angel Gabriel would not have visited Hagar twice, once after each of these two incidents; an honour no woman had received till then!

3. The Firstborn and Heir of Abraham

From the time of Adam the Divine Laws on the rights, privileges and position of the *"First born"* who is the heir, are recorded in the Torah as follows:

> "If a man has two wives, one beloved, and another hated, and they have borne him children, both the beloved and the hated; and if the firstborn son be hers that was hated:

> "*Then it shall be*, when he maketh his sons to inherit that which he hath, that he *may not* make the son of the beloved firstborn before the son of the hated which is *indeed the firstborn*:

"But he *shall acknowledge the son of the hated for the firstborn, by giving him a double portion of all that He hath: for He is the beginning of his strength; The right of the firstborn is His*" (Deuteronomy 21: 15-17).

Under these laws Ishmael was not only the firstborn but also the heir of Abraham!

Further, the under mentioned passage of the Old Testament shows that Sarah was opposed to God's laws, hence she is portrayed as a sinner in the Holy Bible:

"Wherefore she (Sarah) said unto Abraham ... for the son of this bondwoman shall not be heir with my son, even with Isaac" (Genesis 21: 10).

Thus the Holy Bible proves that Sarah was not only a jealous woman but she was also a sinner and was overriding Abraham all the time according to the Holy Bible.

That God not only upheld Ishmael as the seed of Abraham but also protected him from his babyhood is seen from the following passages of the Holy Bible:

"And God heard the voice of the lad (*i.e.* the baby Ishmael); and the angel of God called to Hagar out of heaven, and said unto her, What aileth thee, Hagar? fear not; for God hath heard the voice of the lad (Ishmael) where he is (under the shrub and has caused a spring of water to burst forth out of the ground).

"Arise, lift up the lad and hold him in thine hand; for I (the Lord, God) will make him a great nation (because he is Abraham's seed as confirmed in Genesis 21: 13).

"And God opened her eyes, and she saw a spring of water (sprouting out of the ground where the little hands and legs of baby Ishmael were hitting the ground, because this spot where he was lying was a blessed spot); and she went (running), and filled the bottle with water, and gave the lad to drink (as he was too small even to drink by himself).

"And God was with the lad; and he grew up and dwelt in the wilderness, and became an archer" (Genesis 21: 17-20).

Abraham recognised Ishmael not only as his first born but also as more beloved than Isaac. That God accepted this position also will be clear from the Holy Bible:

"And Abraham said unto God, O that (my beloved) Ishmael (might be blessed with a child instead of Isaac to me in my old age and) live before thee!

"And (God said through the Angels sent to destroy Sodom and Gomorrah) as for Ishmael I have heard thee (Abraham): Behold I have blessed him, and will make him fruitful, and will multiply him exceedingly; twelve princes shall he beget, and I will make him a great nation" (Genesis 17: 18 and 20).

Therefore the following passage of the Holy Bible must be a fabrication for God does not lie!

"And God said unto Abraham ... for in Isaac shall thy seed be called" (Genesis 21: 12).

4. The Twelve Princes

In Genesis 17: 20 we read that God had promised that Ishmael would be blessed with twelve princes.

The names of these twelve sons of Ishmael are to be found in Genesis 25: 13-15. Their father Prince Ishmael was not a king of any place but lived the life of an archer in the wilderness of Paran (Genesis 21: 20-21), Hence the question of his sons being called princes for this reason does not arise. None of his twelve sons were kings of any place. They all lived as one joint family. Their descendants are the Arab Nation. They were only a single unit or nation. Then what is the reason or meaning behind God addressing them as "twelve princes" in the Holy Bible?

The only logical reason for their being called princes is because their grandmother Princess Hagar was third in the line of succession to the throne of Egypt, her brother Amenemhait II, being the first and his son the second in the said line. Therefore Prince Ishmael was (fourth in the line of succession to the throne of Egypt. Accordingly the children of Prince Ishmael were called hereditary princes!

As Princess Hagar was the daughter of the Pharaoh Senusrit I and Queen Nufrit who ruled over Egypt from 1971 to 1928 B.C. is it not very strange indeed to call her a "Bond-maid" in the Holy Bible? When a wonderful and fabulous engineering feat was performed by digging a canal from the River Nile to the Red Sea to enable the Pharaohs to alleviate the necessities of Hagar, could such a person by any stretch of the imagination be a slave girl or rather was she not the rightful princess of Egypt? Is it not very wrong to describe a "Princess" of a ruling Kingdom as a "Bond-woman"?

In spite of every effort to run down Princess Hagar and Prince Ishmael the forgers of the Holy Bible have been exposed as they overlooked and forgot to delete the word "Princes" from the Holy Bible:

> "And as for Ishmael, I have heard thee: Behold, I have blessed him, and will make him fruitful, and will multiply him exceedingly; twelve *Princes* shall he beget, and I will make him A (*Single*) Great Nation (and not twelve princedoms or nations)" (Genesis 17: 20). The emphasis is on "A (*Single*) Great Nation".

5. The Reason for These Forgeries

One feels rather puzzled as to what could be gained out of these forgeries.

The prime reason apparently is to misguide the world to

believe that the promised seed of Abraham through whom the whole world would be blessed is going to come out of the descendants of Isaac instead of Ishmael. Hence the interpolation of the name of Isaac in place of Ishmael in Genesis 22: 2 as pointed out earlier.

They knew from the under mentioned passages of the Holy Bible that the promised seed would be from that son of Abraham, who was being taken to be sacrificed.

The relevant passage of the Holy Bible confirms this:

"And said, By myself have I sworn, saith the Lord, for because thou hast done this thing and hast not withheld thy son, *Thine only son*:

"That in blessing I will bless thee, and in multiplying I will multiply thy seed (*i.e.* Ishmael thy Only son at this point of time) as the stars of the heaven, and as the sand which is upon the sea shore; and thy seed (Ishmael) shall possess the gate of his enemies;

"And in thy seed (Ishmael) shall all the nations of the earth be blessed; because thou hast obeyed my voice" (Genesis 22: 16-18).

As we go on we shall read the numerous forgeries that have been incorporated in the Holy Bible to misguide the world from the promised seed of Abraham, through whom the world would be blessed. Thus several passages have been falsified of the Holy Bible with this ambitious purpose to lead astray millions of innocent people all over the world. But by distorting passages in the Holy Bible can one ever hope to stop or alter God's decrees and decisions? Is it not the height of folly on the part of mischief-makers, whereby they misguide many millions?

6. Jesus Proves the Forgeries

Jesus had confirmed to his disciples the forgeries introduced by the Jewish Rabbis in Genesis, the first book of Moses, on pages 101-105 of *"The Gospel of Barnabas"* edited and translated by Lonsdale and Laura Ragg (See *Destruction or Peace*, Chapter 12: F-12) as follows:

> "Then said Andrew: 'Thou hast told us many things of the Messiah, therefore of thy kindness tell us clearly all.' And in like manner the other disciples besought him.

> "Accordingly Jesus said: 'Everyone that worketh, worketh for an end in which he findeth satisfaction. Wherefore I say unto you that God, verily because He is perfect, hath not need of satisfaction, seeing that He hath satisfaction in Himself. And so, willing to work, He created before all things the soul of His messenger, for whom He determined to create the whole, in order that the creatures should find joy and blessedness in God, whence His messenger should take delight in all His creatures, which He had appointed to be his slaves. And wherefore is this so, save because thus He hath willed?

> "Verily I say unto you, that every prophet when he is come hath borne to one nation only the mark of the mercy of God. And so their words were not extended save to that people to which they were sent. But the messenger of God, when he shall come, God shall give to him as it were the seal of His hand, insomuch that he shall carry salvation and mercy to all the nations of the world that shall receive his doctrine. He shall come with power upon the ungodly, and shall destroy idolatry, insomuch that he shall carry salvation and mercy to all the nations of the world that shall receive his doctrine. He shall come with power upon the ungodly, and shall destroy idolatry, insomuch that he shall make Satan confounded; for so promised God to Abraham, saying: "Behold in thy seed I will bless all the tribes of the earth; and as thou hast broken into pieces the idols, O Abraham, even so shall thy seed do".

THE LIFE OF ABRAHAM

"James answered: 'O Master, tell us in whom this promise was made; for the Jews say "in Isaac," and the Ishmaelites say "in Ishmael".

"Jesus answered: 'David, whose son was he, and of what lineage?'

"James answered: 'Of Isaac; for Isaac was the father of Jacob, and Jacob was the father of Judah, of whose lineage is David.'

"Then said Jesus: 'And the messenger of God when he shalt come of what lineage will he be?

"The disciples answered: 'Of David'.

"Whereupon Jesus said: Ye deceive yourselves; for David in spirit calleth him lord, saying thus: 'God said to my lord, sit thou on my right hand until I make thine enemies thy footstool. God shall send forth thy rod which shall have lordship in the midst of thine enemies.' If the messenger of God whom ye call Messiah were the son of David, how should David call him lord? Believe me, for verily I say to you, that the promise was made in Ishmael, not in Isaac'.

"Thereupon said the disciples: 'O master, it is written in the book of Moses, that in Isaac was the promise made.'

"Jesus answered with a groan: 'It is so written, but Moses wrote it not, nor Joshua, but rather our rabbis who fear not God. Verily I say unto you, that if ye consider the words of angel Gabriel, ye shall discover the malice of our scribes and doctors. For the angel said *"Abraham, all the world shall know how God lovest thee; but how shall 'the world know the love that thou bearest to God? Assuredly it is necessary that thou do something for love of God."* Abraham answered: *"Behold the servant of God is ready to do all that which God shall will."*

"Then spoke God, saying to Abraham:

"*Take thy son, thy firstborn Ishmael, and come up the mountain to sacrifice him*" (Genesis 22: 2).

How is Isaac firstborn, if when Isaac was born Ishmael was several years old?" (Ishmael was born when Abraham was 86 years old—Genesis 16: 16. Isaac was born when Abraham was 100 years old—Genesis 21: 5. Thus Ishmael was 14 years old when Isaac was born).

"Then said the disciples: Clear is the deception of our doctors: therefore tell us thou the truth, because we know that thou art sent from God.'

"Then answered Jesus: *'Verily I say unto you, that Satan ever seeketh to annul the laws of God; and therefore he with his followers, hypocrites and evil doers, the former with false doctrine, the latter with lewd living, today have contaminated almost all things, so that scarcely is the truth found. Woe to the hypocrites: for the praises of this world turn for them into insults and torments in hell.*

"I therefore say unto you that the messenger of God is a 'splendour' that shall give gladness to nearly all that God hath made, for he is adorned with the spirit of understanding and of counsel, the spirit of wisdom and might, the spirit of fear and love, the spirit of prudence and temperance; he is adorned with the spirit of charity and mercy, the spirit of justice and piety, the spirit of gentleness and patience, which he had received from God three times more than he hath given to all his creatures. O blessed time, when he shall come to the world: *Believe me that I have seen him (and have done him reverence, even as every prophet hath seen him): seeing that of his spirit God giveth to them prophecy (i.e. prophethood)'* And when I saw him my soul was filled with consolation, saying: "O Mohammed, God be with thee, and may He make me worthy to untie thy shoe latchet, for obtaining this I shall be a great prophet and holy one of God".

"And having said this, Jesus rendered his thanks to God."

H. Building the Holy House of God Almighty

The Kaabah at Mecca was a place of pilgrimage for Angels from 2,000 years before the advent of Adam (page 103, Vol. I, *Tafirhul Askia Fil Ahwal Ul Ambia*).

When Adam and Eve committed their first act of disobedience they were sent out of the "Garden of Eden" and exiled on the face of the earth. For what the act of disobedience was and its consequences refer to see *Destruction or Peace*, Chapter 20: A, B, C, D, and E.

Adam cried and asked God for forgiveness but this was not granted until he made a reference in his prayers saying "O Creator! Please forgive my sins in the name of that beloved of Yours whose name appeared with Your (God's) name in Heaven". The Hebrew text of the Holy Bible even today gives the name of the "Beloved of God" (see *Destruction or Peace*, Chapter 17: C 6) as Muhammad. This sentence was: "*La Illaaha Illal laahu Mahummadur Rosoolullah*" (Translation from Arabic into English: There is none worthy of divine worship except Allah and Muhammad is the messenger of Allah) see *Destruction or Peace*, Chapter 8: I. Immediately upon this reference to the name of Muhammad the promised seed through whom the world would be blessed, God Almighty forgave Adam and Eve and reunited them on the ninth day of the lunar month of 'Zil Haj' on the plains of "Arafat", which means "re-union".

On this plain there is a small hill named "Rahmat" which means "Blessings". It was here that Adam and Eve prayed the whole day and thanked Allah for His Mercy. At sundown they left for Kaabah, which is about 12 miles from this place. They spent the night en route at Muzdalfah about 4 miles from Arafat. On the morning *i.e.* the tenth day of 'Zil Haj' the Angel Gabriel took them to the Kaabah and showed them how to perform Hajj. (Page 103,

Vol. I, *Tafrihul Askia Fil Ahwal Ul Ambia*). Thus the first pilgrimage of Hajj was undergone by man. Eve spent her life in the vicinity of Kaabah and lies buried at Jeddah about 30 miles away.

Adam performed the pilgrimage of Hajj 40 times during his lifetime (page 107, Vol. I, *ibid*).

The building of the Kaabah was bodily lifted up to heaven just before the great Deluge of 2370 B.C. (page 104, Vol. I, *ibid*).

In 1885 B.C. when Abraham was 133 years old, he was ordered by God to go to Mecca or the wilderness of Paran (as it was then called) and rebuild the Kaabah (page 224, Vol. I, *ibid*), with the aid of Ishmael who was then 47 years old and had been dwelling over there from the time he was a few months old. Several angels also assisted them in the rebuilding which was done on the old original foundations which Ishmael dug up again (pages 225-235, Vol. I, *ibid*).

These angels brought stones for the building from various mountains and hills which were going to be declared holy later on. These included mount Zion on which the temple of Jerusalem was to be built.

The sacred stone known as "Aswad", a white stone from heaven was fitted in one of the corners of the Kaabah's outer wall foundation. When anyone kissed this stone it had the effect of drawing out evil thoughts from the person concerned and making him purer in his thoughts and deeds. As it drew out the sins of mankind, its original white colour gradually became blacker. Now it is generally blackish in colour except for a few small greyish white spots.

Abraham's finger and hand-imprints were found on this stone at the time of setting "Aswad" in the corner. These hand-prints of Abraham were mistaken by ignorant people at a later stage as faded carvings of idols on it (page 230, Vol. I, *ibid*).

A few of the numerous references appearing in the Qur'an are given hereunder, which will explain satisfactorily the importance of Kaabah or House of God rebuilt by Abraham and Ishmael at Mecca.

The prayer of Abraham for a prophet from the descendants of Ishmael, who will recite the revelations of God Almighty and guide men to goodness and piety is also contained in these passages. The only prophet born from the descendants of Ishmael is Muhammad, who was born and brought up at Mecca. Hence the prayer of Abraham at the time of rebuilding the Kaabah was fulfilled in the coming of the Holy Prophet Muhammad (peace of Allah be on him).

A few of the relevant passages are quoted hereunder:

"And (remember) when his Lord tried Abraham with (His) commands, and he fulfilled them He said: Lo! I have appointed thee a leader for mankind. (Abraham) asked: And of my offspring (will there be leaders)? He said: My covenant includeth not wrongdoers.

"And when We (Allah) made the House (at Mecca) a resort for mankind and, sanctuary, (saying): Take as your place of worship the place where Abraham faced (to pray). And We (Allah) imposed a duty upon Abraham and Ishmael, (saying): (Rebuild and) Purify My House for those who go around and those who meditate therein and those who bow down and prostrate themselves (in worship).

"And when Abraham prayed: My Lord! Make this a region of security and bestow upon its people fruits, such of them as believe in Allah and the Last Day, He answered: As for him who disbelieveth, I shall leave him in contentment for a while, then I shall compel him to the doom of fire—a hapless journey's end!

"And when Abraham and Ishmael were raising the foundations of the House, (Abraham prayed): Our Lord! Accept from us (this duty). Lo! Thou, only Thou, art the Hearer, the Knower.

"Our Lord! And make us both "Muslims" (*i.e.* submissive unto Thee) and of our seed, a nation of "Muslims" (*i.e.* submissive unto Thee), and show us our ways of worship, and relent toward us. Lo! Thou, only Thou, art the Relenting, the Merciful.

"Our Lord! And raise up in their midst (*i.e.* the children of Ishmael) a prophet from among them who shall recite unto them Thy revelations, and shall instruct them in the Scripture and in wisdom and shall make them grow. Lo! Thou, only Thou, art the Mighty, the Wise. (From the children of Prophet Prince Ishmael only one single Prophet has come—*i.e.* "Muhammad" in answer to this prayer of Abraham).

"And who forsaketh the religion of Abraham save him who befooleth himself? Verily We (Allah) chose him in the world, and Lo! in the Hereafter he is among the righteous.

"When his Lord said unto him: '*Aslim*' (*i.e.* Surrender)! he said: '*Aslamto*' (*i.e.* I have surrendered to) the Lord of the entire creation.

"The same did Abraham enjoin upon his sons, and also Jacob, (saying): O my sons! Lo! Allah hath chosen for you the (true) religion; therefore die not unless you are "Muslims" (*i.e.* as one who has surrendered unto Him).

"Or were ye present when death came to Jacob, when he said unto his sons: What will ye worship after me? They said: We shall worship thy God, the God of thy fathers, Abraham and Ishmael and Isaac. The One God, and unto Him we are 'Muslims' (*i.e.* surrendered).

"Those are a people who have passed away. Theirs is that which they earned, and yours that which ye earn. And ye will not be asked of what they used to do.

"And they say: Be Jews or Nazarenes, then ye will be rightly guided. Say (unto them, O Muhammad): Nay, but (we follow) the religion of Abraham, the upright, and he was not of the idolaters.

"Say (O Muslim): We believe in Allah and that which is revealed unto us and that which was revealed unto Abraham, and Ishmael, and Isaac, and Jacob, and the tribes and that which was given to Moses and Jesus (*i.e.* the Torah and Evangel respectively) and that which the prophets received from their Lord. *We make no distinction between any them*, and unto Him we are "Muslims" (*i.e.* as one who has surrendered unto Him).

"And if they believe in the like of that which ye believe, then are they rightly guided. But if they turn away, then are they in schism. And Allah will suffice thee (for defence) against them. He is the Hearer, the Knower.

"(We take our) colour from Allah, and who is better than Allah at colouring? We are His worshippers.

"Say (unto) the people of the Scriptures, (*i.e.* the Jews and the Nazarenes): Dispute ye with us concerning Allah when He is our Lord and your Lord? Ours are our works and yours, your works. We look to Him alone.

"Or say ye that Abraham, and Ishmael and Isaac, and Jacob, and the tribes were Jews or Nazarenes? Say: Do ye know best, or doth Allah? And who is more unjust than he who hideth a testimony which he hath received from Allah? Allah is not unaware of what ye do" (Qur'an 2: 124-140).

The building of this altar to Allah and that the surrounding area would be the chosen land for the descendants of Abraham is also mentioned briefly in the Torah as:

"And the Lord appeared unto Abram, and said, Unto thy seed will I give this land: and there builded he an altar unto the

Lord, who appeared unto him" (Genesis 12: 7).

I. The Voice of Him That Crieth in The Wilderness Inviting Mankind to The Way of Allah

When Abraham completed the rebuilding of Kaabah with the assistance of his first born son Ishmael and performed Hajj, he was ordered by God to climb up the surrounding hills and announce three times in a loud voice "Come for Hajj Pilgrimage to Bait-Ullah (*i.e.* House of God, which is now ready (*i.e.* rebuilt and purified), O mankind! either on foot or on transport from far-off lands" (extract from Qur'an 22: 26-27).

"Oh my Lord: There is not a single person or thing, not even an animal or a bird or a tree in this wilderness of Paran (Mecca) which is in the middle of the desert, who is there to hear my voice and come to pray at your "Bait-Ullah"? I am a voice that crieth in the wilderness inviting mankind to the way of Allah" (page 243, Vol. I, *Tafrihul Askia Fil Ahwal Ul Ambia*).

The reference to this call of Abraham from the top of the hills of the wilderness in the desert in compliance with God's orders is mentioned in the Holy Bible in the following passage:

> "The voice of him that crieth in the wilderness, prepare ye the way of the Lord, make straight in the desert a highway for our God" (Isaiah 40: 3).

Besides Abraham there has been only one other prophet of God who was ordered to make a similar public proclamation which was also fulfilled by the deliberate Will of God from the very same hills around Mecca, thereby inviting mankind to the worship of the One and Alone, the Almighty Creator.

At the end of the third year of Holy Prophet Muhammad's teachings, he received the following order at Mecca:

> "O thou enveloped in thy (woollen) cloak,

"Arise and warn!

"Thy Lord magnify,

"Thy raiment purify,

"Pollution shun!

"And show not favour, seeking worldly gain!

"For the sake of thy Lord, be patient!" (Qur'an 74: 1-7).

Till now Muhammad had been preaching the message only to relatives and friends. So the next morning he ascended one of the surrounding hills and called out to the inhabitants just as Abraham had done 2,500 years earlier.

It was the custom amongst the Meccans that whenever anybody had some very important information to give concerning the welfare of the city and its population, he would climb up the hill and shout out calling all the people, who would come to listen, leaving aside all other work. Accordingly all the elders of the town assembled to hear the momentous message that Muhammad had to give to them.

Muhammad asked them: "If I say there is an army of enemies on the other side of this hill would you believe me?"

They replied with one voice: "O Muhammad! you have never lied in your life and that is the reason why we have given you the title of 'AL-AMIN', the trustworthy. Therefore if you say there is an army of enemies on the other side of this hill we would implicitly believe you".

Then Muhammad explained that the chief reason for which he had called them was to tell them that there is no God save and except Allah, the one and the Alone, and he further pointed out the wretched folly of idolatry in the face of the tremendous laws of day and night, of life and death, of growth and decay, which all manifest the power of Allah and attest his sovereignty.

So annoyed were the Qureysh that they turned their backs upon him and left him speaking alone to the vast surrounding wilderness.

This incident in Muhammad's life which reproduced the call of Abraham in the wilderness of the desert is also mentioned in the New Testament:

> "For this is he that was spoken of by the prophet Esaias, saying, The voice of one crying in the wilderness, Prepare ye the way of the Lord, make his paths straight" (St. Matthew 3: 3).

> "As it is written in the book of the words of Esaias the prophet, saying, The voice of one crying in the wilderness, Prepare ye the way of the Lord, make his paths straight" (St. Luke 3: 4).

Since no other prophet besides only these two have climbed upon a hill in the desert and exhorted mankind to the true worship of God Almighty, these three references including the one from Isaiah 40: 3 quoted earlier must evidently be in relation to either one or both of them.

When Abraham asked God: "O Lord! there is nobody over here to hear my call and answer it", God Almighty informed him that it was for Abraham to give the call in the wastes of Paran (Mecca) and it was up to Him to get the call made by one calling in the desert wilderness, answered (page 243, Vol. I, *Tafrihul Askia Fil Ahwal Ul Ambia*).

To-day we see several millions of people answering this call of Abraham each year with the answer:

"Labbaik—Allah Humma Labbaik

Labbaik—La Sharika laka Labbaik

Innal hamda waniamata laka wal mulka

La sharika laka".

Translation: "I am present—Oh Allah I am present! I am present —Oh One who has no equals I am present! Indeed All Praise and good deeds and all kingdoms are yours. Oh One who has no equals".

They start reciting this answer to Abraham's call the moment they leave their homes for Mecca. These millions of Muslims come from each and every continent of the world, all speaking various languages, with different cultures, of diverse nationalities but all clothed in the same pilgrim's robe for men—only two unstitched pieces of white linen cloth—right from the kings, presidents, ministers of various countries down to the poorest of the poor. They are all dressed in one manner allowing no distinction of any kind whatsoever between one man and another from the fairest white to the darkest brown and black in colour. All are bonded in one universal brotherhood of equality, love and peace—AL-ISLAM (*i.e.* all surrendered to the will of God—Thy Will be done on earth as it is in Heaven).

As soon as these pilgrims arrive at Mecca, they go straight to "Mukam-E-Ibrahim" *i.e.* "Station of Abraham" and offer prayers. Then they go round the Kaabah seven times as Abraham and Ishmael had done.

Thereafter they drink the Holy Sacred Water from the well of Zam Zam, which saved the baby Ishmael. They then make the seven trips between Safa and Marwah and pray as Princess Hagar had done, running where she ran and walking where she walked. They spend the whole day at Arafat on the ninth day of Zil Haj and the night at Muzdalfah just as Adam and Eve had done upon being pardoned. Then they stone the three Satans at Monah with seven pieces of stones just as Abraham had done, and sacrifice the lamb at Monah in memory of the ram that was sacrificed instead of Ishmael. Finally they come back to the Kaabah at the wall of wailing where the Prophet Jacob son of the Prophet Isaac had cried for his son Joseph, when he was sold by his brothers. It was here that Jacob came to know that his beloved son Joseph was alive and he would meet Joseph in his old age before his death. The Muslims pray here for the grant of their wishes just as Jacob the grandson of Abraham had done.

In short the Muslims whilst on the Hajj Pilgrimage recall every single incident connected with prophets Adam, the first man, Abraham, Hagar, Ishmael and Jacob. The Prophet Moses was only one of the numerous Jewish prophets who had gone for Hajj Pilgrimage from the descendants of Isaac to Mecca.

When Moses reached "Raoha" a place some miles away from Kaabah he took two blankets with one he covered the lower part of his body and with the other the upper portion. This is called the wearing of the "Ehram" or Pilgrim's robe worn by Muslims (page 233, Vol. I, *Tafrihul Askia Fil Ahwal Ul Ambia*).

Moses went reciting "*Labbaik* ... (*etc.*)" just as Muslims do even today.

When Moses reached the hill "Safa" he heard the voice of God Almighty saying:

"Labbaik Abdi Anamaka"

Translation: "I am present, Oh my slave (Moses), I am with you"

Upon hearing this Moses fell onto the ground and worshipped the Lord.

All the Jewish Prophets whenever they had any great difficulties, went for the Hajj pilgrimage to the Kaabah and prayed over there and their difficulties were solved.

The "Wall of Wailing" at Kaabah derives its name from the lamentations of the Prophet Jacob when he was separated from

Joseph. Hagar and Ishmael lie buried on this side of the Wall of the Kaabah.

This "Bait-Ullah" (or House of Allah) was the place towards which Adam and Eve faced in their prayers. Abraham and all believers also turned their face towards Kaabah whilst praying. It was only after the building of the Temple of Jerusalem by the Prophet King Solomon (peace of Allah be on him) that the Jews were ordered to face towards Jerusalem in their prayers. This is confirmed in the following passage from the last of the Heavenly Books.

> Lo! the first Sanctuary appointed for mankind was that at "Becca" (Mecca), a blessed place, a guidance to the peoples;
>
> "Wherein are plain memorials (of Allah's guidance); the place (Kaabah) where Abraham stood (*i.e.* faced) to pray; and whosoever entereth it (for Hajj pilgrimage), is safe. The (Hajj) pilgrimage to the "Bait-Ullah" is a duty unto Allah for mankind (from the time of Adam and Eve), for him who can find a way thither. As for him who disbelieveth, (let him know that) lo! Allah is Independent of (all) creatures.
>
> "Say O People of the Scriptures (*i.e.* Jews and Nazarenes)! Why disbelieve ye in the revelations of Allah, when Allah (Himself) is Witness of what ye do (then have ye no fear that He is watching ye and will punish ye)?" (Qur'an 3: 96-98).

Thus the call of one crying in the wilderness in the middle of the desert is answered every year by the circumcised children and followers of Abraham—the Muslims in their millions. The manner in which they greet one another, the co-operation and goodwill they show on the occasion of the Hajj Pilgrimage in spite of the differences of languages, manners, customs, colour of their skin, and social status make one realise that mankind *is but one family and we are all brothers and equals*; Here is the best kind of unity for the human race despite its diversity.

Here certainly is a cement which is actually moulding millions from different countries before our eyes into one brotherhood of love each year at Bait-Ullah or House of Allah. Therefore here is something available to the educated to study as to how we could get rid of the curse of God, which broke up the unity of mankind at King Nimrod's tower of Babel. This unity can once again be achieved by following the call of Abraham, the destroyer of Nimrod, the main cause for the curse of God at Babylon; by forsaking Nimrod's teachings of only begotten son of God born of the great virgin mother queen of the heavens, the trinity in unity, the lamb of the heavens come to save the baptised sinners by sitting on the right hand of God, the laws of God being a curse, sacramental feasts converting the sinners into pure sinless gods, the sign of the cross the initial letter of TAM-MUZ or "Fire the perfecter" and all other such Blasphemies and manifestations of idolatry *etc.*

The living example of the millions of Muslims (*i.e.* those surrendered to the Will of Allah) performing Hajj each year comprising different nationalities, races, cultures and languages from all over the world, is indeed an irrefutable proof of unity and Universal Brotherhood. It could be the answer to:

How to achieve a universal Brotherhood!
"International Peace and goodwill amongst mankind"

Chapter 5

Important events connected with Prophets

God Almighty has blessed each of his messengers with something exceptional. For the purpose of our study it will suffice to dwell on some of the noteworthy events.

Quite often God Almighty chooses to prove His laws with various types of miraculous exceptions to convince mankind that He is the Supreme Lord of all. He does whatsoever pleases Him. There is none to question His Authority. He has no equals and none comparable with Him in any way.

A. Miraculous Births

The most wonderful birth in human history has been that of Adam who was created in a unique manner by an act of God, without the necessity of either a Father or a Mother.

Eve is the next most miraculous, being created out of Adam but without any mother.

Lastly, the birth of Jesus from the womb of the Virgin Mary, without a father.

Thus God has shown that he can create human beings in any of the three unnatural ways, *viz:*

- Adam—without any Father or Mother.
- Eve—without any Mother but out of a Man, Adam.

- Jesus—without any Father but out of the Virgin Mary.

B. Raising the Dead to Life

The first man to raise the dead to life was Abraham: When God bestowed upon him the title of "Khalil-Ullah" *i.e.* friend of Allah (Qur'an 4: 125) he was informed by the Angel Gabriel that God had blessed him with the powers to raise the dead to life. This miracle is briefly described in the Qur'an as under:

> "And when Abraham said (unto his Lord): My Lord! Show me how thou givest life unto the dead. He said: Dost thou not believe? Abraham said: Yea, but (I ask) in order that my heart may be at ease. (His Lord) said: Take four of the birds (*i.e.* four different species. Abraham took a peacock, an eagle, a dove, and a cock), and cause them to incline unto thee (*i.e.* teach each of them to come flying when you call their respective names and when these birds have been trained then cut them up into small pieces and mix their pieces together). Then scatter a portion of this mixture of cut up pieces on each of the (several surrounding) hills, and call them, (and you will see before your eyes how the scattered parts will come flying from the various directions of the particular type of bird which you have called and you will see how) they will come to thee, (reassemble and come back to life) in haste. And know that Allah is Mighty, Wise" (Qur'an 2: 260).

For further details please refer to page 200, Vol. I, "*Tafrihul Askia Fil Ahwal Ul Ambia*".

The second well-known incident of raising the dead to life was that of the son of a widow with whom Prophet Elijah was living. When the child died, Eiijah laid the widow's son on his own bed and placed his own body over the dead child and prayed to God thrice and the child came back to life (I Kings 17: 17-24).

The third popular episode of raising the dead to life is quoted here from the Holy Bible:

> "And Elisha died, and they buried him. And the bands of the Moabites invaded the land at the coming in of the year.
>
> "And it came to pass, as they were burying a man, that, behold, they spied a band of men and (through fear of being caught by this band of men and in order to save time) they cast the (dead body of) the man into the sepulchre of Elisha: and when the (dead) man was let down, and (no sooner had it) touched the bones of Elisha, he revived, and stood up on his feet" (2 Kings 13: 20-21).

From this incident it is further clarified that those who have spent their lives in the path of God are not really dead but their powers are still active. This is indeed a very important incident and clear proof of the most wondrous ways in which the Almighty showers His blessings upon His beloved even long after they completed their earthly span of life. Thus blessing them with eternal bliss and happiness—the proof that there is a reward of Heaven for those who surrender themselves to the Will of God.

After these prophets, the next to raise the dead to life was Jesus. He restored to life a widow's son at Nain (St. Luke 7: 11-16).

As far as Islam is concerned almost all leading saints have raised the dead to life and thousands of miracles of this type can be quoted with full references and detailed data. Hence even though this is indeed a great miracle yet it is nevertheless extremely common amongst the saints of Islam. For details refer to *Destruction or Peace*, Chapter 17: F-2.

C. Some Unique Miracles

You will read in greater detail about some of the unparalleled Miracles of Muhammad in *Destruction or Peace*, Chapter 17: F, 1-6.

1. The splitting of the Moon into two halves!
2. Raising the sun from the Western horizon after it had set.
3. The bringing out of streams of water from his fingers in a cup of water, in the wilderness to supply the requirements of a whole army of 34,000 men and all accompanying animals!

D. The Visit of Angel Gabriel to various Prophets

On page 35, Vol. II, *"Tafrihul Askia Fil Ahwal Ul Ambia"* it is recorded that the Angel Gabriel visited some of the prophets as under:

- Adam had the honour of 12 visits.
- Enoch had the honour of 4 visits.
- Noah had the honour of 50 visits.
- Abraham had the honour of 42 visits.
- Moses had the honour of 400 visits.
- Jesus had the honour of 10 visits.
- Muhammad had the honour of 26,000 visits.

There were several other prophets who have received visits from angels. But as they are not so well known they have not been included in the above chart. Some of the famous ones include Prophets Lot and Zakariah. The three blessed ladies who received direct visits from Angels are Princess Hagar, the second wife of Abraham, the Virgin Mary, mother of Jesus, and Amena, mother of Muhammad.

E. Raised Bodily Alive To Heaven

There is evidence available that four prophets were honoured by

God to be taken up in a living condition bodily to Heaven, *viz*:

1. Enoch was raised to Heaven bodily at the age of about 365 years (Genesis 5: 21-24).

2. Elijah was taken bodily to Heaven alive in the presence of Elisha in a flaming chariot (2 Kings 2: 9-15).

3. Jesus was raised bodily in a live condition to Heaven in the presence of his followers (St. Luke 24: 50-51 and Acts 1: 9).

4. Muhammad was raised bodily to heaven, shown around and returned to earth as described in *Destruction or Peace*, Chapter 17: E-9.

The first two of these four have gone to Heaven and will not lead earthly lives any more, even though they may appear in bodily form temporarily for specific purposes just as Elijah appeared in a cave and had a private discussion with Muhammad in the presence of his disciples and Jesus re-appeared to guide his disciples.

Of the remaining two, Muhammad led an earthly life for over twelve years after this miraculous incident.

Jesus will also come again to earth and lead a normal life for a period of about 40 years (see *Destruction or Peace*, Chapter 29: C, 9-10). Then will Jesus marry, have children, and rule the Earth under one universal religion thus fulfilling the promise of "Iesus Nazarenae Rex Iudaei" or "Jesus of Nazareth a King out of Jews" (see *Destruction or Peace*, Chapter 29: C-10).

F. The Three Adams

For the differences between prehistoric men and ourselves and whether modern man has evolved out of the prehistoric men or Adam was a creation have been dealt with in detail in *Destruction or Peace*, Chapter 17: B, 1-6. Until then let us take the various religious scriptures at their face value.

We are all familiar with Adam the first man and Eve his wife from whom the generations of mankind have come (Genesis 1: 27-28). Hence he is rightly termed the father of the human race.

When men became wicked God Almighty destroyed them by the great deluge about 2370 B.C. (Genesis 7: 1-24.) save and except Noah and his three sons and their wives. All the different nations of today are from the three children of Noah.

Hence Noah is not only the second of the modern Adams as compared to the prehistoric man but he is also the most significant because the present people of the world are divided in to three basic races from his three sons; Shem, Japheth and Ham (page 166, Vol. I, "*Tafrihul Askia Fil Ahwal Ul Ambia*". See also *Destruction or Peace*, Chapter 17: B, 1-6.

The third Adam is also a prophet like the first two but there is a divergence between him and the others. The first two Adams are fathers of all mankind but the third is only the father of the nations of believers. Also all male members belonging to the third are circumcised. The Holy Bible refers to him as:

> "Neither shall thy name any more be called Abram, but thy name shall be Abraham; for a father of many nations have I made thee" (Genesis 17: 5).

To make a distinction between the believing children of Abraham and the non-believers, a covenant was made at the same time by God:

> "*This is my covenant which ye shall keep, between me and you and thy seed after thee: Every man child among you shall be circumcised.*
>
> "*He that is born in thy house and he that is bought with thy money, must needs be circumcised: and my covenant shall be in*

your flesh for an everlasting covenant.

"And the uncircumcised man child whose flesh of his fore skin is not circumcised, that soul shall be cut off from his people (i.e. those belonging to Abraham); he hath broken my covenant" *(Genesis 17: 10, 13-14).*

Therefore the uncircumcised people cannot be the followers of Abraham, the father of nations of believers.

G. The Chosen People of Allah

It is an admitted fact that the Jews have always claimed to be the chosen people of Allah because they are the descendants of Isaac, the second son of Abraham. We all know that every time the Israelites transgressed the Divine laws they were punished and every time they repented they were forgiven by God. For taking to the religion of Nimrod, the City of Jerusalem and its temple were razed to the ground and the irony of it was that the Jews were made captives in 607 B.C. by Babylon itself, whose religion they were following (2 Kings 25: 1-21 and Jeremiah 52: 8-15).

From the Holy Bible we come to know that another set of people were also blessed.

"And as for Ishmael, I have heard thee (Abraham): Behold, I have blessed him, and will make him fruitful, and will multiply him exceedingly and I will make him a great nation (Genesis 17: 20).

Thus the Holy Bible confirms that the children of Ishmael have also been blessed by God to become a great nation.

These Ishmaelities at Mecca took to idolatry just as their brethren the Israelites did at Jerusalem. They still called the Kaabah "Bait Ullah" or the "House of Allah", but the chief objects of worship were a number of idols, which were called intermediaries to plead before Allah for the wicked sinners.

When Jerusalem and its holy temple were demolished and the Israelites punished by being taken as slaves to Babylon for adopting the teachings of King Nimrod, *i.e.* the worship of Baal, the Sacred Heart and his initial "Tau", the cross of Tammuz then the Ishmaelites of Mecca certainly also deserved a similar punishment, when they took to idolatry.

History informs us that Abraha, the Abyssinian ruler of Al Yemen, had sent a large army of 70,000 soldiers equipped with fighting elephants under General Aryat against the Ishmaelites (page 142, Vol. 1, "*Siratun Nabi*" by Sulaiman Munsoorpuri, sixth edition). His purpose was to destroy Kaabah, raze Mecca to the ground and make its inhabitants slaves just as Nebuchadnezzar, King of Babylon, had done to Jerusalem in 607 B.C.

The Ishmaelites, seeing this formidable army, fled into the surrounding hills helplessly to watch their homes being effaced. When challenged to come out and fight, they replied: "You have come to destroy '*Bait-Ullah*'. *Since it is the House of Allah let Him defend it*".

The watching Meccans were much impressed to note that the leading elephant when urged to lead the charge upon Mecca and Kaabah simply refused to advance and all the elephants started running back towards Yemen. This delayed the attack by a few minutes. Then came swarms of an unknown type of green-coloured flying creatures named in the Qur'an as *Ababil*. These *Ababils* shot bullets (described as stones because of their hardness) at the attackers. The bullets went right through the troops and the elephants and emerged from their bodies on the opposite side smashing all bones in their path and burning and disfiguring completely the parts of the body through which they passed. Thus in a few minutes the entire army of the Yemeni king had been totally annihilated (pages 771-774, Vol. 1, *Trafrihul Askia Fil Ahwal Ul Ambia*).

These *Ababils* then flew away and nobody knows from where they came and where they went or what they were—except that it was by Allah's Will.

Some of these so-called stones or bullets were later on picked up by a few Meccans and preserved until Prophet Muhammad became famous. The following passage was revealed in the early part of Prophet Muhammad's preaching's at Mecca:

"In the name of Allah, the Beneficent, the Merciful.

"Hast thou not seen how thy Lord dealt with the owners of the Elephants?

"Did He not bring (all) their stratagem to naught,

"And sent against them swarms of *Ababil*

"Which pelted them with (bullets which appeared like) stones of baked clay.

"And destroyed and mutilated them like things devoured" (Qur'an 105).

The Jews have called themselves the chosen people of Allah but the Christians claim that they are "Sons of god". For example:

"But as many as received him, to them he gave power to become the *sons of god*, even them that believe on his name" (St. John 1: 12).

"The Jews and Christians say: We are sons of Allah (the claim of the Christians) and His loved ones (the claim of the Jews). Say (in reply): Why then doth He chastise you for your sins? Nay, ye are but mortals of His creating. He forgiveth whom He Wills and chastiseth whom He wills. Allah's is the sovereignty of the heavens and the earth and all that is in between and unto him will ye (eventually) return" (Qur'an 5: 18).

This miraculous saving of Mecca when all hope was abandoned and the defenders had fled away, proves that the

Ishmaelites were treated by God in a manner more beneficent than the Israelites. One is naturally puzzled and curious to know why the Ishmaelites were given such preferential treatment under conditions identical with the destruction of Jerusalem.

The answer apparently is any one or both of the following reasons:

1. Ishmael was not only the first born of Abraham but also the true heir of Abraham the father of the nation of believers. Hence his children were not only entitled to, but actually they also received greater privileges from God than the so-called chosen people, the Israelites, as is clear from the above historical event.

2. The promised seed through whom the world would be blessed was going to be born at Mecca amongst the Children of Ishmael within the next few days, as a blessing for his sake.

IMPORTANT EVENTS CONNECTED WITH PROPHETS

H. Genealogical Tables

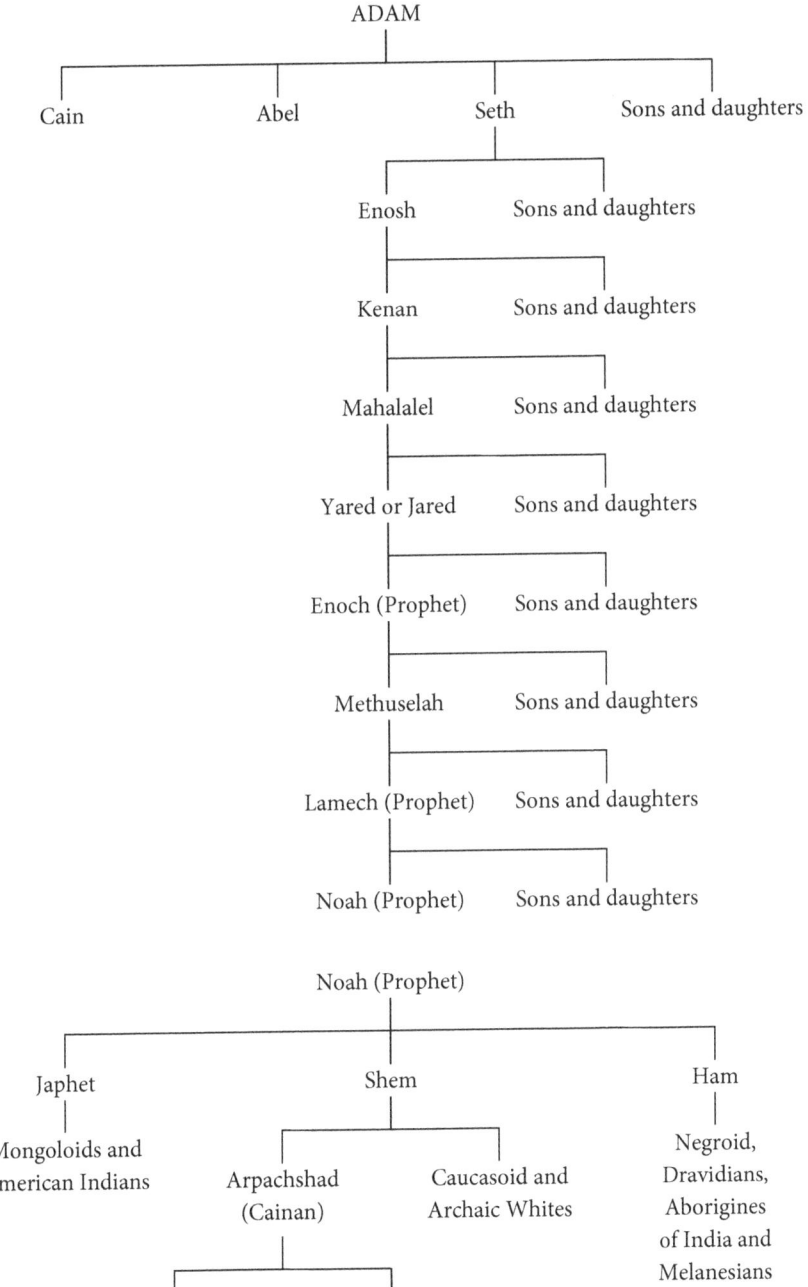

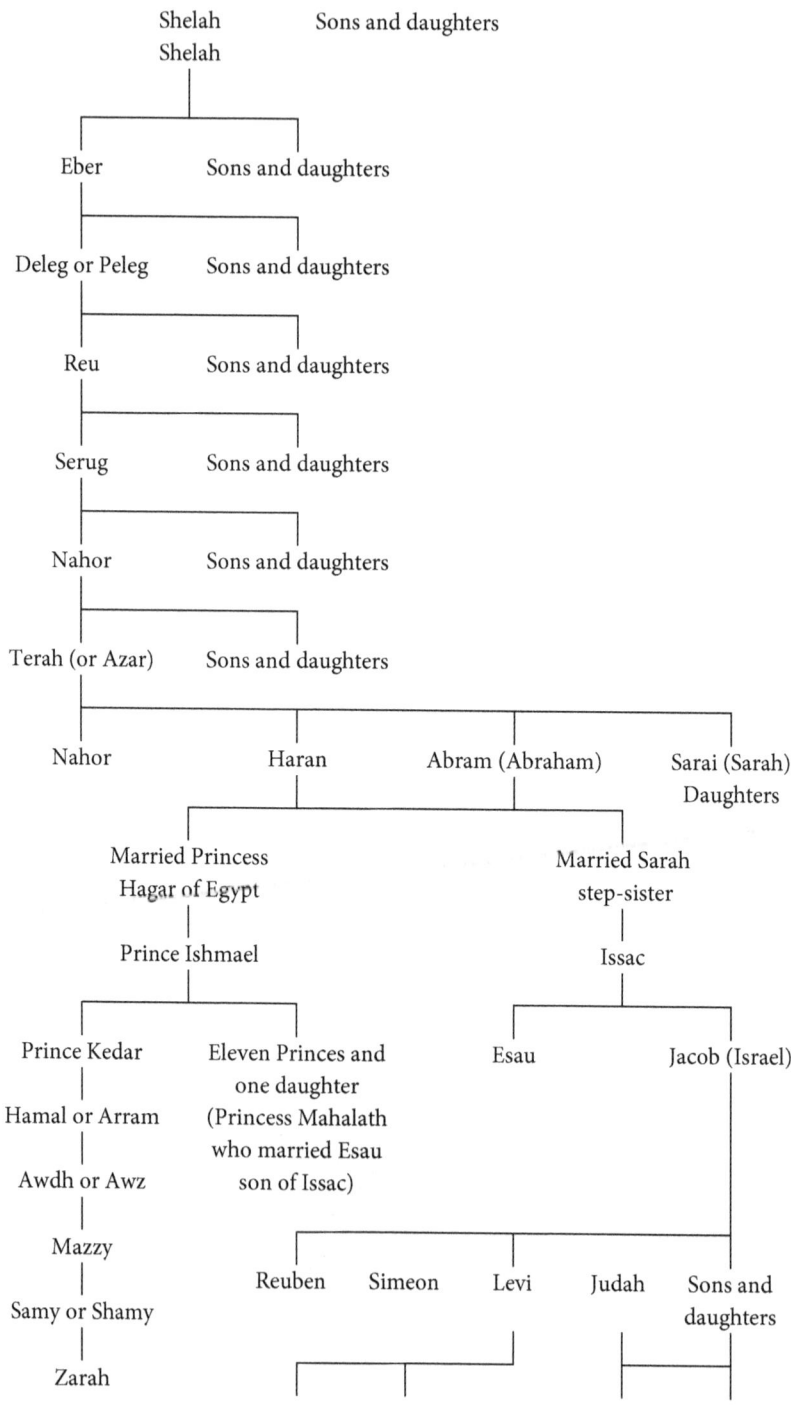

IMPORTANT EVENTS CONNECTED WITH PROPHETS

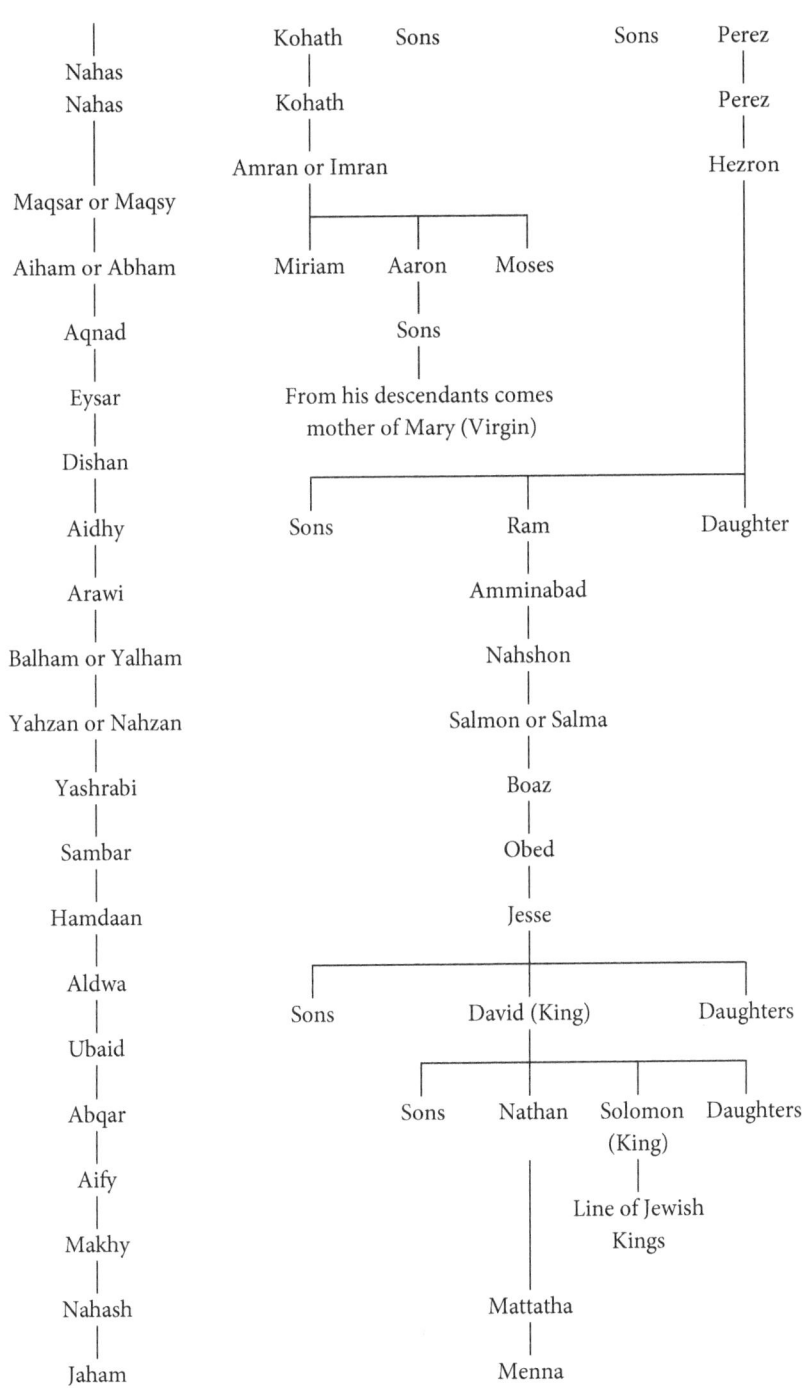

Taunj	Melea
Taunj	Melea
Ydlaf or Tdlaf	Eliakim
Baldas	Jonam
Haza	Joseph
Nashid	Judas
Awwam	Symeon
Ubbi	Levi
Qumwal	Matthat
Yuz	Jorim
Aus	Eliezer
Salaman	Jesus
Humaisa	Er
Ubad	Elmadam
Adnan	Cosam
Maad	Addi
Nazaar	Melchi
Mudhar	Neri
Elyas	Zerubbabel
Mudrekah	Rhesa
Khuzaimah	Joanan

IMPORTANT EVENTS CONNECTED WITH PROPHETS

Kananah	Joda
Nadhar	Josech
Nadhar	Josech
Malek	Semein
Tehr	Mattathias
Ghalib	Maath
Luwaij	Naggai
Kaab	Esli
Murrah	Nahum
Kublab	Amos
Qussa	Mattathias
Abdul Munaf	Joseph
Hashim	Jannai
Abdul Muttaleb	Melchi
Abdullah	Levi
Ahmed, Muhammad	Matthat
(May Allah bless them)	Heli (Father of Mary)
	Mary (Virgin)
	Jesus (May Allah bless them)

I. Heavenly Titles to Eight Chosen Prophets

Eight of the chosen prophets were blessed with divine titles. These are called *"Qalima"* or recitations. They are the proclamations of faith for the followers of the particular prophet concerned.

The first person to be thus honoured was Adam, the original father of the human race. The *"Qalima"* for his children was:

"La Ilaaha Illal Lahu Adam Shafiullah"

Translation: "There is none worthy of divine worship except Allah (and) Adam has been forgiven by Allah".

This was conferred upon Adam when he performed the first Hajj at "Bait-Ullah" at Mecca.

Thus the Almighty has made it clear for mankind that Allah is the Forgiver of sins. Men must never give up hope in Allah for forgiveness. This is the essence of the first *"Qalima"*.

The second person to be blessed with the *Qalima* was Noah:

"La Ilaaha Illal Laahu Nooh Najibullah"

Translation: "There is none worthy of divine worship except Allah (and) Noah is the one who was saved by Allah (from destruction by the deluge)".

This Qalima brings home very vividly that everything was destroyed by the great deluge save and except Noah and his three sons and their wives. Allah gave them the following order:

"And God blessed Noah and his sons, and said unto them, Be fruitful, and multiply, and replenish the earth" (Genesis 9: 1).

At the same time Allah did not forsake his people and let them wander about without a prophet to guide them to the Will of Allah, the right path of "Thy Will be done on Earth as it is in Heaven". This guide when man made the second start was Noah.

Hence the second *Qalima* is that man's safety lies not only with Allah but also in carrying out His Will.

The third person to be thus honoured is Abraham with the following *Qalima*:

"*La Ilaaha Illal Laahu Ibrahim Khalil ullah*"

Translation: "There is none worthy of divine worship except Allah (and) Abraham is the friend of Allah".

The emphasis this time is on the fact that "Abraham is the friend of Allah". Hence all the circumcised children of Abraham *i.e.* the Ishmaelites and the Israelites and all others following the teachings of Abraham become the chosen people, belonging to the "Friend of Allah". Thus the full implications of the meaning of the name "Abraham" is "A father of Nations of believers in Allah".

We may recall here the "Everlasting Covenant" made between God and Abraham that every man-child from amongst the followers and children of Abraham "*must be circumcised*" (see *Destruction or Peace*, Chapter 7: E).

Thus a permanent distinction is made between the circumcised followers of Abraham and the uncircumcised but baptised followers of Nimrod, the cursed.

The fourth *Qalima* is:

"*La Illaha Illal Laahu Ismail Zabiullah*"

Translation: "There is none worthy of divine worship except Allah (and) Ishmael (is the one who willingly offered himself as) the sacrifice to Allah".

Thus Ishmael was accorded special honour and blessings from the Creator according to the Holy Bible, *viz*:

1. That God would bless and multiply his descendants as the stars are in the heavens and as the sands are on the

sea shores (Genesis 22: 17).

2. That from his descendants would be the promised seed through whom the whole world would be blessed (Genesis 22: 18).

The fifth *Qalima* is:

"*La Illaha Illal Laahu Musa Kalimullah*"

Translation: "There is none worthy of divine worship except Allah (and) Moses (is the one who) spoke to Allah".

Thus Moses had the honour of being the first human being to speak directly with Allah.

The sixth is:

"*La Illaha Illal Laahu Dawood Khalifatullah*"

Translation: "There is none worthy of divine worship except Allah (and) David is the Viceroy Allah".

To proclaim his Viceroyalty, God asked all people to turn towards Jerusalem instead of Mecca as before in prayers. Thus a very great honour was bestowed upon David, who was also blessed with a divine book.

The seventh is:

"*La Illaha Illal Laahu Eesa Ruhallah*"

Translation: "There is none worthy of divine worship except Allah (and) Jesus is from the spirit of Allah".

His miraculous birth is given prominence in this *Qalima*.

The last is:

"*La Illaha Illal Laahu Muhammadur Rasoolullah*"

Translation: "There is none worthy of divine worship except Allah (and) Muhammad is the messenger of Allah".

J. Heavenly Books

A very large number of prophets have been blessed periodically with heavenly messages ranging from a single order or rule in one's life-time to numerous orders or extensive messages. Only very few of these have been preserved in the various religious and historical records available today, especially when it is realized that there were about 144,000 religious elders (or divine messengers) to the Holy Bible (Revelation 7: 4). We do not even know their names, when they were born, in which parts of the world and to which communities they preached. The only reliable and relevant information available is quoted hereunder:

> "And verily We (Allah) have raised **in every Nation a Messenger**, (proclaiming): Serve Allah and shun false gods. Then (there were) some of them (peoples of the various nations) who followed Allah's guidance, and some of them (there were) upon whom (their own evil deeds and) errors had a complete hold. Do but travel in the land and see the nature of the consequences of the deniers (like the destruction of the cities of Pompeii in Italy, Sodom and Gomorrah in the Dead Sea, Babylon in Iraq and so many others)!" (Qur'an 16: 36).

> "Lo! We (Allah) have sent thee with the Truth, a bearer of glad tidings and a warner; **And there is not a nation but a warner hath passed among them**" (Qur'an 35: 24).

We find from the Qur'an that only four Divine Books were revealed by God Almighty through four different prophets to the world. They are:

1. Touriath (Torah or the first 5 books of the Holy Bible *viz*: Genesis, Exodus, Leviticus, Numbers and Deuteronomy) through Musa or Moses.

2. Zabourah (Psalms or the 19th book of the Holy Bible) through Dawood or David.

3. Engil (Evangel) through Eesa or Jesus.

4. Qur'an through Muhammed.

1. Torah

The necessity of the Torah, the first of the Divine Books, is quite clear. Primitive man required a book of rules for his conduct. This book comprises numerous Heavenly Messages. They contain various Divine Orders, laws, historical records, miracles, foretelling's, *etc.* and form a complete teaching for primitive man to make him civilized and law-abiding. When this set of Divine Books was subsequently forged and false statements were incorporated, the world was in need of further guidance.

2. Pslams

The second of the Heavenly Books comprises hymns in praise of God Almighty and contains certain foretellings. These hymns were sung to music as practised and taught by King David.

They were used both in the public services of Israelites and also in their private devotions. Poetical songs accompanied with music enthused the listeners and the singers with great love and devotion of God and even led them to ecstasy in contemplation of the Divine Creator.

Some of the most beautiful passages in English literature are to be found in this book. Of all the books of the Bible, this is one of the most widely read and sung, not only amongst the Jews but also in most Christian churches of today.

These Psalms were disclosed to Prophet David through Angel Gabriel, the bearer of God's messages to the prophets, and were recorded by King David in his own handwriting in the Hebrew language.

These Holy Scriptures were destroyed when Jerusalem was razed to the ground in 607 B.C. Thereafter the Jews again came very much under the influence of Babylon during their captivity. They changed their week from Saturday, being the first day of the week to Sun-god's day or Sunday. Hence their Sabbath was changed from Friday, the last day of the week from the time of Adam to Saturdays. The Saturday Sabbaths are still being observed by the Jews.

The Prophet Ezra re-wrote the Torah and the Psalms. But they were soon fabricated by the Jews. Ibn Hazm (d. 456 A.H. / 1064 A.D.) has proved in his works that at least 57 passages in the Old Testament have been falsified. The result was that the "Original Teachings" of God were once more lost.

3. Evangel

Hence to Jesus was sent the *Evangel* to correct the corruptions and falsifications that had been forged into these holy Heavenly books as confirmed in the following passage:

> "Think not that I am come to destroy the (Mosaic) law, or the (teachings of the earlier) prophets: I am not come to destroy, but to fulfil (and thus bring back into existence what have been spoilt or destroyed after the Jews came under the pagan influence of Babylon)" (St. Matt. 5: 17).

Thus the Evangel is the third of the four Heavenly Books. It contained those divine messages which were revealed to Jesus by the Angel Gabriel as also the answers given by Jesus to the various questions put to him on a wide range of issues. It was dictated personally by Jesus in the Hebrew language, his own mother tongue, during his stay on earth and before his ascension. It was immediately recorded in Hebrew in Aramaic script by several Jewish scribes, all of whom were his close companions and disciples.

The most famous of these was Levi, son of Alphaeus. Levi was by profession a "Publican" *i.e.*, a collector of tolls and customs imposed upon persons and goods crossing Lake Gennesaret at Capernaum. Papias, in the first half of the second century says that the Evangel of Jesus was written by Levi in the Hebrew Aramaic Script. The same statement is to be found in the writings of other early fathers (page 64, part IV, section XXV—Summary of the books of the New Testament being an appendix under the heading: "Helps to The Study of The Bible" in the *Oxford Bible For Teachers*—printed at 91 & 93 Fifth Avenue, New York in 1896 by the publisher to The University of Oxford).

St. John is reported to have written down the Evangel and the Revelations, both in Hebrew Aramaic, a few years after the destruction of Jerusalem by the Romans in 70 A.D. from the notes of the dictations given by Jesus when he was on earth. This Hebrew Evangel by St. John was similar to the one recorded by Levi.

These three abovementioned originals were seized from the possession of Arius by the pagan roman Emperor Constantine in 325 A.D. at the council meeting called by him in Nicaea in Asia Minor. Unfortunately these were burnt and destroyed immediately under orders of Constantine as we shall read later in see *Destruction or Peace*, Chapter 12: F, 2-8.

The Evangels of Jesus recorded by Andrew and Barnabas during the life of Jesus in the Hebrew Aramaic script were also similar to that of Levi. These escaped destruction at the hands of Emperor Constantine because they were not in the possession of anybody at Nicaea as they were somewhere in Alexandria. These were the recognised Genuine Canonical Gospels until 325 A.D.

Such have been the affirmations of the early fathers of the Church and the findings of Christian scholars.

Emperor Constantine issued an order in 325 A.D., that anybody found possessing copies of the Evangel similar to those in the possession of Arius and not burning them instantly would be punished with death. Naturally, out of fear, these Original Evangels of Jesus recorded by Jewish scribes in Hebrew Aramaic were suppressed. Eventually they were handed over to the Pope in 382 A.D. Details of the various incidents about the burning and suppression of the "Original" teachings of Jesus are given later in see *Destruction or Peace*, Chapter 12: F, 1-12.

Hence owing to the destruction and/or suppression of the Original Hebrew Aramaic Evangel of Jesus, the world for the third time stood in need of a book of "Divine Guidance" after 325 A.D.

The following quotation from Jesus confirms that there was only one religion from the very beginning and that "only" four major divine scriptures are all that will come on earth:

> "Jesus answered: 'Everything that conformeth to the book of Moses, that receive ye for true; seeing that God is one, the truth is one; whence it followeth that the doctrine is one and the meaning of the doctrine is one; and therefore the faith is one. Verily I say unto you that if the truth had not been erased from the book of Moses, God would not have given to David our father the second. And if the book of David had not been contaminated, God would not have committed the Gospel to me; seeing that the Lord our God is unchangeable, and hath spoken but one message to all men. Wherefore, when (Muhammad) the messenger of God shall come, he shall come to cleanse away all wherewith the ungodly have contaminated my book'." (Page 285, Gospel of Barnabas by Lonsdale & Laura Ragg, Clarendon Press, Oxford, 1907).

The details of the fourth and the last of the "Divine Scriptures" referred to by Holy Jesus in the above Gospel are given in *Destruction or Peace,* Chapter 18: A-J.

Chapter 6

Buddhism

A. Gautama Buddha

The world was deeply influenced by a great religious teacher approximately five hundred years before the birth of Jesus. Gautama was his clan name, and Buddha was his title which means "The Enlightened One". At the age of 29 years he gave up his kingdom. He forsook his palace at midnight without telling anybody. It was a painful decision for him—he stood only for a moment by his beloved sleeping wife and baby son. His will was of iron. From being a prince of this world he became the prince of ascetics and his fame spread abroad "like the sound of a great gong hung up in the sky".

After six years of rigid self-mortification, he had reduced himself to a faltering skeleton. One day, when in this condition, he was attacked by violent pains and fell down unconscious. When he recovered his senses, he realised that to break open the secrets of the universe, one had to adopt a "middle way" between ascetic self-denial and sensual indulgence. The subsequent events have shown how right he was.

B. The Eight Beatitudes

Gautama sat under a certain "Pipal" tree, afterwards called the "Bo Tree" or the "Tree of Knowledge", in meditation. It was here that he gained enlightenment. It was from here that he got up and made his soul-stirring speech which enthralled the world with his eightfold path of salvation for the perfection of mankind. See *Destruction or Peace,* Chapter 12: J for a comparison of these beatitudes with the teachings of Christianity.

C. The System of Guru or Spiritual Guides

Great indeed was the impact of these Eight Beatitudes, which comprised the teachings of Buddha. His five close friends and monks, who had decided to boycott him when he had embarked on the middle road between asceticism and self-indulgence, were now so impressed by his superior gift of application that after his enlightenment they just sat and watched him intently.

From here the cult of the "Guru" *i.e.* the learned ascetic teacher and his disciples spread to the Middle East. By the time Jesus was born this system had secured a firm root even in the Middle East as well as in the Persian and Roman Empires.

D. The Spread of Buddhism

Buddhism spread like wild fire throughout India and from there to Afghanistan, Ceylon, Burma, Siam, Indo-China, Malaysia, Indonesia, Tibet, China, Russia, Mongolia and Japan.

Its impact was so very profound in Persia that the Persians incorporated all the eight beatitudes and the various incidents in the life of Buddha into their own Nimrodic faith. This hybrid religion became known popularly as Mithraism. Mithraism spread from Persia throughout the Roman Empire. It reached Britain in 70 B.C.

Thus developed the cult of enlightened celibate sages, each with their hundreds of disciples throughout the Middle East.

This is the background in which Christianity had its origin!

Part 2
THE RELIGIONS OF THE ADVANCED WESTERN CIVILISATION

Chapter 7

The Miraculous conception and birth of Holy Jesus

The finest known description of the ancestry, the circumstances of the dedication of the Virgin Mary to the service of God, the miraculous birth of Holy Jesus and how he miraculously proved the purity of his mother against the accusations of Jewish ladies, when he was only a couple of hours old and what was his mission are given from the Qur'an hereunder:

A. The Lineage of the Mother of the Virgin Mary

> "Lo! Allah preferred Adam and Noah and the Family of Abraham and the Family of Imran (the father of Moses) above (all his) creatures.
>
> "They were descendants one of another, Allah is Hearer, Knower" (Qur'an 3: 33-34).

B. The Dedication of the Virgin Mary by Her Mother from Before Her Birth

> "(Remember) when a woman (*i.e.* a female descendant from the renowned family) of Imran (*i.e.* the father of Moses and Aaron) said: My Lord! I have vowed unto Thee that which is in my belly as a consecrated (offering). Accept it from me. Lo! Thou, only Thou, art the Hearer, the Knower!' (Qur'an 3: 35).

C. The Birth and Dedication of Virgin Mary to the Service of God

> "And when she was delivered she said: My Lord! Lo! I am delivered a female (child)—Allah knew best of what she was delivered—the male is not as the female; and lo! I have named her Mary, and lo! I crave Thy protection for her and for her offspring from Satan the outcast" (Qur'an 3: 36).

D. The Virgin Mary received food from Heaven when inside a Locked Room!

Because the Virgin Mary had been dedicated to the service of God by her mother from even before her birth, she was not permitted according to rule to be brought up as a normal child under her parents' guidance at home. She had to be entrusted to the care of the High Priest to be brought up in the Temple of Jerusalem, trained to lead a pure life dedicated to the service of God Almighty.

Accordingly the Virgin Mary was placed under the care of her cousin Prophet Zakariah. He used to keep her locked in a small room of the temple. This was the sanctuary where Mary used to stay and pray all the time. Zakariah would open the door only once a day to hand her food. It so happened that he forgot to give her any food for three days consecutively. When he opened the door of the room on the fourth day with much concern for her wellbeing, he was extremely surprised to find that she had inside the sanctuary beautiful fresh food such as he had never before seen in his life. The Qur'an briefly refers to this incident:

> "And her Lord accepted her (Mary) with full acceptance and vouchsafed to her a goodly growth; and made Zachariah her guardian. When Zachariah went into the sanctuary where she (Mary) was (locked without any food for three consecutive days), he found that she had food. He said: O Mary! Whence

cometh unto thee this (food)? She answered: It is from Allah. Allah giveth without stint to whom He will" (Qur'an 3: 37).

E. Zakariah Prays for a Child from within the sanctuary of the Virgin Mary

So impressed was Zakariah at this that he prayed:

> "Then Zachariah prayed (from within the sacred sanctuary of Mary) unto his Lord and said: My Lord! (Who has bestowed upon Mary such precious gifts also) bestow upon me of Thy bounty a goodly offspring. Lo! Thou art the Hearer of prayers" (Qur'an 3: 38).

F. Zakariah foretold of the birth of Prophet John

> "And the angels called to him as he stood praying in the sanctuary (of Mary): Allah giveth thee glad tidings of (a son whose name will be) John, (who cometh) to confirm a message from Allah, lordly, chaste, a prophet of the righteous.
>
> "He said: My Lord! How can I have a son when (old) age hath overtaken me already and my wife is barren? (The angel) answered: so (it will be). Allah doeth what He will.
>
> "He said: My Lord! Appoint a token for me. (The angel) said: The token unto thee (shall be) that thou shalt not (be able to) speak unto mankind (for) three days except by signs. Remember the Lord much, and praise (Him) in the early hours of night and morning" (Qur'an 3: 39-41).

G. The Virgin Mary is Blessed by God and Preferred Above Women of Creation

> "And when the angels said: O Mary! Allah hath chosen thee and made thee pure, and hath preferred thee above the women of creation.
>
> "O Mary! Be obedient to thy Lord: prostrate thyself and bow

with those who bow (in worship)" (Qur'an 3: 42-43).

H. The Virgin Mary's Engagement to be Married

"This is of the tidings of things hidden. We (Allah) reveal it unto thee (Muhammad). Thou was not present with them when they threw their pens (to know) which of them should be the guardian of (*i.e.* would be married to) Mary, nor was thou present with them when they quarrelled (thereon)" (Qur'an 3: 44).

I. The Virgin Mary foretold of the Birth of Holy Jesus without any human contact and before she is married!

"And remember when the angels said: O Mary! Lo! Allah giveth thee glad tidings of message from Him, whose name is the Messiah, Jesus, son of Mary, illustrious in the World and the Hereafter, and one of those brought near unto Allah.

"He will speak unto mankind in his cradle and in his manhood, and he is of the righteous (Qur'an 3: 45-46).

"She said: My Lord! How can I have a child when no mortal hath touched me? Neither have I been unchaste?" (Qur'an 19: 20).

"He (Allah) said (through the angel): So (it will be). Allah createth what He will. If He decreeth a thing, He saith unto it only: Be! And it is" (Qur'an 13: 47).

J. The Virgin Mary Miraculously Conceives Jesus without Human Contact

"He (the angel) said: So (it will be). Thy Lord saith: It is easy for Me. And (it will be) that We (Allah) may make of him a revelation for mankind and a mercy from Us, and it is a thing ordained.

"And she (Mary) conceived him, and she withdrew with him

to a far place (*i.e.* on the outskirts of the city of Bethlehem)' (Qur'an 19: 21-22).

K. Jesus Miraculously speaks on Childbirth and consoles His Mother

When Mary got her first pains of the birth of Jesus, she was sitting under a dry, dead tree. As soon as her pangs of child-birth started this tree miraculously became fresh and green. All its dry flowers opening out blossomed immediately. Muslims all over the world collect reverently the dry flowers of this tree till this day. After this wondrous incident: the dry flowers of this tree have been named "The flower of Marium" or "The flower of the Virgin Mary". Whenever any child is born in a Muslim's house the Surah Marium (Chapter 19 of the Qur'an named after "The Virgin Mary") is read and the dry flower of Marium placed in a clean bowl of water. As the flower opens out so does the child come out of the womb of the mother. Observation has shown that if there is going to be any complication, this flower will not open out properly or fully and if the child is going to be stillborn or die on birth then the flower often is strangely attacked by insects thus indicating what is going to happen. As this tree did not give Mary enough seclusion for the child-birth she moved into a hollow space nearby under a palm tree. The Qur'an has recorded the miraculous happenings at the time of the birth of Jesus as follows:

> "And the pangs of childbirth drove her unto the trunk of the palm tree. She said: 'Oh! would that I had died ere this (child's birth without any father) and had become a thing of naught (*i.e.* dead and), forgotten':

> "Then (Jesus as he was coming out of the womb of his mother miraculously) replied unto her from below her, saying: 'Grieve not. Thy Lord hath placed a rivulet beneath thee'.

> "(And the child Jesus said): 'shake the palm-tree toward thee,

thou wilt cause ripe dates to fall upon thee'.

"(And the child Jesus said): So eat and drink and be consoled. And if thou, meetest any mortal, say: Lo! I have vowed a fast unto, the Beneficent, and may not speak this day to any mortal" (Qur'an 19: 23-26).

L. The New Born Child Jesus miraculously speaks and defends the Virginity of Mary

"Then she brought him to her own folk, carrying him. They said: O Mary! Thou hast come with an amazing thing (of shame that you have got a child even before you have been married)!

"Oh Sister (this is an Eastern term of respect to address a woman) of (the descendants of) Aaron (brother of Prophet Moses, the son of Imran)! Thy father was not a wicked man nor was thy mother a harlot!

"Then she pointed to him (Jesus). They said: How can we talk to a new born child, who is in the cradle?

"'He (Jesus) spoke (from his cradle even though he was just a few hours old and said): Lo! I am the slave of Allah, He hath blessed me with a book of Scriptures (*i.e.* Evangel) and hath appointed me a prophet.

"And hath made me blessed where-so-ever I may be, and hath enjoined upon me prayer and alms-giving so long as I remain alive.

"And (hath made me) dutiful toward her (the Virgin Mary) who bore me, and hath not made me arrogant, unblest.

"Peace be on me the day I was born, and the day I die, and the day I shall be raised alive (to heaven)!

"Such was Jesus, son of Mary! (this is) a statement of the truth concerning which they doubt" (Qur'an 19: 27-34).

M. Jesus a Prophet for the Jews and His Miracles

"And He (The Lord) will teach him (Jesus) the Scripture and wisdom, and the Torah and the Evangel.

"And will make him a messenger unto the children of Israel, (and Jesus will tell them): Lo! I come unto you (*i.e.* the Jews) with a sign from your Lord. Lo! I fashion for you out of clay the likeness of a bird and I breathe into it and it is a bird, by Allah's leave. I heal him who was born blind, and the leper and I raise the dead by Allah's leave. And I announce unto you what ye eat and what ye store up in your house. Lo! herein verily is a clear evidence for you, if ye are believers" (Qur'an 3: 48-49).

N. Jesus teaches He is not Son of God but the Brethren disbelieve

"It befitteth not (the Majesty of) Allah that He should take unto Himself a son. Glory be to Him! When He decreeth a thing, He saith unto it only: Be! And it is.

"And (Jesus has taught) lo! Allah is my Lord and your Lord (See St. John 20: 17), so serve Him. That is the right path.

"The sects (*i.e.* the Brethren) among them differ (from the Nazarenes): but woe unto the disbelievers from the meeting of an awful Day (of Judgment)" (Qur'an 19: 35-37).

O. The Birth of Adam is More Miraculous

"Lo! The likeness of Jesus with Allah is as the likeness of Adam. He created him (Adam) out of dust, then He said unto him: Be! And he is.

"This is the truth from thy Lord, so be not thou of those who waver.

"Lo! This verily is the true narrative. There is no God save

Allah, and lo! Allah is the Mighty, the Wise" (Qur'an 3: 59-60).

God has thus given a pre-eminent place to Adam over Jesus according to verse 59 of Chapter 3 of the Qur'an quoted before, because Adam was created without either any father or any mother, whereas Jesus, at least, had a virgin mother.

When Adam had no right or claim to Divinity and nobody calls Adam, the son of God, then Jesus, whose birth is far less miraculous than Adam's, surely cannot have any such claim in Divinity by any stretch of the imagination. Some people in spite of these facts call Jesus "Son of god".

Further we have read earlier in Chapter 7: D that Abraham had offered food, a roasted calf, to the angels sent for the destruction of Sodom and Gomorrah (Qur'an 11: 69-70; and 51: 21-33. They had refused to eat because angels do not require human food for their sustenance. But both Jesus and Mary required human food just like any other mortal. Hence both Jesus and the Virgin Mary were human beings and in a stage which was lower than that of spirits, who did not require food to remain alive. The Angels are not called "God" or "sons of God." Therefore if someone is in a stage which is lower than that of Angels then surely they also cannot be called son of God or mother of God! This is brought out beautifully in the last of the Heavenly Books:

> "The Messiah, son of Mary, was no other than a messenger, messengers (the like of whom) had passed away before him. And his mother was a saintly woman. And they both used to eat (earthly) food. See how We (Allah) make the revelations clear for them, and see how they (the Christians) are turned away!" (Qur'an 5: 75).

In St. John 20: 17 Jesus has clarified beyond any doubt that God is as much his God as our God that he is a brother to other human beings and not a divine being. This passage of the Bible reads as follows:

> "... but go to my brethren, and say unto them, I ascend unto my Father, and your Father; and to my God and your God".

This statement of Jesus is also confirmed in the Qur'an:

> "They surely disbelieve who say: Lo! Allah is the Messiah, son of Mary. The Messiah (himself) said: *O Children of Israel, worship Allah, my Lord and your Lord.* Lo! Whosoever ascribeth partners unto Allah, for him Allah, hath forbidden Paradise. His abode is the Fire (Hell). For evil-doers there will be no helpers" (Qur'an 5: 72).

That Jesus has never made any claims to divinity is clarified further beyond doubt in the Holy Bible as under:

> "And Jesus said unto him, Why callest thou me *good (master) there is none 'good (master)' but One, that is,* God" (St. Mark 10: 18 read with *"good master"* from verse 17 *ibid*).

The last of the Heavenly Books confirms this teaching of Jesus as follows:

> "(And Jesus said) Lo! Allah is my Lord and your Lord, so worship Him. That is the straight (correct) path" (Qur'an 3: 51).

P. Jesus's Miraculous Birth Confirmed

The birth of Jesus without any father is indeed one of the greatest miracles by which God Almighty has shown that He can do just what pleases Him, and that there is none who can be compared with His Majesty. This has been confirmed in the *"Gospel of Barnabas"*, pages 3-5 as follows:

> "In these last years a virgin called Mary, of the lineage of David, of the tribe of Judah, was visited by the angel Gabriel from God. This virgin, living in all holiness without any offence, being blameless, and abiding in prayer with fastings,

being one day alone, there entered into her chamber the angel Gabriel, and, he saluted her, saying: 'God be with thee, O Mary'.

The virgin was affrighted at the appearance of the angel; but the angel comforted her, saying: 'Fear not, Mary, for thou hast found favour with God, Who hath chosen thee to be mother of a prophet, whom He will send to *the people of Israel* in order that they may walk in His laws with truth of heart.' The virgin answered: 'Now how shall I bring forth sons, seeing I know not a man?'. The angel answered: 'O Mary, God Who made man (*i.e.,* Adam the first man) without a man (*i.e.,* without any parents) is able to generate in thee man without a man (*i.e.,* without a father), because with Him nothing is impossible.' Mary answered: 'I know that God is Almighty, therefore His will be done.' The angel answered: 'Now be conceived in thee the prophet, whom thou shalt name Jesus: and thou shalt keep him from wine and from strong drink and from every unclean meat, because the child is an holy one of God.' Mary bowed herself with humility, saying: 'Behold the handmaid of God, be it done according to thy word.' The angel departed, and the virgin glorified God, saying: 'Know, O my soul, the greatness of God, and exult, my spirit, in God my Saviour; for He hath regarded the lowliness of His handmaiden, insomuch that I shall be called blessed by all the nations, for He that is Mighty hath made me great, and blessed be His Holy Name".

On page 7 of *ibid* is recorded:

"Joseph being a righteous man, when he, perceived that Mary was great with child, was minded to put her away because he feared God. Behold, whilst he slept, he was rebuked by the angel of God, saying, 'O Joseph, why art thou minded to put away Mary thy wife? Know that whatsoever hath been wrought in her, hath all been done by the will of God. The virgin shall bring forth a son, whom thou shalt call by the name Jesus; whom thou shalt keep from wine and strong drink and from every unclean meat, because he is a holy one of God from his mother's womb. He is a prophet of God sent unto the *people of Israel*, in order that he may convert Judah to His heart, and that Israel may way walk in the law of the Lord, as it is written in the Law of Moses. He shall come with great power, which God shall give him, and shall work great miracles, whereby many shall be saved'.

"Joseph, arising from sleep, gave thanks to God, and abode with Mary all his life, serving God with all sincerity".

Thus it will appear that the following items:

a. Wine

b. Strong drinks

c. Every unclean meat (*i.e.* swine flesh).

were forbidden to Jesus throughout his life because he was a holy and pious prophet sent by God *for the correction of the Jews to the original laws of Moses* (St. Matthew 5 :17 and 10: 5-7 where Jesus says: *Go rather to the lost sheep of the House of Israel*).

Chapter 8

The day and date of the birth of Holy Jesus

St. Luke, Chapter 2: 7-10 gives evidence that Jesus was born before the winter rains had set in, because the shepherds were still keeping their flocks in the open pasture land all night.

The last of the Heavenly books also confirms briefly this fact as follows:

> "And We (Allah) made the son of Mary and his mother a portent, and We (Allah) gave them refuge (at the time of the birth of Jesus) on a height, a place of flocks and water springs" (Qur'an 23: 50).

Dean Farrar in his *"Life of Christ"* has remarked that Jesus was not born on the 25th December because the Bible mentions the shepherds as being that night with their flocks in the fields. Heavy rains start from before mid-October and carry on throughout the winter in Judaea. Hence the birth of Jesus must have been at the latest about the end of September or beginning of October, *i.e.* before the winter rains had set in.

This is also confirmed on page 133 of *"Your Will be done on Earth"*, published by Watch Tower Bible and Tract Society of Pennsylvania in 1958.

On page 5 column 3 of the March 1971 issue of *"The Plain Truth"* is an article by the researcher Garner Ted Armstrong on

Jesus where he confirms that Jesus was not born anywhere near Christmas.

The Muslims believe that Jesus was born on a *Friday* on the *10th* day of the Lunar Month of *Muharram* which corresponds to the 10th day of the Jewish Seventh Lunar Month. *The tenth day Jewish Seventh Lunar Month* called *Ethanim* corresponds to 26th September in the year 1 B.C.

Hence the time as deduced from St. Luke, the Jewish calendar, the research of Dr. Farrar, the findings of the Watch Tower Bible and Tract Society; The Plain Truth and the Islamic system of calculation all seem to concur that the date of the birth of Jesus was the 26th September in the year 1 B.C.

The Muslims further believe that *Friday* the *10th* day of the Lunar Month of *Muharram* is a special chosen day of the Almighty Creator, Who has effected on this particular and auspicious day, date and month throughout the ages many wondrous events of far-reaching consequence besides the birth of Jesus. For further elucidation just a few of the important events that took place on this day, date and month throughout creation are enumerated below:

1. The commencement of the creation of the Universe out of the Holy Spirit, or Word of God.

2. The creation of our Earth from out of the Sun.

3. The creation of Adam the First man in the autumn of 4026 B.C. (Genesis 1: 27).

4. The Ark of Noah touched the ground on top of Mount "Ararat" after the great deluge on this day, date and month in 2369 B.C. (according to the Holy Bible the date is 7 days or just one week later, see Genesis 8: 4).

5. Abraham came out alive from the huge fire into which he

was catapulted by King Nimrod in 2001 B.C. (See *Destruction or Peace*, Chapter 6: F).

6. In 1919 B.C. the destruction of Sodom and Gomorrah, the twin cities of Lot, which are lying submerged in the Dead Sea (Genesis 19: 24-29).

7. Jacob was reunited with his beloved son Joseph, the prime minister of Egypt (Genesis 45 and 46).

8. David slays Goliath (1 Samuel 17: 23, 33-51).

9. The escape of Jonah from the stomach of the giant whale, approximately after three days and three nights (Jonah 1: 15-17).

10. The martyrdom on this day, date and month in the year 680 A.D. of Hazrat Imam Hussain, grandson of Prophet Muhammad, with most of the male members of the families related to Muhammad at Karbala as foretold in the Holy Bible. (See *Destruction or Peace*, Chapter 26: C-1).

11. To commemorate this day, date and month as being the day of their escape from Egypt under Moses and the drowning of Pharaoh and his forces, the Jews were ordered to "Fast" on this date every year, and to keep it holy. This can be seen from the following orders appearing in the Old Testament:

"And this shall be a statute forever unto you: that in the seventh month, on the tenth day of the month, ye shall afflict your souls, and do no work at all, whether it be one of your own country, or a stranger that sojourneth among you" (Leviticus 16: 29).

"And the Lord spake unto Moses, saying,

"Also on the tenth day of this seventh (lunar) month (called

Ethanim) there shall be a day of atonement: it shall be a holy convocation unto you; and ye shall afflict your souls, and offer an offering made by fire unto the Lord.

"And ye shall do no work in that same day: for it is a day of atonement, to make an atonement for you before the Lord your God.

"For whatsoever soul it be that shall not be afflicted in the same day, he shall be cut off from among his people.

"And whatsoever soul it be that doeth any work in that same day, the same soul will I destroy from among his people.

"Ye shall do no manner of work: it shall be a statute forever throughout your generations in all your dwellings.

"It shall be unto you a Sabbath of rest, and ye shall afflict your souls: in the ninth day of the month at even (Sunset), from even (Sunset) unto even (Sunset), shall ye celebrate your Sabbath" (Leviticus 23: 26-32).

Similar references are found in other places in the Old Testament showing how very important this particular date and month is.

From this evidence it is established conclusively that the definite date of the birth of Jesus was Friday the tenth day of the seventh Jewish month called Ethanim, which corresponds to Friday the tenth of Muharram or 26th September in the year 1 B.C., because this is one of the chosen dates of Almighty God, for doing something awe-inspiring and having a far-reaching effect upon humanity. And further that Jesus had thus been honoured greatly by the Lord of all creation by causing such a marvellous birth on such an important day, date and month.

Therefore it is clear from these facts, that the 25th December is not at all connected with the birth of Jesus. It is indeed most unfortunate that nowhere in the whole world is the birth of Jesus of Nazareth, son of the Virgin Mary being celebrated on the 26th September according to the Solar Calendar or the 10th day of the Seventh Jewish lunar month of Ethanim or Muharram. Whose birthday are the Christians then celebrating on the 25th December in each year?

Chapter 9

The teachings of Holy Jesus

Introduction

If our aim is world peace and goodwill, then we must fully appreciate, understand and realise the religious faiths and beliefs of those nations who are today the leaders of our scientific progress and achievements—"The European Group of Nations".

For many centuries they have believed in Jesus. Yet some of them in Eastern European countries have now openly renounced him, whilst the other European Nations have more or less followed suit covertly. You see the Churches on every Sunday morning lying almost deserted in the Christian countries with not even half a per cent of the population attending them. In many Churches throughout Europe you see a congregation of as few as only a dozen people on Sundays, all of them very old, usually over sixty years of age, some so old that they can hardly walk. One naturally feels distressed at seeing the European peoples flocking to concerts of "Pop music", "The Beatles:" *etc.* instead of a Church service on a Sunday! One asks: "Why is it thus?"

Religion has often been the binding factor between man and his fellow beings but unfortunately it has not been so with Christianity as will be clear from the very few extracts given here from pages 496-498 of "*Babylon The Great Has Fallen*":

"As the American nation grew and spread from coast to coast, its separation of Church and State by the National Constitution resulted in its lands becoming the home of more than two hundred religious sects, all of which professed to be Christians.

"Christendom as a whole became rent apart with religious sects, Roman Catholic, Eastern Orthodox and Protestant. In South Africa 1,400 religious sects have grown up among the Bantu people since 1910, when Christendom's missionaries poured in, according to an Associated Press despatch published from Johannesburg, South Africa, on August 12, 1957. **Today the religious situation in Christendom is a mockery of the Christian unity that Christ taught his disciples.**

"The Reformation movement of the sixteenth century led to **shameful religious persecution by both Protestants and Catholics, and to frightful religious wars**".

One is rather puzzled and wonders why Christendom has become an obstacle to unity between the same basic group of people—The European Nations? After all, they all accept the same religious book The Holy Bible!

This can be gauged easily from the numerous public expressions being made daily by the various groups of Christians, *e.g.*:

When one says "God is only one" it is contradicted with: "God is a Trinity in Unity".

If some insist "that "Jesus is not divine" others explain: "Christ is the only begotten son of god".

A group contends "Mary is Mother of god and queen of the Heaven" whereas another sect pays hardly any recognition to her!

Hundreds of such contradictions are now in circulation and for each they quote a reference from the Holy Bible as their source of authority. Surely all these conflicting statements and beliefs cannot be correct. Nor can all the references quoted from the Holy Bible be authentic. One is rightly confused as to why there are all these contradictions in a Holy Book of God, which should be simple and easily understood by the masses. The indisputable answer is that the Original Hebrew Texts of the "Evangel" containing the preaching's of Jesus were simple and clear. They left no scope whatsoever for any contradictions or confusion and misrepresentations. But unfortunately, these originals are no longer available. They were either burnt and destroyed completely in 325 A.D. or suppressed as we shall read later on.

The result is that the Christians, groping in the dark for the truth, have brought out over a dozen versions of the Holy Bible in the English language alone, not to mention the Bibles in Greek, Latin, French, Spanish and other foreign languages. Some of the well known English versions:

1. The Holy Bible by John Wycliffe in 1382-1383
2. New Testament by William Tyndale in 1525-1526
3. Miles Coverdale's version in 1535.
4. Matthew's Bible in 1537 (by John Rogers) with revision in 1539 (by Richard Taverner).
5. The Great Bible in 1539.
6. The Geneva Bible in 1560.
7. The Bishop's Bible in 1568.
8. The Rhemish Bible in 1582, which was later revised into The Douay Bible.
9. The Authorised Version of King James I in 1611.
10. The Revised Version in 1881.
11. The American Standard Version in 1901.

12. The Revised Standard Version in 1952.

13. The New World Translation of the Holy Scriptures.

These multifarious versions of the Holy Bible unfortunately, instead of bringing about unity and love between one Christian and another have become the source and cause of not only disputes, dissensions, but even wars amongst them and what is more important, have broken up the Christians into numerous different sects and groups. Instead of unity, the different versions have brought about disunity.

Many great thinkers and teachers have very rightly viewed these developments with grave concern. They have set out in search of the truth from time to time during the past 1500 years. They are also desperately seeking the correct path which even now may bring about unity amongst the hundreds of factions of Christians. No solution is yet in sight. Could the undermentioned causes be the reasons?

1. The material upon which a Christian is prepared to rely has to be only "The Holy Bible".

2. Many even know that the Original Hebrew Texts of the Holy Bible are no longer available.

3. Christians know for a fact that many of the traditions, rites, rules and regulations are from Pagan or Gentile sources and have no connection with the doctrines of Jesus.

Unless the original teachings of Jesus can be reconstructed to disclose the discrepancies in the Holy Bible, there is no hope for a common basis for goodwill amongst the Europeans. Without unity amongst them, world peace cannot be achieved. Hence this is the *sine qua non*. *This research has been undertaken to meet just this challenge.*

1. Period: The Birth of Jesus

Jesus was circumcised on the eighth day (St. Luke 2: 21). When the Virgin Mary had purified herself after 40 days, a sacrifice was made for Jesus at the temple according to Jewish law (St. Luke 2: 22-24).

2. Period: 29-33 A.D.

Jesus at the age of about 30 years began to preach (St. Luke 3: 23).

He went to the temple of Jerusalem and tried his utmost to root out the evil practices that had crept into the Jewish religion and to bring them once again to the correct path (St. Matthew 21: 12-3; St. Mark 11:15-18; St. Luke 19: 45-46; St. John 2: 13-16).

Jesus went all over Galilee in Judaea for three years teaching to the Jews (St. Matt. 4: 23).

Jesus did not advocate a schism or a separate religion from that of the Jews. His teachings were merely a continuation of the Jewish faith but in its correct original form.

He made this absolutely clear in the following terms:

> "Think not that I am come to destroy the (Judaic) law, or (teach against the earlier Jewish) prophets: I am not come to destroy (Judaism), but to fulfil (and bring Judaism to its original)" (St. Matt. 5: 17).

Jesus and all his followers being Jews by birth naturally spoke only in their mother tongue *i.e.* Hebrew.

Therefore all that he taught, prophesied and did, were recorded in Hebrew because Jesus had come to teach "*to none but unto the Jews only*" (Acts 10: 36 and 11: 19).

From these Biblical records it is apparent that Jesus not only taught the Jewish law but he also lived the life of a Jewish preacher

(St. Matt. 10: 5-7).

The Divine "Evangel" revealed to Jesus through the Angel Gabriel and dictated by him during his lifetime could have been only in Hebrew as it was meant to correct the falsifications in the Torah of Moses which was in Hebrew. Further, the Evangel was documented with the sole object of guiding the Israelites, whose language was Hebrew (page 285, *Gospel of Barnabas*).

That this message of Jesus dictated and recorded in his lifetime was a divine one is proved by the Holy Bible:

> "For I (Jesus) have not spoken out of my self (*i.e.* of my own accord); but (this is the message which) the Father sent me, He gave me a commandment (through Angel Gabriel, as to) what I should say, and what I should speak" (St. John 12: 49).

> "He that loveth me not and keepeth not my sayings (*i.e.* the Evangel); and the word (*i.e.* the Evangel) which ye hear is not mine but the Father's which (He) sent (to) me (through Angel Gabriel)" (St. John 14: 24). ·

3. Jesus is lifted bodily to Heaven

Jesus at the age of about 33 years was lifted bodily to heaven when alive in the presence of witnesses (Acts 1: 9).

During his earthly life he had managed to gather a following of about 120 people, all of whom were Jews (Acts 1: 15).

Jesus did not give his followers the nomenclature Christians. **His followers were the Jews.**

4. The Knowledge of the coming of Jesus

The Jews were aware of the coming of Jesus. This will be clear from the following passages, where John, the predecessor to Jesus has been questioned by the Jews:

"And this is the record of John when the Jews sent priests, and Levites from Jerusalem to ask him, who art thou?

"And he confessed, and denied not; but confessed, I am not the Christ (the word Christ was coined in 325 A.D. as we shall read later).

"And they asked him, what then? Art thou Elias? And he saith, I am not. Art thou that Prophet? And he answered No" (St. John 1: 19-21).

B. The World in which the Christian Church was Born

Since the Old Testament had been corrupted and several passages altered, many Jews were unable to recognise Jesus. This led to the persecution of Jesus and his followers. Even the word "Jesus" is a corrupted form of the Hebrew name "Eisa" or "Eisu".

1. About 35 A.D.

After the departure of Jesus, the oppression did not stop. There lived a young Jew named Saul of Tarsus, later on known as St. Paul. He was not only a hater of Jesus but also the worst possible enemy of his teachings the Evangel.

The Bible records of him:

"And (Saul) cast him (Stephen) out of the city, and stoned him (till he was dead): and the witnesses laid down their clothes at a young man's feet, whose name was Saul (St. Paul).

"And they stoned Stephen, (who was) calling upon God, and saying, Lord (of) Jesus, receive my spirit" (Acts 7: 58-59).

"As for Saul, he made havoc of the church entering into every house, and haling men and women committed them to prison" (Acts 8: 3).

"And Saul, yet breathing out threatening's and slaughter against the disciples of the Lord, went unto the high priest,

"And desired of him letters to Damascus to the synagogues, that if he found any of this way, whether they were men or women, he might bring them bound unto Jerusalem" (Acts 9: 1-2).

So bitter was the persecution of Saul that the followers of Jesus had to scatter to save themselves.

"Now they which were scattered abroad upon the persecution that arose about Stephen travelled as far as Phenice and Cyprus, and Antioch, preaching the word to none but unto the Jews only" (Acts 11: 19).

2. The Conversion of St. Paul

Saul of Tarsus found that he could not destroy the teachings of Jesus by persecution, from the outside, as the followers of Jesus were getting scattered. He then thought of joining the faith to deceive the people (Acts 9: 3-18) by falsely stating that he had met Jesus, who asked him to convert, so that he might subvert the entire teachings of Jesus. The very first words he uttered after his alleged conversion were nothing but pure and simple blasphemy *i.e.* the pagan sun worship theories of Nimrod combined with Buddhism which was then prevalent in this area under the name of Mithraism. With the sole object of confounding the believers he, straightaway, preached blasphemy as will be evident from the following passage:

"And when he had received meat, he was strengthened. Then was Saul certain days with the disciples which were at Damascus.

"And straightaway he (Saul or St. Paul) preached **Christ** (This word was coined in 325 A.D.) in the synagogues, **That He is the Son of god**.

"But all that heard him were amazed; and said: *Is not this he that destroyed them which called on this name in Jerusalem,* and came hither for that intent, that he might (destroy the religion of Jesus and) bring them bound unto the chief priest?

"But Saul increased the more in strength and confounded the Jews (who were the followers of Jesus) which dwelt at Damascus, proving that this is very **Christ** (since this word was coined by Constantine in 325 A.D., this must have been written after 325 A.D.)

"And when Saul was come to Jerusalem, he assayed to join himself to the disciples: but they were all afraid of him, and believed not that he was a disciple" (Acts 9: 19-22 and 26).

C. The Origin of the Christian Churches

1. About 36 A.D.

Saul (St. Paul) got the golden opportunity a year after his professed conversion to found the *"Religion of Brethren"* in co-operation with Peter and half-a-dozen dissidents with the object of destroying the strict teachings of God as revealed through Jesus and recorded in the **Evangel**.

Shortly after his supposed conversion, he propounded that the only way by which they could avoid the persecution from the Jews was not just to concentrate upon preaching to their Jewish circumcised brothers, friends and relatives. So far they had been preaching as Jesus had ordered during his life to teach only to the circumcised Jews—*the lost sheep of the House of Israel* (St. Matt. 10: 5-7).

2. The Decision to preach to Other than Jews

Saul pointed out that they had to attract the attention of the Centurions and the "Gurus" or the religious monks and try to convert these Gentiles. He explained that if they made only one such convert, then all their hundred or more followers along with their families, slaves and dependants totalling a thousand or more would all be converted automatically together with the head of their organisation. Therefore each such conversion would mean a thousand or more followers at a time. The plan was very interesting indeed! As these Centurions and Monks were very influential people amongst the Gentiles, all persecution from the Jewish quarters would accordingly have to stop.

3. How to attract people to convert to the Brethren Faith

Now the serious problem arose as to what would attract them. With the idea of destroying the teachings of the Evangel, Saul (St. Paul) the enemy of Jesus suggested, as follows:-

a. We cannot ask these important people to be circumcised otherwise they will not join our faith.

b. We cannot ask them to follow the Mosaic Laws, because it was too difficult for the Gentiles to lead perfect lives according to God's Laws, and further these great men would not agree to conform to such strict rules. They had to have something attractive, familiar and simpler than the teachings of Jesus.

c. They were believers in Mithra (the changed name of King Nimrod) being the only begotten son of Sun-god. That he was born of the great Virgin Mother, Queen of the heavens. That he was the lamb of the heavens, the saviour, who had come on earth to sacrifice his life to save sinners; that he was trinity in unity with the sun-god. To enter this faith one had to be baptised instead of promising to follow the Mosaic Laws as taught by Jesus, and partake of sacramental foods and drinks to become the pure sinless deity. Observe the eight beatitudes of Buddha *etc.*

d. It was therefore St. Paul's suggestion that this religion of

Mithraism be adopted as the basis of attracting these wise, educated, influential Gentiles with the following changes *viz*:

  i. Replace the name of Mithra by Jesus.

  ii. Replace the name of Queen Semiramis by Virgin Mary.

  iii. Add all the miracles of Jesus.

  iv. Add on one additional miracle because Bacchus was the inventor of the gift of wine by saying that Jesus turned water into wine at a marriage ceremony as against wine being strictly prohibited to Jesus according to the Evangel—*The Gospel of Barnabas* as read in *Destruction or Peace,* Chapter 10: P.

  v. Adopt the whole religion of Mithraism, as if these were the teachings of Jesus. Thus ignore the under-mentioned curse of Jesus:

"Whosoever therefore shall break (even) one of the least (*i.e.* smallest) of these (Mosaic) commandments, and shall teach men so, he shall be (cursed to the lowest hell *i.e.*) called the least in the Kingdom of Heaven: but whosoever shall follow (these Mosaic Laws *i.e.*) do and teach them (to other people), the same shall be (blessed to great positions and respect *i.e.*) called great in the Kingdom of Heaven" (St. Matt. 5: 19 see also Revelation 22: 18-19).

The curse of Jesus is also confirmed in the last Heavenly book as follows:

"Those of the children of Israel who went astray were cursed by the tongue ... of Jesus, son of Mary. That was because they rebelled and used to transgress" (Qur'an 5: 78).

Thus it is explicit from the Holy Bible that *"Nobody"* has had or will ever have any right whatsoever to change any of the teachings of Jesus nor any of the Mosaic Laws, which have been fully incorporated in the Evangel and yet call himself a follower of Jesus. Therefore anybody breaking any of these laws is condemned to the lowest hell by the curse of Jesus, as still recorded in the Holy Bible (St. Matt. 5: 19 and Revelation 22: 18-19).

"If ye love me (Jesus), keep my commandments" (St. John 14: 15).

Thus the religion propagated by St. Paul, which was aimed at destroying the teachings of Jesus, appeared very attractive to the Gentiles because of the miracles, including the raising of the dead and bringing back to life and the actual birth of Jesus from a truly virgin Mary.

4. The First Pagan to Convert to the Brethren Faith

On this basis Peter accepted the first uncircumcised person into their "Brethren" faith about 36 A.D. He was the Roman Centurion named Cornelius (Acts 10: 1-48). Then followed the mass scale conversions of the pagan Gentiles into the faith of the "Brethren".

5. Jesus refused to convert Pagans to his Religion even though they had implicit Faith, which even the Jewish Followers of Jesus did not have

The Holy Bible discloses that Jesus taught to none but Jews (Acts 11: 19). Even though the "Roman Centurion" had absolute faith in him (St. Luke 7: 1-10) yet Jesus did not think it correct to convert this centurion even with circumcising because Jesus had come to save the Jews and not the pagan Gentiles. The reason evidently was that Jesus was well aware that this would be made an excuse to change the religion of God as taught by him into paganism, idolatry, blasphemy and adultery. Therefore, he avoided it, so as not to give any chance whatsoever to mischief makers to alter his religious precepts at a later stage!

Here is a quotation from page 91 of Madras Lectures on Islam—Series No. 2—"*The Cultural Side of Islam*" by the English Research Scholar Pickthall delivered in January 1927 (published in 1937):

> "Even Christ himself, as several of his sayings show—for instance, when he asked if it were meet (*i.e.* correct) to take the children's (*i.e.* Hebrew race) bread and throw it to the dogs (*i.e.* how pagan disbelievers were treated by the Jews), and when he declared that he was sent only to the lost sheep of the House of Israel—seemed to regard his mission as to the Hebrews only;".

6. Jesus commands that his teachings are for Jews and not others

> "These twelve Jesus sent forth, and *commanded them, saying, go not into the Gentiles,* and *into any city of the Samaritans enter ye not.*
>
> "*But go rather to the lost sheep of the House of Israel.*
>
> "*And as ye go, preach, saying, the kingdom of heaven is at hand*" (St. Matt 10: 5-7).

From these it will be clear that Jesus has forbidden anybody from teaching his religion to anybody but the Jews. Further his mission is only "*for the lost sheep of Israel*".

7. The Protest of the Nazarenes to the Brethren

St. John, the Apostle and heir of Jesus, along with about 112 out of the 120 original followers of Jesus requested that at least the new converts be circumcised and be persuaded to follow the laws of

Moses, which were the laws taught by Jesus (Acts 11: 2-3; 15: 1-5). The six dissidents disagreed (Acts 15: 6-24). This group comprising Peter, Paul and half a dozen others thus formed their own religion known as "Brethren" (Acts 11: 1) and thus severed their connections with the original religion of Jesus, (Acts 15: 9-25) by breaking the everlasting covenant of God Almighty (Genesis 17: 12-14) in spite of the protests of almost all (*i.e.* St. John and 112 out of the 120) disciples (Acts 11: 2-3).

8. The Brethren faith break away from the Nazarenes or followers of Jesus

Peter and his religion of the Brethren by this record of the Holy Bible showed:-

a. They had no regard for the *Everlasting Covenant of God.*

b. They thus considered themselves cleverer and more intelligent and learned than *God Almighty Himself.* Is not this *pure and simple Blasphemy*?

c. Such persons as Peter and Paul who break the everlasting covenant of God, commit Blasphemy and misguide men surely cannot be guides for mankind. Far less have they any claims to be *Apostles of Jesus*: Especially when they are violating his commands to preach *only to the lost sheep of Israel* and not to the Gentiles and Samaritans (St. Matt. 10:-5-7).

9. In 47-48 A.D.

Paul, who never recognised Jesus or his teachings, the Evangel, displays publicly once again his utter disregard of the curses of Jesus on those who changed God's message as taught by him. Thus Paul openly commences to preach contrary to the Laws of God and the Evangel dictated by Jesus during his life on earth, as will be seen from the few quotations given hereunder:

    a. Jesus is Saviour (Acts 13: 23)

    b. Jesus is begotten son of god. (Acts 13: 33)

    c. That Jesus preached forgiveness of *Sins if you just believe in him.* (Acts 13: 38-39).

Hence it meant to the Pagan Gentile converts that *all sins were fully justified and encouraged by the Brethren. If they believed in the name, of Jesus they could commit as many sins as they pleased fearlessly even though they were in fact forbidden by Jesus and also prohibited under the laws of Moses as taught by Jesus in the Evangel* (Acts 13: 39).

10. The Warning of Jesus

Beware of the Day of Judgment on which you will be raised from the dead and will have to give an account of your deeds on earth. And I warn you that you will not attain heaven without good deeds. Beware on this day a sinner with a sin as small as *one jot or one tittle shall in no wise escape from the (Mosaic) law, and enter into heaven until he or she abides by and fulfils all the (Judaic) Laws* (St. Matt. 5: 18).

> "For the eyes of the Lord are over those who do good and right deeds (as required by the Jewish Law) and His ears are open unto their prayers; but the face of the Lord is against them that do evil (in disregard of the Judaic law)" (1 Peter 3: 12).

11. The Second Protest in 49 A.D.

St. John, the apostle and the 112 disciples of Jesus *i.e.* "the Nazarenes" again protested against these false teachings of Paul as they were contrary to the preachings of Jesus and the Evangel saying:

> "Except ye be circumcised (and follow the Evangelical laws) after the manner of Moses ye cannot be saved" (Acts 15: 1).
>
> Paul thus had a serious dispute with the believers in Jesus (Acts 15: 2).
>
> "Saying, this fellow (*i.e.* Paul) persuadeth men to worship God contrary to the (Mosaic) Law (as taught by Jesus)" (Acts 18: 13).

From the above it will be explicit that Paul was taken by the faithful disciples of Jesus not only as a hater of Jesus but that after his alleged conversion he also continued to teach such things, as were fundamentally contradictory to, the doctrines of Jesus. According to these faithful disciples of Jesus, Paul's teachings without a doubt were calculated to destroy and obliterate the pure religion of Jesus from the face of the earth.

When the disciples of Jesus started protesting against the teachings of Saul, a conference was called by the "Brethren" under the chairmanship of Peter. It was attended amongst others by the following persons, the members of this conference were:

1. Peter (Acts 15: 7).
2. James the brother of Judas (Acts 15: 13).
3. Simeon (Acts 15: 14).
4. Judas, brother of James (Acts 15: 27).
5. Salias (Acts 15: 27).
6. Mark (Acts 15: 39).
7. Saul of Tarsus (St. Paul).

At this meeting of the "Brethren" it was resolved:

a. To forsake the teachings of Jesus.

b. To adopt a new religion based on the teachings of King Nimrod, *i.e.* Mithraism.

c. To replace the name of Baal with its translation of "The Sacred Heart" and the names Mithra or Nimrod with the already famous name of Jesus.

d. That the *Gentiles need not be circumcised when they accepted this new faith (of the Brethren)* (Acts 15: 19) *even though this meant the breaking of the everlasting covenant of God with Abraham* (Acts 15: 24).

e. That neither the Pagan converts nor should the disciples be burdened any longer with the following of the Mosaic Laws taught by Jesus (Acts 15: 9-11 and 24).

f. Following the Mosaic Laws would amount to tempting God to punish them for having broken the said divine laws. (Acts 15: 10). Thus in effect violating the following teachings of Jesus in the Holy Bible:

"Think not that I am come to destroy the (Judaic) law, or the (teachings of the Jewish) prophets; I am not come to destroy (these teachings), but to fulfil (them)" (St. Matt. 5: 17).

"*For I (Jesus) say unto you, that except your righteousness* (*i.e.* good deeds done on earth in accordance with the Mosaic Law) *shall exceed the righteousness* (*i.e.* good deeds done on earth in accordance with the Mosaic Law, which are equally applicable to the followers of Jesus as the Jews) *of the scribes and Pharisees, ye shall in no case enter into the kingdom of heaven*" (St. Matt. 5: 20).

g. That it is immaterial what sins a Christian commits, so long as he believes in Jesus (as the only begotten son of god), he shall be saved by his grace just like they (that took all the trouble to follow the Mosaic law. Hence good deeds were not only irrelevant but they were to be looked down upon—Acts 15: 11).

Accordingly these Nimrodic principles became the foundation in 49 A.D. for the development of the Churches of Peter (Antioch), Mark (Alexandria), and Paul (Rome), which adopted the Pagan sun worship religion prevailing in these areas but instead of using the names Baal, the Sacred Heart or Tammuz and the sign of the cross, or Mithra, the saviour, the only begotten son born of the virgin, *etc.*, they merely replaced them with the already famous name of Jesus and gave him all their titles *e.g.* the Sacred Heart, the only begotten Son, the Saviour come to save the world by the sacrifice of his life, *etc.* Thereby they raised the status of Jesus in course of time from "A Man" to "Son of god" to fit in with the pagan mythology of the "Virgin giving birth to the only begotten son of the Sun god, who sacrificed his life to save sinners".

Therefore, the religion taught by the "Brethren" was completely at variance with that of Jesus. It had no real or any imaginary connections except for the incorporation of the name of Jesus. They enlarged upon his miracles as their best and most convincing argument. This is thus the beginning of the display of utter disregard for Jesus and his threat to disown such corruptors of his religion on the "Day of Judgment". This refers to those who changed his teachings of observance of the Mosaic Laws and the doing of good deeds failing which one could not hope to attain heaven.

The message of Peter on behalf of the "Brethren" to the Pagan converts was as under:

> Forasmuch as we have heard, that certain (people *i.e.* St. John and the Nazarenes) which went out from us have troubled you with words, subverting your souls saying, *Ye must be circumcised and to keep the (Mosaic) Law: to whom* (the Nazarenes) *we* (*i.e.* the Brethren) *gave no such commandment.*

"It seemed good (enough) unto us, (the Brethren) being assembled with one accord, to send chosen men unto you with our beloved Barnabas and Paul,

"We have sent therefore Judas and Salias, who shall also tell you the same things by mouth" (Acts 15: 24-25 and 27).

Thus started orally the new religion of the "Brethren" in contradiction to the "Evangel", the message of God through Jesus.

This is confirmed by St. John in the Holy Bible:

"And the world passeth away, and the lust thereof: but he that doeth the will of God abideth for ever.

"Little children, it is the last time: and as ye have heard that anti-christ shall come, *even now are there many antichrists*; whereby we know that it is the last time.

"*They (the Brethren) went out from us (the Nazarenes), but they were not of us (the followers of Jesus) for if they had been of us (the followers of Jesus), they would no doubt have continued with us (the followers of Jesus); but they (the Brethren) went out that they might be made manifest (i.e. become world famous on account of the new popular religion they have originated in the name of Jesus thus they made clear) that they were not at all of us (the followers of Jesus)*" (I John 2: 17-19).

D. The warnings of Jesus that he disowns Peter

Did Jesus authorise St. Peter in terms of the Holy Bible to:

1. Accept Gentiles and Samaritans and others who were not Jews into the faith without being circumcised?

2. Do away with the Judaic Law and to treat it as a curse?

3. Alter the religion taught by Jesus?

From the Holy Bible it is confirmed that Jesus had warned

Peter in his original name of Simon that Satan is going to possess him as follows:

> "And the Lord said, Simon, Simon behold *the Satan hath desired to have you, that he may sift you as wheat.*" (St. Luke 22: 31).

From the Holy Bible it appears that Jesus has informed Peter repeatedly in the presence of two or three witnesses as required under the law—Deuteronomy 17:6, that on the Day of Judgment when Peter would approach him, Jesus would disown Peter, because he was aware that Peter and those like him would destroy the teachings of Jesus and turn his religion from God worship into paganism, idolatry and blasphemy.

When one has been disowned repeatedly and warned by Jesus in the presence of witnesses how can such a one be described as an apostle of Jesus? What right has he to call himself an apostle of Jesus? How can such a person be the guide to followers of Jesus? What is the value of anything taught by Peter and his associates especially when it is aimed at effacing the teachings of Jesus?

The witnesses to the warning of Jesus to Peter were:

1. John, the son of Zebedee (St. Matt. 4: 21).
2. Andrew.
3. James, the son of Zebedee (St. Matt. 4: 21).

This warning to Peter is quoted hereunder from the Holy Bible:

> "And as he sat upon the Mount of Olives over against the temple, Peter and James and John and Andrew asked him privately.
>
> "And Jesus answering them began to say, Take heed lest any man (even from amongst those present here—a direct

reference to Peter and those like him) deceive you.

"For many shall come in my name (*i.e.* claiming to be the Apostles of Jesus), saying I am sent by (or chosen by Jesus) Christ and (such like Peter) shall deceive many" (St. Mark 13: 3, 5-6).

Jesus has clarified further in the Holy Bible that he would disown Peter and those like him on the Day of Judgment:

"Not everyone that saith unto me, Lord, Lord, shall enter into the Kingdom of heaven (*i.e.* faith in Jesus is not sufficient); but he that doeth the will (*i.e.* does good deeds and follows the Judaic Laws) of my father (*i.e.* the Creator), Which is in heaven.

"Many will say to me in that day (of Judgment), Lord, Lord, have we not prophesied in thy name? and in thy name done many wonderful works?

"And then will I (Jesus) profess unto them, I never knew you (because you did not follow my teachings): depart from me, ye that work iniquity (by saying "Faith" is sufficient and good deeds and the Judaic law of God are a curse)" (St. Matt. 7: 21-23).

Thus Jesus has clarified before witnesses as required under the Law (Deuteronomy 17: 6) to Peter that he was fully aware, of what mischief Peter and his associates would do after his Ascension. And Jesus has warned that on the Day of Judgment, Jesus was going to disown Peter and his followers and chase them away for the harm they would do to the religion of God as taught by Jesus.

Jesus knew very well what was going to happen in the future to his religion and who is going to change and demolish it.

Since John, his heir and Andrew and James (brother of John, the son of Zebedee) were going to remain on the right path, *this warning was a direct and indisputable reference to Peter, who was the fourth and an indirect reference to Paul and their followers, i.e. the Brethren.*

Jesus has expressed further his disappointment at Peter for his inability to pray for an hour to save himself from the temptations of Satan when praying at the Garden as follows:

> "And he cometh unto the disciples, and findeth them asleep, and saith (only) unto Peter: What, could ye not watch with me one hour? (Jesus did not say so to the sons of Zebedee because he knew that they would remain on the right road and that all his references and warnings related only to Peter. He thus kept the same two witnesses out of the previous three also on this occasion, one of whom was to be his only Apostolic heir).
>
> "(Jesus orders Peter) Watch and pray that ye (Peter) enter not into temptation (of the Satan, who is going to have you as warned earlier—St. Luke 22: 31) ...
>
> "He (Jesus) went away again the second time, and prayed ...
>
> "And he came and found them asleep again (*i.e.* Peter and the two sons of Zebeedee *i.e.* John and James the two witnesses of the previous warning to Peter. Thus Jesus kept witnesses regularly against Peter, which shows he fully knew about Peter) ...
>
> "(Again Jesus awoke Peter warning him to pray otherwise the Satan would have him as warned in St. Luke 22: 31, saying this is the third and final chance Peter had of saving himself from the Satan if he prayed with Jesus and woke up John and James a second time so that they might be witness to his warnings to Peter). And he left them and went away again, and prayed the third time, saying the same words (of warning to Peter).
>
> "Then cometh he (Jesus after he had finished his prayers) to his disciples and saith unto them (to Peter in absolute disappointment and to John and James as his witnesses), Sleep on now, and take your rest (as the hour of prayer for safety from Satan for Peter had already passed) ..." (St. Matt. 26: 40-

45).

Then there are the six famous denials of Peter in the Holy Bible before the cock crows. These occurred thrice at the house of Annas (St. John 18: 17-18 and 25-27) and again thrice at the Palace of Caiphas (St. Matt. 26: 69-75; St. Mark 14: 66-72). These six denials of Peter in one single night clearly show how little was Peter's faith in Jesus.

Jesus has made it clear in the Holy Bible that if anyone denies him *even once in public* then Jesus would disown him in heaven:

> "*But whosoever shall deny me before men, him will I also deny before my father (i.e. the Creator) which is in heaven*" (St. Matt. 10: 33).

> *Since Peter has denied Jesus six times in public* (see Destruction or Peace, Chapter 12: H-3), *therefore Peter is a person disowned by Jesus* hence absolutely unfit to represent Jesus according to the Holy Bible.

The Holy Bible confirms further that God Almighty has given no right to anybody to change even an iota from the religion of God as can be seen from the following quotations:

> "For I testify unto every man that heareth the words of the prophecy of this book, if any man shall add unto these things, God shall add unto him the plagues that are written in this book" (Revelation 22: 18).

> "Ye shall *not add* unto the work which I command you, *neither shall ye diminish ought from it*, that ye may keep the commandments of the LORD your God which I command you.

> "Know therefore this day, and consider it in thine heart, *that the LORD He is God in heaven above*, and upon the earth beneath: there is NONE ELSE.

> "Thou shall keep therefore His statutes, and His

commandments, which I command thee this day, that it may go well with thee, and with thy children after thee, and that thou mayest prolong thy days upon the earth, which the LORD thy God giveth thee, (This is a commandment) for ever" (Deuteronomy 4: 2, 39-40).

If anyone deviates from the laws of God Almighty then he is either:

a. Assuming to be cleverer than God Almighty so that he can change His orders—but that is impossible and also a blasphemy as no man can ever compare his knowledge with that of God Almighty, or,

b. The changer of the law is a sinner.

In both the cases such a person has no right whatsoever even to pretend before the world that he is an Apostle of Jesus. The people of the world are forbidden by the above Biblical orders to follow such mischief makers. Otherwise they surely will suffer dire consequences.

Even if such a person were an "appointed Apostle" of Jesus, from the moment he discarded the law or taught disobedience to the Mosaic Law, he would cease automatically to be an apostle of Jesus. Thus he would become an apostle of the devil instead of Jesus.

Jesus has made this quite evident by the following curse:

"Whosoever therefore shall break (even) one of these least (*i.e.* the smallest of these Mosaic) commandments, and shall teach men so, he shall be (cursed to the lowest hell *i.e.*) called the least in the kingdom of heaven but whosoever shall do (*i.e.* follow these Mosaic commandments) and teach them (to other people), the same shall be called (*i.e.* blessed to) great (positions and respect) in the Kingdom of Heaven" (St. Matt. 5: 19).

As such, a person who invokes upon himself the curse of Jesus, can by no stretch of the imagination be one of his Apostles.

Further, Jesus has clarified by his prayer in the Bible that he prays for only those few who would keep to his teachings and thus belong to him and not for the rest of the world:

"I pray for them: I pray not for the world, but (only) for them, which Thou hast given me; for they are Thine (*i.e.* those who are observers of your Judaic Laws and Commandments)" (St. John 17: 9).

The last Heavenly Book corroborates the above teachings of Jesus as follows:

"But when Jesus became conscious of their disbelief, he cried: Who will be my helpers in the cause of Allah? The disciples (St. John and the 112 out of the 120) said: We will be Allah's helpers. We believe in Allah and bear thou (O Jesus) witness that we are "Muslims" (*i.e.* we have surrendered ourselves to the Will of Allah—Thy will be done).

"Our Lord! We believe in that which (Evangel) thou hast revealed (through Jesus) and we follow him, whom thou hast sent. Enrol us among those who are witnesses (to the truth.)

"And they (Peter and Paul and the Brethren) schemed (against John and the 112 believers in Jesus) and Allah is the best of schemers" (Qur'an 3: 52-54).

E. The Origin of the Non-Hebrew Gospels

In 50 A.D.: Paul commences to write letters of advice for the new Pagan converts inviting other Gentiles to join this new religion of which he and his "Brethren" are the founders. These letters of Paul in course of time became the first man-made "Gospel" and that too in a non-Hebrew tongue *i.e.*, a language alien to Jesus, as against the Divine Original Hebrew Evangel of Jesus (see also *Destruction or Peace,* Chapter 8: J-3—The Evangel).

They compiled eventually their own *Holy Bible* in the non-Hebrew languages of the Gentiles as opposed to the original *Evangel* personally dictated by Jesus in Hebrew before being lifted to heaven and recorded in Aramaic script by several Jewish scribes including Levi, Andrew and Barnabas. They had recorded it during the period that Jesus was preaching, and it was also noted by John there and then but reproduced in book form a few years after the Romans ravaged Jerusalem in 70 A.D. All these Jewish scribes were not only the companions but also numbered among the 120 disciples of Jesus (Acts 1: 15).

About 56-58 A.D.: The Pagan converts to the faith of the "Brethren" had become numerous. They required a book of instructions. The Evangel was not acceptable to them! A Gentile of Antioch who was by profession a physician whose name was Luke (Colossians 4: 14) became a faithful companion of Paul. Luke was an acknowledged scholar. At Paul's request and on the basis of the information given by Paul to him, he wrote the "Gospel of St. Luke". This is the second series of man-made writings, which is again in a Non-Hebrew language—*i.e.*, not for Jews but for the Gentile converts.

About 58-60 A.D.: When St. John and the Nazarenes, the true followers of Jesus, heard of the false gospel of Luke they started showing the Pagan converts the Hebrew "Evangel" of Jesus.

This gave rise to bitter feelings between the Nazarenes and the Brethren; who had already increased to some thousands in number. The Pagan converts were mostly Romans in authority. They commenced immediately a systematic persecution of the Nazarenes, who by 62 A.D. had to flee for their lives from Jerusalem as foretold by Jesus (St. Luke 21: 20-24).

About 60-65 A.D.: It appears that because Paul had got his

THE TEACHINGS OF HOLY JESUS

friend Luke to write out a gospel, Peter likewise influenced his friend Marcus, another intellectual of the time, to compile a book also. This became the third series of man-made writings in a non-Hebrew language for the Pagan converts to counteract the Original Hebrew "Evangel" of Jesus.

This new religion of the "Brethren" appears to be based upon the undermentioned quotations which spelt the death-knell of the teachings of Jesus and the Evangel:

> "But that no man is justified by the law in the sight of God, it is evident: for the just shall live by the faith.
>
> "And the laws is not of faith: but the man that doeth them shall live in them.
>
> "CHRIST" (this word was coined by Constantine in 325 A.D. hence this must have been written thereafter) has redeemed us from the curse of the law, being made a curse for us: for it is written, cursed is every one that hangeth on a tree" (Galatians 3: 11-13). These are purely Nimrod's teachings.

That the religion of these "Brethren" is that taught by King Nimrod at the "Tower of Babel", the Church of Babylon, is even confirmed by St. Peter in the Holy Bible when be requested St. Mark to write out a Gospel paying due respect to the teachings of this temple of Babylon and to greet with a kiss this gospel when written and prepared as follows:

> "The *Church* (Tower of Babel) that is *at Babylon* elected together with *You* (*i.e.* founded by *You*—King Nimrod) Saluteth *You* (*i.e.* King Nimrod, the only begotten son of God who was born of the great Virgin mother, queen of the heavens, the lamb come to save sinners): and so doth Marcus (St. Mark the gospel writer) my son.
>
> "(When the gospel of St. Mark on King Nimrod replacing it with the name of Jesus is prepared) Greet Ye one another with a kiss of Charity. Peace be with you all that are in *Christ* (this

word was coined in 325 A.D.) Jesus Amen" (I Peter 5: 13, 14).

Babylon has always upheld one religion (page 23 of *Babylon the Great has Fallen!*), that of King Nimrod from the time of the curse of God at the Tower of Babel. This is re-iterated in the Holy Bible:

> "Babylon hath been a golden cup in the Lord's hand, that made *All the earth Drunken*; the nations have drunken of her wine; *Therefore the Nations are mad*". (Jeremiah 51:7)

F. The Spread of Christianity

1. The Brethren Faith

The spread of the Brethren faith of Peter and Paul was very rapid until 70 A.D., when Jerusalem was destroyed by the Romans.

Thereafter; as they were considered a branch of the Jewish faith, they came under the persecution of the Romans. Therefore they had no option but to show that there was a great difference between the Jewish faith and that which the Brethren were following. Rather the latter was identical with the Mithraic faith of the Romans. In fact the Brethren claimed that their faith, even though it appeared similar to Mithraism, was definitely superior in the following respects:

- a. Jesus was actually born of a virgin named Mary as against the mythological story of Nimrod the only begotten son of sun-god through the virgin queen of the heavens.
- b. All the people of Judea had actually witnessed the wonderful miracles performed by Jesus including the raising of the dead to life.

Because of these two arguments, the Brethren faith continued to spread amongst the pagans.

2. The Church receives Royal Patronage

On the 28th October, 312 A.D. the Roman Emperor Constantine the Great was declared the Chief Augustus and Pontifex Maximus by the Roman Senate after he had defeated his rivals.

In January 313 A.D. Constantine, in his capacity of Pontifex Maximus, published his famous edict of toleration in favour of those professing the Brethren and the Nazarene faiths, both of which claimed Jesus to be the founder of their religion. Thus Jerusalem was again opened to the followers of Jesus.

In 321 A.D., Constantine enacted his first law which would apply equally to his pagan as well as Christian subjects *viz*:

Henceforth *"Dies Solis"* or Sun-god's day was to be observed as the "Sabbath day by all his subjects irrespective of their religious beliefs".

Hence the Christians were obliged to observe the Pagan sun-god's day as their "Sabbath" instead of "Fridays" as was being observed by the followers of Jesus, who did not eat meat on Fridays nor kill animals for food but observed Fridays as the holy day for prayers.

In 325 A.D. King Constantine had his son-in-law Emperor Licinius killed. Thus he became the sole Monarch of the Eastern and Western Roman Empires. By this unifying action he gained great power and respect.

He wanted to consolidate this position by having a common universal religion for all his subjects whether pagan or otherwise. He was even anxious to end all religious rifts between the Brethren faith and Mithraism on the one hand and the Brethren and Nazarenes on the other. If all his subjects professed only one faith, it would mean much greater strength and unity for his whole empire. That was his ideal. Just as he had unified the

Eastern and the Western Roman Empires into one consolidated Roman Empire, so also did he want to do the same thing with the religion of all his subjects.

On studying the various religions prevalent in his empire, he found that Mithraism and the Brethren faith were rather similar. The two arguments of the Brethren on the miraculous birth of Jesus and his numerous miracles being witnessed by a large number of people impressed him very much.

Accordingly in 325 A.D. the pagan Constantine in one of his first acts as sole emperor of the Eastern and Western Roman Empires and as Pontifex Maximus called together a religious council for settling the disputes between the diverse religions professing to originate from Jesus. This was the first step towards his objective of unifying all religions into one single faith for his subjects.

On pages 477-478, of *"Babylon the Great has Fallen!"* one reads the following:

> *Unbaptized Constantine, the pagan Pontifex Maximus, called for all the Christian episcopal or overseers throughout the empire to meet in council, not in Italian Rome, but in Nicaea, near Nicomedia, in Asia Minor. Of all these overseers, only about one-third, or 318, are reported to have come; and even this figure is understood to be too high. But why should these overseers, if they were Christians, obey a pagan Pontifex Maximus and let him dictate in Christian matters? Because of the attendants whom the bishops brought along, the number of men present at the Council may have been between 1500 and 2000. Constantine himself attended this first Council of Nicaea and he, as Pontifex Maximus and not as the religious bishop of Rome presided over the council. It was conducted, not in Latin, but in Greek, and the Nicene Creed that resulted was in Greek. The Latin Church had only seven delegates present, two of these being presbyters who represented the bishop of*

Rome.

"Those who upheld the trinity were championed by the young archdeacon Athanasius of Alexandria, Egypt. Those who opposed it and who showed from the (original handwritten Hebrew) Scripture that Jesus Christ was less than God his Father were championed by Arius, a presbyter. For about two months the two sides wrangled. Arius maintained that 'the son of god was a creature, made from nothing; that there was a time when he had no existence; that he was capable of his own free will of (doing) right and wrong,' and that, 'were he in the truest sense a son, he must have come after the Father, therefore the time obviously was when he was not, and hence he was a finite being.' When Arius rose to speak, a certain Nicholas of Myra hit him in the face. Afterwards, as Arius talked on, many stuck their fingers in their ears and ran out as if horrified by the old man's 'heresies.'

"Finally Pontifex Maximus Constantine made his decision and came out in favour of the trinitarian teachings of Athanasius (because they fitted in with the existing Mithraism and would help him to unify the religion of all his subjects). So the Nicene Creed on the "Trinity" was issued and enforced. Later, for resisting this, Arius was banished to Illyria by Constantine's order".

From this finding of the Watch Tower Bible and Tract Society it will be quite clear that there are still many true followers of Jesus who believe in his teachings:

"But in vain they do worship me (Jesus), teaching for doctrines the commandments of men" (St. Matthew 15: 9).

"Jesus saith unto her (Mary Magdalene) ... but go to my brethren, and say unto them, I ascend unto my Father and your Father; and to my God, and your God" (St. John 20: 17).

These statements of Jesus thus clarify beyond any doubt the following issues:

a. The worship of Jesus is in vain.

b. That Jesus is the brother of mankind.

c. That the "God" of mankind is equally the "God" of Jesus.

d. That the "Father" of mankind is also the "Father" of Jesus or in other words, God, out of respect, has been referred to in numerous passages of the Holy Bible as "The Divine Father" which only means that "The Creator" of mankind is also "The Creator" of Jesus. It does not by any stretch of the imagination mean "Father" in the physical sense. Otherwise each human being becomes divine according to the above statement of Jesus—that would indeed be an absurdity!

Therefore if Jesus was divine as decided upon by Constantine, the Pagan Pontifex Maximus, in 325 A.D. at the Council of Nicaea at the suggestion of Athanasius, then in that case, according to the above quotation from the Holy Bible, the entire human race, who are the brethren of Jesus, must each be equally divine! If Jesus is declared son of god then it follows that his brethren *i.e.* every human being must also be the sons of 'God'! But Jesus has made no claim whatsoever to divinity anywhere in the Holy Bible. He has never said I am "God the son" or "Only begotten son of God" or "Trinity in Unity". His above statement "my God and your God" therefore clearly establishes the heresy of Athanasius and Constantine.

All lovers of Jesus will naturally be very much shocked to find that because Arius and two fellow bishops refused to renounce the teachings of Jesus and worship Jesus which is something in vain and useless according to the Holy Bible they were banished and the **Original teachings of Jesus were declared heresies!** Can the teachings of Jesus ever be heresies?

The definition of Arianism as it appears in a standard English

Encyclopaedia (The Penguin) may here be appropriately quoted. Though it is described as a heresy in the Encyclopaedia, the particulars given rather lend support to the arguments of the true believers in Jesus, and this clearly shows it to be the authentic teachings of Jesus:

> "**Arianism.** Christian heresy named after Arius, about A.D. 256-336, a priest of Alexandria who taught that Jesus was not co-eternal with God the Father but created by Him and therefore in some sense inferior. Condemned by the Council of Nicaea A.D. 325 and bitterly opposed by Athanasius (later Bishop of Alexandria), it was embraced by many pagan converts to Christianity especially among the Goths and Germans, but from the 6th century gradually died out, though held by individuals (including allegedly Milton) at various times throughout Christian history; ..."

On page 1357, Vol. 3, of *"The Reader's Digest Great Encyclopaedic Dictionary"* one reads:

> "**Arianism.** Doctrine held by Arius of Alexandria (c 250-335) and his followers, who denied that God the Son was truly divine, con-substantial and coeternal with the Father, but was created by him".

From the above definition given by the Reader's Digest, it would appear that all Christians do not hold Arianism *i.e.* the original teachings of Jesus as heresies. Those who follow Constantine and Athanasius do, but the lovers of Jesus do not!

The following list of dates on *Trinity* might be of interest to all seekers of the truth:

A.D. 33: "I ascend unto my Father and your Father and to my God and your God" (St. John 20: 17).

A.D. 57: The Brethren about this time are teaching: "For there is *One God,* and *one mediator between God and man, the man Jesus*" (1 Timothy 2: 5).

A.D. 96:	About this time Clement wrote that Jesus was sent by God and the Apostles by Jesus.
A.D. 120:	The creed of the Apostles became known to the Church as: "I believe in God the Father, the Almighty".
A.D. 230:	Origen writes against prayers being offered Jesus, which is in accord with the teachings of Jesus, that prayers to him are in vain (St. Matthew 15: 9).
A.D. 260:	Sabellius teaches: *Father, Son* and *Holy Spirit* are three names for the same god.
A.D. 300:	No trinitarian form of prayer is yet known to the Church.
A.D. 310:	Lactanius (orthodox father) writes: "*Jesus never calls himself God*".
A.D. 320:	"*Jesus teaches us to call his Father the True God and to worship Him*".
A.D. 325:	History bears testimony to the fact that Christos or Christ the name coined by Emperor Constantine after the Greek letter "X", was declared con-substantial with the Father by the Council of Nicaea. To enforce the Divinity of Christ, there followed that horrifying and inhuman slaughter of thousands of innocent people, who refused to accept the Divinity of Christ conferred on him by the said Council, not only in Europe but in the sacred city of Jerusalem as well.
A.D. 381:	The Council of Constantinople gives the finishing touch to *the doctrine of "three persons in one god"*.
A.D. 383:	The Emperor Theodosius threatens to punish all who will not believe in and worship the Trinity.

At the first Council of religious heads at Nicaea, not the Pope of Rome but Constantine in his capacity as Pontifex Maximus issued a number of regulations to be observed by the members of the Church. These canons included:

a. The Greek letter "X" pronounced as "*chi*" to represent the first letter of the name of the founder of their religion just as the upright sign of the Cross stood for "Tau" or the first letter of the name of Tammuz, the title of Nimrod.

b. From the Greek letter "X" he coined the name Christos or Christ (in English) for the founder of this religion.

c. His birthday to be celebrated at the Winter Solstice, the birthday of Nimrod-Mithra and called "X-mas" pronounced "Christmas".

d. That henceforth the followers of the Christ were given a special name called Christians. Thus this is the origin of Christianity.

e. He decided on which *Dies Solis* or Sun-god's day of the year "Easter" should be regularly held,

f. That God instead of being one and alone as taught by Jesus was reduced to a "Trinity in Unity" according to Nimrod's teachings as in Mithraism.

g. Anyone not accepting these doctrines was to be persecuted, Arius along with two Bishops being exiled for this very same reason.

h. All documents which showed that Constantine, the Great Pontifex Maximus, was forcing pagan Mithraism into the religion which he named Christianity, were destroyed by his orders. This resulted in God's curse falling upon Constantine causing the destruction of the Roman Empire, about which we shall read later.

3. The Burning of the Evangel and other Hebrew texts

Accordingly the original Evangels of Jesus written by Levi, son of Alphaeus and St John in Hebrew Aramaic Script along with the Revelation of St. John also in Hebrew were seized from the custody of Arius and burnt at the suggestion of St. Athanasius, the archdeacon of Alexandria, who wrote out in the Greek language at the Royal Command the "Holy Bible" we now have incorporating the word "Christos" or "Christ" which was coined by Constantine in 325 A.D. at the council of Nicaea. Further, the language is Greek *i.e.* the language of Constantine the Pagan Pontifex Maximus's choice and not Hebrew the language of Jesus or Latin, the official language of the Roman Empire till 312 A.D. Therefore the "Non-Hebrew Gospels" have nothing to do with the real teachings of Jesus which had to be burnt because these differed materially from the Greek manuscripts thus prepared in or after 325 A. D.

All these burnings of the original Hebrew books and records and letters of protests as also that everything has been done to humour Constantine are confirmed in the following passage:

> "It was indeed significant that in the early fourth century one of the first acts of Constantine, when by his presence, he gave countenance to the new status of the Church at the Council of Nicaea, should be the receiving of numerous petitions of complaints from bishops against their fellow bishops. **It is recorded that he burned them**" (page 14 of *"Islam and Christian Theology"* Part 1: Vol. One—Preparatory Historical Survey of the early period by J. Windrow Sweetman, published by Lutterwood Press; London 1945. See *Destruction or Peace*, Chapter 8: J-3—Evangel).

In Socrates, Schol. Eccl. Hist. 1.1.c. 9 we are informed:

a. That an edict was issued by Emperor St. Constantine the pagan head of the Nicaean Council of 325 A.D.

b. The order decrees that all the writings in the hands of Arius be burnt. Thus the Original Evangel of Jesus in Hebrew Aramaic script dictated personally by Jesus during his life and noted down by the Scribe Levi as also the Original Gospel of St. John and the Revelation *etc.* all in Hebrew Aramaic script were seized from the custody of Arius and burnt.

c. This edict further orders that anybody concealing any documents containing the same teachings as that of Arius and not immediately producing these and committing them to the flames would be punished with death.

d. That those who persisted in preaching what Arius advocated would be anathematised, excommunicated, imprisoned, banished, fined, beggared and starved.

Not only was the Original Evangels of Jesus written by Levi and John thus destroyed along with many Hebrew books of the New Testament but even Arius and two other Bishops who voted with him were also tortured, excommunicated and exiled for their persistence in preaching the authentic teachings of Jesus! Their banishment is referred to in page 26 of "*A Popular History of the Catholic Church*" by Philip Hughes published by Burns & Oates, London, 1958.

On page xiv of the Preface to the Second Edition of the "*Apocryphal New Testament*" published by William Hone of Ludgate Hill, London, 1820, it is again borne out:

> "... an edict published by Constantine, in which he decrees that all the writings (similar to those seized from the possession) of Arius (*i.e.* the Original Hebrew Aramaic Evangel personally dictated by Jesus to Jewish Scribes) should be burned and anybody concealing any writings composed by him, and not immediately producing them, and committing them to the flames, should be punished with death".

4. The Religion of the Founder of "The Church of Christ"

It is stated on pages 202-205 of "*The Two Babylons*" by the Rev. Hislop that Constantine the Great, saw (in a dream) a flaming Cross in the heavens under the "SUN" (his patron god) bearing the words "*In hoc signo vinces*" (*i.e.* "By this sign you will conquer"). This was before the council of Nicaea. This occurred during his campaign against his opponent Maxentius in 312 A.D. whom he defeated. Since then Constantine had boundless faith in the magical "Sign of the Cross". He therefore founded his "Church of Christ" or Christianity upon it in 325 A.D.

The royal founder of "The Church of Christ" may have chosen to put forward his adoption of the Cross as the sign of his new religion, but the fact remains that Apollo was his patron deity, and remained so throughout his life, as the seal and coinage of Emperor Constantine demonstrate.

Hence it is evident that Constantine, while claiming to be a Christian was in fact a Sun worshipper and that his pagan belief was responsible for the adoption of the "Sign of the Cross" of "Sun-god". This is proved further beyond any doubt by the resolutions he adopted at this first Council of religious bishops held under his Presidency.

Constantine got this Council to ratify his decree of 321 A.D. changing the Sabbath day from "Fridays" to "*Dies Solis*" or the day of "Sun-god Sol", whose symbol was the Cross.

He believed in Trinity of Sun-worship comprising:

1. Jupiter as god of gods,
2. Apollo as son of god Jupiter and
3. Leto, the virgin mother of Apollo.

This influenced Constantine to accept Trinity as propagated

by St. Athanasius. This theory fitted in beautifully with his pagan religious belief in the Trinity in unity of gods of Sun-worshippers. Thus started what is known as the "Blessed Trinity" or the "Nicene Creed" or "The Church of Christ" and "Christianity".

That explains why even after two months of efforts and in spite of showing him the Original Handwritten Evangel of Jesus in Hebrew Aramaic Script by Levi and St. John and the Revelation of St. John also in Hebrew, Arius failed to convince Emperor Constantine.

Naturally it follows that if such were the true facts, then God's curse must have fallen upon the religion founded by Constantine. The terrible devastation it caused for Europe is recorded later.

5. The Character of the Originator of "The Church of Christ"

History informs us that the founder of The Church of Christ was as follows:

- a. King Constantine cruelly tortured his wife to death by drowning her in boiling water!
- b. He also arranged the murdering of the following members of his family and relatives:
    1. His own son Crispus
    2. The husband of his sister Anastasia
    3. The twelve year old son of his sister Constantia
    4. The husband of his sister Constantia
    5. His own father-in-law Maximilian Hercules.
- c. He also ordered the slaughter of a large number of people, who were not so closely related to him.

In spite of all these murders of innocent people The Church of Christ has bestowed upon its founder the title of "Saint".

6. The Reasons for Founding "The Church of Christ"

Emperor Saint Constantine asked the pagan priest Supator to give him absolution from the Sin of the murder of his own father-in-law. But Supator, the Mithraic priest, refused in spite of being tortured. In a temper Constantine decided not only to kill this priest but he also resolved to destroy Mithraism as well and thus declared himself to be a Christian! This cannot by any stretch of the imagination be called a conversion, rather it emanated out of his hatred against justice. Hence The Church of Christ has been born out of a revulsion for truth and justice—principles which are so very far removed from the teachings of the gentle Jesus.

The European Research Scholar John Devenport has shown (pages 137-138 of "*Mohammed and the Koran*" by J. Davy & Son, London, 1882) that all the horrible atrocities committed in the name of holy Jesus were the result of the wicked teachings of this Roman Emperor Saint. He has commented about him as follows:

> "... the least sanction or authority for the horrible atrocities afterwards perpetrated in his (Jesus's) revered name? To whom, then it may be asked, are they attributable? The answer is easy—*To the Emperor Constantine, falsely surnamed the Great ... The Emperor, who, from political motives exclusively, had embraced Christianity, but who, on account of his cruelty, has justly been called A Second Nero, presided over the Famous Council of Nicaea ... in which the Doctrine of Christ's Divinity was, for the First Time Established*".

7. The Destruction of Mithraism

From these actions of the pagan Roman Emperor it becomes clear that to achieve his objects:

a. To destroy Mithraism because its priest refused him absolution for the murder of his father-in-law, and

b. To have one unified religion for all his subjects be they pagans or otherwise,

Constantine did not hesitate to take any action—harsh, unfair or unreasonable. His principal of life therefore was:

"It does not matter what destruction is involved, everything is fair. So long as the object is achieved—it is fully justified".

Constantine incorporated in the Greek Holy Bible this principle of his as follows:

Think not that I am come to send *Peace* on earth: I am not to send *Peace but the Sword*" (St. Matt. 10: 34).

Let us compare and see how very contrary are these teachings of Emperor St. Constantine the originator of the word "Christos" and The Church of Christ from the real teachings of Jesus:

"This is my Commandment, that ye love one another, as I have loved you" (St. John 15: 12).

"These things I Command you, that ye love one another" (St. John 15: 17).

"... For they that take (to) the sword (to impose their will upon others) shall (one day) perish with the sword" (St. Matthew 26: 52).

The Christian religion thus formed had the full backing and encouragement of the Roman Kings that followed "Saint Constantine the Great Roman Emperor", the founder of Christianity.

Those who were the wardens of "The Church of Christ" in those days never failed to do two things according to historical records, until Christianity fully triumphed over Mithraism *viz*:

1. Christian Churches incorporated all the popular pagan cults into their faith.

2. The Church took particular pains to obliterate and burn all available pagan records and libraries in order to remove all evidence as to the origin from which their Christian faith was derived and which if allowed to remain, would clearly show that the Christian religion had its origin in a faith not only so alien to that of Jesus but in something which was even hated and despised by Jesus as also cursed repeatedly by God, the most famous curses of God being at the Tower of Babel and again in the respective destructions of Jerusalem in 607 B.C. and 70 A.D.

The thoroughness with which these sun-worship records of Nimrod's faith were destroyed by The Church of Christ can be visualised from the extermination, not only by the burning of the Alexandrian Library some fifty years after the death of the Great Roman Emperor St. Constantine but also the killing of Hypatia, the great teacher and priest of the sun-worship cult as well as its librarian.

8. The Religion of the Sword in one Hand and the Holy Bible in the other

While reading the history of the Church of Christ, one cannot but be convinced that the Christian Church founded by Constantine had used the sword and fire in wiping out every trace and memory of Sun-worship in its original form. It was incorporating anything and everything of the heathen forms of worship into its own teachings and traditions in order to make the new faith popular. They were not interested in teaching the religion of Jesus, but were only anxious to make as many converts as possible who would call themselves the followers of the faith of the second

Nero, the Roman Emperor St. Constantine (*i.e.* Christians).

Copernicus could not do better service in this direction to the Christo—Pagan Church, to which he belonged, than to introduce his solar system and substitute it for the Ptolemaic—a mere reference to which system would easily show the origin of the Christian Mysteries, and the dates of the Church festivals.

There were several treatises setting forth the religion of Mithra, but "everyone of these have been destroyed", says Robertson on page 325 of '*Pagan Christ*', "by the care of the Church and it is remarkable that the treatise of Firmices is mutilated at passage (V) where the writer seems to be accusing Christians of following Mithraic usages". In this respect, Professor Murray says:

> "the polemic literature of Christianity is everywhere triumphant, (because) the books of the Pagans have been destroyed (by the Christian Church)".

When the Christians landed in Mexico they were greatly surprised to find that their religious belief in the only begotten son of god, the lamb who had come to save sinners with the sign of the cross and all the Christian customs and beliefs were already being followed here, and had been so for several thousands of years. It was the sun-worship of Nimrod which had been scattered from Babylon by the curse of God Almighty at the Tower of Babel. Here also the Christians used violent means forcibly to convert them to Christianity by means of their superior armaments and guns. They again destroyed all evidence that this pagan religion had its origin from the same source as Christianity, which certainly was not from Jesus of Nazareth, the son of the Virgin Mary.

That coercion has been used by the Christian Churches in obliging the pagans to convert themselves to it is further evident from the fact that in 988 A.D., Vladimir the Great of Russia married Anna the sister of Emperor Basil II. He had himself baptised. He had the idolatrous images of Peroun and other gods cast into the Dnieper River. At this action the people wept, but they yielded to Vladimir's demand for them to be baptised as Christians.

Vladimir's son nearly completed the forced conversions of the Russians, who thus became members of the Orthodox Church of Constantinople.

Page 37 of Volume 24 of "*The Encyclopedia Americana*", Edition 1929 reads:

> "Russian paganism did not vanish when the Christian Gospel began to be preached. It survived in the popular language, sayings, traditions, domestic life and even religious beliefs. As late as the 18th century, serpents were adored in some remote villages. Eugenius Golubinsky, the great historian of the Russian Church, declares that Russia was baptized in the ninth century, but not Christianized".

9. The Origin of the Canonical Gospels

On page 270 of "*The Apocryphal New Testament*" by William Hone, London, 1820, it is reported that Athanasius, Bishop of Alexandria, wrote out the New Testament, which is exactly the same as the New Testament we now have before us today. From this it will be obvious that the Greek Manuscripts of the New Testament incorporating the words "Christos", or "Christ", coined by Constantine in 325 A.D. and in the language of Constantine's choice *viz*: in Greek, instead of Hebrew, the mother tongue of Jesus, or Latin, the language of the Roman Empire, were the works of Athanasius, the destroyer of the original Evangels of Jesus written by Levi and John in Hebrew Aramaic script. Thus the New Testament before us does not include the original works of Matthew (or Levi to call him by his original Hebrew name) and

St. John *etc.*, but is the work of the destroyer of the Original Evangel and his collaborators.

It will be clear from the undermentioned quotations of English Biblical Research Scholars that this falsification of the Bible and its endorsement as the "Canonical Gospel" was not only carried out under the instructions of Emperor St. Constantine, the founder of "The Church of Christ", but was also inspired by fear of him as also to placate him as stated in page XIV of ibid:

> "Let us, with the illustrious Jortin, consider a council called, and presided over by this Barbarian Founder of the Church Militant: by what various motives the various Bishops may have been influenced; as by reverence to the Emperor or to his counsellors and favourites, his slaves and eunuchs; by the fear of offending some great prelate, as a Bishop of Rome or of Alexandria, who had it in his power to insult, vex, and plague all the bishops within and without his jurisdiction; by the dread of passing for heretics, and of being calumniated; reviled, hated, anathematised, ex-communicated, imprisoned, banished, fined, beggared, starved, if they refused to submit; by compliance with some active leading and imperious spirits; by a deference to the majority; by vanity and ambition, by a total ignorance of the question in debate, or a total indifference about it; by private friendships; by enmity and resentment; by old prejudices; by hopes of gain; by an indolent disposition; by good nature; by the fatigue of attending, and a desire to be at home; by the love of peace and quiet; and a hatred of contention, & c.
>
> "Whosoever takes these things in to due consideration will not be disposed to pay a blind deference to the authority of general councils but will rather be inclined to judge that 'the council' held by the Apostles at Jerusalem was the first and the last in which the Holy Spirit may be affirmed to have presided".

Therefore many lovers of Jesus would be surprised to find

from the records of Christian Bible scholars that what is now known as the "Canonical" New Testament has been written in or after 325 A.D. for the sole purpose of the gratification of Emperor St. Constantine, the founder of "The Church of Christ". All matters included are arbitrary for the purpose of having a uniform religion for all his subjects, be they pagan Gentiles following Mithraism or the followers of Jesus. Therefore no consideration was given to the teachings of Jesus. The specific objective was to have one single unified religion for all the subjects of the Roman Empire.

Dr. H. Spencer Lewis, Ph.D., has disclosed in his study *"The Secret Doctrines of Jesus"* that since the Nicaean Council until 1870 A.D.,

> "Twenty ecclesiastic or church council meetings were held in which **man** alone decided upon the text of the Bible. Self-appointed judges in the four Lateran Councils between 1123 and 1215 A.D., decided to expurgate from the Bible those sacred writings which did not please them!"

10. The Stoppage of the Spreading of the Nazarene Faith

Confusion naturally followed the burning in 325 A. D. of the two Original Hebrew Evangels of Jesus recorded by Levi and John after they were seized from the possession of Arius at the Nicaean Council meeting and the issue of the decree by Constantine that anybody found possessing similar Original Hebrew Evangels and not burning the same would be put to death immediately. The Hebrew Aramaic Evangel of Jesus by Barnabas and Andrew which were being read as the "Canonical Scriptures" until 325 A.D. in the churches of Alexandria were hidden instantly by lovers of Jesus somewhere in Alexandria. That is how they escaped destruction in 325 A.D.

In or about 367 A.D. St. Athanasius, the author of the Greek Manuscripts and the destroyer of the Original Evangels of Jesus by Levi and John in Hebrew Aramaic Script, by a letter announced what he considered to be the correct or canonical gospels. He naturally declared his own works *i.e.* the Greek Manuscripts of the New Testament, which we now have, as "Canonical".

In 367 A.D. he also issued a list of those Original Hebrew Evangels of Jesus which he knew had escaped destruction in 325 A.D. and which proved clearly the falsity of the "Canonical Greek Gospels". In this list amongst others, figures the "Evangelium Barnabe". Everybody knew that if they made over these original Hebrew texts to Athanasius, he would surely destroy them, as had been the fate of the Evangels by Levi and John. Therefore no one submitted these "Originals" to Athanasius, who died disappointed. The curse of God that fell on Athanasius is described later.

Some years after the death of Athanasius, apparently under pressure from the Roman Rulers a meeting of the Church Council was called in 382 A.D. Pope St. Damasus I as head of this meeting sanctioned the list of Gospels in Greek prepared by St. Athanasius as "Canonical". He also approved of the list of "Aprocryphal Gospels" as prepared by St. Athanasius, which included "Evangelium Barnabe" or the Evangel of Jesus (recorded) by Barnabas. This Pope required these Apocryphal Gospels in the Original Hebrew Aramaic Script to be surrendered to him or his successors. Thus since 382 A.D. these original Hebrew Evangels have been in the "Private" library of the Popes at the Vatican. Nobody is allowed to read them unless he is the trusted representative of the Pope.

The lovers of Jesus were shocked at the burning of the two Hebrew Evangel of Jesus recorded by Levi and John, as also the Revelation of John at the Nicaean Council and the decree of

Constantine that anybody found possessing such Hebrew Originals and professing that God is one and alone and Jesus is not the begotten son of god and not accepting "Trinity in Unity" as promulgated by him would be burnt at the stake. So great was the effect upon the Nazarenes that the spread of the true doctrines of Jesus was halted from the year 325 A.D. whilst the Pagan Nimrodic teachings of "The Church of Christ" received a great impetus.

11. The Apocryphal Gospels

The word "Apocryphal" has originated from the Greek word "Apokrupha" which means hidden or secret (writings). According to *"The Reader's Digest Great Encyclopaedic Dictionary"* (page 51c, Vol. 1) the word "Apocrypha" represents:

> "Those books of the Old Testament, which "were included in the Septuagint (Greek Old Testament) but were not originally written in Hebrew, are not counted genuine by the Jews, and are excluded from the canon". Also applied to … a number of early Christian writings (Gospels, Epistles, Acts, *etc.*) some of which were at one time included in the New Testament canon".

Bible students therefore know that *the Jews have rejected as Canonical anything which was not originally written in Hebrew.*

On page 7 of *"Helps to the study of the Bible"* by the Rev. Charles H. H. Wright, D. D., Ph.D., given at the back of the "Holy Bible" (King James Version) published by The Bible Mediation League of Ohio and printed in Great Britain by Collin's Clear Type Press, one reads:

> "GREEK—All the books of the New Testament have come down to us in Greek only. It is a question whether St. Matthew's (or to call him by his original Jewish name "Levi") was not composed originally in Hebrew. If that be so, the

original is lost, for only the Greek version is extant".

Lovers of Jesus naturally ask: Since the Jews have rejected books of Greek origin as "Apocryphal" and spurious and recognized the Hebrew versions only as "Canonical", then why should they not also reject the Greek Manuscripts as "Apocryphal" and counterfeit especially in the light of the findings of Christian scholars as read here before and insist upon the Hebrew Originals only as being Canonical? Surely they contend that in all these years somebody or other must have had an opportunity to read one of these originals in the Pope's confidential library and if it was not possible to smuggle the original out, then at least to make a translation of it in a small note book or some loose sheets of paper?

Various Christian scholars have prepared lists of "Apocryphal" Gospels, which their research shows were genuine and accepted as the Canonical Gospels until 325 A.D.

William Hone published in 1820 from London, *"The Apocryphal New Testament"*. A portion of the list of contents of this book with the remarks made about them by the highest English Church Authorities is reproduced hereunder:

I. CORINTHIANS	"These are 'The Genuine
II. CORINTHIANS	Epistles of the Apostolic
BARNABAS	Fathers: being together with
EPHESIANS	the Holy Scriptures of the New
MAGNESIANS	Testament, a complete
TRALIANS	collection of the most primitive
ROMANS	Antiquity for about a hundred
PHILADELPHIAN	and fifty years after Christ' says
SMYRNAEANS	William (Wake) Lord Bishop
POLYCARP	of Lincoln, afterwards Lord
PHILLIPPIANS	Archbishop of Canterbury."

I. HERMAS—VISIONS
II. HERMAS—COMMAND
III. HERMAS—SIMILITUDES

It will thus be clear from the above findings of Church Authorities that these ancient Gospels are genuine.

12. The Gospel of Barnabas

When the Italian translation of the Gospel of Barnabas was disclosed by J. F. Cramer to John Toland in 1709 A.D., who made the Spanish translation, there arose a big controversy over the authenticity of this Gospel throughout Europe during the eighteenth century. A lot of research was done. Some of the interested English scholars were:

- Dr. Holme, Rector of Hedley
- Dr. Thomas Monkhouse, Fellow of Queen's College, Oxford, who also prepared an English translation from the Spanish MS (manuscript).
- Dr. White Bampton, Lecturer in 1784 *etc.*

The following opinions have been expressed in favour of the writings of Barnabas who was a companion of Jesus and one of the 120 original converts to the teachings of Jesus, by the Reverend Ancient Fathers of the Church of Jesus, learned Christian scholars and also Church Authorities:

> "It has been cited by Clemens Alexandrinus, Origen, Epusebius, and Jerome, and many ancient Fathers. Cotelerius affirms that Origen and Jerome esteemed it genuine and canonical; Dr. Bernard, Savilian Professor at Oxford, not only believed it to be genuine but that it was read throughout, in the churches at Alexandria, as the canonical scriptures were. Dodwell supposed it to have been published before the Epistle of Jude, and the writings of both the Johns Vossius, Dupuis,

Dr. Cane, Dr. Mill, Dr. S. Clark, Whiston and Archbishop Wake also esteemed it genuine" (page 143 of the *Apocryphal New Testament* by William Hone, London, 1820).

The Arab Christian Scholar Dr. Khalil Sahadat Bey of Cairo after conducting a research on the Italian version of the "Evangelium Barnabe" *i.e.* the Evangel of Jesus (recorded) by Barnabas informs:

1. Barnabas was a Jew from Cyprus and one of the companions of Jesus as also his disciple.

2. The Evangel by Barnabas comprises the teachings, advice and dictations of Jesus recorded in the Hebrew language in Aramaic Script in the presence of Jesus, before he was lifted to heaven. Hence it contains the complete, true, original teachings of Jesus.

3. The Evangel of Jesus by Barnabas also contains the full story of Jesus from his birth to his ascension, as found in the four canonical gospel, but the volume of additional matter in Barnabas is totally missing from the canonical gospels very often leaving a missing link which shows that something has been deliberately deleted from the canonical Gospels.

4. The Evangel of Jesus by Barnabas was recognised as the canonical gospel till 325 A.D. and was read regularly in the churches at Alexandria as the canonical gospel, according to the early Fathers of the Church.

5. The Original Evangel of Jesus recorded by Barnabas in the Hebrew Aramaic Script escaped destruction in 325 A.D. because it was somewhere in Alexandria and had not been taken to the church council meeting which was called by Emperor Constantine at Nicaea, in Asia Minor. Otherwise it would also have been burnt.

6. Athanasius the cursed by God, in 367 A.D. declared by letter a number of original works dictated personally by Jesus and recorded by Jewish scribes before his ascension as "Apocryphal". This included "Evangelium Barnabe" in Hebrew Aramaic script.

7. In 382 A.D. Pope St. Damasus I as head of the Church Council approved the list of Apocryphal Gospels as prepared by Athanasius. This list included "Evangelium Barnabe" and required that the same be surrendered to the Pope.

8. The Evangel of Jesus by Barnabas was referred to by the ancient authors in the "Decree of Gelassius". *Therefore the Evangel of Jesus by Barnabas did exist but the Church holds that the contents of it can never be known because it is either lost or destroyed!*

9. In 1585 A.D. an Italian priest named Peretti became Pope Sixtus V.

10. The Italian monk Fra Marino was a close friend of Pope Sixtus V, and therefore Fra Marino was granted special permission by Pope Sixtus V to read the secret books in the Pope's library.

11. Fra Marino could read the Hebrew language in the Aramaic script. When Fra Marino read the Original Evangel of Jesus recorded by Barnabas in Hebrew Aramaic Script in the Pope's library in 1585 A.D., he was so impressed that he took a few loose sheets of paper, some of them of different quality, or as readily available to him, and formed them into a small "Pocket-size" note book about 6¼" x 3¼" containing 255 leaves, and after completing the translation he bound them with thin stiff boards, covered with leather having a thickness of a little

over 1½ inches. In this little pocket book he translated the Gospel of Barnabas over a period of several days from the Original Hebrew Aramaic into Italian in his own handwriting in a free running style and not with printed letters as would have been the case if a book was prepared for record purposes.

12. Fra Marino became a Muslim in accordance with the instructions of Jesus as given in the Evangel recorded by Barnabas.

13. Fra Marino died without disclosing the contents of his Italian translation of the Gospel of Barnabas. Hence it has remained unknown to the Muslims.

14. This Italian translation of the Gospel of Barnabas passed from hand to hand for a period of about 110 years without its contents being known to the Muslims and eventually reached J. F. Cramer, who was the Counsellor to the king of Prussia shortly after 1700 A.D.

Lonsdale and Laura Ragg inform us in their introduction to the Gospel of Barnabas published by Clarendon Press (1907) as follows:

On pages x and xi:

"Our Italian M. S. was acquired in Amsterdam 'by J. F. Cramer, and lent by him to John Toland in 1709. Four years later, in 1713 (as the dedicatory preface observes) Cramer presented his prize to the illustrious Connoisseur Prince Eugene of Savoy: and eventually it found its way, in 1738, in company with the rest of that prince's library into the Hopbibliothek at Vienna, where it now reposes.

"Further back than the beginning of the eighteenth century, we have no certain traces of the Codex, though an ambiguous reference in the preface to the (NOW LOST) copy of the

Spanish version, seen and described by Sale in 1734, may possibly indicate that our Italian Manuscript was once in the library of Pope Sixtus V (1585-1589)".

On page xliii:

"Thus much we may say with confidence. The Italian "Barnabas" is, to all intents and purposes, *an original work*".

On page xliv:

"It is the work of one, whose knowledge of the Christian Scriptures is considerably in advance of his familiarity with the Scriptures of Islam: presumably, therefore, of a renegade from Christianity".

The Spanish version, which is not available now, must be the work of John Toland the great Spanish Scholar. This Gospel of Barnabas was a translation from the Italian Manuscript and should be dated around 1709 A.D.

Thus the Spanish Manuscript was written over 120 years after the Italian MS. if the date of the writing of the Italian Manuscript is fixed around 1585 A.D.

The Italian Manuscript was in the Imperial Library at Vienna at the beginning of this century when Lonsdale and Laura Ragg copied the Italian text and translated it into English.

George Sale, on page X of his note "To the Reader" in his translation of *"The Koran"* (the correct spelling should be Qur'an) has made the following observation about the Spanish Gospel of Barnabas:

"There is a preface prefixed to it (*i.e.* the Spanish M.S.) wherein the discoverer of the original (Hebrew) M.S. who was a Christian Monk, called Fra Marino, tells us that having accidentally met with a writing of Irenaeus (among others), wherein he speaks against St. Paul, alleging, for his authority, the Gospel of Barnabas, he became exceeding desirous to find this Gospel; and that God, of His Mercy, having made him very intimate with Pope Sixtus V., one day, as they were together in that Pope's library, His Holiness fell asleep, and he to employ himself, reaching down a book to read, the first he laid his hand on proved to be the very gospel he wanted: overjoyed at the discovery, he scrupled not to hide his prize in his sleeve; and, on the Pope's awakening, took leave of him, carrying with him that celestial treasure, by reading of which he became a convert to Mohammedanism.

"This Gospel of Barnabas contains a complete story of Jesus Christ from His birth to His ascension; and most of the circumstances in the four real Gospels are to be found in them".

Thus George Sale admits that this Gospel of Barnabas contains the complete story of Jesus as found in the four canonical Gospels put together. If that be so then the Gospel of Barnabas cannot be a forgery at all! Rather this research scholar has called it a "celestial treasure" thereby confirming without any doubt that this "Gospel of Barnabas" contains the true and correct teachings of Jesus. Otherwise how can it be regarded as a "celestial" *i.e.* heavenly treasure?

George Sale confirms that he never saw the Original (Hebrew) manuscript nor its translation into Italian by the Christian Monk Fra Marino. He claims that he was given in 1734 A.D. by Dr. Holme, Rector of Hedley in Hampshire, only the Spanish manuscript of this Gospel, which was of course a translation of the Italian translation of the original Hebrew Aramaic Gospel in the Pope's Private library. Hence he has made the above remarks about the theft of the Hebrew manuscript from the library of Pope Sixtus V. apparently on a mere speculation, as will be seen hereafter from the remarks of Lonsdale and Laura Ragg who not only saw the Italian manuscript but transcribed and translated it. If the Original Hebrew Gospel of Barnabas, dictated during the time that Jesus was on earth, was stolen by the Christian Monk Fra Marino as alleged, then the said Original would have got disclosed just as the Italian manuscript has been! But the fact that it has not fallen into the hands of the public shows that the Original Hebrew Manuscript is still in the Pope's private library and that Fra Marino had made only an Italian translation of it.

Lonsdale and Laura Ragg in their preface to the Gospel of Barnabas inform us:

1. The Spanish manuscript went from Dr. Holme, Rector of Hedley to Dr. Thomas Monkhouse, Fellow of Queen's College, Oxford.

2. Dr. Monkhouse gave the original text of the Spanish manuscript and a translation of the Gospel of Barnabas to Dr. White Bampton, Lecturer, in 1784. So we know that the Spanish manuscript was in existence until 1784 A.D. and that there was also an English translation thereof.

3. When Lonsdale and Laura Ragg tried to inspect this Spanish manuscript around 1902-1906 A.D. it could not be traced anywhere. They have remarked of it: "which has since unfortunately disappeared from view". They did not even find the English translation of the Spanish Manuscript.

4. In the Original Italian Manuscript of the Gospel of Barnabas, which they have copied and translated into English, there is however no reference whatsoever to the effect that the Christian Monk Fra Marino stole the (Hebrew) Original from the Pope's library. The charge made by George Sale in his note of 1734 A.D. of theft against Fra Marino is therefore false according to both the Italian Manuscript and fact that the Original Hebrew

scripture has not fallen into the hands of the public just like the Italian Manuscript which should have been the case had it been stolen because both these would have been together had the Original Hebrew Gospel been taken out of the Vatican. Further, if the original could be taken out then what was the necessity for Fra Marino to make an Italian Translation? In fact the Italian Translation by Fra Marino goes to show that it was not possible to remove the Original Hebrew Gospel of Jesus recorded by Barnabas during the life of Jesus from the private library of the Popes. Hence Fra Marino had to translate same in his own handwriting and for his convenience in his mother tongue *i.e.* Italian.

Fra Marino's claim that he translated it into Italian from the Original Hebrew Aramaic Manuscript written by Barnabas himself and lying in the Pope's library, which he read with the permission of Pope Sixtus V. amongst other books seems much more plausible for three very obvious reasons *viz*:

a. The Italian manuscript is in the size of a small notebook which could easily be hidden in a priest's flowing robes. In fact Fra Marino used to carry a few sheets of paper every day and when alone in the library he used to translate into Italian the Evangel of Jesus recorded by Barnabas in the Hebrew Aramaic Script. This process continued for a number of weeks before he had translated the full book. The Italian language did not exist at the time of Jesus!

b. It is in fast running handwriting, which would not be the case if it were the original. In the original one would expect well-formed printed letters in a much larger sized book if such an important Gospel was being documented to be preserved in the Pope's library.

c. The very fact that the Italian priest Fra Marino converted to Islam on the basis of the book in the Pope's library suggests that what he had seen with his own eyes must have been the original document in Hebrew Aramaic written during the life of Jesus by Barnabas, a companion of Jesus. Otherwise it could never have convinced him that it was the true and authentic teachings of Jesus in accordance with which he accepted Islam. As a matter of fact, the Gospel of Barnabas contains a lot of information given by Jesus, which is totally missing from the so called Canonical Gospels.

The readers of this study would be anxious naturally to have some more concrete evidence as to whether this Italian Manuscript of the Gospel of Barnabas was several centuries old and stolen by Fra Marino from the private library of the Pope during the time of Pope Sixtus V (1585-1590) or was written on paper manufactured during the second half of the sixteenth century and in a style of handwriting that was prevalent around 1585 A.D. which means that it was a translation into Italian by Fra Marino in his own handwriting from the Original in Hebrew Aramaic written during the life of Jesus and lying concealed in the Pope's private library. Lonsdale and Laura Ragg provide us with the required proof on pages xiv-xv of their introduction to this gospel which reads:

> "The paper is described by Toland as 'Turkish', and Denis follows him; but a careful examination scarcely bears out this judgement. There are, in fact, two leaves (ff. 107 and 108) that might be described as delicately gummed and polished; but these are entirely different in character from the rest—yellow, thin and smooth. All the remaining pages are of a somewhat coarse and stout 'cotton-paper', and a close inspection reveals a water-mark such as no oriental paper ever bore. The anchor within a circle, says M. Briquet, is distinctively Italian; and the form which that sign assumes in the present case belongs,

according to the same distinguished expert, to the second half of the sixteenth century.·

"The handwriting cannot, of course, be of greater antiquity than the paper on which it is written and probability is in favour of its being not very much later. The specimen photograph which we give of the first page, together with one from the middle of the book, will offer fairly adequate material for a positive Judgement as to the date of the script. Its general style will be seen to be that of the latter half of the sixteenth century. A fairly close resemblance to it can be found in certain Venetian MSS. of 1543, 1563, and 1564 in the Archivio di Stato, and of 1550, 1562, and 1567 in the Archives of St. Mark's. The most exact parallel that we have seen—remarkable for the reproduction of the characteristic *p* and *h* of our codex—is, however, a document in the latter collection, which bears the signature 'Franc Vianello, Segretario Ducale', and the date April 15, 1584".

So the Italian Manuscript was written on paper manufactured in Italy during the second half of the sixteenth century *i.e.* after 1551 and before 1600 A.D., and in a style of writing which was prevalent in 1584 A.D. Hence it must have been the handwriting of Fra Marino during the period of the reign of Pope Sixtus V *i.e.* around 1585 A.D.

Thus it is proved conclusively that the Italian Manuscript has come out of the original Hebrew Aramaic Text of "Evangelium Barnabe" in the Pope's private library. Hence it must be the true and accurate teachings of Jesus. If it did not contain the precise teachings of Jesus then it could not possibly be preserved in the Pope's confidential library since 382 A.D. It will be remembered as recorded earlier that Pope St. Damasus I had issued an order in 382 A. D. to the effect that anybody possessing the "Evangelium Barnabe" amongst others should surrender the same to the Pope. Hence the original Hebrew M.S. of this Gospel, written during the life of Jesus by Barnabas himself, had been preserved in the Pope's library ever since 382 A.D. from which Fra Marino had made the Italian translation during the time of Pope Sixtus V *i.e.* around 1585 A.D. on paper manufactured in Italy in that period and in a handwriting style which was current around 1584 A.D.

Secondly, if this Hebrew Gospel was not authentic then why should the Christian monk Fra Marino take the trouble to translate it into Italian, his mother tongue, in 1585 A.D. Why should he want to have a copy of this Gospel for his personal record? Hence his translation in fast running handwriting into a small pocket size notebook is understandable.

Finally, why should Fra Marino, a monk attached to a Pope, have forsaken Christianity and converted to Islam of his own accord unless he was fully convinced beyond doubt that the Hebrew Original of this Gospel which he read in the Pope's library, was one of the very few Gospels which had escaped destruction in 325 A.D. and was the original document written by Barnabas, himself, during the lifetime of Jesus—hence the true unadulterated teachings of Jesus, son of the Virgin Mary, as against the Canonical New Testament we now have before us, which is based on the Greek Manuscript of the New Testament written in 325 A.D. and thereafter by Athanasius to humour Emperor St. Constantine, the Founder of the Church of Christ (pages XIV and 210 of *The Apocryphal New Testament* by William Hone, London, 1820).

Lonsdale and Laura Ragg state it took them four years to translate this Italian Manuscript of the Gospel of Barnabas into English. They were assisted in this task by Padre Minocchi of Florence, Professors Nallino and Casareo of Palermo, Professors Guidi and Nonaci of Rome, Professor Grescini of Padua, Commendatore Malagola of the Venetian Archivio, Professor J. Ritter von Karabacek, Director of the Imperial library at Vienna and his colleague Dr. Rudolp Beer. Would the learned priest of Florence and all these reputed scholars and Italian savants have assisted in the translation into English of this book if it was not the absolute truth?

Thousands of copies of the Gospel of Barnabas were published by the Clarendon Press of Oxford University in 1907. The author of this thesis had been trying to get a copy of this book for many years but not a single copy seemed to be available anywhere. After years of searching one copy was eventually traced in the British Museum, London. A photocopy of this Gospel of Barnabas was obtained eventually from the British Museum, London through the kind assistance of his English Correspondents.

One feels puzzled as to why there was so much difficulty in obtaining even one copy of this Gospel. The answer is given by Frederic C. Grant of the Union Theological Seminary of the U.S.A. He has revealed that the Church took deliberate steps to suppress this Gospel of Barnabas by Lonsdale and Laura (M. Roberts) Ragg published by Clarendon Press, 1907.

At this disclosure many seekers after the truth will feel highly distressed and anxiously ask:

1. Certainly now there is no fear of persecution by the Roman Emperors. The Roman Empire has disappeared many centuries ago.

2. If the Gospel of Barnabas was the true translation of the Evangel of Jesus recorded by Barnabas then the Church has committed a serious mistake in suppressing the original teachings of Jesus. If it is not then there was no need whatsoever to suppress the Gospel of Barnabas, because any intelligent person upon reading it would realise that it is not correct hence it would be ignored

automatically. Suppression always does much more harm and invariably leaves the impression that the truth is being hidden!

3. When the work of Barnabas is admitted by leading authorities of the church as containing the genuine teachings of Jesus and was recognised as such until the Nicaean Council of 325 A.D. then why is it not being publicized by the Vatican? Why should the world have to depend on the Italian translation made secretly by the Italian monk Fra Marino, as a friend of Pope Sixtus V in 1585 A.D. from the Hebrew original?

4. What happened to the Spanish Manuscript? Did it suffer the same fate as the Evangel of Levi and John in 325 A.D. at the hands of The Church of Christ?

5. What happened to the English Translation of the Spanish Manuscript? Was it destroyed or suppressed deliberately just like the thousands of copies of the Gospel of Barnabas published by the Clarendon Press in 1907 A.D.?

Here are two small extracts from the speech delivered on Sunday, 24th July, 1927 to Christians at the general assembly of 15,000 members of the International Bible students at Toronto, Canada by President Rutherford of the Watch Tower Bible & Tract Society:

> "... with great pomp and glory that unholy system rides upon the backs of the peoples. Without the support of the common peoples that wicked system called "Christendom" could not survive. When the peoples withdraw their support therefrom 'Organized Christianity', which is a part of Babylon or the Devil's organisation, will fall like a great millstone into the sea.

> "... But instead of heeding the message from the word of God, the rulers of the world, to wit, those constituting the unholy alliance, walk on in darkness and continue to oppress the

peoples. The doom of "Organized Christianity" or Babylon is sealed: ..." (page 312 of Watch Tower, dated 15th October 1927).

The Holy Bible also warns thus about the devastations of the Nuclear Holocaust:

"And he cried mightily with a strong voice, saying Babylon the great is fallen, is fallen and is become the habitation of devils, ...

"For all nations have drunk of the wine of the wrath of her fornication, and the kings of the earth have committed fornication with her, and the merchants of the earth are waxed rich through the abundance of her delicacies.

"And I heard another voice from heaven, saying, Come out of her (the religion of Babylon now known as The Church of Christ), my people, that ye be not partakers of her sin, and that ye receive not of her plagues.

"For her sins have reached unto heaven, and God hath remembered her iniquities.

"Reward her even as she rewarded you, and double unto her double according to her works: in the cup she hath filled, fill to her double.

"How much she hath glorified herself, and lived deliciously so much torment and sorrow give her: for she saith in her heart, *I sit a Queen, and am no widow and shall see no sorrow.*

"Therefore shall her plagues come in *one day, death, and mourning, and famine; and she shall be utterly burned with fire: for strong is the Lord God, who judgeth her.*" (Revelation 18: 2-8)

With this Biblical warning about the destruction of Babylon which according to The Watch Tower Bible Society refers to Christianity, one and all should feel apprehensive about the future welfare of the Powerful Nations. Because their destruction in a

Nuclear Holocaust would certainly also mean the devastation of many unprepared and neutral nations. It will surely have very serious world-wide consequences—a disaster of unimaginable magnitude will take place suddenly in one single day without any prior warning, according to Biblical Prophecies.

To indicate the means whereby mankind can escape from such a terrible calamity is the sole object of this treatise.

G. Accept the Teachings of which Jesus?

Jesus of Nazareth, son Of the Virgin Mary, has taught:

> "A new commandment I (Jesus) give unto you. That ye love one another; as I have loved you, that ye also love one another" (St. John 13: 34).

As against the above teaching of Jesus, history shows that for the past seventeen centuries since the Nicaean Council of 325 A.D. Christians of one sect or belief or place have fought, murdered and burnt at the stakes millions of fellow Christians of another sect or place with incredible viciousness. They have not even spared the lives of the aged infirm, the helpless women and innocent children all believing in the very same Holy Bible and professing to be followers of a *Jesus*.

Mothers who presumably believed in the same Jesus but lived under different governments have fervently prayed that Jesus grant their sons success in battle over neighbouring European kingdoms and nations. This must have been enormously confusing to whichever Jesus, if any, who heard those impassioned pleas.

Immediately the question arises, which *Jesus*?

The *Jesus* that taught:

> "But I (Jesus) say unto you, Love your enemies, bless them

that curse you, do good to them that hate you, and pray for them which despitefully use you, and persecute you" (St. Matthew. 5:44).

— or —

Constantine, who to justify the numerous murders at his own instigation, got the following forgery inserted into the Greek Holy Bible that his Jesus Christ has announced:

"Think not that I am come to send *peace* on earth: I am not to send *peace*, but the *sword*" (St. Matt. 10: 34).

It's *easy* to spot such hypocrisy. Today double standards are prevalent everywhere owing to the real teachings of Jesus being contradicted in the Greek Holy Bible itself by Constantine's theories in the name of Christ and Jesus Christ causing confusion, and confounding the devotees of Jesus as to which Jesus they should follow?

A believer in Jesus shooting a machine gun at any human being irrespective of caste, colour or creed in spite of the injunction of Jesus to love one's enemies is as purely hypocritical as a policy of peace through war, success though cheating, or happy marriages through adultery.

The Original Teachings of Jesus

1. ON GOD

The original teachings of Jesus	Nimrodism	Christianity today
That Jesus never claimed divinity will be apparent from the Holy Bible. **a. The First Commandment of Jesus:** "And Jesus answered him, *The First of all the Commandments is*, Hear O Israel; *The Lord our God is one Lord* (*i.e.*one Who has no father, mother, husband, virgin wife, brother, sister, begotten son, daughter or any other form of equal): "And thou shalt love the Lord thy God with all thy heart, and with all thy soul, and with all thy mind, and with all thy strength; this is the first commandment" St Mark 12: 29, 30). **b. The Parting advice of Jesus:** "Jesus saith then unto her (Mary Magdalene) ... but go to *my brethren*,	The first and only man to claim divinity in the world is Nimrod, the mighty hunter in rebellion against God. (Genesis 10: 9). We have read earlier that King Nimrod of Babylon had taught that god consisted of trinity in unity comprising: 1. Shamash (the Sun god or father of the gods). 2. Sin (the Moon god or Nimrod or Baal, the Sacred Heart or Tammuz, the only begotten son of god). 3. Ishtar (goddess queen of the heavens or Semiramis or Rhea or the Great Virgin Mother of god). This teaching of Trinity in unity spread, all over the world from Tower of Babel when God disrupted the unity of mankind by His curse, which changed the languages of	As against the teachings of Jesus that God is one and alone, *i.e.* one who has neither any begotten son nor virgin wife *etc.*, we find that Nimrod's teachings of god as a trinity in unity incorporated in the manmade books of the Bible as follows: 1. god the Father 2. god the Son 3. god the Holy Ghost (St. Matt. 28:19) In the Trinitarian Monastery at Madrid the Christians worship an image of the Triune god with three heads on one body representing god the Father, god the son, and god the Holy Ghost. In India for the past 3,500 years "Trimurti" or a god with three heads on one body or a trinity in unity has been worshipped.

The original teachings of Jesus	Nimrodism	Christianity today
and say unto them, I ascend … to my God and your God" (St. John 20: 17). Thus it is evident that the first commandment and the parting words of Jesus are the same. God is one and alone and not a multiple in one god as in the faith of the Gentiles. He is as much the God of Jesus as the God of all mankind. We are all the brethren of Jesus, who is therefore not divine in any way, unless all mankind are also divine, and that would be the height of absurdity. The following is a quotation from page 487 of "The Gospel of Barnabas"; "Jesus answered : Believe me, Barnabas, that every sin, however, small it be, God punish with great punishment, seeing that God is offended at sin. Wherefore, since my	the people in 2239 B.C. (Genesis 11: 1-9). The names have altered from place to place due to the haunting Curse of the Tower of Babel, but the basic religion of Nimrod has continued.	The Hindu god Siva also has three faces or heads on one single body. He has been worshipped since the time of the Mohenjodaro civilization which existed more than three millennia ago. These teachings of "A trinity in unity" have originated from King Nimrod, the mighty hunter in rebellion against God (Genesis 10: 9) and are certainly not the doctrines of Jesus son of the virgin Mary but are in fact absolutely contrary to his teach-ings.

The original teachings of Jesus	Nimrodism	Christianity today
mother and my faithful disciples that were with me loved me a little with earthly love, the righteous God hath willed to punish this love with the present grief, in order that it may not be punished in the flames of hell. And though I have been innocent in the world, since men have called me "God", and "Son of God", God, in order that I be not mocked of the demons on the day of judgement, hath willed that I be mocked of men in this world by the death of Judas, making all men to believe that I died upon the cross. And this mocking shall continue until the advent of Mohammed, the Messenger of God, who, when he shall come, shall reveal this deception to those who believe in God's law; "Having thus spoken, Jesus said: 'Thou art just, O Lord our God, because to Thee only		

THE TEACHINGS OF HOLY JESUS

The original teachings of Jesus	Nimrodism	Christianity today
belongeth honour and glory without end'."		

2. ON ONLY BEGOTTEN SON OF GOD

The original teachings of Jesus	Nimrodism	Christianity today
Jesus never claimed that he was the Only begotten son of God. Rather he affirmed that he was an inferior being and a servant of God according to the Holy Bible: "For my father (*i.e.* God) is greater than I (Jesus)" (St. John 14: 28). "Verily, verily, I (Jesus) say unto you, The servant (*i.e.* Jesus) is not greater than his Lord (God); neither he (*i.e.* Jesus) that is sent greater than He (God) that sent him (Jesus)" (St. John 13: 16). "And when he (Jesus) had gone forth into the way, there came one running, and kneeled to him, and asked him Good Master, what shall I do that I may inherit eternal life?	As read earlier, Nimrod had propagated that he had been created through a virgin woman as the only begotten son of god, who had come on earth to save sinners by the sacrifice of his life. That he is: 1. The only begotten son. 2. The shepherd. 3. The redeemer. 4. The Sin-bearer. 5. The well beloved son. 6. The healer. 7. The light-bringer. 8. The liberator. 9. The deliverer. 10. The slain to save sinners. 11. The one who would be seated on the right side of the Sun-God on	The Christians believe that Christ the only begotten son of god born of the virgin Mother, had come on earth to save sinners by the sacrifice of his life. That he is: 1. god's only begotten son. 2. The good shepherd. 3. The redeemer. 4. The gift of god to man to ransom his sins. 5. The well beloved son. 6. The healer of souls. 7. The giver of the Water of Everlasting Life. 8. The sinless. 9. The bread of life. 10. The price of sin. 11. Seated on the right hand—thus having superior position to God on

The original teachings of Jesus	Nimrodism	Christianity today
"And Jesus said unto him, why callest thou me Good (Master, when I Jesus am His servant)? There is none Good Jesus never claimed that he was the Only begotten son of God. Rather he affirmed that he was an inferior being and a servant of God according to the Holy Bible: "For my father (*i.e.* God) is greater than I (Jesus)" (St. John 14: 28). "Verily, verily, I (Jesus) say unto you, The servant (*i.e.* Jesus) is not greater than his Lord (God); neither he (*i.e.* Jesus) that is sent greater than He (God) that sent him (Jesus)" (St. John 13: 16). "And when he (Jesus) had gone forth into the way, there came one running, and kneeled to him, and asked him Good Master, what shall I do that I may inherit eternal life? "And Jesus said unto him, why callest thou me	the day of Judgment—dispensing Judgment—forgiving his baptised followers, and condemning the doers of good deeds and the followers of the "Laws of God" for their small mistakes because they believed in the Justice of God. Nimrod, is not a man but the only begotten son of Sun-God—hence: his function is that of the one and only mediator between God and men.	the day of Judgment, forgiving baptised sinners and condemning to hell for their small mistakes, the doers of good deeds, *i.e.* the followers of the "Laws of God", because they believed in the Justice of God. That all these above claims about Christ being son of god are later fabrications, is proved by the following passage in the New Testament written by the "Brethren" themselves a few years after Jesus had already been lifted to heaven: "For there is (only) *One God*, and one mediator between God and men, the *Man* Christ Jesus" (1. Timothy 2: 5). Hence Jesus was considered a "*Man*" and not the only begotten son of god when this was written by St. Paul *i.e.* about 50-55 A.D. That the above statement has also been

The original teachings of Jesus	Nimrodism	Christianity today
Good (Master, when I Jesus am His servant)? There is none Good (Master) but one, that is God, but if thou will enter into (eternal heavenly) life, (then) keep the (Mosaic) Commandments (which I have come to correct and teach)"—(St. Matt. 19: 16-17 and St. Mark 10: 17-18). Here is a quotation from page 127 of "The Gospel of Barnabas": "And having said this, Jesus smote his face with both his hands, and then smote the ground with his head. And having raised his head, he said: *'Cursed be everyone who shall insert into my sayings that I am the son of God.'* At these words the disciples fell down as dead, whereupon Jesus lifted them up saying: 'Let us fear God now, if we would not be affrighted in that day (of Judgment)". On page 487 of ""The Gospel of Barnabas" it is	Nimrod is the Saviour, come to save the world of sinners by the sacrifice of his life.	copied from Nimrodism will be clear from the following passage in the Holy Bible, which contains the last prayer of Jesus as: "I (Jesus) pray for them (that are my followers): I pray not for the world (because I am not the mediator between God and men), but for them, (only) which thou hast given me; for they are thine" (St. John 17: 9). Hence from this passage in the Bible, it is clear that the claims now being made by the Christians that Christ is the "Saviour" is not in accordance with the teachings of Jesus, but concurs with Nimrodism, which has been incorporated at a later stage in the Greek man-made New Testament *e.g.*: "And we have seen and do testify that the Father sent the Son to be the Saviour of the world. Whosoever shall confess

The original teachings of Jesus	Nimrodism	Christianity today
again confirmed that Jesus is not God nor son of God and that this is a lie, will be proved when Muhammad, the Messenger of God shall come. The last of the divine scriptures also reiterates the above teachings of Jesus as: "The Messiah (Jesus) WILL NEVER SCORN TO BE A SLAVE UNTO ALLAH (this is therefore the meaning of the statement of Jesus quoted above from St. Matt. 19: 16-17 and St. Mark 10: 17-18 that only God is the "Good Master" hence Jesus must accordingly be His humble servant or slave as mentioned in St. John 13:16), nor will the favourred angels. Whosoever scorneth service to (*i.e.* adoration of) Him (Allah) and is proud, all such will be assembled unto Him (for punishment in Hell fire)" (Qur'an 4: 172). Jesus was questioned		that Jesus is the Son of god, god dwelleth in him, and he in god" (1 John 4: l4-15).

The original teachings of Jesus	Nimrodism	Christianity today
after being lifted to heaven by God if he had preached the blasphemy of only begotten "Son of God". His reply is reproduced hereunder from the last of the divine scriptures: "And when Allah questioned: O Jesus son of Mary! Didst thou say unto mankind: Take me and my mother for two gods besides Allah? He replied: (O Allah) Be glorified! It was not mine to utter THAT TO WHICH I HAD NO RIGHT. If I used to say it, then Thou knewest it. Thou knewest what is in my mind and I know not what is in Thy mind. Lo! Thou only Thou art the knower of things hidden. "I spoke unto them only that which Thou commandest me (teaching): worship Allah, my Lord and your Lord (St. John 20: 17). I was a witness of them (only) while I dwelt among them, and when Thou tookest me, Thou wast the Watcher		

The original teachings of Jesus	Nimrodism	Christianity today
over them. Thou art witness over all things" (Qur'an 5: 116-117).		

3. ON SONS OF GOD

The original teachings of Jesus	Nimrodism	Christianity today
As read herebefore when Jesus has not claimed to be a son of God then anybody having pretensions to be "the sons of God" surely commits blasphemy. This is confirmed also in the last of the Divine Scriptures: "… and Christians say: The Messiah is the son of Allah. That is the sayings of their mouths. They imitate the sayings of those who disbelieved of old (*i.e.* Nimrod the mighty hunter in rebellion against God). How perverse are they! "They have taken as lords besides Allah, their priests and their monks (when they perform the Holy sacraments and hear their confessions) and the Messiah, son of	We have read earlier that Nimrod at the feast of his birthday at the "Magical Well" taught magic and gave powers to as many as believed in him "to become sons of god" (see *Destruction or Peace*, Chapter. 5: E-7, C). Thus Nimrod not only called himself the only begotten son of god but those of his followers, who believed in him were given powers to become sons of god. Even though they did not have any miraculous births or any other logical basis yet they maintained this fantastic claim!	Nimrod's blasphemous teachings on "sons of god" are to be found incorporated in the Holy Bible: "But as many (people) as received him, to them he gave power to become sons of god, even to them that believe in his name" (St. John 1: 12). "For as many as are led by the Spirit of god, they are the sons of god" (Romans 8: 14). "For ye are all the children of god by (having) faith in Christ …" (Galatians 3: 26). "Behold, what manner of love the Father hath bestowed upon us, that we should be called the sons of god: therefore the world knoweth us not, because it knew him

THE TEACHINGS OF HOLY JESUS

The original teachings of Jesus	Nimrodism	Christianity today
Mary, when they were bidden (by Jesus) to worship only one God (St. Mark 12: 29-30). There is no god save Him (St. Mark 10: 17-18). Be He glorified from all that they ascribe as partner (unto Him)" (Qur'an 9: 30-31). Jesus has clarified further in the Holy Bible: "*But in vain they do worship me, teaching for doctrines the commandments of men*" (St. Mathew 15: 9).		not. "Beloved, now are we the sons of god, and it doth not yet appear what we shall be: but we know that, when he shall appear, we shall be like him; for we shall see him as he is". "And every man that hath this hope in him purifieth himself (and becomes sinless), even as he (Christ) is pure and sinless)". (1 John 3: 1-3).

4. CHRISTMAS

The original teachings of Jesus	Nimrodism	Christianity today
Jesus was born before the winter rains had set in to prevent the shepherds from keeping their flocks in the open fields at night (St. Luke 2: 7-10) *i.e.* on 26th September as earlier research shows. Then the Angel Gabriel, who brought the good tidings to Mary, of her impending pregnancy	The sun-worshippers' legends are based upon zodiacal calculations *viz*: in the last week of December on a clear night, one sees overhead the three bright stars (called the three Kings) of the belt of Orion pointing to the East. Soon rises Sirus (called the Herald of the sun-god or the Messianic	Uesener has recorded that by an order of Pope Liberius, the celebration of the date of birth of Jesus was fixed at 25th December in the year 353-354 A.D. so that it may correspond to the "Nativity of Sun" *i.e.* the birth date of Mithra! The entire Mithraic Legends had already been incorporated under

The original teachings of Jesus	Nimrodism	Christianity today
without human contact (St. Luke 1: 26-38) must have appeared sometime around the middle of December so as to give 9 months and 10 days as the normal period for the birth of Jesus. But unfortunately the Christians do not hold any festival relating to the pregnancy of Mary, around the middle of December or the miraculous birth of Jesus on 26th September 1 B.C. If the Christians were the followers of Jesus, surely they would be celebrating his birthdate and not that of Nimrod, the mighty hunter in rebellion against God. In fact the celebration of Christmas was started several centuries later with a view to dislodge the hold that Mithraism had gained upon the people living around the Mediterranean and the Europeans. This was after several of the original Evangels of Jesus were burnt and destroyed in 325 A.D.,	star) the brightest of all the hosts of heaven. It is followed by the rising of the constellation of Virgo or Virgin at about midnight, which announces the birth of son of god Sun by the virgin. Daylight hours in the Northern Hemisphere reach their minimum intensity on the 24th December. This was taken to indicate that the rule or power of darkness and evil is at its height. At this stage a saviour, the only begotten son born of the virgin mother is come not only to stop darkness becoming more extensive but also to get the daylight or goodness to proliferate as he grows bigger. Hence if this pagan Nimrod is born at midnight on the 24th / 25th December, then each day as he will slowly grow bigger so also the daylight starts to increase each day gradually from this date.	orders of Emperor Constantine in the man-made New Testament in Greek, the language of Constantine's choice, including the Pagan story of the Messianic Star, the three kings from afar paying homage (St. Matt. 2: 9-11) *etc.* *"The Golden Bough"* by Sir James George Frazer on pages 357-358 reads: "Among the gods of eastern origin who in the decline of the ancient world competed against each other for the allegiance of the West was the old Persian deity Mithra. The immense popularity of his worship is attested by the illustrative monuments of it which have been found scattered in profusion all over the Roman Empire. "In respect both of doctrines and of rites, the cult of Mithra appears to have presented many points

THE TEACHINGS OF HOLY JESUS

The original teachings of Jesus

whilst the remaining original, Evangels in Hebrew had been hidden for fear of persecution.

The following passage appears on pages 102-103 of *"The Two Babylons"* by the Rev. A. Hislop:

"That festival, called Lady-day is celebrated at Rome on the 25th March, in alleged commemoration of the miraculous conception of our Lord in the womb of the Virgin, on the day when the angel was sent to announce to her the distinguished honour that was to be bestowed upon her as the mother, of the Messiah. But who could tell when this annunciation was made? The scripture gives no clue at all in regard to the time. But it mattered not. Before our Lord was either conceived or born, that very day now set down in the Popish calendar for the 'Annunciation of the

Nimrodism

The Messianic star (*i.e.* Sirus) announced the birth of "gon of god" and the three Kings from afar (the three stars in Orion's belt) paid homage to him.

This is the common basis for the birth of the son of the sun-god in all the countries, irrespective of the varied names of the son or the virgin mother, which were changed from place to place due to the curse of Almighty God which changed the languages of the builders of "Babel" (see *Destruction or Peace*, Chapter. 5: E-7; F-1 and G).

Christianity today

of resemblance not only to the religion of the Mother of the gods but also to Christianity. The similarity struck the Christian doctors themselves and was explained by them as a work of the devil, who sought to seduce the souls of men from the true faith by a false and insidious imitation of it. So to the Spanish conquerors of Mexico and Peru, many of the native heathen rites appeared to be diabolical counterfeits of the Christian sacraments!

"However that may be, there can be no doubt that the Mithraic religion proved a formidable
rival to Christianity, combining as it did a solemn ritual with aspirations after moral purity and a hope of immortality. Indeed the the new born sun by the image of an infant which on his birthday, the winter solstice, they

The original teachings of Jesus	Nimrodism	Christianity today
Virgin' was observed in Pagan Rome in honour of Cybele, the Mother of the Babylonian Messiah. Now it is manifest that Lady-day and Christmas day stand in intimate relation to one another. Between the 25th of March and the 25th of December there are exactly nine months. If then the false Messiah was conceived in March and born in December, can anyone for a moment believe that the conception and birth of the true Messiah can have, so exactly synchronised, not only to the month, but to the d a y? Lady-day and, Christmas day, then are purely Babylonian".		brought forth and exhibited to his worshippers. No doubt the Virgin who thus conceived and bore a son on the twenty-fifth of December was reckoned the winter solstice, and it was regarded as the Nativity of the Sun, because the day begins to lengthen and the power of the sun to increase from that turning-point of the year. The ritual of the nativity, as it appears to have been celebrated in Syria and Egypt, was remarkable. The celebrants retired into certain inner shrines, from which at midnight they issued with a loud cry, "The Virgin has brought forth. The light is waxing". The Egyptians even represented the new born sun by the image of an infant which on his birthday, the winter solstice, they brought forth and exhibited to his worshippers. No doubt the Virgin who thus

The original teachings of Jesus	Nimrodism	Christianity today
		conceived and bore a son on the twenty-fifth of December was the great Oriental goddess whom the Semites called the Heavenly Virgin or simply the Heavenly goddess; in Semitic lands she was a form of Astarte. Now Mithra was regularly identified by his worshippers with the sun, the Unconquered Sun, as they called him; hence his nativity also fell on the twenty-fifth of December. The Gospels say nothing as to the day of Christ's birth, AND ACCORDINGLY THE EARLY CHURCH DID NOT CELEBRATE IT. In time, however, the Christians of Egypt came to regard the sixth of January as the date of the Nativity, and the custom of commemorating the birth of the Saviour on that day gradually spread until by the Fourth century it was universally established in the East. "But at the end of the

The original teachings of Jesus	Nimrodism	Christianity today
		third or the beginning of the fourth century the Western Church, which had never recognised the sixth of January as the day of the Nativity, adopted the twenty-fifth of December as the true date and in time its decision was accepted also by the Eastern Church. At Antioch the change was not introduced till about the year 375 A.D".

5. THE SIGN OF THE CROSS

The original teachings of Jesus	Nimrodism	Christianity today
Jesus was fully aware that the sign of the Cross was a symbol, which had already been cursed by God Almighty not only because of Nimrod at the tower of Babel, but also when some Jewish women were weeping for Tammuz (the pagan Babylonian god Nimrod who was represented by the sign of the Cross) at the Northern Gate of the Temple of Jerusalem. In fact God Almighty was	Among the Babylonians an upright cross was a sacred magical symbol to ward off evil. In the Hebrew alphabet, such a cross was the original form of their letter "T" (or Tau). So the cross was the initial letter of the name of the Babylonian god Tammuz or "Fire, the Perfecter", or Nimrod. Its worship was thus the worship of "Tammuz" or Bacchus or Nimrod.	Nowhere in the Bible is it mentioned that the Cursed Pagan sign of the Cross is to be worshipped by the Christians.

Clement in his list of Christian; symbols, does not mention the sign of the Cross. Hence it does not date from the crucifixion!

On pages 204-205 of *"The Two Babylons"* by the Rev. A. Hislop one reads: |

The original teachings of Jesus	Nimrodism	Christianity today
so infuriated at this incident that He ordered them to be killed—vide the Holy Bible: "… he brought me to, the door of the gate of the Lord's house which was towards the north; and behold there sat (Jewish) women weeping for Tammuz" (Ezekiel 8: 14). "Slay utterly old and young, both maids, and little children, and women … and begin (these killings) at My sanctuary …" (Ezekiel 9: 6). As read earlier, in accordance with the above curse of God Jerusalem, the sacred city of not only the Jews but also of Jesus, was completely demolished for this reason in 607 B.C. (see *Destruction or Peace*, Chapter. 6: M). Further this sign of the Cross represents the throwing of Prophet Abraham, the friend of God, into the fire by	The cross has thus been venerated by sun-worshippers throughout the world for many centuries before the so called Christian era. This worship has spread from Babylon to Mexico and South America on one hand, and throughout Asia, Europe and the Mediterranean countries on the other as we have read earlier in *Destruction or Peace*, Chapter 5: F-2.	(With reference to Christendom) "and the Tau, the sign of the cross, the indisputable sign of the Tammuz, the false Messiah, was everywhere SUBSTITUTED in its stead" (*i.e.* "X" or Chi as in Christos which was introduced by King Constantine in 325 A.D) Thus the adoption of the magical sign of the cross shows that Christianity came under, the corrosive influence of the spell of Nimrod, which has robbed Christians of their will power and reasoning! Otherwise they would have stayed surely far away from this intoxicating sign which is not only a cursed symbol in the eyes of Jesus, but also despised by him. During this century, a cross has been discovered in Ireland with a crucified effigy, but it is the effigy of "Mithra" as a Persian Prince and not that of Jesus, because the head of the one crucified

The original teachings of Jesus	Nimrodism	Christianity today
Nimrod for having broken Idols, as read earlier in *Destruction or Peace,* Chapter VI: F. Hence the Cross is a sign hated by both God and Jesus because it represented Nimrod, the mighty hunter in rebellion against God (Genesis 10: 9), and his attempts to wipe out the teachings of "God is One" by replacing it with "trinity in unity"! The last of the Heavenly Books repeatedly stresses "… Follow not the footsteps (*i.e.* do not imitate anything) of the devil (Nimrod). Lo! he is an open enemy for you" (Qur'an 2: 168).		bears a Parthian coronet arid not the crown of thorns. This identifies it with the old Mithraic cult. Thus the sign of the cross and the crucifixion came from Mithraism into Christianity. Hence the sign of the cross has nothing to do with Jesus nor with any incident in his life.

The original teachings of Jesus	Nimrodism	Christianity today

6. ON CIRCUMCISION

The original teachings of Jesus	Nimrodism	Christianity today
The centurion of the town of Capernaum had a sick servant. He asked Jesus to pray for his servant and not bother to come to his house as he was fully confident his servant would get cured! "… speak the word only and my servant shall be healed" he said (St. Matt. 8: 8; St. Luke 7: 7). When Jesus heard this he was very much moved and declared: "Verily I say unto you, I have not found so great faith, no, not in Israel" (St. Matt. 8: 10; St. Luke 7: 9). Yet Jesus did not convert this believing centurion and all his servants as well as the 100 soldiers under him and their families even though they all had such ardent faith in Jesus. This one conversion would have	The difference between the pagan followers of Nimrod and the believing followers of Abraham, the father of the nations of believers in God Almighty has been circumcision of the males from the very inception of these two basic religions. 1. Those who are circumcised cannot fall easily a prey to the magical influence of Nimrod. 2. Those uncircumcised are usually much too intoxicated even, to realise what blasphemies they utter! It should be noted here that when anyone approaches the two fallen angels in the underground chamber of Babel (see *Destruction or Peace,* Chapter 5: D) where they are hung upside down in the well	"The Brethren" broke the everlasting covenant of God with Abraham, by inviting the uncircumcised Cornelius, a centurion of the Roman Army in 36 A.D. to convert into their faith (Acts 10: 1-48). Immediately they became victims of the spell of Nimrod upon humanity as warned in the Holy Bible: "Babylon hath been a golden cup in the Lord's hand that made all the earth drunken: the nations have drunken of her wine: THEREFORE THE NATIONS ARE MAD" (Jeremiah 51: 7). Many of the true believers in Jesus warned the Brethren converts: "And certain men (*i.e.* the Nazarenes which included St. John and the 112 out of the 120 believers in Jesus) which

The original teachings of Jesus	Nimrodism	Christianity today
meant anything from 500 to 1,000 converts but Jesus did not convert them! Why? Why was he content with only 120 converts (Acts 1: 15) and all of them only the circumcised Jews! Jesus was fully aware that because the Jewish King Ahab, son of Omri, had married the pagan Princess Jezebel, daughter of the uncircumcised Ethbaal, king of the Zindonians the whole Jewish nation had been corrupted into Nimrodism (1 King 16: 29-33) Just one contact brought several Jewish kings under the magical spell of Nimrod resulting eventually in the effacement of Jerusalem in 607 B.C. because of Nimrodism and its sign of the cross and the feast of Easter! He therefore wanted to ensure that his teachings were not corrupted and destroyed by inviting the	of punishment, both Horus and Marduk warn the persons that they would lose their souls if they were to learn the art of magic (Qur'an 2: 102). If they insisted then they were asked to go and urinate at another well in the same chamber (pages 134-139, Vol. 1, *Tafrihul Askia Fil Ahwal Ul Ambia*). Therefore circumcision plays such a vital role as to distinguish forever the pagan followers under the magical spell of Nimrod and the circumcised children and followers of Abraham, the friend of Allah.	came down from Judaea taught the "Brethren" (*i.e.* the converts of Peter, Paul and the dissidents to Jesus) and said, Except ye be circumcised (according to the covenant of Abraham and follow the Judaic Laws) after the manner of Moses, ye cannot be saved" (Acts 15: 1). That the Brethren being overcome under the hypnotic spell of Nimrod paid no heed to the teachings of Jesus of Nazareth is evident from: "And being brought on their way by the church, they passed through Phenice and Samaria, declaring the conversion of the *Gentiles*; and they caused great joy unto all the *Brethren*" (Acts 15: 3). "Forasmuch as we (the Brethren) have heard, that certain (people *i.e.* Nazarenes) WHICH WENT OUT (*i.e.* who

The original teachings of Jesus	Nimrodism	Christianity today
uncircumcised people, as he was fully aware of the bewitching influence of Nimrod. Therefore Jesus not only refused to accept the uncircumcised pagan centurion who had absolute faith in him but he also never preached to nor converted the uncircumcised. This is clear from the following passage in the Holy Bible: "… Preaching the word to none but unto the (circumcised) Jews only" (Acts 11: 19). Jesus ordered his disciples to preach only to the Jews and not to the uncircumcised pagans as follows: "These twelve Jesus sent forth, and commanded them, saying, Go not into the way of the Gentiles, and into any city of the Samaritans enter ye not: "But go rather to the lost sheep of the house of		have broken away) FROM US HAVE TROUBLED You with words, subverting your Souls, saying: ye must be circumcised and keep the (Mosaic) Laws (taught by Jesus): to whom (*i.e.* the Nazarenes) WE (the Brethren) GAVE NO SUCH COMMANDMENT" (Acts: 15: 24). 'Consequently it is clear from this that the authority of the Brethren came from themselves. The words "WE (i.e. THE BRETHREN!) GAVE NO SUCH COMMANDMENT" being very significant! Thus it makes explicit that it is "the Brethren" who have broken away from the teachings of Jesus of Nazareth, by following their own whimsical desires and think themselves to be even cleverer than Jesus and the Divine Evangel. If this is not "Blasphemy" of the worst type,

The original teachings of Jesus	Nimrodism	Christianity today
Israel" (St Matt. 10: 5-6). Jesus himself was circumcised when he was eight days old (St. Luke 2: 21).		then what is it? St. John has corroborated that it is the Brethren who have broken away from the teachings of Jesus as shown earlier in *Destruction or Peace,* Chapter 12: C-12 according to the Holy Bible.

7. ON SABBATH DAY

The original teachings of Jesus	Nimrodism	Christianity today
Jesus regularly observed the Sabbath Day throughout his life as is confirmed in the Holy Bible: "And he (Jesus) came to Nazareth, where he had been brought up: and, as his custom was, he went into the synagogue on the Sabbath day, and stood up for to read" (St. Luke 4: 16). "And (Jesus) came down to Capernaum, a city of Galilee, and taught them on the Sabbath days" (St. Luke 4: 31). According to tradition	According to Nimrod's teachings of Sun-worship, he started the week from Sunday or Sun-god's day. This was the first day of their week. The Sabbath observed by the Prophets on Friday, the last day of the week, was with the idea of asking God for the forgiveness of one's sins actually committed during the whole of the week which ended on Friday, so that they could start the next week from Saturday in a purer condition.	The Christians observed till now two of the rules of the Sabbath of Jesus *viz*: 1. Not to eat meat on Fridays. 2. Not to kill any animal for food on Fridays. But according to the decree of King Constantine issued in 321 A.D. they changed the weekly day of prayer and rest in conformity with the pagan system of observing "Dies Solis" or Sun-god's day or the first day of the pagan week instead of Friday the

The original teachings of Jesus	Nimrodism	Christianity today
Jesus taught the observance of Sabbath from sunset on Thursday to sunset on Friday as follows: 1: Not to light any fires or to cook any food. 2. Not to kill any animal for food. 3. Not to eat any meat. 4. Not to do any manual labour. 5. To spend the day in prayers, good deeds, attending synagogues, reading the Torah and preaching, thus keeping the day holy. "When it was day, Friday morning, early, Jesus, after prayers, assembled his disciples and said unto them: 'Let us sit down (in prayers); for even as on this day God created man of the clay of the earth" … then Jesus sat down and praised God (page 281, Gospel of Barnabas). This was the system of observing the Sabbath on Friday, which was the	The Pagan's objective of observing the Sabbath was not forgiveness of one's sins or purity. On the contrary it was adhered to with the sole object of having good luck throughout the duration of the week that they observed Sunday as the most powerful "sun god's day" or the first day of the week as their prayer day. This teaching of Nimrod spread all over the world when God's curse broke up the unity of mankind at the tower of Babel and the peoples were scattered from there.	seventh day of the week of the Prophets from the time of Adam thus showing a greater respect for King Constantine's sun worship as compared with the teachings of Jesus and the earlier prophets, from the inception of the creation of mankind. The research scholar Garner Ted Armstrong has written on page 5 of the March 1971 issue of *"The Plain Truth"* as follows: "Read about the Jesus whose mother had a large family (Matthew 13: 55-56), who is Lord of the Sabbath, not Sunday," (St. Mark 2: 28). So it will be clear that Jesus's sabbath was not on a Sunday but on *Fridays, i.e. the day they were forbidden to eat meat* and to refrain from killing any animal for food! In 321 A.D., Constantine

The original teachings of Jesus	Nimrodism	Christianity today
last or seventh day of the week from the time of Adam as shown earlier (see *Destruction or Peace,* Chapter 4: B and C).		ordered: Henceforth "Dies Solis" or Sun-god's day was to be observed as the Sabbath day by all his subjects! (see *Destruction or Peace,* Chapter 12: F-2).

8. ON MEAT WITH BLOOD FORBIDDEN

The original teachings of Jesus	Nimrodism	Christianity today
We find from the Holy Bible that the first occasion where permission was given to mankind to eat meat was after the great deluge. Before that only vegetables and fruits were eaten. This order on Noah reads: "Every moving thing that liveth shall be meat for you; even as the green herb have I given you all things. "But flesh with the life thereof, which is the blood thereof, shall ye not eat" (Genesis 9: 3-4). The Angel Gabriel came	King Nimrod spent his long life only in exciting rebellion against God Almighty. He is described in the Holy Bible as follows: "And Cush begat Nimrod: he began to be a mighty one in the earth. "He was a mighty hunter in rebellion before the Lord. Wherefore it is said Even as Nimrod the mighty hunter in rebellion before the Lord" (Genesis 10: 8-9). He always considered the laws of God All mighty a curse and took the greatest pleasure in	The Christians by following the system of Nimrod by killing animals with one stroke by either chopping off the head or by paralyzing the brain with an electric shock or a stroke on the head are eating meat with blood still in it. Thus the Christians accord greater respect by their deeds to the principles of Nimrodism as against God All mighty's orders forbiding the eating of "Blood". If this is not "Hero worship of Nimrod" and "Blasphemy against

The original teachings of Jesus	Nimrodism	Christianity today
and showed how this order was to be carried out, *viz*: the animal's or bird's wind pipe and the two main arteries on the two sides of the wind pipe in the neck were only to be cut with a sharp knife, causing instantaneous death without injuring the spinal cord, so that the brain could still operate the heart of the animal or bird for a few minutes after death until all blood in the body flows out of it through these two cut main arteries. When all the blood had been pumped out in this manner then only would the animal or bird become fit for eating. Any animal or bird which died of itself or was killed by another animal or by strangulation (Leviticus 17: 15-16) or by chopping off its head in one stroke thus injuring the spinal cord or otherwise impairing the functioning of the heart in	not only breaking them but also getting others to follow his mischievous teachings. Hence his title "Nimrod" which means "Let us rebel". Quite naturally he considered the rules of killing an animal and taking out its blood before eating it an unnecessary waste of time and effort. So he pretended that in killing an animal or a fowl in the manner ordered by God All Almighty was to cause great torture to the animal or bird concerned. Thus he posed himself as a great preventer of cruelty to animals and birds. The proper way of killing an animal or a bird according to Nimrod without causing any pain or torture was to chop off the head of the animal or bird in one stroke or even to wring the neck of the birds, if they are small, as that would cause instantaneous death with the	God", then what is it? For full details of the Divine Laws that "BLOOD IS FORBIDDEN" as observed by Jesus please refer to: "And wherever you live, you must not eat the blood of any bird or animal. Anyone who eats blood must be cut off from their people." (Leviticus 7: 26-27) "I will set my face against any Israelite or any foreigner residing among them who eats blood, and I will cut them off from the people. For the life of a creature is in the blood, and I have given it to you to make atonement for yourselves on the altar; it is the blood that makes atonement for one's life. Therefore I say to the Israelites, "None of you may eat blood, nor may any foreigner residing among you eat blood." "Any Israelite or any foreigner residing among you who hunts

The original teachings of Jesus	Nimrodism	Christianity today
pumping the blood out of the body through cut arteries or an animal dying a natural death were forbidden as food because the process of the brain causing the heart to pump the blood out of the body through the two cut main arteries was impaired. Hence such meat, which was with blood, was forbidden to be eaten by the descendants of Noah, from whom the present human race has come about. The followers of Jesus also conformed to this law as is evident from the following passage in the Holy Bible: "That ye abstain from meats offered to idols, and from things strangled, and from fornication" (Acts 15: 29).	least possible torture. Thus he used to eat meat with blood still in it.	any animal or bird that may be eaten must drain out the blood and cover it with earth, because the life of every creature is its blood. That is why I have said to the Israelites, "You must not eat the blood of any creature, because the life of every creature is its blood; anyone who eats it must be cut off." "Anyone, whether native born or foreigner, who eats anything found dead or torn by wild animals must wash their clothes and bathe with water, and they will be ceremonially unclean till evening; then they will be clean. But if they do not wash their clothes and bathe themselves, they will be held responsible." (Leviticus 17: 10-16) "Do not eat any meat with the blood still in it." (Leviticus 19: 26) and you will realise that the punishment for eating meat with blood is "death" and the

9. ON FOOD LAWS—SWINE FORBIDDEN AS FOOD

The original teachings of Jesus	Nimrodism	Christianity today
		person will be cut off from God's blessings!

The original teachings of Jesus	Nimrodism	Christianity today
The swine, which belongs to the wild-boar family, was abominable to Jesus and his followers because:	Swine flesh was eaten under Nimrodism as an abusive revenge on the flesh of Abraham, who was responsible for the violent death of their only begotten son of the sun-god (see *Destruction or Peace,* Chapter 6: K).	The Christians by enjoying swine flesh, (something hated by Jesus) thus identify themselves with the followers of Nimrodism.
1. It was one of the animals of god Tammuz. Hence it was a special item of meat offered to Idols.		By taking swine flesh at the feast of Christmas, the birth date of Nimrod, they prove categorically that they eat it only to express their hatred for Abraham, the architect of the death of their Messiah.
2. Swine flesh was eaten by the pagans on festive occasions with a view to take an abusive revenge upon the one who was responsible for the violent death of Nimrod, their only begotten son of sun-god born of the great virgin queen of the heaven as read earlier (see *Destruction or Peace,* Chapter 6: I, J and K).	Therefore every eater of swine flesh is ipso facto a hater and an enemy of Abraham, the friend of God All mighty.	
3. The man, who was responsible for the violent death of Nimrod was Abraham the		Can such people ever be the followers of Jesus of Nazareth the son of the Virgin Mary? We have already read in see *Destruction or Peace,* Chapter 10: P, that all his life Jesus had been forbidden repeatedly the following items as recorded in "The Gospel

The original teachings of Jesus	Nimrodism	Christianity today
ancestor of Jesus and his followers. Therefore eating swine flesh meant the eating of the flesh of their own great ancestor Abraham.

4. Swine flesh was also strictly forbidden to Jesus and his followers the circumcised Jews under the divine Laws:

"And the swine, because it divideth the hoof, yet cheweth not the cud, it is unclean unto you: ye shall not eat of their flesh, nor (even) touch their dead carcase" (Deuteronomy 14: 8) also similar order is in (Leviticus 11: 7 and 8), which is as follows "And the pig, though it has a divided hoof, does not chew the cud; it is unclean for you. You must not eat their meat or touch their carcasses; they are unclean for you."

5. If the carcass of a swine is even accidentally touched, then it would render one | | of Barnabas":

a) Wine
b) Strong drinks
c) Every unclean meat.

Therefore the followers of Jesus cannot indulge in wine (even for sacramental purposes) or in strong drinks or swine flesh on festive or any other occasions.

That Jesus refused to drink wine because it was prohibited will be evident from the following Biblical quotation:

"And they gave him (Jesus) to drink wine mingled with myrrh: but he received it not" (St. Mark 15: 23). |

The original teachings of Jesus	Nimrodism	Christianity today
unclean for the rest of the day until the sunset when the new day commenced: "The carcases of every beast which divideth the hoof, and is not cloven footed, nor cheweth the cud, are unclean unto you: every one that toucheth them shall be unclean. "And whosoever beareth ought of the carcase of them shall wash his clothes, and be unclean (for the rest of the day) until the even (*i.e.* sunset when the new day starts)" (Leviticus 11: 25 and 26). Hence it is evident from these passages that no follower of Jesus can even touch swine flesh under any circumstances whatsoever, let alone eat it!		

The original teachings of Jesus	Nimrodism	Christianity today

10. ON IDOLATRY

The original teachings of Jesus	Nimrodism	Christianity today
"Little children keep yourselves from idols. Amen" (1 John 5: 21). "Wherefore, my dearly beloved, flee from idolatry" (1 Corinthians 10: 14). "And what agreement hath the temple of God with idols? ..." (2 Corinthians 6: 16).	As recorded earlier Nimrodism taught that praying before idols was prayer to the deity. This is the belief of the pagans. This is the commencement of idolatry after the deluge. (see *Destruction or Peace,* Chapter 5: F-1).	Many Christians pray before idols. Just like the pagans they believe that prayers before idols are prayers to the deity! Are they not thus giving preference to Nimrodism over the teachings of Jesus, son of Mary? Are not such idolaters?

11. ON MARRIAGE

The original teachings of Jesus	Nimrodism	Christianity today
Marriage is a blessing and that there is no restrictions on the number of wives can be seen from the following Biblical quotations: "And God blessed Noah and his sons, and said unto them, Be fruitful, and multiply, and replenish the earth. "And God spake unto Noah, and to his sons with him saying:	We have read earlier that Nimrod planned to reunite the different groups, when God's curse broke up the unity of mankind at the tower of Babel (Genesis 11: 1-9) by preaching as follows (see *Destruction or Peace,* Chapter 5: H): 1. That nobody would be permitted to marry a relative but that marriage should be contracted with some	1. Only one wife to be allowed. 2. The husband and wife should be from different families. 3. Marriages between cousins not normally allowed. From the above it is explicit that the Christians preferred and accepted the teachings of Nimrod as against God's

The original teachings of Jesus	Nimrodism	Christianity today
"And I, behold, I establish My covenant with you, and with Your seed after you; "And you, be ye fruitful, and multiply; bring forth abundantly in the earth, and multiply therein" (Genesis 9: 1, 8, 9, 7). "Whoso findeth a wife findeth a good thing, and obtaineth the favour of the Lord" (Proverbs 18: 22). "Who can find a virtuous woman? For her price is far above rubies" (Proverbs 31: 10). The teaching of Jesus found in the New Testament is cited: "Marriage is honourable in all (be they priests or nuns or ordinary people) …" (Hebrews 13: 4). That marriage amongst cousins is encouraged can be seen from the following Biblical quotation: "… but he shall take a virgin of his own people	other group, so that unity and friendship may flourish amongst the different groups and thus they could re-unite and undo what God Almighty had done to split the Unity of mankind. 2. If a person had more than one wife there could be quarrels between the wives which would mean a dispute between three or more family groups. Thus it was a possible source of disunity. Hence only one wife was his order of the day. 3. To support this theory he preached that marriage in the same family meant the same blood and that this was detrimental to the health of their children.	orders taught by Jesus. The result of following Nimrodism must inevitably bring a curse of Almighty God upon the Christian group of nations. As an example the world sees that during the last World War many of the young German men were killed. There were left approximately five women to one man in the marriageable age group. If one man can marry only one wife, what happens to the remaining four women? Are they not human beings according to the Christian Church? Must they be denied the right of married life? Was this the purpose for which they were created by the Almighty that they should be reduced to prostitution, being denied their rights to marry and lead honourable lives in accordance with the laws of God? (See

The original teachings of Jesus	Nimrodism	Christianity today
(*i.e.* a cousin) to wife" (Leviticus 21: 14).		*Destruction or Peace,* Chapter 19: E-3).
a) **Marriage laws according to the Bible:** According to Biblical laws you cannot marry the following, and any one breaking these laws is to be put to death:		Can these ever be the laws of God? Or are the Christians merely blindly following the teachings of Nimrod, the accursed, and thus bringing God's scourge upon themselves?
1. Pagans and Idolaters (Leviticus 20: 1-6).		It was for this life of shame that many places were destroyed by God's curse from time to time. Sodom, Gomorrah, in the days of Lot, Babylon, Pompeii etc.—not to forget the great deluge in the time of Noah! Should not the Europeans beware that God's curse will overtake them if they do not give up Nimrod's cursed principles of having only one wife and a free license for prostituting any number of other women!
2. Another living man's wife (Leviticus 18: 20; 20: 10).		
3. Father, mother, son, daughter (Leviticus 18: 6-8).		
4. Do not prostitute thy daughters (Leviticus 19: 29).		
5. Sister, father's daughters (*i.e.* stepsisters), mother's daughters (*i.e.* half-sisters) (Leviticus 18: 9; 20: 17).		
6. Father's wives (*i.e.* Stepmothers) (Leviticus 18: 8; 20: 11).		The answer to such tragic situations in Europe is to follow the teachings of God Almighty.
7. Daughter-in-law (Leviticus 18: 8; 20: 11).		

The original teachings of Jesus	Nimrodism	Christianity today
8. A woman, her daughter, her daughter's daughter, her son's daughter (Leviticus 18: 17). 9 Wife's mother (Leviticus 20: 14). 10. Mother's sisters or Father's sisters (Leviticus 18: 12, 13; 20: 19). 11. Uncle's wife (Leviticus 18: 14; 20: 20). 12. Brother's wife as long as brother is alive (Leviticus 18: 16; 20: 21). 13. Wife's sister as long as the wife is alive (Leviticus 18: 18). 14. Another man's wife or a prostitute however beautiful or attractive she may be (Leviticus 20: 10). 15. Another man for wife (Leviticus 18: 22; 20: 13). 16. Any animal for sexual pleasures (Leviticus 18: 23; 20: 15 and 16). All others you can marry from amongst your		Look at the Arabs! They have on rare occasions married more than one wife (See *Destruction or Peace*, Chapter 19: E-3, F and G), all cousins of one another and see how very contentedly they are living in perfect harmony amongst themselves. They have from the time of Abraham some 4,000 years back, married amongst cousins, without suffering any ill-health, thus disproving totally the teachings of Nimrod! By marrying between cousins, the wives being cousins and knowing one another from childhood co-exist very happily and well. This would not be so if they were not interrelated. Therefore this is the only way by which the Europeans can rid themselves of prostitution, which is haunting them and eroding their morality. Instead of

The original teachings of Jesus	Nimrodism	Christianity today
relatives without any restrictions on the number of wives a man may have! These are the teachings of Jesus who had come not to destroy the Mosaic Laws but to fulfil them (St. Matthew 5: 17).		living a clean honest life, they are living a life of deceit and shame, owing to their man-made laws of restricting marriage to only one wife. Thus this is proving a curse for the Europeans and is destroying their family lives (See *Destruction or Peace*, Chapter 19: G—Polygamy and the West).

This cankerous principle of Nimrod of having only one wife and so many women available without any hope for decent honourable lives is the cause of the various "Nudist Cults", "Exchange of mates", "Call Girls", and the "Free for all living styles" now raging throughout the European assortment of nations and America (*Destruction or Peace*, Chapter 23: C-8). |

12. ON MONASTICISM

The original teachings of Jesus	Nimrodism	Christianity today
a) **The Holy Bible shows Jesus is against Monas-**	We have read earlier that King Nimrod encouraged monasticism to	Many of the Christian sects by observing Monasticism thus

The original teachings of Jesus	Nimrodism	Christianity today
ticism "Now the Spirit speaketh expressly, that in the later times some (*i.e.* Peter and his group the Brethren) shall depart from the faith (of Jesus), giving heed to seducing spirit, and doctrines of the devils (*i.e.* Nimrod and his teachings like Mithraism); "Speaking lies in hypocrisy; having their conscience seared with a hot iron; "FORBIDDING TO MARRY …" (1 Timothy 4: 1-3). "MARRIAGE is honourable in ALL (be they priests or nuns or ordinary people) and the bed undefiled: but whoremongers and adulterers God will judge" (Hebrews 13: 4). **b) Marriage is compulsory for priests under the Holy Bible** That the Priests of Jesus MUST BE married people is proved from the	prevent the birth of Abraham, whereby he hoped to destroy the truth and thus prevent the light of the Almighty Creator being spread on the face of the earth! (see *Destruction or Peace,* Chapter 6: A, B and C). Thus monasticism is an expression of hatred to Abraham, the father of the nations of believers (see *Destruction or Peace,* Chapter 7: E and 8: F). Thus it was King Nimrod who formulated	identify themselves as the followers of Nimrod! Therefore they are the enemies of Abraham! One who is an enemy of Abraham is ipso facto also an enemy of Jesus, who is one of his descendants. Is that what Christianity is? A religion of hatred to both Abraham and Jesus! St. Peter the originator of the "Brethren" was a married man.

The original teachings of Jesus	Nimrodism	Christianity today
following passages of the Holy Bible: "**This is a true saying** (of Jesus), if a man desire the office of a '**BISHOP**', he desireth a good work. "**A bishop then must be blameless, the husband of one wife**, vigilant, sober, of good behaveiour, given to hospitality, apt to teach; "**Not given to wine,** no striker, not greedy of filthy lucre; but patient, not a brawler, not covetous; "One that ruleth well his own house, having his children in subjection with all gravity; "*(For if a man know not how to rule his own house, how shall he take care of the Church of God?*" (1 Timothy 3: 1-5). "Likewise must the 'DEACONS' be grave, not double-tongued, not given to ... wine, not greedy of filthy lucre;	the first anti-marriage laws, with the object of preventing the birth of Abraham (see *Destruction or Peace,* Chapter 6: C). Therefore all who follow these unnatural laws and observe celibate monasticism are surely the followers of Nimrod, the enemy of Abraham, the ancestor of Jesus. Hence the various orders of celibate priests and nuns all over the world, under whatever names, are all the enemies of the children of Abraham, including Jesus!	**In 867 A.D.:** Adrian II a married man became Pope. Therefore the following anti-marriage laws, contrary to the precepts of Jesus, must have been copied from Nimrodism: "... It is good for a man not to touch a woman" (1 Corinthians 7: 1). "I say therefore to the unmarried and widows, It is good for them if they abide (unmarried) even as I" (1 Corinthians 7: 8). "... He that is unmarried careth for the things that belong to the Lord, how he may please the Lord; "But he that is married careth for the things that are of the world, how he may please his wife. "There is a difference also between a wife and a virgin. The unmarried woman careth for things of the Lord, that she may be holy both in body and in spirit: but she that is

The original teachings of Jesus	Nimrodism	Christianity today
"And let these also first be proved; then let them use the office of a deacon, being found blameless. "Even so must their wives be grave, not slanderers, sober, faithful in all things. *"Let the deacons be the husband of one wife, ruling their children and their own houses well"* (1 Timothy 3: 8-12). **c) Celibacy is a bad thing according to God in the Holy Bible** Every true religion, which had come from the One and only God through anyone of the numerous prophets of God, has invariably	The following quotation is from page 220 of "The Two Babylons" by the Rev. A. Hislop: "The effects of its (monastic celibacy) introduction (by Nimrodism from Babylon) were most disastrous. The records of all nations where priestly celibacy has been introduced have proved that, instead of ministering to the purity of those condemned to it, it has only plunged them in the deepest pollution. The history of Tibet, and China, and Japan, where the Babylonian institution of priestly celibacy has prevailed from time immemorial, bears testimony to the abominations that have flowed from it. The excesses committed by the celibate priests of Bacchus in Pagan Rome in their secret Mysteries, were such that the Senate felt	married careth for the things of the world, how she may please her husband" (1 Corinthians 7: 32-34). These are nothing but the doctrines of Nimrod (see *Destruction or Peace,* Chapter 6: C). In 1123 A.D.: At the first Lateran Council, it was clearly passed that PRIESTS and NUNS from that date onwards were forbidden to marry! Hence it is absolutely obvious that this law on celibacy did not exist at the time of Jesus and those that followed him. It is something which was innovated eleven centuries later! In fact this unnatural and Pagan law is solely responsible for priests, bishops and cardinals taking mistresses. Alexander VI fathered at least four illegitimate children before

The original teachings of Jesus	Nimrodism	Christianity today
preached against "Monasticism", since the time of Adam till date: "And the Lord God said, It is not good that the man should be alone; I will make him an help meet for him" (Genesis 2: 18). The teachings of Jesus as well as of St. Paul, one of the founders of the Brethren faith, also confirms in the Holy Bible that only married men can be priests of the Church and not the celibate priests and nuns as in paganism! "This is a true saying (of Jesus) if a man desire the office of a Bishop, he desireth a good work. "A BISHOP then MUST BE blameless, THE HUSBAND OF ONE WIFE" (1 Timothy 3: 1-2). "Let the DEACONS BE THE HUSBANDS OF ONE WIFE, *ruling their children and their houses well*" (Timothy 3: 12).	called upon to expel them from the bounds of the Roman Republic. In Papal Rome the same abominations have flowed from priestly celibacy, in connection with the corrupt and corrupting system of the confessional, insomuch that all men who have examined the subject have been compelled to admire the amazing significance of the same divinely bestowed on it, both in a literal and figurative sense, 'Babylon the Great, THE MOTHER OF HARLOTS AND ABOMINATIONS OF THE EARTH'" (Revelation 17:5).	becoming the Pope in 1492 A.D. Historian Henri Daniel Rops estimated that in the 15th century in Burgundy, half of the children born, were out of prostitution indulged in by Priests, Bishops and Cardinals. **In 1836:** "The Rev. M.H. Seymour shows that the total number of births in Rome in one year was 4373 of which no fewer than 3160 were born out of illicit relationships with the priests" (Moral Results of Romanish System, page XLIX in Evening with Romanists). "When Pope' Paul V mediated the suppression of licensed brothels in the "Holy City", the Roman Senate petitioned against his carrying his design into effect, on the ground that the existence of such places was the ONLY means of HINDERING THE PRIESTS FROM SEDUC-

The original teachings of Jesus	Nimrodism	Christianity today
		ING THEIR WIVES AND DAUGHTERS!" (Pages 220 of "The Two Babylons" by the Rev. Alexander Hislop, The 6th American Printing of 1953).
	As seen earlier King Nimrod taught Monasticism as part of his policy of revolt against God and His friend Abraham, the father of the circumcised believers (see *Destruction or Peace,* Chapter 6: C).	Often young attractive virgins going alone for confession into the secluded confines of the Church have realised too late that they are coming out of a brothel and not a place of worship of God, with their chastity lost to the one they were looking upon as their guide in religious and spiritual matters! They have experienced sin in the Church at the hands of the "Forgiver" of their sins, the hearer of their confessions!
d) General Order of God that a Priest must Marry		Hence this unnatural Pagan Law of Nimrod has made the clergy a danger to the dignity and purity of the society.
The particular orders for priests were as follows (Jesus being from the family of the Jewish priests) and these form part of the laws that Jesus taught:		
"And the Lord said unto Moses, speak unto the priests, the sons of Aaron (the Virgin		Even though Jesus gave no permission to practise Monasticism

The original teachings of Jesus	Nimrodism	Christianity today
Mary's Mother being from this particular family), and say unto them. "And he (the priest) SHALL (*i.e.* compulsorily) take a wife in her virginity. "A widow or a divorced woman, or profane, or an harlot, these SHALL he not take: but he SHALL (compulsorily) take a virgin of his own people (*i.e.* a near relative, a cousin) to wife. "Neither shall he (the priest) profane his seed among his people: for I the Lord do sanctify him" (Leviticus 21; 1, 13-15). **e) Divine Confirmation that Monasticism was not taught by Jesus** That this was the divine message in the Evangel given by God Almighty to the world through	This Pagan Law of King Nimrod has not brought any dignity, honour, perfection and reverence for the "Celibate Priests" all over the world. On the contrary it has brought disgrace, dishonour and imperfection. Because such a law is not only a disobedience to God, being against the call of nature but it has also been devised for the sole purpose of preventing the fulfilment of God's will i.e. the birth of Abraham, the ancestor of Jesus (see *Destruction or Peace*, Chapter 6: A, B and C).	and celibacy, yet the Christians took to it after the lapse of many Centuries. By doing so whom are they following? To whom do they show greater respect; THE REAL JESUS — or — NIMROD? *i.e.* Constantine's CHRIST ?

The original teachings of Jesus	Nimrodism	Christianity today
Jesus is confirmed again by the last of the Heavenly books as follows: "And We (Allah) verily sent Noah and Abraham and placed the Prophethood and the (Divine) Scriptures among their seeds, and among them there is he who doeth right, but many of them are evil livers. "Then We (Allah) caused our messengers to follow in their footsteps (*i.e.* Noah and Abraham); and We (Allah) caused Jesus, son of Mary, to follow (the Judaic Laws, taught and practised by the earlier prophets) and gave him the Evangel, and placed compassion and mercy in the hearts of those who followed him. But Monasticism (*i.e.* the different celibate priestly and nunnery schools) they (the Christians) invented (by copying the pagan teach -ings of Nimrod)—We		In January, 1966 a group of Italian Priests had petitioned the Pope to relieve them from the obligation of celibacy, arguing that it was an intolerable burden and the rule had no basis either in the scriptures or natural law. If Christianity or Nimrod's teachings as it is called in modern times is a curse for mankind, then there can be no solution for the upliftment of man and his salvation unless and until mankind submits to God's laws, without altering a single letter of it.

The original teachings of Jesus	Nimrodism	Christianity today
(Allah) ordained it not for them—only seeking Allah's pleasure (by leading normal married lives in the right way). Hence they (the Christians) observed it not with the right observance. So We (Allah) give those of them who believe (and follow the Evangel *i.e.* the Nazarenes) their reward but many of them (*i.e.* the Christians) are evil-livers." (Qur'an 57: 26-27).		

13. THE APOSTLES

The original teachings of Jesus	Nimrodism	Christianity today
The Jews were many thousands when they escaped from Egypt under Moses, but the latter appointed only one Apostle i.e. Joshua after him to guide the large numbers belonging to the twelve different tribes of Jews. In 2 Kings 2, we read of Elijah having appointed Elisha to be his Apostle	Nimrod, the great astronomer, as we have read earlier invented the theory of the twelve heavenly guides or the twelve constellations of the Zodiac, from which he showed that all those born under their influence had common characteristics and on this basis Horoscopes and forecasts were invented by him. Hence	Since Jesus did not appoint the twelve apostles, then from where did this theory of the twelve guides come about? Was it not from Nimrodism? Is it not with the object of misguiding the world to accept such utterly incompetent people as St. Peter and St. Paul who have been disowned by Jesus according to the

The original teachings of Jesus

and heir after him.

Similarly King David was appointed heir to Prophet Samuel and David appointed Solomon after him as apostle for the whole Jewish race. In fact, the whole of the Old Testament is full of such evidence that only one guide was nominated at a time for all the twelve tribes of the Jewish nation.

The Holy Bible gives us the following information:

"And in those days (i.e. those that followed after Jesus was raised to heaven) Peter stood up in the midst of the disciples, and said, (the number of names together were about a hundred and twenty)" (Acts 1: 15).

By no stretch of imagination can it be suggested that an apostle is required for the guidance of every 10 disciples or more than one apostle as necessary

Nimrodism

the twelve sections of influence were a *sine qua non* as far as his teachings were concerned! (see *Destruction or Peace,* Chapter 5: F-5).

This is the Pagan basis for the twelve guides or the twelve heavenly Apostles.

Christianity today

Holy Bible? (see *Destruction or Peace,* Chapter 12: D and H-3).

Jesus has publicly declared that St. Peter is a Satan e.g.:

"But he (Jesus) turned, and said unto Peter, *Get thee behind me Satan*: thou art an offence unto me: for thou savourest not things that be of God, but those that be of men.

"For what is a man profited, if he shall gain the whole world and lose his soul? ..." (St. Matthew 16: 23 and 26).

The original teachings of Jesus	Nimrodism	Christianity today
to guide 120 converts to the faith of Jesus.		
According to tradition Jesus also appointed only one heir. He is John the son of Zebedee (St. Matthew 4: 21) the writer of the Evangel and the Revelation both in the Hebrew Language in Aramaic Script. His works were seized from the possession of Arius along with the Evangel by Levi and burnt in 325 A.D. under orders of Emperor Constantine. These were replaced by St. John, the Revelation and St. Matthew respectively—all written in Greek—*a language foreign to Jesus!*		

14. ON SIN AND HOLY COMMUNION

15. FORMALITIES TO ENTER THE FAITH OF THE REAL JESUS

The original teachings of Jesus	Nimrodism	Christianity today
1. "And Jesus answered him THE FIRST OF ALL THE COMMANDMENTS IS: Hear, O Israel; THE LORD OUR GOD	God is a trinity in unity. Nimrod is the only begotten son of Sun-god, born of the virgin queen of the Heavens, come to	God is a trinity in unity. Christ is the only begotten son of god, born of the virgin mother, come to save

The original teachings of Jesus	Nimrodism	Christianity today
IS ONE LORD (i.e. one who has no father, mother, husband, virgin wife, brother, sister, only begotten son, daughter or any other form of equals):	save sinners by the sacrifice of his sacred and precious life.	sinners by the sacrifice of his sacred and precious life.
"And thou shalt love the Lord thy God with all thy heart, and with all thy soul, and with all thy mind, and with all thy strength: *this is the first commandment*" (St. Mark 12: 29-30).		
2. To face towards Jerusalem	To face towards the East the rising place of the Sun	*To face the East instead of towards Jerusalem*
— and —	— and —	— and —
3. To make a pledge to observe the Mosaic Laws of God from now onwards.	To be baptised from the sacred founts of Alpheus and Peneus which would clean up one's polluted sins just as the Augean stables were cleaned instantly.	*To be baptised with water.*
4. To be circumcised within 8 days.		
Jesus hated *"Baptism"* because it represented the magical rites to bring one under the spell of Nimrodism, due to which Jerusalem, the Sacred City of his ancestors, had been destroyed in 607 B.C. as	The Pagan mythology tells us that when the Only begotten son of Sun-god was baptised, the Sun descended in resplendent glory and	"And Jesus, when he was baptised, went up straightway out of the water: and, lo, the heavens were opened unto him, and he (alone)

The original teachings of Jesus	Nimrodism	Christianity today
read before. That Jesus was never baptised and that he did not baptise anybody is recorded in the Holy Bible as follows: "Though Jesus himself baptised not (neither himself nor others) …" (St. John 4: 2). Hence there can be no question of the followers of Jesus practicing the pagan sun worshippers' rites of "Baptism" for bringing them under the spell of King Nimrod, the Cursed, in the light of the following Biblical warning: "Babylon hath been a golden cup in the Lord's hand, that made all the earth drunken: the nations have drunk of her wine: therefore the NATIONS ARE MAD (to suggest God coming down on earth to declare "*This is my beloved son in whom I am well pleased*" when God has no son nor any other form of equals. He	announced: "*This is my well beloved son in whom I am well pleased*". Two of the Cuneiform Tablets, which were dug up by German Excavators in 1903-1904 at Kalah Shargat, the site of ancient Assur 'one of the cities built by Nimrod' give the following account of Nimrod's religious teachings: Baal is taken prisoner. Baal is tried in the House on the Mount (the Hall of Justice). Baal is smitten (wounded).	saw the spirit of God descending like a dove, and lighting upon him: "And lo a voice from heaven, saying, *This is my beloved son in whom I am well pleased*" (St. Matthew 3: 16-17; St. Luke 3: 21-22). As Jesus was not baptised and did not baptise anybody according to the Holy Bible (St. John 4: 2) then all that is in the Holy Bible to the contrary is nothing but a fraud introduced to suit the Pagan converts and to deceive the world! The Non-Hebrew versions of the Bible show: Jesus is taken prisoner. (St. Mark 14: 46; St. John 18: 12). Jesus is tried in the House of the High Priest and the Hall of Justice (of Pilate). (St. Mark 14: 56-65; 15: 2-15). Jesus is scourged. (St. Matthew 27: 26). Together with Jesus, two

The original teachings of Jesus	Nimrodism	Christianity today
is One and Alone)" (Jeremiah 51: 7). According to Nazarene tradition it is stated that Judas, the betrayer, whilst going with the Jews to capture Jesus was separated from the group in the darkness. Immediately, by the will of God, his face and features changed to those of Jesus. When Judas came to rejoin the seekers after Jesus, he was captured by the Jews, who believed that he was Jesus in spite of his protests. This captive explicitly denied before Pilate that he was Jesus. Pilate, being satisfied, refused to take any action. Again before Herod the victim disclaimed that he was Jesus. Herod took a basin of water, in accordance with his Jewish Custom, and washed his hands of the accused man's blood to indicate that he found him innocent. This	Baal is led away to the Mount. Together with Baal a malefactor is led away and put to death. Another, who is also charged as a malefactor, is released. Thus he is not taken away with Baal. After Baal has gone to the Mount, the city breaks out into tumult, and fighting takes place in it. Baal's clothes are carried away. A woman wipes away the heart's blood of Baal which is flowing from a drawn-out weapon (? spear). Baal goes down into the Mount away from the sun and light, disappears from life, and is held fast	malefactors are led away and put to death (St. Mark 15: 27-28), another (Barabbas) is released to the people, and thus not taken away with Jesus (St. Matthew 27: 17, 20, 21 and 26-36). At the death of Jesus, the veil in the temple is rent, the earth quakes, the rocks are rent asunder, the graves are opened, and the dead come forth into the holy city. (St. Matthew 27: 50-53). Jesus's robe is divided among the soldiers (St. Matthew 27: 35; St. Mark 15: 24; St. John 19: 24). A spear is thrust into Jesus' side and there is out flow of water and blood. (St. John 19: 34). Mary Magdalene and two other women busy themselves with ministerring unto him (i.e. washing the wounds and embalming the body). (St. Matthew 27: 55-56, St. Mark 15: 40-41). Jesus, in the grave, in the

The original teachings of Jesus	Nimrodism	Christianity today
infuriated the persecutors. Subsequently for the safety of the alleged Jesus from the infuriated crowd, he took Judas into protective custody for the night and asked the accusers to appear in Court the next day. By now the Jews knew very well that they would not be able to substantiate their charges against the supposed Jesus and they became desperate. So in the early hours of the morning when prison guards were sleepy, they surprised them, took out the supposed Jesus and put him to death instantaneously in spite of protests till the last moment that he was Judas and not Jesus. The Holy Bible confirms that Jesus was unhurt and alive after the alleged crucifixion: "And as they thus spake, Jesus himself stood in the midst of them, and saith unto them, Peace be unto you.	in the Mount as in a prison. Guards watch Baal imprisoned in the stronghold of the Mount. A goddess sits with Baal; she comes to tend him. They seek for Baal where he is held fast. In particular, a weeping woman searches for him at the "Gate of Burial". When he is being carried away, the same lamented: "O, my brother! O, my brother!" Baal is again restored to life (as the Sun of spring), he comes again out of the Mount. His chief feast, the Babylonian New Year's festival in March at the time of the spring equinox, is celebrated as also his triumph over the Power of Darkness (*cp*. The creation hymn "Once when on high" as the New Year's festival	rock tomb. (St. Matthew. 27: 60; St Mark 15: 46) goes down into the realm of the dead ("descent into hell" dogma). Guards are set over the tomb of Jesus. (St. Matthew. 27: 62-66). Mary Magdalene and the other Mary sit before the tomb. (St. Matthew. 27: 61). Mary Magdalene, the other Mary and others came to the tomb to seek Jesus where he is behind the door of the tomb. (St. Matthew 28: 1; St. Mark 16: 1-2; St. John 20: 1). Mary stands weeping before the empty tomb because they have taken her Lord away. (St. John 20: 11-13). Jesus' restoration to life, his rising from the grave (on a morning of dies Solis or Sun-god Sol's day). (St. Matthew 28: 5-7; St. Mark 16: 6; St. Luke 24: 1-10).

The original teachings of Jesus	Nimrodism	Christianity today
"But they were terrified and affrighted, and supposed that they had seen a spirit (because Jesus was supposed to have been killed).	hymn). *A few other Pagan references:* Osiris was betrayed by Typhon slain and dismembered. He was interred but came back to life.	His festival, approximately at the spring equinox, is also celebrated as his triumph over the "Power of Darkness". (Colossians 1: 12-13).
"And he said unto them, why are ye troubled? And why do thoughts arise in your hearts?" "Behold my hands and my feet, that it is I myself: handle me, and see; for (a man who has been killed and if he then appears he is) a spirit (and it) hath not flesh and bones, as ye see me have.	Every year the maidens wept for Tammuz (Ezekiel 8: 14) and then rejoiced over his resurrection. Easter (*Anglo-saxon Eostre* or *Ostera*) is nothing more than Ishtar or Semiramis, the virgin mother, Queen of the Heaven, who is also the goddess of Light and Spring.	
"And when he had thus spoken, he showed them his hands and his feet (to see and feel that they were safe and sound and without any kind of injury of the alleged attack by Jews. Thus he showed that the Jews had neither succeeded in capturing nor killing him and that it was Judas whom the *Jews had murdered*, as confirmed by Jesus on	In her honour the festival of Easter was celebrated everywhere on the first Sunday, after the Full moon about the Spring Equinox for many thousands of years before Jesus (see *Destruction or Peace*, Chapter 5: F-1). Hot-Cross buns and painted eggs were	Jesus was betrayed by Judas, crucified, interred in the rock grave but he came back to life. Every year the Christians mourn the crucifixion of

The original teachings of Jesus	Nimrodism	Christianity today
page 487 of *The Gospel of Barnabas* quoted here before in Column No. 1, of see *Destruction or Peace*, Chapter 12: G-I. "And while they yet believed not for joy, and wondered he said unto them, Have ye here any meat (because when one has been killed or died he cannot anymore eat human food thereafter)? "And they gave him a piece of a broiled fish, and of a honey comb. "And he (Jesus) took it, and did eat before them (thus proving before several witnesses as recorded in the Holy Bible that definitely he had not been killed by the Jews and that he was still unharmed and alive, and not risen after death)" (St. Luke 24: 36-43). Jesus was not killed but was raised bodily in live condition after the alleged crucifixion. This is evident from the Holy	distributed and eaten in all Middle East countries, including Egypt as also in the British Isles and Ireland. The practice continues even now in Christendom at the time of Easter. In *"Pagan and Christian Creed"* page 39: "The triumph of the Sun-god was, therefore and quite naturally ascribed to the influence of Aries (The Lamb of the Heavens). The lamb thus became the symbol of the Rising Saviour and of his passage from the underworld into the height of heaven". In *"The Golden Bough"*, by Frazer, pages 348-356, you read about the Phrygian virgin-born son of god who was bled to death hanging crucified from a pine-tree. His blood renewed the fertility of the earth and thus, brought new life to humanity. He also	Christ and rejoice his resurrection. The date of the crucifixion is another stumbling block in the way of a seeker of truth, because here he finds the date of Good Friday corresponds closely with the date of the passions of the various age-old pagan deities. The same is the case with the time of the resurrection. No doubt we find its mention in the Gospel as occuring near the date of the Passover Feast. But this was a time honoured date in the Pagan world. Hence the Gospel writers have copied all this from Nimrod's teachings.

THE TEACHINGS OF HOLY JESUS

The original teachings of Jesus	Nimrodism	Christianity today
Bible: "… While they beheld, he (Jesus) was taken up (by angels); and a cloud received him out of their sight. "And while they looked steadfastly towards heaven as he went up, behold, two men stood by them in white apparel; "Which also said, Ye men of Galilee, why stand ye gazing up into heaven? This same Jesus, which is taken up from you into heaven, shall (on the day of the Battle of Armageddon) so come (back to earth) in like manner as ye have seen him go into heaven" (Acts 1: 9-11). The following passages from the last of the Heavenly Books also confirm that Jesus was never crucified: "And because of their saying: We slew the Messiah, Jesus son of Mary, Allah's Messenger	rose from the dead. "In celebrating his death and resurrection, his image was fastened to a pine-tree cut in the form of a cross on March 24th and the day was called the "Day of Blood" since on that day the deity was bled to death. The image was then laid in a tomb, when there was wailing and mourning, but the coming night changed their sorrow to joy. The Tomb was found empty on the next morning *i.e.* 25th March, when the festival of the resurrection was celebrated. These rituals included a baptism of blood and a sacramental meal". In Prescott's "*Conquest of Mexico*" Volume I, page 60, we find that Quetzalcoatle, son of Virgin Chimalman was crucified, when the sun was darkened and withheld its light. His second coming was looked for so eagerly that when Cortez	The movable nature of Easter between March and April according to the moon phases clearly shows that: a) If the crucifixion of Jesus had really taken place, then this festival would take place on a fixed date. Hence this festival has nothing to do with the crucifixion. b) Further, it is common knowledge that new life starts budding after the "Full Moon" occurring during the spring Equinox. Hence this festival is nothing but the worship of Ishtar or Eostre or Ostera, the goddess of Light and spring, the ruler of the zodiac, Queen Semiramis, the mother of Nimrod! c) The lamb is the symbol of the Pagan "Sun god's son rising from the dead" during the period of Aries or

The original teachings of Jesus	Nimrodism	Christianity today
—They slew him not nor crucified him, but it appeared so unto them; and lo! those who disagree concerning it are in doubt thereof; they have no knowledge thereof save pursuit of a conjecture; they slew him not for certain. "But Allah took him up (bodily into the Heaven) unto Himself. Allah is ever Mighty, Wise" (Qur'an 4: 157-158). "(And remember) when Allah said: O Jesus! Lo! I am gathering thee (from the earth) and causing to ascend (to heaven) unto Me, and am cleansing thee of those (Peter and the dissidents etc.) who disbelieve in thee and the Evangel) and am setting those who follow thee above those who disbelieve until the Day of Resurrection. Then unto Me ye will (all) return and I shall judge between you (i.e. the Nazarenes, the true followers of Jesus and the Christians, the followers	appeared, the Mexicans greeted him as the returning "god". Countless such examples from different places and the varied religions of the sun worshippers can be cited here. Thus it will be seen that even though Mexico had been cut off from the rest of the world for many thousands of years, perhaps right from the time their group left Babylon, yet their religion of sun-worship has not differed in its main features save and except for the names of the "Virgin Mother" and the "Only Begotten Son" because of God's curse at the tower of Babel which changed the languages of the people overnight.	the Constellation of the Lamb. Thus it does not represent Jesus and his crucifixion. d) The effigy of Jesus on the Cross with a crown of thorns is nothing but a copy of Mithra on the Cross wearing a "Parthian" coronet (this has been already referred to earlier). This discovery of the cross in Ireland with Mithra crucified clearly proves that the entire story of the crucifixion of Christ has been copied from Mithraism and has nothing to do with The Real Jesus. The fixing of the particular "Dies Solis" or Sun-god Sol's day on which Easter is to be celebrated by the Christians was done by Emperor Constantine in 325 A.D. at the Nicaean Council. Hence, this may be taken as the proper origin of the story of the Crucifixion of Christ and his

The original teachings of Jesus	Nimrodism	Christianity today
of Peter and the dissidents and Paul, Marcus etc.) as to that wherein ye used to differ. "As for those who disbelieve I shall chastise them with a heavy chastisement in the world (in the battle of Armageddon) and the Hereafter; and they will have no helpers (in Jesus). "As for those who believe and do good works, He will pay them their wages in full. Allah loveth not wrongdoers. "This (which) We (Allah) recite unto thee (O Muhammad) is a revelation (to you) and a wise reminder (to the Christians)" (Qur'an 3: 55-58).		resurrection, as can be seen from the following passage: "Easter began everywhere more of custom than any commandment either of Christ or any Apostle" (Hist. Ecclosiast lib. V, Chapter. 22).

H. The Permanent Sacrifice to Save Sinners

The present Christian religions seem to be interwoven around King Nimrod's theory of the "Only begotten son of god come to save sinners by the sacrifice of his life". It is the *"sine qua non"* of their whole faith. Hence it is necessary to analyse the various aspects of the great sacrifice as found in the Holy Bible.

1. "The Powers of Darkness"

The Holy Bible gives us the following information:

> "When I was daily with you in the temple, ye stretched forth no hands against me: *but this is your hour, and the Power of Darkness*" (St. Luke 22: 53).

From this it appears beyond doubt that during daylight hours (*i.e.* when the sun is in the heavens) the Jewish Priests had no power to molest "the Christ" but when the sun sinks and darkness sets in, then Christ and his god, evidently "the sun", are helpless against "*the Powers of Darkness*"!

As far as God Almighty is concerned His Power is the same all the time. It is the same by night as by day. In fact the phenomena of day on half the earth and at the same time night on the other half is caused by the daily rotation of the earth. Hence *Night* in one part or *Day* in another does not make the least difference to God's powers. Therefore the only natural inference of this quotation from the Holy Bible attributed to Christ can be one of the two undermentioned situations—Which Jesus?:

    i.   EITHER

That according to the Holy Bible, Christ was a believer in and a worshipper of the sun as his god and his powers in daylight and his helplessness in darkness. Hence the Jesus of the Holy Bible is King Nimrod!

    ii.   OR

The *REAL JESUS*, which Jesus was a worshipper of the True God Almighty, then the writers of the Gospels in Greek *i.e.* Luke, Marcus *etc.* were sun-worshippers and not worshippers of God Almighty—The God of the *Real Jesus*.

The above quoted statement from the "Holy Bible" attributed

to the *Christ* of Constantine's creation on "the Powers of Darkness" must be false because the *Real Jesus* was not by any stretch of the imagination a believer in the sun as a god or in the imagination "Powers of Darkness" or in the theory of the weakness of his enemies during daylight hour. Such were the fantasies of the sun-worshippers, who were ignorant of the fact that the rays of the sun always covered half the earth with sunshine all the time, whilst the other half was simultaneously in darkness as the earth rotated.

Therefore the whole story of the crucifixion built upon "the Powers of Darkness" is not only false but also copied from pagan mythologies of Nimrod, the saviour, who had sacrificed his life to a violent death at the hands of Abraham and his God to protect his religion and become the "Sin bearer" come to save the baptised sinners of the world (see *Destruction or Peace*, Chapter 6: I and J). Is not all this nonsense—an absolute insult to the intelligence of the modern educated man and a blasphemy against God Almighty? The *Real Jesus* certainly was not a blasphemer. But Constantine's Christ, who is none other than Nimrod, was! Which *Jesus* should the Christians follow?

2. The Crucifixion

The Greek Holy Bible written for the pagan converts has recorded the incidents which were supposed to have taken place during "the reign of the *Powers of Darkness*" in a single night as follows:

a. The Last Supper (St. Matthew 26: 26-28; St. Mark 14: 22-24; St. Luke 22: 15-20).

b. The decision to betray Jesus was taken by Judas only after this "Last Supper" (St. John 13: 2). It must have taken at least about 3/4 hours to come to such a serious decision as to betray one's teacher and guide, a holy saintly person without any faults and daily performing wonderful miracles!

c. Judas goes to the Jewish High Priest after the "Last Supper" and asks what he would be paid if he betrayed Jesus (St. Matthew 26: 14-15; St. Mark 14: 10-11; St. Luke 22: 3-5).

d. After a bargain is made and an agreement has been arrived at, the "High Priest" orders a number of men to be gathered and armed to capture Jesus (St. John 18: 3). A few hours would surely be necessary for all this.

e. Judas leads these armed men to the various places where Jesus is likely to be found (St. Matthew 26: 16; St. Luke 22: 6).

f. The agony in the garden for at least three hours till a very late hour in the night (St. Matthew 26: 36-45; St. Mark 14: 32-41; St. Luke 22: 39-46).

g. Judas arrives with armed men at this very late hour in the night, possibly 1 a.m. or even later (St. Matthew 26: 47; St. Mark 14: 43; St. Luke 22: 47; St. John 18: 3).

h. Jesus asked the armed men, "Whom seek ye?" They answered "Jesus of Nazareth", Jesus replied "I am he". As soon as Jesus said: "I am he", all the armed men were hurled backward by an unseen power with such great force that all of them collapsed and fell to the ground—fainted (St. John 18: 4-6).

i. Jesus is betrayed by the "Kiss" Of Judas (St. Matthew 26: 48-49; St. Mark 14: 44-45; St. Luke 22: 47-48).

j. Peter chops off the ear of Malchus, the Jewish leader of the men come to arrest Jesus, but Jesus healed his ear by his touch (St. Matthew 26: 51; St. Mark 14: 47; St. Luke

22: 49-51; St. John 18: 10).

k. In spite of these two miracles *viz.* of the soldiers being hurled backward to the ground and the healing of the chopped-off ear of Malchus, the soldiers, instead of running away to save their lives, and Malchus, instead of being grateful for the miraculous healing of his chopped-off ear, have the audacity to arrest and bind Jesus! Is that what the Holy Bible wants us to believe? (St. Mark 14: 46; St. John 18: 12).

l. Jesus is taken first to the house of Annas (St. John 18: 13).

m. Jesus is tried by Annas and interrogated (St. John 18: 19-23) for several hours. What could be the time of the same night when Jesus is sent to the High Priest?

n. Jesus is bound by Annas and sent to the palace of Caiaphas, the high priest (St. John 18: 24).

o. Caiaphas the Chief Priest then gathers the elders from amongst the Jews and counsels that it would be expedient if one man should die (St. John 18: 14). All this must have taken several hours. What could be the time of the same night?

p. Thereupon the Chief Priest, the elders and all the Council tried to collect evidence against Jesus to put him to death but found none (St. Mark 14: 55). This must have taken them several hours. What could be the time of the same night?

q. They blindfolded Jesus and struck him on his face saying "Prophesy, who it is that smote thee?" (St. Luke 22: 64). Thus they tortured Jesus for several hours in an effort to break him. What could be the time of the same night?

r. Having failed to break the patience of Jesus, they decided to gather false evidence against Jesus. So they sent for dishonourable witnesses at this time of the dead of night! Many witnesses were gathered from their houses after being woken up from their sleep at the dead of night and brought to the High Priest (St. Matthew 26: 59-60; St. Mark 14: 56). Then they were taught by the High Priest what to say but when they came before Jesus, they declined to give false evidence. This was a process taking many hours of coaching for each person (St. Matthew 26: 60). The night of the *Powers of Darkness* of a single might must have continued for at least 100/150 hours to enable so much to be done! Is that what the Holy Bible wants us to believe?

s. Under the Jewish Law, before any man can be accused of any crime at least two witnesses are required (Deuteronomy 17: 6 and 19: 15). Hence at least two witnesses have to be forced or induced to give false evidence against Jesus. At long last two persons agree to make false statements (St. Matthew 26:60).

t. But many of the testimonies of these two perjurers were contradictory and did not agree (St. Mark 14:56). This must have taken at least another 8 or 10 hours—all during the *Powers of Darkness* of a single night—The special night with its "*Powers of Darkness*" during which the "god of the Christ" (*i.e.* the sun) was helpless! The night still continued in spite of all these many hours of the Powers of Darkness and yet the sun was not late in rising the next morning!

u. Then followed a lengthy examination of Jesus, arguments and counter arguments *etc.* on how to frame charges of death against Jesus that would convince the Roman Governor. Say another 10/15 hours were necessary, yet the single night still continued according to what the Holy Bible wants us to accept! Nevertheless the sun was not late in rising the next morning!

v. Thereupon the Jews at the palace of the High Priest start hitting Jesus on the face, spitting upon him and tormenting him (St. Matt. 26: 67; St. Luke 22:63). All this must have taken some time. The single night very strangely still persisted according to the Holy Bible!

w. At last in desperation the Jewish High Priest frames a charge of blasphemy and demands that Jesus be put to death (St. Luke 22 : 70-71). The framing of the charge must have taken another several hours. The single night still endured with its *"Powers of Darkness"*.

x. Jesus is bound and led to the Hall of Judgment (St. John 18: 28) at this unearthly hour of the night, when no Court of Justice is held! According to the Holy Bible, the time was early in the night and before they had their meal of the "Feast of the Passover" (St. John 18:28).

y. The Holy Bible wants us to believe that at this unnatural hour of the night, when the world is asleep, Pilate without being woken up comes out and the Jews bring various charges against Jesus during the period of the *"Powers of Darkness"* of a single night. Pilate questions Jesus. Jesus answers, and after a detailed examination of the charges Pilate pronounces Jesus innocent (St. Luke 23: 1-4). The Bible wants us to believe that this Court was held in the dead of night! Further, it took many hours and yet the *"Powers of Darkness* of this special night continued"! Also the sun was not late in rising on the next morning!

z. The Jews became desperate and accused Jesus of inciting revolt throughout Jewry, beginning from Galilee to this place *i.e.* Jerusalem (St. Luke 23:5).

aa. When Pilate heard the name of Galilee he transferred the case to Herod for Galilee was in Herod's jurisdiction (St. Luke 23: 6-7).

bb. Jesus is then taken under escort during the *"Powers of Darkness"* of the single night and produced before Herod at that unearthly hour of the night. Herod very strangely happens to be in Jerusalem on that night instead of somewhere in Galilee, the area under his jurisdiction! Herod is not woken up! Herod is very glad to see Jesus, as he had been anxious and desirous of meeting Jesus for whom he had the highest regard and respect (St. Luke 23: 8).

cc. The Chief Priest and the scribes vehemently accused Jesus before Herod (St. Luke 23:10).

dd. Herod questioned Jesus for a long time but could not find any sign of guilt!

ee. Herod, a king of the Jews, puts his gorgeous royal purple robe on Jesus to show his respect for this great man whom he found innocent. After that the Gospel writers want the world to believe that Herod had a sudden fit of insanity for no rhyme or reason, because Herod and his men of war, we find, mocked Jesus at that unearthly hour of the night and sent him back to Pilate, instead of setting Jesus free and punishing the wicked Jews for bringing false accusations against an innocent man (St. Luke 23:11).

ff. When Pilate found that Jesus was returned again in the dead of night wearing the royal purple robe to show that he was found innocent by the man under whose jurisdiction Jesus was, Pilate was obliged under Roman

Law to set him free, as he was found to be innocent.

gg. When Jesus was brought for trial, the wife of Pilate sent an urgent message to Pilate that she had had a dream which showed that if the innocent Jesus was not set free then they would suffer severely. This request from one's wife would be an imperative command for any sane husband (St. Matthew 27:19).

hh. According to Roman Law under these circumstances Pilate was obliged not only to have set Jesus free but also to have punished the Jews for bringing a false charge. Instead the Greek Gospel writers for the pagan converts want the world to believe that for no rhyme or reason Pilate also got a sudden, inexplicable attack of insanity and he offered to set the innocent Jesus free in lieu of Barabbas, a criminal! (St. Matthew 27:21; St. Mark 15:7-11). How absurd indeed!

ii. The Jews refuse this offer and ask that Jesus be killed and Barabbas, the murderer, released (St. Matthew 27:21; St. Luke 23:18). All this during the *"Powers of Darkness"* of a single night! which must have been at least 200/250 hours long instead of the usual 12 hours at the time of spring equinoxes!

jj. The Gospel writers then want to make the world believe that the superstitious Roman Governor Pilate gets a further fit of temporary insanity. That he ignores his beloved wife and the dream of warning. That he is prepared to get himself punished severely and his family ruined by ordering the crucifixion of the innocent Jesus! The crown of thorns, the scourging *etc.* must have taken several hours. All this after his wife had warned her husband to release the innocent Jesus or suffer dire consequences! Hence it was impossible for Pilate to allow the murder of Jesus under any of these circumstances. Yet The Holy Bible wants the world to believe it was so (St. Mark 15:12-20).

kk. The length of the night during the spring Equinox is twelve hours all over the world and not 250/300 hours as the writers of the Holy Bible seem to pretend as without that, so much could not have possibly taken place during the *"Powers of Darkness"*.

ll. The Holy Bible has made no claims that this night was an exceptionally long night lasting for say about 300 hours or having the length of a month of nights without the sun rising even once in all this period, instead of only 12 hours as is a fact.

mm. Therefore the multiplicity of the various events recorded in the gospel as taking place during the "Rule of the *Powers of Darkness*" of one single night makes the whole Gospel story not only an impossibility but also a complete absurdity and a clear fabrication. It does bring to mind the following advice of Jesus himself:

"But if thine eye be evil, thy whole body shall be full of darkness. If therefore the light that is in thee be darkness, how great is that darkness!" (St. Matthew 6:23).

It was God's plan to save Jesus from the ignominy of death at the hands of his enemies! The Bible disgraces Jesus with a punishment reserved only for criminals by giving him a death on the Cross, but The Gospel of Barnabas and the Qur'an give honour to Jesus that God saved Jesus from death on the Cross by replacing him with Judas and instead raised Jesus to heaven alive before a vast multitude. This theory of Jesus' substitution by Judas was accepted by numerous followers of Jesus. Some of them were known as:

1. The early Basildians
2. The Veselins
3. The Corinthians
4. The Carpocates
5. The Dositors
6. The Armingus
7. The Nazarenes

These early converts to the faith of Jesus knew very well what had actually taken place before their very eyes as against the invention of the story of the *Crucifixion of Christ* some 300 years later!

It is now for the intellectuals to decide which of the theories they are going to follow?

EITHER

Those of the early followers of Jesus who maintain that *The Real Jesus was never crucified but bodily lifted to heaven in a live condition* (Acts 1:9).

OR

Nimrod's theory that he sacrificed his life to save his baptised sinners *i.e.*—What Constantine has incorporated into the Greek Holy Bible and that he was raised up from the dead in a spiritual condition as the "*Ares*" or the lamb of the heavens?

3. St. Peter Denies Jesus Six Times in a single Night!

The Holy Bible tells us that on this eventful night, at two different places St. Peter denied six times all connections with Jesus as under:

Jesus is taken first to the house of Annas (St. John 18:13) and is questioned there (St. John 18:19-23).

St. Peter denied Jesus three times at the house of Annas before the cock crowed twice (St. John 18:16-18, 25-27).

Jesus is bound by Annas and sent to the palace of Caiaphas, the High Priest (St. John 18:24).

St. Peter followed Jesus to the palace of Caiaphas (St. Matthew 26:57-58; St. Mark 14:54).

For the second time the same night St. Peter once again denied thrice all connections with Jesus but this time at the palace of Caiaphas and that these three denials were made again before the cock crowed twice (St. Matthew 26: 69-75; St. Mark 14: 66-72).

Therefore according to the Holy Bible Peter denies Jesus thrice before the cock crows twice on two separate occasions at two different places and at two different parts of the night. Once he rejects him at the house of Annas between 1 a.m. and 3 a.m. Then he sits down and cries and again thrice before the cock crows twice at the palace of Caiaphas between 4 a.m. and 6 a.m. during the same night and finally Peter sits down and cries again. For such an incident to take place once in a lifetime is more than an improbability but to take place twice according to the Greek Bible in the same night with Peter denying Jesus six times and crying after each of these two sets of incidents makes it absolutely unbelievable.

Is it logically possible for such an important personage as the saint and founder of the Brethren Churches to have denied Jesus six times in the same night? And that also twice between the times the cock crowed twice at each of the two separate places? Can such ten coincidences have taken place twice in the same night in two different sets of five incidents each at two different spots?

To any intelligent mind, are not such records of six denials and four cock crowing's all so well synchronised at two diverse sites in a single night a basic impossibility?

In any ease, the Holy Bible makes it clear that Jesus has warned that anybody denying him even once before the public would be disowned by Jesus in Heaven before God in the following passage:

> "But whosoever shall deny me (Jesus) before men (*i.e.* in public), him will I deny before my Father which is in heaven" (St. Matthew 10:33).

Therefore according to the Holy Bible, St. Peter is a *person* who has not only been disowned by Jesus but he was also warned by Jesus in his original name of Simon that Satan was going to have him:

> "And the lord (Jesus) said, Simon, Simon, behold; Satan hath desired to have you, that he may sift you as wheat" (St. Luke 22:31).

When Peter failed to improve, then Jesus declared as under:

> "But he (Jesus) turned, and said unto *Peter, Get thee behind me, Satan*: thou art an offence unto me: for thou savourest not things that be of God, but those that be of men.
>
> "For what is a man profited, if he shall gain the whole world, and lose his own soul?" (St. Matthew 16: 23, 26).

4. Courts of Justice do not function at night!

Courts do not function at the dead of night to try criminals! Hence the Gospel story is inconceivable and devoid of any truth!

5. False witnesses at dead of night

The calling of perjurers at 4 a.m. and the arrival of many of them after many hours of search makes it basically impossible for it to have happened during the *"Powers of Darkness"* of a single night. Further, it is quite absurd to suggest that the High Priest instead of praying and preaching was spending his life in maintaining a list of false witnesses, *Who Testify in The Courts*, with their residential addresses! Hence to call "many" false witnesses as described in the Bible would ordinarily take many nights. Therefore it is quite impossible for so many witnesses to have appeared in a single night. Hence this part of the Bible is also basically untrue.

6. The unexplained and absurd fit of sudden insanity of both Herod and Pilate during the "Powers of Darkness"!

The insane orders of Herod and Pilate only as far as Jesus is concerned during the *"Powers of Darkness"* of the particular night further make the Gospel story a complete fiction and an absurdity. Neither of the two men were "MAD"! Both revered Jesus as shown earlier from the Holy Bible. The question of their torturing Jesus or wanting to exchange him for a criminal and not putting the Jewish High Priest up for trial for bringing false charges against Jesus during the night are all unacceptable to the educated mind of any intellectual.

7. The belated admission exonerating the Jews

Recently the Pope has exonerated the Jews from the charge of crucifying Jesus. This could not have been possible if Jesus had in fact been crucified!

8. The Falsity of the Crucifixion

The whole story of the Crucifixion of Christ and that "Christ gave his life to save sinners" on account of which he would be sitting on the right hand of God dispensing judgment is false as is proved by the following statement of Jesus found in the Nazarene Scripts discovered at Constantinople:

> "I shall not judge men or call them to account. He, who sent me, will do this".

(Page 58, *"Time"* The Weekly Magazine—Asia Edition dated 15th July 1966).

This is also confirmed in the Holy Bible as follows:

> "And if any man hear my words (Evangel), and believe not, I judge him not: for I came not to judge the world ...

> "He that rejecteth me, and receiveth not my words, hath one (God) that Judgeth him ..." (St. John 12: 47-48).

9. Origin of Easter according to the Church

"Easter (the celebration) began everywhere more of (Pagan) custom than any commandment either of Christ or any Apostle" (Hist. Ecclesiast. lib. V, Chapter 22).

10. The origin of The Crucifixion of Christ on The Cross

The discovery in Ireland of an effigy of Mithra hung on a cross wearing a Parthian coronet shows clearly that this is the origin of the story of Christ being hung on a cross wearing a crown of thorns. This theory had been in existence for many centuries before the birth of Jesus. This is the true origin of the Crucifixion of Christ which was incorporated into Christianity when it adopted the "Cross" of Constantine *i.e.* in or after 325 A.D.

11. The Revelation by European Research Scholar

"The Golden Bough" by Sir James G. Frazer—Abridged Edition published 1953, pages 350-361 reads:

> "Thus it appears that the Christian Church chose to celebrate

the birthday of its Founder on the twenty-fifth of December in order to transfer the devotion of the heathen from the Sun to him, who was called the Son of Righteousness. If that was so, there can be no intrinsic improbability in the conjecture that motives of the same sort may have led the ecclesiastical authorities to assimilate the Easter Festival of the death and resurrection of their Lord to the festival of the death and resurrection of another Asiatic god which fell at the same season. Now the Easter rites still observed in Greece, Sicily, and Southern Italy bear in some respects a striking resemblance to the rites of Adonis, and I have suggested that the Church may have consciously adapted the new festival to its heathen predecessor for the sake of winning souls to Christ. But this adaptation probably took place in the Greek-speaking rather than in the Latin-speaking parts of the ancient world; for the worship of Adonis, while it flourished among the Greeks, appears to have made little impression on Rome and the West. Certainly it never formed part of the official Roman religion. The place which it might have taken in the affections of the Vulgar was already occupied by the similar but more barbarous worship of Attis and the Great Mother. The death and resurrection of Attis were officially celebrated at Rome on the twenty-fourth and twenty-fifth of March, the latter being regarded as the spring equinox, and therefore as the most appropriate day for the revival of a god of vegetation, who had been dead or sleeping throughout the winter. But according to an ancient and widespread tradition Christ suffered on the twenty-fifth of March, and accordingly some Christians regularly celebrated the Crucifixion on that day without any regard to the state of the moon. This custom was certainly observed in Phrygia, Cappadocia, and Gaul, and there seem to be grounds for thinking that at one time it was followed also in Rome. Thus the tradition which placed the death of Christ on the twenty-fifth of March was ancient and deeply rooted. It is all the more remarkable because astronomical considerations prove that it can have had no historical foundation. The inference appears to be inevitable that the Passion of Christ must have been arbitrarily referred to that date in order to harmonise with an older festival of the spring equinox. This is the view of the learned ecclesiastical historian Mgr. Duchesne, who points out that the death of the Saviour was thus made to fall upon the very day, on which, according to a widespread belief, the world had been created. But the resurrection of Attis, who combined in himself the characters of the divine Father and the divine son, was officially celebrated at Rome on the same day. When we remember that the festival of St. George in April has replaced the ancient pagan festival of the Parilia; that the festival of St. John the Baptist in June has succeeded to a heathen Midsummer festival of water; that the festival of the Assumption of the Virgin in August has ousted the festival of Diana; that the feast of All Souls in November is a continuation of an old heathen feast of the dead; and the Nativity of Christ himself was assigned to the winter solstice in December because that day was deemed the Nativity of the Sun; we can hardly be thought rash or unreasonable in conjecturing that the other cardinal festival of the Christian church—the solemnisation of Easter—may have been in like manner, and from like motives of edification, adapted to a similar celebration of the Phrygian god Attis at the vernal equinox.

"At least it is a remarkable coincidence, if it is nothing more, that the Christian and the heathen festivals of the divine death and resurrection should have been solemnised at the same season and in the same places. For the places which celebrated the death of Christ at the spring equinox were Phrygia, Gaul, and apparently Rome, that is, the very regions in which the worship of Attis either originated or struck deepest root. It is difficult to regard the coincidence as purely accidental. If the vernal equinox, the season at which in the temperate regions the whole face of nature testifies to a fresh outburst of vital energy, had been viewed from of old as the time when the world was annually created afresh in the resurrection of a god, nothing could be more natural than to place the resurrection of the new deity at the same cardinal point of the year. Only it is to be observed that if the death of Christ was dated on the twenty-fifth of March, his resurrection, according to Christian tradition, must have happened on the twenty-seventh of March, which is just two days later than the vernal equinox of the Julian calendar and the resurrection of Attis. A similar displacement of two days in the adjustment of Christian to heathen celebrations occurs in the festivals of St. George and the Assumption of the Virgin. However, another Christian tradition, followed by Lactantius and perhaps by the practice of the Church in Gaul, placed the death of Christ on the twenty-third and his resurrection on the twenty-fifth of March. If that was so his resurrection coincided exactly with the resurrection of Attis".

"Attis" is one of the names of Nimrod the only begotten son of sun god as will be seen from *Destruction or Peace*, Chapter 5: F-1, which got changed to this name due to the curse of God at the Tower of Babel see *Destruction or Peace*, Chapter 5: G). Such findings have been recorded by numerous European Scholars.

I. Mithraism

i. "Mithra" in Sanskrit stands for benefactor or saviour. Thus Mithra or Mithras is one of the names of Nimrod which was changed by the people of Persia with the alteration in their language owing to the curse at the Tower of Babel.

It is a common fact that when anyone becomes famous, others try to copy him hoping that some of that fame may also come to them through this imitation.

The impact of the spread of Buddhism on Persia was such that they incorporated all the eight beatitudes and the various incidents in the life of Buddha into their Nimrodic faith. This hybrid religion became known as Mithraism. From here it spread throughout the Roman Empire and even into Britain by 70 B.C. Thus developed in the Middle East and the Roman Empire the cult of the enlightened celibate sage with his hundreds of disciples. This is the origin of the system of patron Saints, in whose names temples were built and schools started. This is the background in which Christianity has had its origin as pointed out earlier (see *Destruction or Peace*, Chapter 9: C).

ii. On page 1350 of Volume III, of the *Readers Digest Great Encyclopaedic Dictionary*, First Edition, published in 1964 one reads:

"MITHRAS.—Ancient Persian deity, associated with the sun or light. His cult is said to have been brought to Rome in the middle of the 1st c. B.C. Later it became widely popular, especially in the army ..."

iii. On Page 569 of Volume II, of ibid one finds:

"MITHRAISM.—The religion of the worshippers of Mithras, which was introduced among the Romans under the Empire and spread over most of North and West Europe during the first three centuries A.D. becoming the Principal rival at that time of Christianity".

J. Buddhistic teachings incorporated into Christianity

On Pages 162-163 of *"The Buddha, The Prophet and The Christ"* by F. H. Hilliard, Ph.D., B. D., (London) published by George Allen & Unwin Ltd., London in 1956 you read:

"The internal evidence for a literary connection between the Buddhist and Christian traditions has been reviewed to some extent by Thomas (in *Destruction or Peace*, Chapter 17 of "*The Life of Buddha*"). There are quite striking parallels which have understandably given rise to the argument that one tradition has influenced the other. In both Buddhist and Christian scriptures we have noticed stories of the miraculous birth of the Founder, of his presentation to a holy man, of his temptation, of his transfiguration, and of miracles, including that of the disciple walking on the water. If, however, Dr. Law's conclusions as to the dates of the formation of the Pali canon are accepted, it seems clear on the whole any suggestion of the Pali writings having been influenced by the Christian scriptures must be ruled out, for it would appear that the final form of the Pali canon was fixed before the end of the first century B.C. (see Dr. B. C. Law's "*A History of Pali Literature*" published in London, 1933)".

Hereafter are given a few comparisons of the Buddhistic teachings which have become incorporated into Christianity through Mithraism in the course of time:

Buddhism	Christianity
The birth of Buddha was heralded in the heavens by a star which was seen rising on the Eastern horizon. It is called the "Messianic Star".	The birth of Jesus was announced in the heavens by "his star" (St. Matthew 2: 2), which was seen rising in the East. It might properly be called the "Messianic Star" (St. Matthew 2: 9-10).
Demonstrations of celestial delight were manifest at the birth of Buddha. The Devas in heaven and earth sang praises to the "Enlightened One" and said: "Today, Bodhisatwa is born on earth, to give joy and peace to men and Devas; to shed light in the dark places, and give sight to the blind".	Demonstrations of heavenly joy were manifest at the birth of Jesus. The angels in heaven and earth sang praises to the "Blessed One", saying "Glory to God in the highest, and on earth peace, good will toward men" (St. Luke 2:13-14).
Buddha was visited by wise men who recognised in this marvellous infant all the characteristics of "a	Jesus was visited by wise men who recognised in this marvellous infant all the characteristics of divinity (St.

THE TEACHINGS OF HOLY JESUS

Buddhism	Christianity
superior being".	Matthew 2: 1 and 9-11).
The infant Buddha was presented with "costly jewels and precious substances".	The infant Jesus was presented with gifts of gold, frankincense, and myrrh (St. Matthew 2: 11).
"When twelve years old, the child Buddha is presented in the temple. He explains and asks learned questions; he excels all those who enter into competition with him".	And when he was twelve years old, they brought him to (the temple at) Jerusalem ... While in the temple among the doctors and elders, and learned men of Israel, he posed several questions of learning, and also gave them answers (St. Luke 2: 42-52).
When Buddha was about to go forth "to adopt a religious life", Mara appeared before him, to tempt him.	When Jesus was about to begin his preaching's the devil appeared before him, to tempt him (St. Matthew 4: 1-7; St. Luke 4: 1-5).
Mara said unto Buddha: "Go not forth to adopt a religious life, and in seven days thou shalt become an emperor of the world".	
Buddha would not heed the words of the Evil One, and said to him: "Get thee away from me".	The devil said to Jesus: "If thou wilt fall down and worship me, I will give thee all the kingdoms of the world" (St. Matthew 4: 8-9; St. Luke 4: 5-7).
After Mara had left Buddha, "the skies rained heavenly flowers, and delicious odours pervaded the air".	Jesus would not heed the words of the Evil One, and said to him: "Get thee behind me, Satan" (St. Luke 4: 8; St. Matthew 4: 10).
Buddha fasted for a long period.	After the devil had left Jesus, "angels came and ministered unto him" (St. Matthew 4: 11).
"On one occasion toward the end of his life on earth, Gautama Buddha is reported to have been transfigured.	
Through Prayers in the name of Buddha, his followers expect to receive their rewards.	Jesus fasted forty days and nights (St. Matthew 4: 2; St. Luke 4: 2).
"Buddha was described as a superhuman organ of light, to whom a superhuman organ of	On one occasion during his sojourn on earth, Jesus is reported to have been transfigured: "Jesus taketh with

Buddhism	Christianity
darkness, Mara or Naga, the Evil Serpent, was opposed."	him Peter, James, and John, and leadeth them up into a high mountain apart by themselves: and was transfigured before them: And his raiment became shining, exceeding white as snow" (St. Mark 9: 2-3).
One day Ananda, the disciple of Buddha, after a long walk in the country, meets with Matangi, a woman of the low caste of the Kendalas, near a well, and asks her for some water to drink.	
She tells him what she is, and that she must not come near him. But he replies: "My sister, I ask not for thy caste nor thy family, I ask only for a draught of water". Afterwards she became a disciple of Buddha.	Through prayers in the name of Jesus, his followers expect to receive the rewards of paradise (Acts 16: 30-31).
	Jesus was described as a superhuman organ of light "the Sun of Righteousness" as opposed by "the old Serpent, the Satan, hinderer, and adversary".
According to Buddha, the motive of all our actions should be piety or love for our neighbour.	
During the early part of his career as a teacher, Buddha went to the city of Benaras, and there delivered a discourse, by which Kondanya, and afterwards four others were induced to become his disciples. From that period, whenever he preached, multitudes of men and women embraced his doctrines. This multitude comprised many thousands of followers at the time of his death.	One day Jesus, after a long walk, cometh to the city of Samaria and being wearied with his journey, sat on a well. While there, a woman of Samaria came to draw water, and Jesus said unto her: "Give me to drink" (St. John 4: 6-7).
	"Then saith the woman of Samaria unto him; How is it that thou, being a Jew, asketh drink of me, which am a woman of Samaria? For the Jews have no dealings with the Samaritans". Afterwards she along with all the Samaritans of her town became the believers of Jesus. (St. John 4: 5-42).
Those who became disciples of Buddha were told that they must "renounce the world", give up all their riches, and avow poverty just as Buddha had done!	
	But Jesus did not convert a single person who was not a Jew. Hence this proves the apparent forgeries

THE TEACHINGS OF HOLY JESUS

Buddhism

When Buddha's time on earth was about to terminate, he, "foreseeing the things that would happen in future times", said to Ananda, his disciple, "Ananda when I am gone, you must not think there is no Buddha: the discourses I have delivered, and the precepts I have enjoined must be my successors, or representatives and be to you as Buddha".

In the Buddhist Somadeva the following is found "To give away our riches is considered the most difficult virtue in the world; he who gives away his riches is like a man who gives away his life: for our very life seem to cling to our riches. But Buddha, when his mind was moved by piety, gave his life like grass, for the sake of others; Why should we think of miserable riches: By this exalted virtue, Buddha, when he was freed from all desires, attained supernatural knowledge, entering into Buddhahood. Therefore, let a wise man, after he has turned away his desires from all pleasures, do good to all beings, even unto sacrificing his own life, that thus he may attain true knowledge".

Buddha's aim was to establish a "Religious Kingdom".

Buddha said: I now desire to turn the wheel of the excellent law. For

Christianity

copied from Buddhism.

"But I (Jesus) say unto you, Love your enemies, bless them that curse you, do good to them that hate you, and pray for them which despitefully use you, and persecute you;" (St. Matthew 5: 44).

During the early part of his career as a teacher, Jesus went to the city of Capernaum, and there delivered a discourse. It was at this time that four fishermen were induced to become his disciples. From that period, whenever he preached, multitudes of men and women followed his doctrines (St. Matthew 4: 13-25).

This huge multitude of men and women numbered as few as only 120 at the time when Jesus was lifted to heaven (Acts 1: 15) and not many thousands as in the case of Buddha upon his death. Hence the false statement of huge multitudes of men and women embracing the doctrines of Jesus brings out glaringly the forgeries incorporate into the Holy Bible from Buddhism. They are not facts concerned with Jesus in any way!

Those who became the disciples of Jesus were told that they must renounce the world, give up all thoughts of worldly riches, and avow poverty (St. Matthew 6: 24-

Buddhism	Christianity
this purpose am I going to the city of Benares, to give light to those enshrouded in darkness, and to open the gate of Immortality to man".	34).
	When Jesus' time on earth was about to end, he told of the things that would happen in future times, and said unto his disciples:
Buddha said: "Though the heavens were to fall to earth, and the great world be swallowed up and pass away: Though Mount Sumera were to crack to pieces, and the great ocean be dried up, yet, Ananda, be assured, the words of Buddha are true".	"Go ye therefore, and teach all nations …"
	"Teaching them to observe all things whatsoever I have commanded you: and, lo, I am with you always, even unto the end of the world. Amen" (St. Matthew 28: 19-20).
Buddha said: "There is no passion more violent than voluptuousness. Happily there is but one such passion. If there were two, not a man in the whole universe could follow the truth. Beware of fixing your eyes upon women. If you find yourself in their company, let it be as though you were not present. If you speak with them, guard well your hearts".	"And behold, one came and said unto him, Good Master, what good thing shall I do, that I may have eternal life?"
	"Jesus said unto him, If thou wilt be perfect, go and sell that thou hast, and give (it) to the poor, and thou shalt have treasure in heaven: and come and follow me" (St. Matthew 19: 16 and 21).
Buddha said: "'A wise man should avoid married life as if it were a burning pit of live coals. Those who cannot live in a state of celibacy should not commit adultery".	"From that time Jesus began to preach, and to say, Repent: for the kingdom of heaven is at hand" (St. Matthew 4: 17).
"Buddhism is convinced that if a man reaps sorrow, disappointment, pain, he himself, and no other, must at some time have sown folly, error, sin; and if not in this life then in some former birth".	Jesus, after his temptation by the devil, went and dwelt in the city of Capernaum. "The people which sat in darkness saw great light; and to them which sat in the region and shadow of death light is sprung up" (St. Matthew 4: 16).

THE TEACHINGS OF HOLY JESUS

Buddhism

Buddha knew the thoughts of others: "By directing his mind to the thoughts of others, he can know the thoughts of all beings".

When Buddha was about to become an ascetic, and while riding on the horse "Kantako", his path was strewn with flowers, scattered there by the Devas.

The Eight Beatitudes

1. "BLESSED are they who know and whose knowledge is free from delusion and superstition.
2. "BLESSED are they, who speak what they know in a kindly, open and truthful manner.
3. "BLESSED are they, whose conduct is peaceful, honest and pure.
4. "BLESSED are they, who earn their livelihood in a way that brings no hurt or danger to any living things.
5. "BLESSED are the tranquil, who have cast out ill will, pride, self-righteousness, and put in their place love, piety and sympathy.
6. "BLESSED are ye when ye direct your best efforts to self-training and self-control.
7. "BLESSED beyond measure are ye, when ye are by this means unwrapped from the limits of selfhood.
8. "And BLESSED, finally are they

Christianity

"Verily I say unto you ... Heaven and earth shall pass away: but my words shall not pass away" (St. Luke 21: 32-33).

"Ye have heard" Jesus is supposed to have said "that it was said of old time, Thou shalt not commit adultery:

"But I say unto you, That whosoever looketh on a woman to lust after her hath committed adultery with her already in his heart" (St. Matthew 5: 27-28).

"It is good for a man not to touch a woman"

"But if they cannot contain, let them marry: for it is better to marry than to burn"

"To avoid fornication, let every man have his own wife, and let every woman have her own husband" (1 Corinthians 7: 1, 9, 2).

"And as Jesus passed by, he saw a man which was blind from his birth. And his disciples asked him, saying, Master, who did sin, this man, or his parents, that he was born blind?" (St. John 9; 1-2).

Jesus could read the thoughts of others. By directing his mind to the thoughts of others, he knew the thoughts of all-beings.

When Jesus was entering Jerusalem,

Buddhism	Christianity
who find rapture in contemplating what is deeply and really true about this world and our life in it." (*Reader's Digest*—August, 1955, page 33, "Buddha, The Enlightened One" by Max Eastman).	riding on an ass "And many spread their garments in the way (in honour of Jesus to ride over them): and others cut down branches off the trees, and strawed them in the way (of Jesus to ride over them)" (St. Mark 11: 7-8).

1. "BLESSED are the poor in spirit: for theirs is the kingdom of heaven" (St. Matthew 5: 3).
2. "BLESSED are they that mourn: for they shall be comforted" (St. Matthew 5: 4).
3. "BLESSED are the meek: for they shall inherit the earth" (St. Matthew 5: 5).
4. "BLESSED are they which do hunger and thirst after righteousness: for they shall be filled" (St. Matthew 5: 6).
5. "BLESSED are the merciful: for they shall obtain mercy" (St. Matthew 5: 7).
6. "BLESSED are the pure in heart: for they shall see God" (St. Matthew 5: 8).
7. "BLESSED are the peacemakers for they shall be called the children of god" (St. Matthew 5: 9).
8. "BLESSED are they which are persecuted for righteousness sake: for theirs is the kingdom of heaven" (St. Matthew 5: 10).

K. Conclusions on the Teachings of the Holy Jesus

It is well known that Jesus began to preach when he was about 30 years old (St. Luke 3: 23).

Jesus was lifted bodily to heaven in the presence of his disciples at the age of about 33 years (Acts 1: 9-11).

Thus Jesus preached in the world for a brief period of about 3 years only, before being lifted bodily to heaven!

In such a short duration it was impossible for Jesus to have taught two contradictory doctrines simultaneously *viz*:

a. The corrected version of the Old Testament.

b. Its contradiction *i.e.* Paganism of Nimrod's Sun-worship that was prevalent under the name of Mithraism with its blasphemies, idolatries and mockeries of God's Laws!

Therefore the question to be decided by the readers for themselves is: What did the *Real Jesus teach*?

a) Were they God's Laws?

or

b) Are God's Laws a curse?

Immediately the question arises: *Which Jesus to accept*?

1. The Admission of the Church Authorities

The research carried out by the Authorities of the Churches confirm that all the present day beliefs of the Christians have originated from pagan sources. For example, the book entitled *"Essay on the Development of the Christian Doctrine"* published in 1878 by John Henry Newman who was made a Cardinal in 1879 by Pope Leo XII reads as follows in Chapter 8 of the 1881 edition, pages 355, 371 and 373.

"Confiding then in the power of Christianity to resist the infection of evil, and to transmute the very instruments and appendages of demon worship to an evangelical use, and feeling also that these usages had originally come from primitive revelations and from the instinct of nature, though they had been corrupted; and that they must invent what they needed, if they did not use what they found; *and that they were moreover possessed of the very archetypes, of which paganism attempted the shadows; the rulers of the Church from early times were prepared, should the occasion arise, to adopt, to imitate, or sanction the existing rites and customs of the populace, as well as the philosophy of the educated class*".

"The use of temples, and these dedicated to particular saints, and ornamented on occasions with branches of trees; incense, lamps, and candles; votive offerings on recovery from illness; holy water; asylums; holy days and seasons, use of calendars, processions, blessings on the fields, sacerdotal vestments, the tonsure, the ring in marriage, turning to the East, images at a later date, perhaps the ecclesiastical chant, and the Kyrie Eleison, *are all of pagan origin, and sanctified by adoption into the church*".

After this candid admission by the authorities of the Christian Churches it is absolutely clear and well established now that the religion presently being preached by the Christian churches is nothing but the *"religion of Babylon"* which was invented by the cursed King Nimrod, "the mighty hunter in rebellion against God" into which have been incorporated, with the passage of time, the teachings of Buddhism. This combined religion was known as Mithraism since more than a century before the birth of Jesus. From 325 A.D. when the Greek Gospels were written, after the destruction of many of the Hebrew Originals, the religion has been renamed after Christos or Christ, the word coined by St. Constantine, the Great Roman Emperor and is known today as Christianity.

2. Has the Church the Right to Sanctify Blasphemy, Idolatry and Wickedness under the Holy Bible?

But do such blasphemies, mockeries and wickedness according to the Holy Bible become consecrated and holy just because the Church has sanctified them?

Let us read a few passages from the New Testament:

"Jesus answered and said unto him, If a man love me, he will keep my words ...

"He that loveth me not keepeth not my sayings: and the word (*i.e.* the Evangel in Hebrew) which ye hear is not mine, but the Father's which (He) sent (to) me (through Angel Gabriel)" (St. John 14: 23-24).

"If ye love me, keep my commandments" (St. John 14: 15).

"For I testify unto every man that heareth the words of the prophecy of this book, if any man (*i.e.* Peter or Paul or Marcus or Luke or Constantine or the Church of Christ or anybody else) shall add unto these things (*i.e.* the Hebrew Evangel dictated by Jesus during his life), God shall add unto him the plagues that are written in this book:

"And if any man shall take away from the words of the book (of Jesus *i.e.* 'Evangel) of this prophecy, God shall take away his part out of the book of (those blessed with eternal) life (of happiness) and out of the holy city (*i.e.* Heaven), and from the things which are written in this book (the Hebrew Evangel)" (Revelation 22: 18-19).

From these quotations it is evident that the authorities of the Christian Churches, if they are followers of the *Real Jesus, then they have no right whatsoever to change even a single word from the original Hebrew Evangel* dictated by Jesus during his life and recorded by the several Jewish scribes in Aramaic script, some of which were burnt and destroyed in 325. A.D., whilst others were misplaced or lost. But the Gospel of Barnabas, one of the Original Hebrew Evangels, though still in existence, is being deliberately suppressed, very surprisingly by the Church of Christ!

3. The Contentions of the Church

The contentions of Constantine's *Jesus, the Christ of Society*, can be summed up as follows:

a. To mock God by calling His Laws a curse contrary to the teachings of the *Real Jesus*.

b. To disobey God's laws and say Christ (*i.e.* Nimrod) has absolved us from the curse of the Laws of God in contradiction to the teachings of the Jesus who is son of the Virgin Mary, a human being, hence not the son of a God!

c. Good deeds are not relevant. The followers of Christ live by the faith that Christ, the son of God, by the sacrifice of his life had redeemed those sinners, who have baptised themselves and eaten sacramental meals, drunk wine and enjoyed swine-flesh! Thus they did everything contrary to the teachings of Jesus of Nazareth who was the son of a human being *viz*: the Virgin Mary, hence not the son of a God.

d. To commit idolatry by praying before "Idols" even though this was forbidden by the *Real Jesus*!

e. To break the everlasting law of circumcision which Jesus, the Jew, and all his disciples, who were also Jews, observed.

f. To commit blasphemy against God by setting up rivals as the "Son of God" and "Trinity in Unity"—the teachings of Nimrod!

g. To eat Abraham's flesh as swine flesh because he is the enemy who destroyed Nimrod, the so-called only begotten son of god.

h. To be baptised to come under the spell of Nimrod, instead of promising to follow the laws of God as taught by Jesus of Nazareth!

i. To call a human being the "Infallible Pontifex Maximus", an

j. honour which is due to none but God Alone.

k. To make *God inferior to Christ* who would sit on the right hand of God and other such blasphemies, profanities and absurdities.

Such absurdities were considered holy and pious things instead of wicked manifestations, according to Christianity just because the Church has adapted and sanctified them!

Thus *God, the Real Jesus and the Evangel* are not of any significance before the Church of Christianity which is supreme and surpasses all of them when it sanctifies something! Does not such a claim of the Christian Church remind one of the following passage in the Holy Bible:

> "BABYLON hath been a golden cup in the Lord's hands that made all the earth drunken: the nations have drunken of her wine (of magical intoxication by baptism and the magical sign of the cross, the initial of Tammuz), therefore the nations are MAD" (Jeremiah 51: 7).

4. Nimrod's Religious Influence

In the Old Testament we find several references as to how the magical charms of this evil genius, Nimrod, will control completely the minds and deeds of the people of the world (even for many millennia after his violent death) in acts of disbelief against God Almighty!

A few quotations are given hereunder:

"For thus saith the LORD GOD of Israel unto me; Take the wine cup of this fury at my hand, and cause all the nations, to whom I send thee, to drink it.

"And they shall drink, and be moved, *and be mad, because of the sword* (this is an apparent reference to Constantine, the founder of the Church of Christ, and his verse of the SWORD, St. Matthew 10: 34, incorporated in the Greek Bible) *that I will send among them.*

"Then took I the cup at the LORD's hand, and made all the nations to drink, unto whom the Lord had sent me:

"To wit, Jerusalem, and the cities of Judah, and the kings thereof, and the princes thereof, to make them a desolation, an astonishment, an hissing, and a curse; as it is this day;

"Pharaoh king of Egypt, and his servants, and his princes, and all his people;

"And all the mingled people, and all the kings of the land of Uz, and all the kings of the land of the Philistines and Ashkelon, and Azzah, and Ekron, and the remnant of Ashdod.

"Edom, and Moab, and the children of Ammon,

"And all the-kings of Tyrus, and all the kings of Zidon, and the kings of the isles which are beyond the sea.

"Dedan, and Tema, and Buz, and all that are in the utmost corners (of the earth),

"And all the kings of Arabia, and all the kings of the mingled people that dwell in the desert.

"And all the kings of Zimri, and all the kings of Elam, and all the kings of the Medes,

"And all the kings of the north, far and near, one with

another, and all the kingdoms of the world, which are upon the face of the earth: and the king of Sheshach shall drink after them.

"Therefore thou shalt say unto them, Thus saith the LORD of hosts, the God of Israel; Drink ye, and be drunken, and spue and fall, and rise no more, because of the sword (*i.e.* Constantine's Christ) which I will send among you" (Jeremiah 25: 15-27).

This clearly proves that according to the Holy Bible the whole world would be affected and influenced by the spell cast by Nimrod, the accursed. Further, the influence of this religion would be so profound that people would follow it blindly just like a drunkard who had lost himself under the influence of intoxication! Further, according to the Holy Bible these followers would be MAD because they would refuse to accept the truth! They would deny the proofs when given to them and would try to twist them and their hearts would be hardened against the true God, just as Nimrod's was until his last breath (see *Destruction or Peace*, Chapter 6: I and J). They would try to perpetuate Nimrod's religion, even knowing that it has been cursed at the Tower of Babel and would lead mankind from disaster to disaster until it is effaced eventually at the Battle of Armageddon.

Chapter 10

The mission of Holy Jesus

A. Introduction

It is accepted universally that Jesus was gifted with powers of performing wondrous miracles, as also with pre-cognition. Thus he was fully aware of those, who would destroy deliberately and systematically his teachings, which unfortunately are now no longer being practised as already seen from the previous chapter.

Jesus not only knew this fact but he also announced publicly that Peter would fall into the hands of Satan and destroy the religion taught by Jesus. This warning of Jesus is in the original name of Peter which was "Simon". This warning is worded:

"And the Lord said, Simon, Simon; behold, Satan hath desired to have you, that he may sift you as wheat" (St. Luke 22: 31).

When Jesus saw that Peter was not improving himself and coming to the true and correct path he declared as follows:

"But he (Jesus) turned and *said unto Peter, Get thee behind me, Satan*; thou art an offence unto me: for thou savourest not things that be of God, but those that be of men.

"For what is a man profited, if he shall gain the whole world and lose his soul? ..." (St. Matthew 16: 23 and 26).

This is exactly what Peter actually did when he preached the foundations of Nimrod's religion *viz*:

    a. "Baptism"

    b. "The Law of God was a curse"

    c. "Good deeds no longer mattered"

    d. "Faith in the Saviour and Sacramental Food and drinks were enough" *etc.*

These anti-God teachings have become the corner-stones of the new Religion of Peter and his collaborator Paul and the dissidents, who formed the Brethren Faith (see *Destruction or Peace*, Chapter 12: C) for teaching to the Pagans.

In course of time, under the chairmanship of Constantine, this religion, which had no affinity with Jesus, has incorporated in it every little detail of the faith, the rites, the dates and the teachings of King Nimrod, the cursed, the mighty hunter in rebellion against God. (See *Destruction or Peace*, Chapter 12: F 1-10; G 1-16 and K 1-4).

Jesus knew fully well what was going to happen to his teachings and through whom and how his followers would destroy eventually the "Evangel" the Divine Book dictated personally by him during his lifetime in Hebrew and noted down in Aramaic Script by Levi, son of Alphaeus, and other Hebrew scribes. Under such circumstances it is quite logical and evident that the teachings of Jesus could never have been his mission on earth, if they were going to be destroyed and not followed!

Indeed something far greater and more outstanding must have been the mission of one who had been favoured by the Almighty to have such a miraculous birth through the Virgin Mary, the only one of its kind in the known history of mankind (see *Destruction or Peace*, Chapter 10), and that also on a chosen day, date and month on which great events of far reaching consequence for mankind have taken place throughout the ages (see *Destruction or Peace*, Chapter 11).

Therefore the following questions pose themselves in everyone's mind:

1. What was the great mission of the *Real Jesus* on earth when it was not his teachings even according to Jesus himself?
2. What evidence is available in support of this from reliable original sources?
3. How can the great mission of the *Real Jesus* be proved by the evidence still available, if any, in the Bible in its present form?

Systematic research on these problems throws a light upon the quest before us. To go into every minute detail would require a much larger book. Hence only a few relative details are quoted hereafter which should suffice to grasp the essence of the Mission of Jesus when it is remembered that Jesus has made it absolutely clear in St. Matthew 5: 17; that he had not come to disrupt the purpose for which the earlier prophets of God had come.

Hence let us start our quest in an organised way to proceed towards our goal "The Mission of Jesus" by taking a look at The Holy Bible.

B. Who is the Promised Seed through Whom the World would be blessed according to the Holy Bible?

The prayer of Jesus in the New Testament just before he was lifted to heaven bodily is quoted hereunder:

> "I pray for them (*i.e.* only the followers of the real Jesus): **I pray not for the World, but (only) for them, Which Thou hast given me ...**" (St. John 17: 9).

Thus it is clear that if Jesus was the Promised seed through whom the world would be blessed he would surely have prayed at this moment particularly for the whole world and not for only his followers! Hence according to Jesus, as recorded in the Holy Bible, he is definitely not that promised seed of Abraham through whom the whole world would be blessed and whose description in the Holy Bible is as follows:

> "... And of the covenant which God made with our fathers, saying unto Abraham, and *in thy seed shall all the kindreds of the earth be blessed*" (Acts 3: 25).

In Galatians 3: 3 we again read that God had informed Abraham "... *in thee (i.e. thy seed) shall all nations be blessed*".

Therefore the real Jesus has shown undeniably in the New Testament according to his own prayer for his followers only and not for the world that he is not that "Promised seed through whom the world shall be blessed" but that personage must be someone else, someone who will be the "Comforter" of the whole world!

This promised seed will therefore have to be a saviour for the whole world. As against that the real Jesus has, unmistakably and without any scope for argument, shown that he had come for the upliftment of only the Jews:

> ... *preaching the word to none but unto the Jews only*" (Acts 11: 19).

> "These twelve Jesus sent forth, and commanded them, saying, *Go not into the way of the Gentiles, and into any city of the Samaritans enter ye not*!

> "But go rather to the lost sheep of the house of Israel" (St. Matthew 10: 5-6).

All these references from the Holy Bible make it explicit that Jesus had come for Jews only and not for the whole world! Even prophet John, the son of Zakariah, the forerunner to Jesus, has informed us in the New Testament that the promised, sought-for Prophet was a different person to Jesus who would be coming with one "Elias" and that both of them would be after Jesus (St. John 1: 19-21 and 25).

Further the Old Testament informs us that the promised Prophet was to be from a brethren tribe to the Jews (Deuteronomy 18: 18) whilst Jesus was a Jew and that the (promised) Prophet would be a blessing and a comfort for the whole world. We are also informed that this Promised Prophet would speak face to face with God as Moses did as a man speaketh unto his friend (Exodus 33: 11) which Jesus never did. Neither is any one claiming in the Bible or elsewhere that Jesus confronted God as Moses did. Hence it is clear that Jesus is not this Promised Seed.

Jesus has himself clarified in the New Testament that he had come not to destroy the Mosaic Laws but to fulfil them (St. Matthew 5: 17) whilst the promised Prophet would come with a complete set of new Laws of God which would remodel and complete the old Mosaic Laws of God (Acts 3: 22-25).

Thus Jesus has shown repeatedly from his prayers and his preaching's that he is not that promised seed of Abraham through whom mankind would be blessed but on the contrary he has come for those who follow him from amongst only the Jews.

In fact Jesus has himself preached about this Promised seed, the Comforter, through whom the whole world would be blessed, in the Holy Bible, as follows:

"If ye love me, keep my commandments.

"And I will pray the father, and he shall give you *another Comforter* (*i.e.* not Jesus himself) that he (this Promised Prophet or the Comforter) may abide with you forever (*i.e.*

Jesus and his teachings have not come to abide forever but only for a temporary intermediary period);

"Even the Spirit of truth (*i.e.* the Holy Spirit from which God has created everything); whom the world cannot receive, because it seeth him not (now), neither knoweth him: but ye know him (from the descriptions I have given of him); ...

"I will not leave you comfortless: I will come to you (again at the time of the battle of Armageddon).

"But the Comforter (*i.e.* Parakletos in Greek; translated into Arabic it becomes Ahmad Rahmat-ul-lil-Aalamin), which is the Holy Ghost (Logos out of which God has created everything, see *Destruction or Peace*, Chapter 17: A 1-8 and B 1-6), whom the Father will send (will tell you what has been taught correctly or incorrectly) in my name, he shall teach you all things, and bring all things to your remembrance, whatsoever I have said unto you" (St. John 14: 15-18 and 26) *i.e.* to say he, the "Comforter" of the world, the promised seed through whom the whole world would be blessed will teach the world all things and thus complete the religion of God on earth which came down step by step. Each time a set of laws was destroyed, another list of laws more elaborate was sent down not only to correct the distortions but also to avoid its destruction by the previous methods (see *Destruction or Peace*, Chapter 15: E; 18: H and I) and bring to the remembrance of the followers of Jesus the various signs given by Jesus with which to recognise him, *viz*:

a. A piece of cloud would shade him by day (page 167, *The Gospel of Barnabas*).

b. He would have the seal of Prophethood on his right shoulder (Isaiah 9: 6).

c. He would speak to God as one friend speaks to another *etc.* (Deuteronomy 18: 18).

d. He would rest under the tree planted by Abraham at

Beersheba (Genesis 21: 33), where only those who would be prophets of God could rest and pray (see *Destruction or Peace*, Chapter 13: H).

e. He would not accept charity but would accept a gift (see *Destruction or Peace*, Chapter 13: I).

f. He would be born at a place which is South of the land of Palestine. He would be a breaker of idols and a destroyer of idolatry just as Abraham had been the breaker of idols (page 223, *The Gospel of Barnabas*).

g. Idols all over the earth will fall down upon the ground and miraculously speak announcing the birth of the promised messenger (page 169, *The Gospel of Barnabas*).

h. "But when the comforter is come, whom I will send unto you from the Father, even the Spirit of Truth, which proceedeth from the Father, he shall testify of me (This means that the promised Comforter when he comes would confirm the miraculous birth of Jesus and that Jesus was not crucified but lifted alive to heaven *etc.*);

"And ye also shall bear witness, because ye have been with me from the beginning (and I have given to you detailed descriptions about him which Arius and the Nazarene priests have confirmed as to the mission of Jesus as will be read hereafter)" (St. John 15: 26-27).

i. He would recite the message of God when in a state of trance, as if divinely inspired:

"Nevertheless I tell you The Truth; it is expedient for you that I (*i.e.* my, teachings the "Evangel") *go away* (*i.e.* be destroyed): *for if I* (*i.e.* my teachings the "Evangel") *go not away* (*i.e.* until the Evangel is not destroyed), *The comforter will not come unto you but if I depart* (*i.e.* when the Evangel is destroyed then after about the same period for which it had existed will become disclosed the Promised Seed through whom the world will be blessed, as shown by the calculations of Arius given hereafter),

I will send him unto you.

"And when he is come, he will reprove the world of sin, and of righteousness, and of judgment:

"Of sin, because they believe not on me (but only pretend because they will use my name to deceive the world by pretending that Christianity is the religion taught by Jesus, when in reality it is Nimrodism);

"Of righteousness, because I go to my Father, and ye see me no more;

"Of judgment, because the prince of this world is judged.

j. *I have yet many things to say unto you, but ye cannot bear them now* (*i.e.* Jesus has not completed the teachings of God on earth because the people cannot bear them now).

k. "*Howbeit when he, The Spirit of Truth* (*i.e.* Logos—see *Destruction or Peace*, Chapter 17: A, 1-8), *is come, he will guide you into all truth* (and not Jesus): *for he shall not speak of himself; but whatsoever he shall hear* (from God), *that shall he speak* (in Arabic Al-Qur'an—see *Destruction or Peace*, Chapter 18): *and he will show you things to come*" (St. John 16: 7-13).

The following passages are from pages 225-227 of "*The Gospel of Barnabas*":

"Then said the Priest: 'How shall the Messiah be called, and what sign shall reveal his coming?'

"*Jesus answered*: 'The name of the Messiah is admirable, for God Himself gave him the name when He had created his soul, and placed it in a celestial splendour. God said: "*Wait Muhammad; for thy sake I will to create paradise, the world, and a great multitude of creatures whereof I make thee a present, insomuch that who so shall bless thee, shall be blessed, and whoso shall curse thee, shall be accursed. When I shall send thee unto the World, I shall send thee as My messenger of salvation, and thy Word shall be true, insomuch that heaven and earth shall fail, but thy faith shall never fail."* '**Muhammad is his Blessed name**'."

"Then the crowd lifted up their voices saying: *'O God, send us Thy messenger: O Muhammad, come quickly for the salvation of the World!'*

Ahmad and Muhammad are the two most popular names of the Prophet of Arabia. For their meaning and origin see *Destruction or Peace*, Chapter 17: A-5.

Sir William Muir says in *"Life of Mahomet"* that the word "Ahmad" might "have been erroneously employed as a translation of Perikalutas in some Arabic version of the *New Testament*".

Barnabas whose personal name was Joseph was a companion of Jesus and one of the 120 Jews who were converted to the faith of Jesus. This Barnabas has recorded as read here before that Jesus has said:

1. God created Paradise, the world and a great multitude of creatures for the sake of Muhammad.

2. Paradise, the world and all created things have been given as a gift from God to Muhammad.

3. Muhammad will come on earth as God's messenger of Salvation, (*i.e.* in Arabic "Rahmat-ul-lil-Alameen", one of the titles given by God to Muhammad).

4. Those who shall follow Muhammad and send blessings upon him will be blessed by God, but those who will disbelieve in Muhammad will be accursed by God.

5. The heaven and the earth will be destroyed eventually but the teachings of Muhammad shall never fail.

Not only Jesus and his disciples but also the Last of the Heavenly Books confirm that the promised seed of Abraham through whom the whole of the UNIVERSE will be blessed is Muhammad and that his religion shall never be demolished:

> "We (Allah) sent thee (Muhammad) not (for any purpose) but as a mercy for the whole creation" (Qur'an 21: 107).

> "He (Allah) it is Who hath sent His messenger (Muhammad) with guidance and the Religion of Truth, that he may cause it to prevail (from the time of the battle of Armageddon) over all religions, however much the disbelievers may be averse (Qur'an 9: 33).

From these it would appear that when the original Evangel in Hebrew Aramaic was burnt and destroyed in 325 A.D. and the Bible in the Greek language was prepared that the proper name Ahmed Rahmat-ul-lil-Alameen was translated into "Parakletos", although in the Arabic translation of the *New Testament* the word "Ahmad" is still there, as observed by Sir William Muir in his book "*Life of Mahomet*".

C. The Promised Comforter according to the New Testament

Jesus has said as recorded in "*The Gospel of Barnabas*" pages 97-99 as follows:

> Then the disciples wept after this discourse, and Jesus was weeping, when they saw many who came to find him, for the chiefs of the priests took counsel among themselves to catch him (Jesus) in his talk. Wherefore they sent the Levites and some of the scribes to question him, saying: 'Who art thou?'

> "Jesus confessed, and told the truth: 'I am not the Messiah.'

> "They said: 'Art thou Elijah or Jeremiah, or any of the ancient prophets?'.

> "Jesus answered: 'No.'

> "Then said they: 'Who art thou? Say, in order that we may give testimony to those who sent us.'

"Then Jesus said: 'I am a voice that crieth, through all Judaea, and crieth: "Prepare ye the way for the messenger of the Lord," even as it is written in Esaias.'

"They said: 'If thou be not the Messiah nor Elijah, or any (of the olden) prophets, wherefore dost thou preach a new doctrine, and make thyself of more account than the Messiah?'

"Jesus answered: 'The miracles which God worketh by my hands show that I speak that which God willeth; nor indeed do I make myself to be accounted as him of whom ye speak. *For I am not worthy to unloose the ties of the hosen or the latchets of the shoes of the messenger of God whom ye call "Messiah," who was made before me, and shall come after me, and shall bring the words of truth (i.e. the Qur'an), so that his faith shall have no end*".

The Jewish Priests had asked these very same questions not only of Jesus but also earlier of Prophet John son of Zakariah. Hence it is apparent that the Jews were awaiting anxiously the arrival of the Promised Prophet. These questions and the answers of Prophet John are quoted herein from the Holy Bible:

"And this is the record of John (son of Zakariah), when the Jews sent Priests and Levites from Jerusalem to ask him, Who art thou?

"And he confessed, and denied not; but confessed, I am not the Christ (this word was coined by Constantine in 325 A.D.).

"And they asked him, What then? Art thou Elias? And he saith, I am not. Art thou that (Promised) prophet? And he answered, No.

"And they asked him, and said unto him, Why baptizes thou then, if thou be not that Christ, nor Elias, neither that (Promised) prophet?" (St. John 1: 19-21 and 25).

From these passages it becomes clear that:-

a. Jews were aware from their holy books that three great personages were going to come whose description or names were:

1. "Jesus" (in the Hebrew language the original name of Jesus is "Eisa". When the Greek language was used the original name of Eisa was corrupted into Jesus by changing the "Ei" into "Je" and adding "us" at the end of it. Thus the correct name of Jesus is "Eisa").

2. "Elias" (In original Hebrew this name was pronounced "Eli" or "Ali" but corrupted by Greek translators into Elias by adding "as" to the end of it).

3. The (Promised) Prophet.

b. From these quotations in their *New Testament* the believers of Jesus were thus fully aware that after Jesus were to come two great personages *viz*:

1. "Elias" or according to the Hebrew pronunciation "Ali".

2. The (Promised) Prophet.

c. Further we find in the *New Testament* that Jesus has been described as:

Jesus, Son of Mary

Jesus, son of man

The Promised Seed

Christ

Son of God *etc.*

But Jesus has never been described as "the Prophet". Hence any reference to 'The Prophet" in the Holy Bible must obviously mean "The (Promised) Prophet" referred to in the above quotations of St. John 1, who was to come after Jesus and further that "The (Promised) Prophet" was very definitely and distinctly quite a different person from Jesus, who has never been described anywhere in the New Testament as "The Prophet"!

Now if one looks at The Acts of the Apostles, one will read the following passages:

> For Moses truly said unto the fathers, *A prophet* shall the Lord your God raise up unto you (twelve tribes of Israel) of your brethren (tribe *i.e.* descendants of Ishmael), like unto me (*i.e.* one who will speak face to face with God just like one converses with his friend—Exodus 33: 11); him shall ye hear in all things whatsoever he shall say unto you.
>
> "And it shall come to pass (after a passage of sometime *i.e.* at the battle of Armageddon), that every soul, which will not hear that (Promised) prophet, shall be destroyed from among the people (of the earth).
>
> "Yea, and all the prophets, from Samuel and those that follow after, as many as have spoken, have likewise foretold (of the coming of this Promised Prophet of the final period) ..." (Acts 3: 22-24).

From the New Testament it becomes explicit that both the Jews as well as the true followers of Jesus are fully aware that *the promised Prophet* will be quite a different person from Jesus and that he would be one of the two great personages that were to come at some stage after Jesus (St. John 1: 19-21, 25).

The fact that they *i.e.* both the Jews and the Nazarenes, the followers of Jesus have recognised Muhammad of Arabia as the Promised Prophet of the final period (as will be read hereafter) makes it clear that if the world is to achieve unity, harmony, love and brotherhood it has to follow the Promised Comforter of the whole world, the Promised seed of Abraham from the brethren tribe to the Jews (*i.e.* the descendants of Ishmael) through whom the whole world would be blessed, as declared by Jesus (see *Destruction or Peace*, Chapter 7: G-8) when he proves that the Bible has been forged, and teaches the cursed pagan religion of Nimrod, by whatever name it may be called including Christianity. It was Nimrodism that broke up the unity of mankind by God's curse upon it at the Tower of Babel (Genesis 11: 6-9) and which will continue to disrupt the unity of mankind so long as it is followed by millions of people, who are drunk and drowned in the intoxication of the spell of Nimrod which God has described in the Holy Bible, as:

> "*Babylon, hath been a golden cup in the Lord's hand that made all the earth drunken*: the nations have drunken of her wine (of magical intoxication by baptism and the sign of the cross); therefore the nations are *Mad*" (Jeremiah 51: 7).

With the present trend of deterioration and dissensions in international relations, resulting in two of the biggest disasters in human history, the two world wars between the Christians, the believers in the same "Holy Bible" and the same "Christ" and that also within a quarter of a century, mankind, especially the Christians seem to be suffering from some form of insanity. It is indeed unbelievable that in spite of the terrific progress of science so much devastation has not only been caused by the two world wars but that even a holocaust is also feared in the near future. One would expect that the advancement in learning should lead to greater understanding, peace and tranquillity for all. Instead we live in a world full of surcharged tension and terror as never known before. Undoubtedly something is wrong. It could be our religion that is misconceived by following the false Jesus Christ. Hence the cause of misunderstanding between man and man as mentioned in the above quoted passage from the Holy Bible, which clearly shows what an all-pervasive influence Nimrodism still has over mankind. Even after 4,000 years we are behaving like those who are insane in spite of all our achievements and advanced scientific knowledge of today!

D. The Promised Prophet honoured as "Lord" in the Holy Bible

Numerous prophets have referred to the "Promised Prophet" in the Holy Bible as their "Lord" *e.g.*:

> "Then said Jesus: 'And the messenger of God when he shall come, of what lineage will he be?'
>
> "The disciples answered: 'Of David.'
>
> "Whereupon Jesus said: 'Ye deceive yourselves; for David in spirit calleth him lord, saying thus: *"God said to my lord (i.e. the saviour), sit thou on my right hand until I make thine enemies thy footstool. God shall send forth thy rod which shall have lordship in the midst of thine enemies."* If the messenger of God whom ye call Messiah were the son of David, *how should David call him lord* (instead of my son or descendant)? Believe me, for verily I say to you, that the promise was made in Ishmael, not in Isaac'." (Page 103, *The Gospel of Barnabas*).

The *New Testament* confirms the same facts as:

> "While the Pharisees were gathered together, Jesus asked them,
>
> "Saying, what think ye of the Saviour, whose son is he? They say unto him, The Son of David.
>
> *"He (Jesus) saith unto them, How then doth David in spirit call him lord, saying,*
>
> *"The Lord (God) said unto my lord (the Saviour), Sit thou on my right hand, till I make thine enemies thy footstool*?
>
> "If David then call him Lord, how is he (the Saviour) his son (*i.e.* descendant)?" (St. Matthew 22: 41-45).

King David has stated in the *Old Testament*:

> *"The Lord (God) said unto my lord (the Saviour), Sit thou at*

my right hand, until I make thine enemies thy footstool.

"*The Lord (God) shall send the rod of thy strength out of Zion* (*i.e.* the Prophethood which was so long with the Jews will go out of Zion or the Jewish kingdom of Jerusalem): *rule thou* (Oh Saviour) *in the midst of thine* (*i.e.* the Saviour will be given dominion over his) enemies!

"The LORD (GOD) hath sworn, and will not repent, *thou* (Oh Saviour) *art a Priest for ever.*

"The LORD (GOD) at thy (the Saviour's) right hand shall strike through kings in the day of his wrath (at the Battle of Armageddon).

"He shall judge among the heathen, he shall fill the places with the dead bodies; he shall wound the heads over many countries" (Psalms 110: 1-2, 4-6).

"Behold, I will send my (Promised) messenger, and he shall prepare the way before me: and the lord (Promised Saviour), whom ye seek, shall suddenly come to his temple, (he is) even the (Promised) messenger of the covenant (made with Abraham when he had taken Ishmael his first born only son for sacrifice), whom ye delight in; behold, be shall come, saith the LORD (GOD) of hosts" (Malachi 3: 1).

Moses in his farewell message has not only called the Promised Prophet, the Saviour as his "lord" but he has also forecast to the Jews concerning the following:

1. That the prophethood which was with the Jews since the time of Jacob would be transferred from Sinai or Palestine to another race.

2. That this promised prophet would become famous all over the world from a place known in those Biblical days as "Seir".

3. That this promised prophet will be revealed at "a Mount at

Paran".

4. That since the people of Paran would force the Promised Prophet to leave his birth place, be would come with an army of 10,000 saintly persons and capture his birth-place.

5. After capturing Paran a fiery law would be established eliminating idolatry for all time.

6. That this Promised Prophet would forgive all the trouble-makers in Paran.

7. That after capturing Paran be would purge the place of idols and sit down and pray with all his followers at the purified temple of God.

8. Moses has commanded by this law that all the Jews follow this Promised Prophet.

9. That this Promised Prophet would be from a tribe of people, who are the brethren of the Jews.

10. That those who will not follow this promised Prophet will be destroyed from amongst the people on the earth at the battle of Armageddon.

Before proceeding further let us pose the questions:

i. According to the Holy Bible where is Paran?

ii. Who was the important Prophet who lived at Paran and was blessed by God according to the Holy Bible?

"And God was with the lad (Ishmael the first born son of Abraham); and he grew, and dwelt in the wilderness, and became an archer.

"And he dwelt in the wilderness of Paran: and his mother took him a wife out of the land of Egypt" (Genesis 21: 20-21).

"And as for Ishmael, I have heard thee (Abraham): Behold, I have blessed him, and will make him fruitful, and will multiply him exceedingly; Twelve princes shall he beget, and I will make him a great nation" (Genesis 17: 20).

PARAN is the place where Ishmael grew up, lived in and died in and is buried there. This place is now called Mecca (see *Destruction or Peace*, Chapter 7: G, H and I).

Now let us refer to the Torah:

"AND this is the blessing, wherewith Moses the man of God blessed the children of Israel before his death.

"And he said, The *Lord* (The Saviour) came from Sinai (*i.e.* the prophethood which was with the Jews at Sinai or Jerusalem came from Jerusalem to), and rose up from Seir (*i.e.* the hill at Madinah) unto them (*i.e.* the Saviour would become famous from Madinah amongst the Jews settled by King Tibba at Madinah to await the arrival of the Promised Prophet, see *Destruction or Peace*, Chapter 13: F), he (the Saviour) shined forth from Cave Hira on Mount Noor or Light which is a mount (at) Paran (Mecca), and he came with (an army of exactly) ten thousands of saints (to capture Mecca and convert the temple of God known as Bait Ullah at Kaabah in Mecca which had 360 idols in it into the *True House of God*): from his right hand went a fiery law for them (the Saviour on his triumphant entry into Mecca, his birthplace, without even a fight, went to each of the 360 idols in "Bait Ullah" at Kabaah and declared before each of them individually as follows:

"The Truth has prevailed, Darkness has vanished away."

As soon as Muhammad made this announcement before one of the idols in the Bait Ullah pointing towards it with his staff, immediately that particular idol would miraculously break loose from its firm base without anyone touching it, then hurl itself onto the floor smashing itself into small fragments. Muhammad repeated his declaration 360 times that day and one by one all the

360 idols in the Kaabah destroyed themselves in the presence of the awestricken pagan inhabitants of Mecca and the army of Muslims from Madinah, see *Destruction or Peace*, Chapter 17: E-24, also miracle No 212 given on pages 101-102 of *Maujizat-e-Muhammadia*. So profound was the effect of this supernatural manner of destroying idolatry that all the pagans of Mecca converted there and then to Islam. The Kaabah was accordingly cleansed of idolatry and purified into a *True house of Allah* or *Bait Ullah* as it was when originally constructed by Abraham and Ishmael—see *Destruction or Peace*, Chapter 7: H. This miraculous incident became the turning point or foundation upon which commenced the abolition of idolatry throughout Arabia in the 8th year of Hijrah and was completed within two years thereafter during the life-time of the Promised Prophet *the Lord of all the earlier messengers*. Arabia till this day is free from idolatry and the Qur'anic Laws of God are still firmly established.

> "Yea, he (the Prophet) loved the people (of Mecca and forgave them all their crimes and their attempt to murder him); all his saints are in Thy hand (*i.e.* they have surrendered themselves to live their lives according to the will and pleasures of God Almighty—AL-ISLAM) and they sat down (in prayers) at Thy feet (at Kaabah, the temple of God in Mecca); every one (of the pagans of Mecca or Paran) shall receive thy words (*i.e.* each and every one of the people of Mecca upon seeing the wonderful kindness with which Muhammad behaved when he captured Mecca and the miraculous manner in which, he destroyed the 360 idols in the Kaabah willingly came to him and received his teachings and converted to Al-Islam or surrender to the will of God).
>
> "Moses commanded us (the Jews, this order of God that when the Promised Saviour comes they should immediately accept him. This order is made into) a law, even (unto) the inheritance of the congregation of Jacob (*i.e.* all the twelve tribes of the Jews who are the descendants of the twelve sons

of Jacob)" (Deuteronomy 33: 1-4).

"I (God) will raise them (*i.e.* for the guidance of the Jews) a Prophet from among their brethren (*i.e.* not a Jew but from their brethren *i.e.*, the Ishmaelite's), like unto thee (Moses *i.e.*, "And the Lord spake unto Moses face to face, as a man speaketh unto his friend"—Exodus 33: 11) and will put my words in his mouth; and he shall speak unto them all that I shall command him (in Arabic sayings are called "AL-QUR'AN". From this it is clear that it would not be necessary for the Promised Prophet to have any worldly knowledge to read and write).

"And it shall come to pass (after the passage of sometime at the Battle of Armageddon) that whosoever will not hearken unto My words which he (the Promised Prophet) shall speak (*i.e.* the Qur'an) in My name, I will require it of (*i.e.*, punish and destroy) him (at the battle of Armgeddon)" (Deuteronomy 18: 18-19).

The only person besides Moses who has spoken face to face with God is Muhammad. No other Prophet has made such a claim, not even Jesus. Further, Muhammad is the only prophet, who in a state of trance, used to recite the Divine words of God, as if they were put into his mouth—hence the name "AL-QUR'AN" or the recitations of a man who did not know how to read or write a single word (see *Destruction or Peace*, Chapter 18 for further details).

The mount thus referred to in Deuteronomy 33: 2 is definitely Cave Hira on Mount "Nur" (*i.e.* "Light") where the first revelation of the Holy Qur'an was made. This mount is on the outskirts of Mecca city or Paran. This Promised Prophet's teachings of *Al-Islam* or *Surrender to the will of God* would spread all over the earth from Seir *i.e.* Madinah had been foretold in the Holy Bible in Deuteronomy 33:1 by Moses in his parting advice not only to the Jews *i.e. the congregation of Jacob* but also to all believers in the Holy Bible!

The name of the Promised Prophet will be "Mohamadeem" still appears in the Hebrew Text of the *Old Testament* as currently in circulation (see *Destruction or Peace*, Chapter 17: C-6).

Therefore, the Bible has prophesied not only the specific city where the Promised Prophet would be born but even the particular mount at Mecca (Paran) from where Allah's revelations of the Qur'an would emanate, that his teachings would spread from Madinah (Seir) and that his name would be Mohamadeem or Muhammad!

E. The Prophecy of Holy Moses

Moses had been blessed by God so that he could speak to Him face to face just as one friend speaks to another. According to tradition, Moses was in the habit of asking God all kinds of questions. Some of them were as under:

1. Is there any man more learned than me at this time on earth? (Qur'an 18: 60-82).
2. Is there anybody who loves you more than I do? (See *Destruction or Peace*, Chapter 20: A).
3. Will there be any prophet who will be greater than me? and so on.

In reply to the third question according to tradition Allah gave the following answers:

> Yes, there would be a prophet whose saints would be such that they would go to Heaven on the Day of Judgment without having to give any account of their deeds on earth. This prophet would speak not only face to face with God Almighty but would also see Him with the naked eye, which none others will achieve. He would not only spread love, goodwill and

brotherhood amongst mankind without any distinction for caste, colour or nationality, but his followers would also eventually establish world peace under a new system of civilisation when the whole world would become one single community of 'Surrender to the Will of Allah'. Wars would then become a thing of the past. This promised Prophet would be a 'Blessing for the whole universe'." Allah also informed Moses that everything which is in the entire universe has been created out of the spirit of this Promised Prophet. Thus he would have influence over even heavenly bodies. He is the Spirit of Light of Guidance to all the Prophets from Adam. He will be born on earth from the descendants of Ishmael, the first-born and heir of Abraham, that is to say from the brethren tribe to the Jews who are from Isaac, the second son of Abraham. He would be the final prophet till the end of the earth".

Then Moses paid his respects to Muhammad and replied that he was desirous of becoming a follower of this great Promised Prophet, so that he might also go to heaven without having to give an account of his deeds, especially for the soldier of Pharaoh, whom he had killed, for whipping an aged Jew.

God Almighty replied:

"You should be satisfied with the honourable position of being one of My great prophets, but I will take you during your wanderings through the wilderness with the Israelites to the temple built by Abraham for My worship where this Promised Prophet will be born and also to the place from where he will spread My final teachings. His name will be Ahmed, and when this great Promised Prophet of the final period of the earth will come, he will mention the teachings of the earlier prophets. You instruct the Jews that they shall leave aside all My teachings given to them through you and all the other prophets before and after you and hearken unto the call of this Promised Prophet".

Further Allah said,

"I will put My words in his mouth and he shall recite only what I shall command him for the benefit of mankind. Whosoever will not listen unto My words which he shall recite in My name, I will punish them severely, and after some lapse of time would come a great 'Battle' in which all disbelievers in this Promised Prophet and his teachings will be cut off from amongst the people of the earth and, God, shall completely destroy such disbelievers".

"Your people will recognise this Promised Prophet of the final period just as they recognise their own children by the following signs:

He shall have the seal of Prophet-hood on his right shoulder.

He will perform all the miracles, which any other prophet has performed before him.

Besides, he shall perform such miracles, which no other prophet shall have performed.

His miracles will not only be witnessed by those near him but also will be witnessed simultaneously by peoples of distant lands even thousands of miles away.

Even though he will be too poor to go to any school and, he would never learn how to read or write a single word, yet he will recite My teachings in a language, which will remain without any parallel in the history of mankind till the end of the earth. This is the interpretation of Deuteronomy 18: 18.

He shall give details of the leading prophets of the World even though he would never have studied their history (St. John 14: 26).

He will bring warring peoples into firm bonds of brotherhood, love and peace.

Money, wealth, riches, position, beautiful girls *etc.*, will not influence him.

Even though he will rule large areas, he will lead a simple, and ascetic life wearing rough woollen clothes with several patches.

His magnanimity of heart and forgiveness will win over many sworn enemies.

He will be the protector of the weak, the poor, the oppressed, the widows and orphans.

He would not accept any charity from anybody but would accept a gift.

Even though a virtual king, he would work for his living and lead a humble life!

He will be raised to Heaven bodily and shall not only speak to God Almighty (Deuteronomy 18: 18) but also see Him with the naked eye—an honour which no other prophet has been given by the Almighty.

He would be a man of very strong character and exemplary will-power.

Whenever he would go under the open sky a wisp of cloud would give shade over him.

He would be born as a posthumous child. He would speak in his cradle. His mother would die when he is only a few years old.

His conduct would be such from his childhood that at the prime of his youth the title of "The Faithful and True" will be conferred upon him (see *Destruction or Peace*, Chapter 25: T and Revelation 19: 11; also see *Destruction or Peace*, Chapter 17: D-30). He would be the bringer of divine help at the Final Battle (Armageddon). His Title would be "THE WORD OF GOD" (see *Destruction or Peace*, Chapter 17: A, 1-8; 25: T and Revelation 19: 13).

"The sacred fire" maintained by the Persian Magi in the "House of fire", in commemoration of the throwing of

Abraham, the idol-breaker, into the fire by King Nimrod, as read earlier in, see *Destruction or Peace*, Chapter 6: F, with the sole object of purging the world of evils, *i.e.* the true divine teachings as propagated by Prophet Abraham, the friend of Allah, and which fire had been burning since the time of Nimrod, whom they called Tammuz or "Fire, the perfecter" or Zoroaster (for reference please see Appendix to *"The Two Babylons"* by A. Hislop, pages 313-317) for the first time in thousands of years would be quenched as an indication of the birth of one who stands for the obliteration of idolatry and paganism on a world-wide basis (see *Destruction or Peace*, Chapter 17: D, 7-11; 17: E, 21-24).

On page 109, Vol. II, *"Tafrihul Askia FilAhwal UlAmbia"* there is a reference to *"Jasbul Qulub Diarul Mahboob"* in which Sheik Abdul Huq Mohaddis Dehalvi has written that on one occasion (during the 40 years of wanderings of the Israelites under the guidance of Moses in the wilderness, when they were being led by God from place to place) they visited the temple of God built by Abraham and Ishmael at Paran (now called Kaabah or Bait Ullah, or House of Allah at Mecca) where Moses prayed with the Israelites. On the return journey they came upon a place which they immediately recognised by the descriptions given in the Torah as "Seir", which is now called Madinah from where the Promised Prophet of the final period would spread the ultimate message of Allah. They halted and prayed there for a considerable period before moving on towards the Promised Land for the Jews. Hence the Jews had not only the exact description of the Promised Prophet, but they also knew that his place of birth would be Mecca and the town from which he would spread his teachings of the Surrender to the will of God would be Madinah.

On page 427 of *"The Gospel of Barnabas"* is given an original quotation from the books written personally by Prophets Moses and Joshua:

"The scribe then said (to Jesus): 'Pardon me, O master, for I have sinned'.

"Said Jesus: 'God pardon thee; for against Him hast thou sinned'.

"Whereupon said the scribe: *'I have seen an old book written by the hand of Moses and Joshua* (he who made the sun stand still as thou hast done), *servants and prophets of God; which book is the true book of Moses. Therein is written that Ishmael is father of the Messiah (Muhammad the Messenger of God),* and Isaac is the father of the messenger of the Messiah (i.e. Jesus, is the harbinger of the coming of the Promised Prophet Muhammad, the Messenger of God who is described in The Gospel of Barnabas as the Messiah). And thus saith the book, that Moses said "Lord God of Israel, Mighty and Merciful, manifest to Thy servant the splendour of Thy Glory". *Whereupon God showed him His messenger in the arms of Ishmael, and Ishmael in the arms of Abraham.* Nigh to Ishmael stood Isaac in whose arms was a child (*i.e.* Jesus), who with his finger pointed to (Muhammad) the Messenger of God, saying: *"This is he for whom God hath created all things"*.

"Whereupon Moses cried out of joy: 'O Ishmael, thou hast in thine arms all the world and paradise! *Be mindful of me, God's servant, that I may find grace in God's sight by means of thy son* (i.e. descendant Muhammad) *for whom God hath made all*."

F. King Tibba, The Re-Builder of "Ya Tibba" or "Yathrib"

On page 110, of Vol. II, *"Tafrihul Askia Fil Ahwal Ul Ambia"* it is recorded that the pagan King of Yemen, whose name was Tibba, had set out to conquer Syria and Iraq.

During his journey he came upon the place now famous as Madinah, which pleased him and he occupied it. He made his son the Governor of this place.

The people of Madinah conspired and murdered this son of King Tibba.

When he received the news of his son's assassination, he returned from Syria to Madinah to take his revenge. He vowed he would wipe out completely that place from the face of the earth, and gave orders for the general massacre of the population of Madinah, and the destruction of each and every house there.

Repeated attempts were made by him day after day but to his great surprise he found that what he destroyed one day was restored to its original state the next morning and that he was merely wasting his time and energy without making any progress whatsoever!

Now amongst the captives which he had taken from Palestine and Syria were four hundred learned Jews who were well versed in the Torah. They explained to king Tibba that he could do whatever he liked but he could never demolish this place because one day it would become the seat of the Promised Prophet of the final period of the earth.

To test their theory further he had a fire lit publicly and asked two of the Jewish elders to walk through the fire carrying the Torah with them. They came out of the fire unharmed. Then he sent two of his priests carrying idols of their supreme god (probably of Fire or Tammuz *i.e.* Fire, the perfecter) but they had hardly put their foot into the fire when they ran out burnt.

This fully convinced King Tibba. He accepted what was written in the Torah about the coming of the Promised Prophet of the final period of the Earth and the spread of his religion from this town of Seir. So he gave up immediately his attempt to destroy Madinah.

Therefore to right the wrong he had already done out of his ignorance in trying to destroy this town, he freed the four hundred Jewish captives. He built a house for each of them at Madinah, gave them each a Jewish slave girl as wife and some money. Thus King Tibba founded a new town. This town was called after his name "Ya Tibba" with the Jewish settlements in and around Madinah with the avowed purpose of awaiting the arrival of the Promised Prophet of the final period of the earth. In course of time the name of this town changed from "Ya Tibba" to "Yathrib" by which name it was known, when Prophet Muhammad came here in 622 A.D.

The leader of these learned Jews was a man called Shahaul. King Tibba wrote a letter and handed it over to Shahaul with instructions that he should hand over this letter to the Promised Prophet, if he came to this town during his life-time, but, if not, then to hand over this letter to his son with the same instructions generation after generation *i.e.* to preserve and hand over this letter to the Promised Prophet whenever his identity was disclosed. Further, that Shahaul was to make him a guest in this house which he built specifically for this purpose and gave to Shahaul to live in. Thus the Yemeni King foretold that the Promised Prophet would stay in this house on his first arrival at Madinah.

In the tenth/eleventh year of Muhammad's preachings in the year 620 A.D., *i.e.*, when, he was just over fifty years old, during the pilgrimage season, he came upon a little group of men, who listened to him gladly. They had come from Yathrib, a city more than two hundred miles away, which has since become world famous as *Madinah, or "City of the Prophet"*. At Yathrib the descendants of the learned Jews had often spoken to the pagans of a Promised Prophet of the final period of the Universe, who was soon to come among the Arabs from the descendants of Ishmael—a brethren tribe to the Jews, both being descendants of Abraham. The Jews descended from Isaac, the second son of

Abraham. This promised Prophet would come on earth to wipe out idolatry just as Abraham had attempted. When he appeared the Jews would join him, because the Jews knew that this Promised Prophet would efface paganism from Arabia. When the men from Yathrib saw Muhammad at the outskirts of Mecca, they recognised him as this Promised Prophet, whom the Jewish rabbis had so often described to them. On their return to Yathrib they narrated what they had seen and heard, with the result that at the next pilgrimage season *i.e.* 621 A.D. a deputation came from Yathrib to Mecca with the sole purpose of meeting the Prophet. This delegation secretly met the Prophet on the outskirts of Mecca at a place known as Aqabah. They met at this place to avoid arousing the suspicions of the Meccans. At this place this delegation swore allegiance to the Prophet in what is known as the "First Pact of Al-Aqabah", the oath they took being that which was afterwards exacted from women converts, with no mention of fighting. They then returned to Yathrib with a Muslim teacher in their company, and soon there was not a house in Yathrib wherein there was not a mention of the messenger of Allah and the great tortures and difficulties he had been facing for the past twelve years and the continuous dangers to his life at Mecca.

In the following year *i.e.* 622 A.D. at the time of pilgrimage, seventy-three Muslims from Yathrib came to Mecca to vow allegiance to the Prophet and invite him to their city. They met the Prophet secretly by night at Al-Aqabah. Here they swore to defend him as they would defend their own wives and children. This is known as the "Second Pact of Al Aqabah". It was then that the Hijrah or the decision to shift to Yathrib, and thus be free from persecutions of the Meccans was decided upon by Muhammad.

In this group of 73 was a young man named Abu-Laila. He was the son of Ayub Ansari, who was a descendant of the learned

Jewish Leader Shahaul, in whose custody the letter of King Tibba was entrusted. Ayub Ansari had secretly given this letter of King Tibba to his son Abu Laila just as he was leaving Yathrib for Mecca as a member of the group of 73 Muslims sent out to invite Muhammad to come over and live in peace at Yathrib. He had instructed his son not to disclose this letter, but to bring it back with him, unless he was asked to produce it by Muhammad. That would be a good test to know if Muhammad was in reality the Promised Prophet. As soon as this group met Muhammad, he miraculously came to know that the letter of King Tibba was with a member of this delegation and he miraculously pointed to Abu Laila and said, "Your name is Abu Laila and you have secretly hidden on your person the letter King Tibba has written to me, please produce it." Everybody was surprised as to how Muhammad recognised Abu Laila, who had come for the first time before the Promised Prophet, and how he knew about this letter, which everyone thought was still at Abu Laila's house in Yathrib.

This letter was produced by Abu Laila and read publicly, for the Prophet Muhammad could not read or write. It was found that the letter was written 1,040 years earlier by King Tibba. (For the original text please refer to page 110, Vol. II, *Tafrihul Askia Fil Ahwal Ul Ambia*). The rendering into English of its contents is as follows:

> "After saying your praise (*Hamd*) and praying for your safety and welfare (*Salaam*), let it be known to you Oh! Muhammad (Peace of Allah be on you) I hereby declare that I have accepted you and have placed my faith on that book, which Allah will send through you and I hereby declare that I have already converted myself to your religion and I hereby accept your God, as the Creator of all things and I hereby accept all rules of the Sariat of Islam, which will come down from Allah through you.

"On the day of Judgment I hereby beg of you to plead for my forgiveness to Allah and do not forget me on this day. I have accepted you and your teachings of Islam from before your coming and I have thus become your first disciple and follower. And to further my claim upon you I have hereby converted myself to the religion of your forefather "Ibrahim Khalilullah" (*i.e.* Abraham, the friend of Allah) and I am now living according to his religious teachings."

"Seal and Signature of Tibba,
King of Yemen"

When Muhammad arrived later that year at Yathrib he was on a camel with Abu Bakr Siddiq. Everybody wanted to invite him to their house. It was difficult to decide where to stay. So Muhammad said, "I will be the guest of the people of the house where my camel stops". The house where the camel stopped and sat down of its own accord was that of Abu Laila's father, Ayub Ansari, the descendant of Shahaul the learned leader of Jews. Thus the foretelling's of King Tibba came true *i.e.* when the Promised Prophet of the Final period of the Universe would come to Yathrib, he would first of all stay as a Guest in this house which he had built specially for this purpose and given to the Learned Jewish Leader Shahaul, in whose custody he had also left his letter for the Promised Prophet.

G. The Learned Jewish Elders and the result of disobedience

As soon as Muhammad arrived at Yathrib and became a guest of Ayub Ansari, the people of the whole town, the Jews, the pagans and the Muslims, all came to see him. He delivered a wonderful speech full of good advice, which made a deep impression upon his listeners (see *Destruction or Peace*, Chapter 17: E-15; also pages 108-112, Vol. II, *Tafrihul Askia Fil Ahwal Ul Ambia*).

Among this crowd was Abdulla bin Salaam, the most learned

of the Jewish elders of the time at Madinah. Abdulla bin Salaam was convinced that Muhammad was undoubtedly the Promised Prophet. He took the first opportunity of coming back to Muhammad when he was more or less alone with just a few Muslims and Ayub Ansari's family members. He told Muhammad that he wished to ask the Prophet a few questions which could not be answered by one who was not a prophet of God. One of his questions was:

What will be the first sign of the destruction of this Earth?

Muhammad replied:

"It will be a 'Fire' going from East to West which will spread indescribable devastation. This will be the first sign of the coming destruction of this Earth".

Upon hearing Muhammad's reply Abdulla bin Salaam admitted that Muhammad was perfectly right, and confessed:

"La Illaaha Illalla wa innaka Rasulallah"

Translation:

"There is no god but Allah and you are indeed the Prophet of Allah".

Thus he became the first Muslim convert after the arrival of the Prophet at Yathrib (page 112, Vol. II, *ibid*).

He asked Muhammad to keep his conversion to Islam a secret. He requested the Holy Prophet to invite the Jews and see what they had to say about him and also regarding his acceptance of the Holy Prophet. During that time he would remain hidden in some interior room in the house.

Accordingly the Jews were invited and Muhammad asked them why they did not admit the fact, which they knew very well, that he was the Promised Prophet of the Final period. They denied that they had already recognised him to be the Promised Prophet.

Then Muhammad asked them what their opinion was about Abdulla bin Salaam. They answered:

"Saiyadena wa ibne Saiyadena, Allamna wa ibne Allamna"

Translation:

"He is a 'Saiyad' (*i.e.* from the descendants of the Jewish Prophets) and the son of a 'Saiyad'.

"He is a most learned 'Doctor' of religious knowledge and the son of a most scholarly religious authority".

Muhammad asked them: "If Abdulla bin Salaam says that I am the Promised Prophet of the final period will you not accept this most learned Saiyad's advice?"

They replied: "May Allah save him from becoming a Muslim". Three times were these questions repeated and thrice the same answers given.

Thereupon Muhammad called Abdulla bin Salaam from his hiding place and he came out reciting the "*Qalima*" i.e. "There is no god save Allah and Muhammad is His Messenger". He informed them that he had asked several questions of Muhammad which none but a Prophet could answer and he had received the correct answers. He also told the Jews: "You know perfectly well that this is the Promised Prophet of the final period" and he proved this by references to the Torah which he was carrying with him.

Abdulla Bin Salaam pointed out further from the Torah (Deuteronomy 18: 18-19) that God had warned Moses that whosoever shall not listen and follow implicitly My (God's) Words, which this Promised Prophet will say in My (God's) name, I (God) shall severely punish by having them cut off from their people and even their menfolk slaughtered, and their women and children sold as slaves. Knowing all this he warned the Jews:

"Why are you doing such things as would deprive you of your homes and force you to leave and may even destroy you and your families. Have you no fear left in your hearts of God Almighty and His powers, which our forefathers have tasted in the past on many an occasion in the past for their disobediences. Have you forgotten all this or do you wish the curse of Allah to fall upon you again and again and thus become losers not only in this earthly life but also of Heaven. Oh! what is wrong with you, my people and brethren?" The Jews angrily left as they could not rebut the references quoted by Abdulla bin Salaam which even gave the name of the beloved Prophet of God as Muhammad. (See *Destruction or Peace*, Chapter 17: C-6, Solomon's Song 5: 16).

In the first year of his reign at Yathrib, Prophet Muhammad entered into a solemn treaty with the Jewish tribes, which secured equal rights of citizenship and full religious liberty for them in return for their support of the new State. But the Israelites' idea of the Promised Prophet was one who would give them dominion and rule over the Arabs and not one who made the Jews who followed the Prophet, brothers of every Arab who might happen to believe as they did. The Jews still wanted to be the superior race or the chosen nation and not be regarded as equals, amongst human beings, without any distinction for caste, colour or nationality.

Till then the Qiblah (the place towards which the Muslims face when praying) had been the temple of God at JERUSALEM. The Jews imagined that the choice implied a leaning towards Judaism and that the Prophet stood in need of their guidance so they were the superior or chosen race. Whereupon the Prophet received a command from God to change the QIBLAH from Jerusalem to the old Original KAABAH, the House of God built by Abraham and Ishmael at PARAN or MECCA. The whole of the first part of Surah 2 (Chapter 2) of the Qur'an relates to these

Jewish controversies.

When the Jews found that they could not use the Promised Prophet for their own ends to give them superiority over the rest, they tried to shake his faith in his Mission and to seduce his followers—a line of conduct in which they were secretly encouraged by some hypocrites professing to be Muslims but who considered they had cause to resent the Prophet's coming to Yathrib, since it robbed them of their local influence. In the Madinah surahs of the Qur'an (Chapters of the Quran that were revealed at Madinah by Angel Gabriel to Prophet Muhammad) there are frequent references to these Jews and these hypocrites.

The reverse which the Muslims suffered on Mt. Uhud in the third year of Hijrah lowered their prestige with both the Arab tribes and with the Jews of Yathrib. Tribes which had been inclined towards the Muslims for the past three years were now inclined towards the Qureysh. The Qureysh were the leading tribes of Mecca. Muhammad was one of them. When Muhammad started preaching that God is one and alone and that idolatry was sacrilege this had turned the Qureysh against Muhammad. They did not stop persecuting Muhammad even after he had gone over to Yathrib. After the incident of Mt. Uhud whenever the Muslims went out of Yathrib in small groups, they were attacked and murdered. Khubeyh, one of his envoys, was captured by a desert tribe and sold to the Qureysh, who publicly tortured him to death in Mecca.

The Jews, despite their treaty, now hardly concealed their hostility. They even went so far in their flattery of the Qureysh as to declare that the idolatry of the pagan Arabs was superior to the worship of the One and only God under Al-Islam—thus committing "Blasphemy".

The natural result was that God's curse fell upon these mischievous Jews. The ringleaders amongst these blasphemers were the Jewish tribes of Bani Nudir. Accordingly they were forced to emigrate from Madinah, leaving behind their hearth and homes. Thus the first curse of God fell upon them as warned in the Torah, that they would be cut off from their people and their estate, if they did not heed the words of God spoken by the mouth of the Promised Prophet.

In the fifth year of the Hijrah, the idolaters made a great effort to destroy Al-Islam in what is known as the War of the Clans or the War of the Trench. On this occasion the Qureysh with all their clans and the great desert tribe of Ghatafan with all their clans, formed an army of ten thousand men and rode against Yathrib. The Prophet on the advice of one Salman Pharsi (see *Destruction or Peace*, Chapter 13: 1) caused a deep trench to be dug before the city, and himself led the work of digging it. The Army of the clans was stopped by the trench, a novelty in Arab warfare. It seemed impassable for the cavalry, which formed their strength. They camped in sight of it and daily showered their arrows on its defenders.

While the Muslims were awaiting the assault, news came that Bani Qureysh, a Jewish tribe of Yathrib which had till then been loyal, had gone over to the enemy. The situation seemed desperate. But the delay caused by the trench had dampened the ardour of the clans, and one who was secretly a Muslim, managed to sow distrust between the Qureysh and their allies, so that they hesitated to act. Then came a bitter wind from the sea, which blew for three days and nights so terribly that not a tent could be kept standing, not a fire lighted, and not a pot boiled. The tribesmen were in utter dismay. On the third night the leaders of the Qureysh decided that the torment could be borne no longer and gave orders to retire. When the tribes of Ghatafan awoke next morning they found the tribes of the Qureysh had departed. They too took up their baggage and withdrew demoralised, without even a skirmish having taken place.

Thus the Muslims were left to face the treacherous Bani Qureysh, who conscious of their guilt fled into their fortress for refuge. Because of God's curse falling upon them, they only begged that they might be judged by a member of the Arab tribe of which they were adherents, instead of the Promised Prophet. The Prophet granted their request. But the judge, upon whose favour they had counted condemned their men to death and their women and children to slavery according to the Mosaic Laws. Thus the punishment, mentioned by God in the Torah for refusing to follow the Promised Prophet about which Abdulla bin Salaam had warned the Jews five years earlier, as read here before, was fulfilled for the second time but in a much harsher manner than that experienced by the Jewish tribes of Bani Nudir, a couple of years earlier. This was "the second curse of God" on the Jews for their disobedience to the Promised Prophet of the final period.

Obviously this incident caused great consternation amongst the Jews, as it reminded them of the destruction of Jerusalem in 607 B. C. when their males were put to the sword and the women and children captured and taken to Babylon as slaves for disobeying the Mosaic Laws of God. Now they realised that either they must accept the Promised Prophet in accordance with the foretelling's of Moses and the prophets before and after him in compliance with the orders of God or alternatively, with a view to take revenge for Bani Qureysh, to prepare such a strong army as would wipe out Muhammad and his teachings from the face of the earth. At this juncture Muhammad's followers were limited to below 5000 men. If the Jews delayed then the number of Muslims would become larger and later on they (the Jews) would not be able to do anything about it. Hence this was a matter of great urgency for the Jews.

The Israelites according to their customary habit of revolting against the wishes of Allah decided upon the latter choice. Therefore for two years they gathered and trained their men at Kheybar, in North Arabia and prepared a vast army of about 50,000 or more, calculated to outnumber the maximum strength of the Muslims.

Accordingly in the seventh year of the Hijrah, they forced Muhammad to lead a campaign against their fully fortified forts of Kheybar and its vast, well-equipped and trained army. Thus they got the Prophet to fall into their well-prepared trap.

Abu Bakr, the Prophet's companion, was commissioned to lead the attack on the first day against the strongest of the forts but he failed to capture it. On the second day, Umar led the attack but with no better result. On the third day, Muhammad gave the command to Ali his son-in-law and declared, "Today I am placing the command in the hands of a person who loves Allah and His Prophet and who never retraces his steps from the field of battle. He shall certainly conquer this fort". This prophecy was fulfilled that very day. This was the lunar month of Safar in the year 7 A.H. or 629 A.D. Hence in spite of severe odds at the battle of Kheybar the Muslims were completely victorious—thus proving once again that none can ever change the decisions of God Almighty for His chosen Prophet.

Henceforth the Jews of Kheybar became the tenants of the Muslims until the expulsion of the Israelites from Arabia during the Caliphate of Omar for their repeated acts of treachery. Thus again the decrees of God Almighty were fulfilled upon the disobedient Jews and they were cut off from what had been theirs for centuries.

It was at Kheybar that a Jewess prepared some poisoned meat for the Prophet of which he only tasted a morsel without even swallowing it, whereupon he warned his comrades that it was poisoned. One Muslim, who had already swallowed a mouthful, died immediately. Muhammad himself, from the mere taste of this poisoned meat prepared by this Jewish lady derived the illness which eventually caused the Prophet to pass away from this earthly life. Thus Muhammad was also one of the prophets, who wore a martyr's crown just like so many of the earlier Jewish Prophets, who were also murdered by the Jews.

The woman who had cooked the meat was sent up for trial on a charge of murder of the one man, who had died, and for the attempted murder of many more. She said that she had done it on account of the continuous humiliation "the Jews had suffered since the advent of Islam for their refusal to convert". So she had done it out of hatred and revenge. Muhammad, the Prophet, upon hearing her reasons for the crime showed the magnanimity of his kindness and forgave this Jewess lady. Thus she was saved from the gallows on a charge of murder.

When the Jews of Yathrib made a pact with Muhammad in the first year of Hijrah, they knew perfectly well that he was the Promised Prophet. Therefore they asked him to pray to Allah that the Israelite be blessed with:

1. Facial Beauty
2. Wealth
3. Knowledge

Accordingly, we find the Jews and Jewesses are beautiful to look at. They have large funds at their disposal and may be considered the wealthiest community. Accordingly they control world finances in quite a big way. Many of the scientific discoveries have come from this community. They were indeed blessed by Prophet Muhammad with all they had asked for.

Because of their repeated treacheries to the Promised Prophet and their refusal to follow God's words spoken through him, the

Jews have brought upon themselves the curse of the Almighty.

Now the American, the British and the French Governments with their well-connived plans of trying to destroy the teachings of this Promised Prophet (see *Destruction or Peace*, Chapter 29: C-2G) created an artificial homeland for the Jews in Palestine—to repay their financial debts to the Jews during the two great world wars out of the lands belonging to somebody else *i.e.* the Arabs. Thus innocent Arabs were massacred and their homes destroyed deliberately. Hence this New State of Israel has been constructed out of the blood of innocent Arab martyrs at the point of the gun with the funds of the Jews. Naturally Israel has made enemies of all those around her. But how long can guns and money prevail over the innocent blood of martyrs (see *Destruction or Peace*, Chapter 29: C-6A to C and C-7A to F)? This is therefore a very potential source for a major conflict involving those in this area and those who have contributed extensively to the artificial creation of Israel by force. God Almighty will sooner rather than later right this injustice as foretold in *Destruction or Peace*, Chapter 29: C-2H as He has always done in the past.

Therefore if world Jewry desire their own good, they must realise that they cannot have any permanent success on earth and eternal peace and happiness in Heaven, unless and until they accede to Allah's command (Deuteronomy 18: 18-19) and follow his teachings through His Promised Prophet of the final period.

The way in which the Jews can contribute to World Peace and harmony and their own happiness is to follow God's command and accept this Promised Prophet and treat all those around them, whom they have made their enemies, as brothers and to give adequate compensation, and relief. And also to rehabilitate those Arabs whom they have thrown out of their homes which they have destroyed by bulldozers at the point of the gun. If they do this, *i.e.* give equal voting rights and give equal opportunities to all in Palestine *i.e.* Israel, the Arabs as to the Jews. They could all become one unit of brothers irrespective of caste, colour or creed and thus unimaginable progress, prosperity, happiness, goodwill and unity would be their lot. This would be a very positive step to World Peace and happiness amongst men of goodwill, which is now threatened in the Middle East by the ill-will caused by the artificial creation of Israel, and by robbing the land from the surrounding Arabs, a source of constant danger not only to International Peace in general but the foretold destruction of Israel also in particular can thus be removed permanently by following the Old Testaments:

> "I will raise (for) them (*i.e.* Bani Israel) up a Prophet from amongst their brethren (*i.e.* Bani Ishmael), like unto thee (*i.e.* "And the LORD spake unto Moses face to face, as a man speaketh unto his friend"—Exodus 33:11), and will put MY words into his mouth: and he shall speak (*i.e.* Al-Qur'an) unto them all that I shall command him.
>
> "And it shall come to pass, (after the passage of sometime at the Battle of Armageddon) that *whosoever will not hearken unto MY words, which he shall speak in MY name, I will require it of* (*i.e.* punish and destroy) him (at the Battle of Armageddon)" (Deuteronomy 18: 18-19).
>
> "We (*i.e.* Bani Israel) have dealt very corruptly against thee (O' LORD), and have not kept Thy commandments, nor the statutes, nor the Judgments, which Thou commandest Thy servant Moses.
>
> "Remember, I beseech Thee, the word that Thou commandedest Thy servant Moses, saying, If ye transgress, I (God) will scatter you abroad among the nations:
>
> "But if ye turn unto ME, and keep MY COMMANDMENTS, and do (*i.e.* follow) them; though there were of you cast out unto the uttermost part of the heaven, yet will I gather them from thence, and will bring them unto the place that I have

chosen to set my name there" (Nehemiah 1: 7-9).

Otherwise Israel is bargaining for the curse of God, which destroyed so many mighty empires in the past.

H. The knowledge of The Nazarenes, the true followers of Jesus, about the Mission of Jesus

1. Sergius, son of Udas, a Nestorian Priest was residing at a place called Beheera about six miles from Beersheba. He saw a caravan of Arabs coming from the South bound for Syria. He noticed that in the clear blue sky a speck of cloud was providing shade to the caravan. He remembered immediately that Jesus had foretold this as one of the signs of the Promised Prophet of the final period. At once he sent out an invitation to the leaders of the Caravan to have some food with him. The Caravan stopped near a tree some distance away. The children accompanying the caravan were left in charge of the animals and the merchandise and the elders came to meet Sergius, the monk, who saw that the speck of cloud did not come along but stayed at the tree where the caravan had stopped. He said to them: "You have left someone behind and it is him I wish to meet". They said: "only the children. So he asked that the children be brought along one by one. When Muhammad son of Abdulla was brought the speck of cloud followed him. On this day, Muhammad was 12 years 2 months and 10 days old. The aged priest ran forward and took Muhammad in his arms with great love and affection and told him: "You have on your right shoulder a mark, I wish to see it". Muhammad showed it to him. He kissed it declaring that: "This is the seal of Prophethood, this child is the Promised Prophet". He enquired instantly as to

who was related to him. Abu Talib said: "He is my son". Thereupon Sergius replied: "You are not speaking the truth because Jesus had predicted that this child will be a posthumous child and his mother would die in his early childhood, so you cannot be his father". At this Abu Talib replied: "You are right, his father was my brother, Abdulla". Then the priest declared that this child was the Promised Prophet of the last period and that Muhammad must not be taken any further and certainly never to Syria because the Jews in Syria would recognise him just as easily as he had recognised him from afar, and as they had killed several of their prophets and had attempted to kill even Jesus, they would surely try to kill Muhammad also. Therefore he forced Abu Talib to send this child back to Mecca from here and warned him never to permit Muhammad to go to Syria. Accordingly Muhammad was returned to Mecca after he had stayed for a few days at Beheera as a guest of this Nazarene—the true followers of Jesus of Nazareth. This was the first trip of Muhammad out of Mecca with a trading caravan (page. 22, Vol. 2, *Tafrihul Askia Fil Ahwal Ul Ambia*). Jesus had informed his followers that a white speck of cloud will gave shade over Muhammad is recorded on page 167 of *The Gospel of Barnabas.*

2. When Muhammad was 24 years 9 months and 6 days old he was declared "AL-AMIN" *i.e.,* "The Faithful and True" by the people of Mecca at a Public Meeting (page 24, Vol. 2, *Tafrihul Askia Fil Ahwal Ul Ambia* also see *Destruction or Peace*, Chapter 17: D-30).

At this time a wealthy widow named Khadija of Mecca was in need of a trustworthy and faithful person to accompany her caravan laden with merchandise for sale to Syria. When she heard of the declaration of "AL-AMIN" she offered the job to Muhammad, which he accepted after consulting his Uncle Abu Talib.

The caravan was placed in the charge of Khazima, a relative of Khadija and her trusted slave named Masira. Muhammad accompanied them as the third member of the party. They left Mecca a few days later bound for Syria.

When this caravan reached Beersheba, they camped at a well and Muhammad took rest under a tree close by. In front of this place lived a Nazarene priest named Nastura. Immediately he saw Muhammad taking rest under this tree he came rushing out and took him in his arms and kissed him. The other two companions asked the aged monk the reason for this strange behaviour.

Nastura explained that Prophet Abraham had planted this grove and had prayed there (Genesis 21: 33) and from that time till now only prophets had come and rested and prayed under it. Jacob was comforted when he had prayed under this tree at Beersheba (Genesis 46: 1-3).

Therefore without doubt this young man was the Promised Prophet of the last period of the earth whose coming had been foretold by all the earlier prophets and that Jesus was the messenger, who brought the glad tidings that the Prophet after him would be the great Comforter of the whole universe, who would complete the religion left incomplete by Jesus (St. John 16: 12-13 and see *Destruction or Peace*, Chapter 13: B).

Nastura warned Khazima that they must not go any further because Muhammad would be recognised by the Jews of Syria. Upon Nastura's insistence they sold their goods at Beersheba. The manner in which Muhammad conducted the sales, his behaviour and good dealings won so much praise and popularity that they earned twice as much profit as they would have earned in Syria. Therefore after selling all their merchandise they returned from there to Mecca (pages 24-25, Vol. 2, *Tafrihul Askia Fil Ahwal Ul Ambia*).

I. The Mission of Jesus by Arius from the line of St. John, the Only Heir of Jesus

According to a tradition Salman Pharsi had given the following information at Madinah, when he converted from the Nazarene faith to Islam in the first year of Hijrah *i.e.* 622 A.D.

Salman was born in a town called Pharas, around 310 A.D. His parents were fire-worshippers, *i.e.* Zoroastrians. He left his family and went in search of worship of the true God. He met Arius, who was the heir to the teachings of Jesus through the line of heirs established by St. John, the first and only heir of Jesus (see *Destruction or Peace*, Chapter 12: G-13). Salman made Arius his religious preceptor and guide. Salman was with Arius when he died in 335 A.D. He converted to the faith of Jesus not by "Baptism" which Arius informed him was the method of entering the faith of "Nimrod". Arius informed Salman that Jesus was never "Baptised". Neither did he "Baptise" anybody nor did he teach "Baptism" (St. John 4: 2). "Baptism" was nothing but the pagan Sun worshippers' method of being initiated into their religion. Baptism was therefore something hated and despised by Jesus. Accordingly Salman Pharsi was circumcised and made to commit himself to observe as under to enter the faith of Jesus. So Salman become a true follower of Jesus by promising to observe the following conditions (see *Destruction or Peace*, Chapter 12: G-15):

a. To believe that God is one and alone, who has no father, mother, brother, sister, husband, virgin wife, only begotten son, daughter or any other form of equals or partners. This is the first Commandment of Jesus and to love God with all his heart, with all his strength and with all his mind and soul (St. Mark 12: 29-30).

b. Jesus is the messenger of God and is therefore not divine (see *Destruction or Peace*, Chapter 12: G-1).

c. To abstain from wine and strong drinks (pages 5 and 7, *The Gospel of Barnabas*) and from forbidden foods *i.e.* swine flesh, any flesh with blood in it or any food offered to idols (see *Destruction or Peace*, Chapter 12: G-9). Not to eat any food offered in the name of idols in sacramental ceremonies as the body and blood of a god and thus commit a communion with Satan.

Because such food and drinks, instead of securing remission of sins as claimed would instead heap greater sins on the partakers of such "Holy Communion" and "Sacred Sacraments" (see *Destruction or Peace*, Chapter 12: G-14).

d. He would observe the holy Sabbath from sunset on Thursday to sunset on Friday. Further, during the Sabbath period, he would not kill any animal or eat meat or do any manual labour or trade. Instead, he would keep this period free for the adoration of God Almighty (see *Destruction or Peace*, Chapter 12: G-7).

e. He would observe the Mosaic Laws as taught by Jesus (see *Destruction or Peace*, Chapter 12: G-15).

f. He would pray to God daily facing towards Jerusalem and not towards the East, the rising place of the sun, as was done by Pagan Sun worshippers.

g. To fear the Day of Judgment when all will be raised up from the dead by God and all will have to give an account of their own deeds on earth and be judged by God (see *Destruction or Peace*, Chapter 12: G-14).

h. No man will bear the burden of the responsibility of the sins of another (see *Destruction or Peace*, Chapter 12: G-14).

i. To attain heaven one had to do good deeds (see *Destruction or Peace*, Chapter 12: G-14).

j. One could become a true lover of Jesus only by following the Commandments of Jesus (St. John 14: 15).

k. Jesus has declared that it is the truth from him that when the "Evangel" or the Divine Message dictated personally by him in Hebrew and noted in Aramaic Script by the Jewish scribe Levi, son of Alphaeus, will be gone from the hands of his true believers and heirs, the Nazarenes, *i.e.* will be destroyed and will exist no more on earth, then after the same interval as existed between his departure from earth and the destruction of the "Evangel", the identity of Ahmad Muhammad, the Promised Prophet will be disclosed. This Promised Prophet will be the Holy Spirit of Truth. As long as the "Evangel" or the Divine scripture dictated by Jesus in Hebrew and noted by Levi during his lifetime will not go away from earth, *i.e.* be destroyed, until then Ahmad Muhammad, the Promised Prophet, the Comforter of the world, who is the Holy Spirit, the messenger of salvation for whose sake everything in the entire universe has been created, will not come (see *Destruction or Peace*, Chapter 13: B).

l. "He shall teach you all things, which I (Jesus) have not yet been able to say to you, because you will not be able to bear them now. He being the Holy Spirit or the Light of Guidance will guide you unto all truths, for he shall not speak from his mouth anything as the words of God save and except whatsoever he shall hear from God Almighty, that he shall recite (*i.e.* Qur'an) and he will show you things to come". He will also confirm the truth of the teachings of the earlier prophets including Jesus. This Comforter will be the final Prophet of God on this earth until the time of restitution of all things (*i.e.* when everything will be resurrected on the Day of Judgment). About this fact, God has spoken by the mouth of all his Holy Prophets since the world began. For example, Jesus quoted that Moses said truly unto their fore-fathers that a Prophet shall the Lord your God raise up for you from your brethren tribe of Ishmael, like unto Moses, who will speak to God as if face to face as a man speaks unto his friend, and him shall you obey in all things whatsoever he shall say unto you· And it shall come to pass after a lapse of some time that every soul, which shall not hear that Prophet, shall be destroyed at the battle of Armageddon from among the people of the earth. Jesus has said that this had been reiterated by all the Prophets from the time of Samuel in the same manner as Moses had said earlier that the teachings of the Final Prophet to this earth will remain until the restitution of the entire Universe on the Day of Judgment. He will be from the brethren tribe of the Jews *i.e.* a descendant of Ishmael whose children are the Arab tribes whilst the Jews are descended from his younger brother Isaac.

m. Jesus has further warned: "Remember ye are the children of the Prophets saying remember the covenant which God Almighty has made with our forefathers saying to Abraham that from his first-born son i.e. from Ishmael shall come the final Prophet of the world, whose teachings will replace all earlier teachings of the Prophets and he will be a Comforter for the whole Universe, which shall be blessed through him (see *Destruction or Peace*, Chapter 13: B and C).

Then Arius wept bitterly and informed Salman that the original hand-written Holy scriptures of Jesus the "Evangel" recorded by Levi which had been handed down generation after generation from St. John, the heir of Jesus to himself as well as the explanations of the Evangel and the life of Jesus and his examples and miracles and the Revelations written by St. John in Hebrew Aramaic Script had been confiscated from him under orders of King Constantine, when he (Arius) was banished to Illyria in 325 A.D. and these original Hebrew Texts were handed over to Athanasius, Bishop of Alexandria, who burnt and destroyed them. He added Athanasius was a preacher of the Babylonian faith of Nimrod started by Peter and Paul in the name of Jesus which advocated that:

i. "God is a trinity in unity" instead of "God is one and alone".

ii. "Christ is the only begotten son of God" instead of "Jesus is a created being hence inferior to God".

iii. "That to enter the religion of Christ you have to be Baptised like the Pagan sun worshippers" instead of "getting oneself circumcised and promising to follow faithfully the teachings of Jesus".

iv. "That to pray facing the East, the rising place of the Sun *i.e.* Sun-worship," instead of "facing towards Jerusalem as taught by Jesus".

v. "That to pray before idols of Christ" instead of "prayers are for God only and that prayer before idols is idolatry and strictly forbidden by Jesus".

vi. "That good deeds no longer mattered so long as you have faith in Christ, the son of God" instead of "You cannot attain Heaven without doing good deeds as taught by Jesus".

vii. "That the laws of God were a curse" instead of "you must live according to the Mosaic Laws as taught by Jesus".

viii. "That Jesus is the Redeemer, the Saviour, the Mediator, *etc.*" instead of "No man shall bear another's burden as taught by Jesus".

ix. "That Jesus has come for the whole world" *etc.* instead of "Jesus has prayed for only his believers as confirmed in the New Testament".

It is thus apparent that the Greek Manuscripts of the Holy Bible now before us are the outcome of the mischief of Athanasius, the destroyer of the "Evangel" and this is further proved by the word "Christos" or Christ being included in the Greek texts now before us—a word coined by King Constantine in the year 325 A. D.

That the Church is aware of this fact will be clear from:

"Papias in the first half of the second century, says that he (Levi son of Alphaeus who is now identified by the Christians as St. Matthew) wrote it (Evangel) in Hebrew Aramaic, and the same statement is found in the statement of early Fathers"· (page 64 of Part IV of the *New Testament* Chapter 25, Summary of the Books of the New Testament of the S.S. Teacher's Edition of The Holy Bible—The Authorised Version—Printed at Oxford University Press, London).

Hence the coming of the Comforter or the Promised Prophet according to the foretellings of Jesus as calculated by Arius was as follows:

Original Evangel (the Holy Bible of Jesus) recorded by Levi son of Alphaeus in Hebrew was destroyed in 325 A.D.

Less 33 years Life of Jesus on earth 33 A.D.

The Original Hebrew Evangel by Levi existed for 292 Years

The year of destruction of the Original Hebrew Evangel is 325 A.D.

Add the period that the Original Bible existed after Jesus 292 years.

The year in which the Promised Prophet of the final period would become renowned all over the known world by the miracle of splitting of the moon is 617 A.D.

This miracle of splitting the moon with full details is narrated in *Destruction or Peace*, Chapter 17: F-6.

That Jesus was the harbinger of glad tidings of the coming of the Promised Prophet of the final period (pages 223 and 167, *The Gospel of Barnabas*). This Prophet would be the only prophet after Jesus and there would be no more prophets born on earth after the Promised Prophet (page 225, *The Gospel of Barnabas*).

There would be no prophets in between, Jesus and the Promised Prophet just as there were no prophets in between John, the son of Zakariah, and Jesus and further that like John, the son of Zakariah, was the "Message bringer" of glad tidings of the coming of Jesus so also would Jesus be the harbinger of the good tidings of the coming of Muhammad (page 167, *The Gospel of Barnabas*).

Hence the real mission of Jesus on Earth was not to propagate his teachings, which were to be destroyed by those who would be his professed followers, but to give glad tidings of the coming of the Promised Prophet, the Saviour of the Universe (page 167, *The Gospel of Barnabas*).

That the Promised Prophet of the final period of the Universe will be born in the City of the "House of God" built by Abraham (*i.e.* at the Kaabah at Mecca) which is south of the land of Palestine (page 223, *The Gospel of Barnabas*). He would be from the descendants of Ishmael the first-born of Abraham, *i.e.* the Arabs (page 105, *The Gospel of Barnabas*). That the people of his native town will not accept him and will revolt against him. That he would come eventually as a leader of men to Yathrib (Madinah) and be accepted by the public as the Promised Prophet. That the Promised Prophet would be a great destroyer of idols and idolatry (pages 167 and 223, *The Gospel of Barnabas*).

That the believers in Jesus would be able to recognise him easily, just as they recognise their own sons by any of these outstanding characteristics:

- He shall have the seal of Prophethood on his right shoulder.
- He shall not accept charity.
- He shall accept a gift of goodwill.

A piece of cloud shall always cover and give shade over his body (page 167, *The Gospel of Barnabas*) and his body would not throw any shadow.

He will be born south of the land of Palestine (page 223, *The Gospel of Barnabas*).

He will be a destroyer of idols and will efface idolatry (pages, 167 and 223, *The Gospel of Barnabas*).

That even though he would not go to any school to learn how to read or write, yet what so ever he would teach, would always be flawless, valid for all time to come, full of logic, simple to understand, easy to follow, meant for universal application and a blessing for the entire universe.

That the final and complete divine message would be put into his mouth and he would utter the same when in a state of trance.

Even though he would rule over large areas yet he would always lead a humble life, earning his livelihood by his own labours, wear simple woollen clothes with numerous patches, have a very kind, generous and forgiving heart towards those who do harm to him, be full of justice, a protector of the weak, widows and orphans and the upholder of the rights of equality for even slaves and also women so that oppression of any description may be banished and idolatry abolished and replaced by love and peace amongst men of goodwill. Thus he would initiate "Universal Brotherhood" irrespective of caste, colour, tribe, race or other national distinctions.

Arius informed Salman Pharsi that he realised that Salman would have a very long life of over three hundred years or more; as such he shall surely have the opportunity of meeting the Promised Prophet. The name of the Promised Prophet would be Ahmad and Muhammad, according to the information given by Jesus and the *Old Testament*. Arius requested Salman to go to Yathrib after his death and to wait there for the coming of Ahmad Muhammad, the Promised Prophet and when he came to leave all that had been taught by him to Salman and to accept Ahmad Muhammad, the Promised Prophet, as ordered by Jesus in the Evangel. That he could easily recognise the Promised Prophet by these three simple signs:

1. That he would have the seal of Prophethood on his right shoulder.
2. That he would not accept any kind of charity.
3. That he would gladly accept a gift of goodwill.

Thus Salman Pharsi in accordance with the advice of Arius, set out for Yathrib after his teacher's death in or about 335 A.D.

On the way he was captured by a roaming band of Arab Bedouins and sold as a slave to the Jews of Yathrib.

He faithfully served ten Jewish masters, having been sold ten times on the death of each previous Jewish master. In this way he spent about 285 years of his life in Yathrib awaiting, the arrival of Ahmad Muhammad, the Promised Prophet.

In 622 A.D. when Muhammad, arrived at Madinah Salman took the first opportunity that same night of testing for himself as to whether or not this was Ahmad Muhammad the Promised Prophet, as foretold by Jesus and all the prophets before him. Salman offered some dates saying *"This is charity"*. Muhammad replied: "I am extremely sorry but I do not accept any charity". So saying he requested Salman to distribute the dates amongst the orphans and the poor that were present there. Thus the first of the signs given by Jesus to recognise Ahmad Muhammad, the Promised Prophet, proved authentic.

On the next occasion Salman again, presented some dates to Muhammad saying it was a gift of goodwill from his side. The Prophet gladly accepted it, ate a few pieces then gave some dates to each of his family member and distributed the rest amongst those present. Therefore the second of the signs given by Jesus to recognise Ahmad Muhammad, the Promised Prophet, was proved.

A few days later there was a funeral amongst the Muslims of Yathrib and Salman Pharsi attended it. As Muhammad went to lend his shoulder to lift the bier, the cloth on his right shoulder was shifted. Salman, who was just behind, saw the seal of "Prophethood". Hence the most vital sign given by Jesus for the recognition of the Promised Prophet was confirmed before his own eyes.

Immediately, with tears of love flowing from his eyes, he fell at the feet of Muhammad and declared before all that this was indeed Ahmad Muhammad, the Prophet of the final period of the Universe, for whose glad tidings Jesus had come on earth and that Almighty God had thus fulfilled the "Sacred Mission" of Jesus. He accepted Islam declaring that with the coming of Muhammad all the teachings of the previous Messengers which had remained incomplete were now to be completed. Then he related his whole life history, which has been given very briefly above.

The Holy Prophet Muhammad collected subscriptions and paid the price for Salman Pharsi and bought him over from his last Jewish master and freed him.

Salman Pharsi died in 35 Hijrah *i.e.* about 659 A.D. at the ripe old age of about 349 years.

J. Roman king Heraclius and the golden casket Sakina from the temple of Jerusalem

The fame of Muhammad as a prophet, who was propagating that God is one and alone had spread far and wide. Heraclius was anxious to find someone who was opposed to this prophet, and yet who would know all about the said prophet. He wanted to check up through such an opponent to satisfy himself whether or not Muhammad was the Promised Prophet according to the Biblical Foretelling's and other records in his possession.

In the year 7 A.H. or 629 A.D. an Arab trading caravan had gone from Mecca to Syria. King Heraclius was then at his palace at Hims. When he heard of the visit of the Meccans, he called for their leader. Accordingly Abu Sufian, the Meccan leader, went into the presence of the Roman Emperor.

Heraclius asked Abu Sufian: "Do you know anything about the claimant to prophethood from amongst your midst?"

Abu Sufian remarked: "Yes, I do know about him from his

very childhood."

Heraclius enquired: "Do you consider him a prophet or an impostor?"

Abu Sufian replied: "Most certainly he is an impostor."

Heraclius retorted: "If he be an impostor then how do you explain that his few men defeated your large armies?"

Abu Sufian admitted that the Meccans, in spite of vast numerical superiority, had lost at Badr but at the battle of Uhad, by a clever ruse, they were able to attack the Muslims from the rear and inflict great losses upon them. Also at their third encounter the Muslims had escaped annihilation, because of the trenches they had dug and so no real battle could be fought.

Heraclius remarked: "These are certainly not the signs of a false Prophet or an impostor. If he were an impostor there should be only one major flare-up and he would keep on rising steadily until his force was spent out and then his end would come in a big drop. But in this case it is clear that sometimes you win and sometimes he wins. These are not signs of falsehood but of truth. Anyway, please tell me, what does he order you to do and what does he forbid you?"

Abu Sufian replied:

1. "He asks us to bow in humility morning and night in prayers in the same way as we make our wives and slaves bow before us.

2. "He asks us to pay taxes on our wealth for the upliftment of the needy.

3. "He forbids us to eat blood, meat of animals dead (due to disease or natural death) or flesh of carcasses of animals (killed by some animal of prey)".

Heraclius explained that the first is supplication to God and is the highest form of adoration of the Almighty Creator. The second is charity which we give also to the poor. The third is something good from all points of view including health, morality *etc.* "All these which you have described are evidence of his purity and not of his being an impostor".

He then enquired from Abu Sufian if Muhammad had ever broken any treaties.

Abu Sufian admitted: "No, not so far, but this time I feel he will break the ten-year treaty signed at Hudeybiyah in 6 A.H."

Heraclius enquired: "What makes you so confident that he will violate this treaty, when he has not broken any treaties before?"

Abu Sufian stated that the Pagan Meccans, in spite of the signed truce of Hudeybiyah, had not only infringed the said treaty by giving help to the tribe of Banu Bakr in their attack on Khuzaa, (a tribe which was on friendly terms with the Muslims,) but when members of the Khuzaa tribe had sought shelter in the sanctuary of Kaabah, there also the Meccans had massacred them. The Meccans fearing revenge had sent him to Madinah for an extension of the treaty of friendship which was refused because Ibn Salim, one of the members of the injured tribe, had told their tale of woe to the Prophet, who was now preparing to attack Mecca. Thus he was preparing to break the treaty of peace and friendship with the Meccans.

Heraclius retorted: "Then it is clear that you are the breakers of this treaty and not Muhammad. Anyway, can you give me your personal estimate of his character?"

Abu Sufian declared proudly that the Meccans had given him the title of "Al-Amin" or "The Faithful and True", when he was only 24 years 9 months and 6 days old and admitted that his character was indeed the best amongst all Meccans.

Heraclius smiled and admitted: "I never expected this truth from his enemy" (for further references please refer to pages 309-310 of *Tarik-e-Waqidi* in Urdu by Navalkishore Press, Lucknow).

Then Heraclius brought out from his treasury a "Golden Casket". He disclosed that this Casket was called "Sakina". The word "Sakina" is derived from the verb *"Taskeen"*. In Hebrew-Arabic *"Taskeen"* means "to satisfy one's belief convincingly". Hence "Sakina" means some evidence which satisfies fully one's belief. This casket "Sakina" or evidence to satisfy totally was given to Adam, the first man, by God and it contained the pictures of all the leading prophets. This casket had been handed over for safe keeping from generation to generation, until it came to Noah and from him step by step to Abraham, and from him to his son Ishmael and from him to his son Prince Kedar, who received orders from God to give it to his cousin Jacob when he was blessed with the title of Israel. As the Israelites would be needing it during their marches under Moses and at the time of the conquest of Palestine etc., it would be carried in their tabernacle.

Whilst as far as the children of Ishmael were concerned until the coming of the Promised Prophet of the final period, they as the special chosen people of God would be protected by God Almighty against all attacks on the Kaabah. Hence even though many of the Arabs of Mecca took to *"Idolatry"* and other corrupt practices they were not punished as the Jews were for their disobedience and pagan worship of Baal and Tammuz (*i.e.* Nimrod). Nor was the Kaabah destroyed just as the temple of Jerusalem was twice destroyed. Nor were their menfolk put to the sword and their women and children sold into slavery, a fate the Jews suffered whenever they reverted to Nimrod's religion. Therefore, it would appear that the descendants of Ishmael received a very favoured treatment from God Almighty, which even the Jews as one of the chosen people did not enjoy as already shown in *Destruction or Peace*, Chapter 8: G. Thus it is obvious that on account of the Promised Prophet Muhammad they enjoyed the most exalted position in the whole of humanity as descendants of Ishmael, the heir of Abraham.

When Prince Kedar (for descendants of Ishmael see *Destruction or Peace*, Chapter 8: H) handed over the golden casket "Sakina" to his cousin at Beershaba, Jacob gave him the glad tidings that on that day a son and heir had been born to him at Mecca whose name would be Hamal and from his descendants would come the Promised Prophet of the final period of this earth, according to a dream God had shown to him the previous night. When Prince Kedar returned to Mecca he found that Jacob's dream was true. That he had after all these years been blessed with a son and heir in his old age through his Arabian wife Gazera (page 289, Vol. 1, *Tafrihul Askia Fil Ahwal Ul Ambia*). This casket was removed from the temple of Jerusalem and taken to Rome in 70 A.D. when the Romans ravaged Jerusalem and looted all its treasures.

After giving all this background, Heraclius opened the casket and showed Abu Sufian the pictures of the important prophets, which were depicted on some kind of silken parchment, commencing from Adam. As soon as the page containing Abraham was shown, Abu Sufian said there was a faint resemblance in this face to that of Muhammad's. Heraclius stated that was his great-grandfather Abraham. When he turned to the next page, Abu Sufian said there was greater resemblance in this face to that of Muhammad. Heraclius said that it was the picture of Ishmael from whose children was to come the Promised Prophet. When the last page was shown Abu Sufian pointed out Muhammad, Ali, Abu Bakr, Osman and Omar. Heraclius replied that in that case Muhammad was indeed the Promised Prophet of the final period and not an impostor. After the capture of Mecca by the Muslims in 8 A.H. when Abu Sufian converted to Islam he made the above statement on the basis of this knowledge that Muhammad was the true Promised Prophet. Upon hearing this the Holy Prophet Muhammad declared that any Meccan taking shelter in the house of Abu Sufian would be forgiven his past crimes against the Muslims. Thus were all the Meccans pardoned.

In the year 7 A.H. Muhammad sent messages to several of the ruling kings of the world inviting them to Islam. Wahiya Qalbi was sent to Heraclius, who also showed him this Golden Casket "Sakina" and gave the above background, informing him that in 70 A.D. when Jerusalem was razed to the ground by the Romans, this golden casket and other treasures of the temple were carried away to Rome. When the page of Abraham was shown, Wahiya Qalbi said the face had some resemblance to that of Muhammad, and when the next page was shown he said there was a very great resemblance between in this face and that of Muhammad. Then Heraclius said that it was the picture of Ishmael, the eldest son and heir of Abraham, from whom would come the Promised Prophet. When the last parchment was displayed Wahiya Qalbi pointed out Muhammad and those around him as Ali, Abu Bakr, Omar and Osman. Heraclius admitted that Muhammad must be Ahmad, the Promised Prophet.

Wahiya Qalbi said to Heraclius: "Since you know very well that Muhammad is the Promised Prophet of the final period then you should convert to Islam." To this he replied: "You go and explain the Islamic teachings to my chief priest, and if he agrees to become a Muslim, I too shall do so". Accordingly Wahiya Qalbi saw the chief priest, who was the son of a holy man named Nathaniel.

This priest asked for the exact date of the birth of Muhammad, which Wahiya Qalbi gave him as Monday the 12th day of the Arabic lunar month of Rabiul Awwal 53 lunar years before Hijrah. He sat and calculated this date and day according to the Roman calendar which would correspond to 20th April 570 A.D. Then he said: "You are right". Because on this very date 59 solar years ago one Monday morning he had been to see Emperor Justin II who ruled as the Roman Emperor from 565 to 578 A.D. This Emperor was not only very well-versed in Law but was also a great astrologer. He was surprised to see the contorted face of his friend so full of worry and anxiety. So he had asked him: "What is wrong with you." In reply Emperor Justin II said: "Today has been born a child with his foreskin miraculously Circumcised from before his birth. Those who will not listen to him when he grows up will be denied Heaven. I know of this from foretelling's of Jesus who had foretold that the day on which all idols all over the world fall by themselves and when the idols are lifted, they will fall again and again each time announcing that today has been born the Promised Prophet of the final period, the Saviour of the Universe, who will destroy idols and idolatry (see page 169, *Gospel of Barnabas* also see *Destruction or Peace*, Chapter 17: D 5-11).

> "This morning I was surprised to find in the Royal Chapel that the beautiful statue of The Christ had very strangely come out of its firm solid base and was lying on the floor. As I lifted the idol of Christ, it said that this day idols all over the world have fallen upon the ground because of the birth of the Promised Prophet, who was born miraculously with his foreskin circumcised from his mother's womb. This child will be a destroyer of idols and idolatry, so out of fear of him we, idols, have fallen down all over the world". This priest replied that it should not be very difficult to find this child from amongst the Jews. To this Emperor Justin II replied that according to his information this child had not been born in a Jewish family but in a community which was related by blood to the Jews, as such he did not know where he had been born. This child is from one Ishmael, the eldest son of Prophet

Abraham (page 105, *The Gospel of Barnabas*).

The chief priest asked Wahiya Qalbi if it was correct that Muhammad was born with his foreskin already miraculously circumcised from before his birth. Wahiya Qalbi confirmed that this was correct.

Then he made several enquiries about Muhammad based upon the foretelling's of Jesus as to the various outstanding features of the Promised Prophet. On being fully satisfied with the answers he got, he declared openly that there was no doubt whatsoever according to the teachings of the real Jesus that Mohammad was the Promised Prophet and the Comforter of the world, who completes the religion of God on Earth and whom the other prophets of old have foretold about.

"I hereby accept Islam". So saying he proclaimed before the public that Muhammad was the Promised Comforter of the world about whom Jesus and the earlier Prophets had foretold. The Christians were so enraged at this statement that they killed this old high Priest on the spot.

Heraclius, seeing this, grew alarmed at his possible fate at the hands of his subjects. Accordingly he decided to postpone his intention of becoming a Muslim in fulfilment of the teachings of the real Jesus. All this happened in the presence of Wahiya Qalbi, who narrated this on his return to Madinah.

K. The causes leading to the surrender of Jerusalem in 16 A.H. / 637 A.D. and its after effects

At the time of the birth of both Jesus and Muhammad, Syria and Palestine were part of the Roman Empire. From their borders started the homeland of the Arab tribes.

You have already read how the Jews living in Arabia started making trouble for Muhammad when he shifted his headquarters

THE MISSION OF HOLY JESUS

from Mecca to Madinah. Their hostility soon affected even the border tribes and skirmishes began to take place. It was to end this mischief and establish law and order that a small band of 3000 Muslims were sent in 8 A.H. Without any cause or provocation this small band of Muslims were attacked by a very large Roman Army comprising over one hundred thousand soldiers under the personal command of Emperor Heraclius himself in what is known as the unprovoked massacre of Muslims at Muta by the Christians.

The Romans, encouraged by their victory, over the Muslims, who were outnumbered to the extent of about 35 Christians to every Muslim, thought they could vanquish and destroy Islam in its infancy because the Muslims were still so few in number.

Therefore in the Year 9 A.H. the Romans prepared to invade Madinah, the very heart of Arabia. Muhammad, however, anticipated their move and marched out with whatever little force he could muster to intercept their advance. When he arrived at Tabuk, the enemy lost heart and did not dare to venture further when they thought of the battle of Muta where only 3000 Muslims without any question of retreat or surrender or flight had fearlessly fought 100,000 Christians to the bitter end. Only a few Muslims were left alive, but the losses of the Romans were almost a quarter of their army or over 25,000 men.

Muhammad never attacked anybody unless they forced him to do so. History is itself witness that Muslims never were the first to shed blood, but when provoked they refused to submit quietly. Thus this struggle was postponed for a time.

The Romans, taking advantage of the temporary lull, decided to join hands with Pagan Iraq to cause further unprovoked aggression on the Muslims in trying to destroy Islam in its infancy. To stop this harassment of the Christians, an expedition under Usama was sent out by Abu Bakr within 19 days after

Muhammad's departure from earthly life, because they were left with no option but to defend themselves.

Abu Bakr accordingly began to make preparations for a campaign in Syria after the completion of the conquest of Iraq. He despatched Khalid bin Sa'id with orders to halt at Tayma and wait for further instructions. He was not to take the offensive and was to confine himself to defending the borders of the infant Islamic state in case he was attacked by the enemy. He was also required to persuade the neighbouring tribesmen, excepting those who had the stigma of apostasy to join him. Khalid bin Sa'id carried out these orders and successfully assembled a host of tribesmen under his banner at Tyama as a precaution against further attacks by Christians.

At a distance of three stages from Tayma, Heraclius the Roman Emperor gathered together Arab tribes of Lakhm, Chassan, and Judham, who dwelt on the borders of Syria, with the object of fighting the Muslims. When the Caliph Abu Bakr was informed of these activities of the enemy, he sent an order to his general: "Proceed—Do not stop. Pray to Allah for help". In compliance with this order, the Muslim forces moved forward and as the enemy dispersed they took possession of his camping ground. The happy result of this skirmish was that the tribesmen who had come to the fight against the Muslims now embraced their Faith. Khalid received fresh orders to march forward but with the necessary precaution of keeping the rear of the army safe. Accordingly he moved on and halted between Zira and Abil. Here he defeated Behan, a Roman chief, who wanted to intercept his march. As Khalid had asked for reinforcements, the Caliph made the necessary arrangements to send him help. Just at about this time the troops that had been sent against the apostates of Yemen, Umar Behrain and Tiham returned to the capital. 'Ikrama and Dhul Kula' Himayari (as scions of the ruling family of Yemen) were also among them. The Caliph now despatched four different armies to Syria under the command of Abu Ubaidah, Shurahbil bin Sufyan, and Amr bin al As. Of these commanders three had to march from various directions towards Balqa or the highlands of Syria, while Amr bin al-As was to proceed through Palestine. They had separate regions assigned to them for conquest, but the combined purpose of their operations was thus expressed, "I know that the Romans will soon be engaged with the Muslims. Hence I wish that the armies of the highlands should have no difficulty in marching to the lowlands, and *vice versa*. They should not be interdependent". Tabari tells us, "it happened as he (the Caliph) had guessed".

The total number of soldiers in the four armies mentioned above was 27,000, excluding Khalid's contingent. When Heraclius heard of the movements of the Muslims, he also made preparations for war on a large scale and encamped at Hims. He decided to despatch separate columns against the various armies of the Caliph in order to stop them from joining together. Theodoric, the brother of Heraclius was sent with 20,000 soldiers against Amr bin al-As; George the son of Theodoric with almost the same number against Yazid bin Sufyan; Darackis against Shurahbil bin Husna and Caycar bin Nestus with 60,000 followers against Abu Ubaidah. The advance-guard of Theodoric encamped at Thinia, on the highlands of Palestine. The Muslims were a little perturbed on seeing the large number of the Roman soldiers and consulted Amr bin al-As who commanded the biggest section of their army. He replied: "My opinion is that we should all unite. The reason for this is that if men like us assemble together then they cannot be defeated simply on account of their numerical inferiority. But if we remain dispersed then none of us will have enough men to meet his opponent, as they have sent separate armies against each of us. Let us all join forces at Yermuk".

The Caliph approved of this opinion and confirmed it thus: "Assemble together so that you become one single army. Break the lines of the infidel army with the Muslim force. Remain convinced of the fact that you are the supporters of the cause of Allah, and that He brings victory to the supporters (of His cause) and degradation to those who do not believe in Him. A group of persons like yourselves cannot be discomfited merely because of numerical inferiority. And indeed groups of ten thousands or even more will be ruined if they take to the path of sin therefore beware of falling on the path of sin. Assemble under your banners at Yermuk and every chief must offer prayers along with his men".

Heraclius also changed his strategy on hearing of these arrangements and ordered his armies to collect at one place. They were to select a site which was wide in the front and narrow in the rear. Theodoric was nominated commander-in-chief of the entire army and George was to lead the vanguard. The right and left wings were placed under the command of Darrackis and Caycar respectively. They were also told that fresh reinforcements would arrive soon under Bahan. In compliance with these instructions of the Emperor, the Roman army encamped at Waqusa on the bank of the Yermuk. They had selected this plain because, protected as it was on one side by the river and on the other by a precipitious hill, it would give the Romans courage and shelter. The Muslims soon realised this, and leaving their own position they moved and encamped in front of the Romans. Thus they were sandwiched between the Muslim army in their front and the hills in their rear. When Amr bin al-As saw this he said to his men, "O People! Be of good cheer. The Romans are now enclosed and few of those who are enclosed can really prosper". For three month the Muslims kept them in this condition, because the river and the hills made it difficult for them to launch an open attack, while the Romans were hesitant to hazard a charge. This confined their activities to petty skirmishes only. But the Romans were beaten in almost every attempt they made. In the month of Safar, when the Caliph received a report of the existing state of affairs; he wrote to Khalid bin Walid that he should hand over immediately the charge of the affairs of Iraq to Muthanna and take his army by forced marches to Syria. Khalid carried out the orders and reached Yermuk in the lunar month of Rabi-ul-Akhir, covering the distance with such rapidity that the legs of his horses gave way. The same day Bahan brought to the Roman army a fresh contingent which was led by priests, who exhorted the soldiers to fight against the Muslims.

It has been recorded by historians that the Romans were two hundred thousand strong while the number of the Muslim soldiers could not have been more than 46,000, including the 9,000 followers of Khalid and certain other reinforcements. But in spite of their numerical superiority, the Romans remained in their trenches for one month even after the arrival of Khalid. The priests did all they could to excite their feelings by telling them that Christianity was in danger. But this had very little effect, and it was not without great efforts that after the lapse of months they came out of the trenches in the month of Jamadi-ul-Akhir.

The Muslim battalions were under separate commands and had no commander-in-chief over them. On receiving information of the movement of the Roman army, they decided that each battalion should fight under the absolute command of its chief. This type of warfare is known among the Arabs as *"Tasanud"*. When Khalid saw this he addressed the entire army and said: "This is an important day which will live down in history. Throwing aside the notions of personal dignity and pride we should follow such a course of action that we make it impossible for the enemy to take advantage of the situation. To fight under separate commands is to divide our strength. You should decide upon a course which will suit the occasion". On being asked to express his own views, he continued, "The Caliph seems to have had an impression that these expedition would be easy. Had he known the conditions that we are actually facing he would have certainly placed the entire charge of the armies in the hands of one commander. Now I am of the opinion that we should have all our forces under one supreme command and every day one of the Amirs (commanders) should bear this responsibility in rotation.

"If you have no objection, then for to-day the supreme command may be entrusted to me". All the Amirs agreed with this proposal and elected him as their commander for that day. As the Romans had drawn up their forces afresh, the Muslim commander also arranged his men in a new order which the Arabs had never seen before. The entire army was split up into forty contingents which were placed under as many experienced chiefs. The soldiers were told that was the most suitable arrangement when the enemy had the advantage of numerical superiority, for this tactic made the army appear twice as strong as it actually was. The middle flank was commanded by Abu Ubaidah, the right wing by Shurabhil bin Husan and Amr bin al-As and the left wing by Yazid bin Abu Sufyan. One of the contingents was under Abdur Rahman-bin Khalid, who was only eighteen years old at that time. After the battle of Badr the Holy Prophet had introduced the practice of getting the Sura "Anfal" recited to the soldiers before fighting commenced. This duty was performed by the "*Qari*" (*i.e.* reciters of the Qur'an), while the *Qass* (*i.e.* storytellers of brave deeds) told stories of valiant deeds of heroes to create fresh enthusiasm among the soldiers so that they might fight fearlessly in the battle. Accordingly Yazid bin Abu Sufyan would go to every contingent and tell the soldiers, "You are like provisions for (supporters of) Arabia and the helpers of Islam, they are like provisions for (supporters of) Rome and the helpers of infidels and idolatry. O Allah! this day is one of Thy great days. Send Thy help to Thy slaves". The army of Islam had one thousand Companions (of the Prophet) of whom one hundred had the distinction of having fought at Badr. When Khalid was arranging the lines of his soldiers, a certain person said: "How vast is the Roman army, and how small is ours". Khalid replied promptly: "No, our army is far mightier than that of the enemy. The superiority of an army does not depend on numbers, it is the resultant victory or defeat that really counts".

The following incident on the field of battle may be related to illustrate the miraculous powers of Truth. The Roman general George, the son of Theodoric, came forward and said indignantly, "Where is Khalid? Let him come near me". Khalid promptly accepted the challenge, and placing his charge in the hands of Abu Ubaidah he went up to the Roman general. 'The two generals now exchanged promises of safety, and then coming close to each other they stood midway between the two armies. George opened the conversation: "Tell me the truth, for free men tell no lies. Do not deceive me, for noble men deceive not. I want to know if your Prophet had received a sword from God, which was bestowed on you and which now is responsible for your victories". "No", said Khalid, "Then", inquired George, "how is that you are known as the sword of Allah?" Khalid replied, "The Almighty Allah sent His Prophet Muhammad (Peace be upon him) to us. He preached Islam to us, but in the beginning nearly all of us kept away from him. Gradually some of us embraced his religion while others remained at a distance and continued to oppose him. I was among those who was against the movement. But soon after Allah changed our hearts, made us to bow our necks and guided us on the right path. When I accepted the guidance, the Holy Prophet said 'O Khalid! you are a Sword from the swords of Allah, which has come out of the scabbard to fight against the infidels'."

"And now among the Muslims I am the deadliest enemy of the infidels". George said, "Khalid, you have told the truth. Now tell me what the message of Islam is". Khalid replied, "To confess that none is to be worshipped except Allah and that Muhammad is His slave and Prophet, and to accept as truth the message that the Prophet has brought from Allah". "What if somebody does not accept it?" asked George. "He should be prepared to pay the *Jizya*" replied Khalid (*Jizya* is a tax payable for maintaining an army to give protection). George now inquired as to the position of a person who accepted Islam. "It is the command of Allah," said Khalid, "*that all Muslims are equal in status, whether they belong to the upper classes or to the lower ones, whether they have accepted Islam earlier or later*". "What about the person who embraces the faith today?" asked George "He will enjoy the same position of equality and in fact, one of precedence", replied Khalid. "How is that possible?" George inquired again. Khalid explained, "*when we accepted Islam the Holy Prophet was alive. He received Divine revelations and preached to us the commands of Allah and we used to see with our own eyes his miracles and powers. In these circumstances our conversion to Islam was inevitable. Today you do not see these things and still you embrace with Faith. Hence you have precedence over us*." George then asked, "Can you swear to me that you have told me nothing but the truth, that you have not deceived me, and that you have made no attempt to please me". Khalid replied, "By Allah! I did not tell you a lie, nor do I hate you or anybody else. I have given the correct answers to what you have asked me. Allah is my Helper". "*Undoubtedly, you are right*", said George, *and throwing away his shield he requested Khalid to instruct him in the teachings of Islam!*

Khalid took him to his tent and after giving him a bath he instructed him in the principles of Islam and made him offer prayers, acting himself as the Imam.

Now that one of their commanders had gone over to the Muslims, the Romans launched a general attack which nearly broke the ranks of the Muslim army, although 'Ikrama and Heritha remained firm. Consequently when Khalid and George came out of the tent they found the Romans penetrating through their lines. Khalid at once cried out to his people, and they responded to his appeal by making a counter charge and pushing the enemy back. Khalid was soon in the thick of the battle, at the head of his forces. Fighting continued with unabated fury till the afternoon, when prayers were offered by mere signs. It was a remarkable sight! George, who was an enemy of Islam in the morning, could now be seen fighting alongside Khalid and launching attacks on the Romans with great enthusiasm and religious fervour. Fortunate as he was, he received martyrdom in the thick of fighting, shortly after offering the prayers which had brought him within the folds of Islam, and thus went triumphantly into the Presence of his Lord. In the evening the Romans began to lose ground, Khalid completed their rout by making a fresh charge with contingents taken from the centre Thus he separated their infantry from the cavalry. The Roman horsemen, unable to bear the brunt of this attack, turned back and fled. The Muslims were happy at this victory but they did not leave their position in pursuit of the fugitives. Having been thus dislodged the Romans took shelter in the trenches, but their victors soon came upon them, and as there was a hill behind them it was not possible for them to escape.

A very large portion of the huge Roman Army was killed and even the tent of their chief, Theodoric; the father of George, was seized by Khalid. After the conclusion of the battle, Magrib prayers were offered, as its time was about to expire. Even after this crushing defeat of the Romans, stray fighting continued throughout the night and Khalid had to supervise operations from Theodoric's tent.

The number of Muslims who were slain in this action is stated to have been as low as 3,000 whilst the losses of the Roman Army were over two hundred thousand. Does this not show clearly that God Almighty must have intervened actively? It was this unbelievable victory which caused a great impression upon the minds of the Romans about the purity and the truth of the teachings of Al-Islam. This incident opened for the Muslims immense possibilities of furthering the teachings of "Surrender to the will of God".

Another remarkable incident of this campaign may also be noted here. Before the battle, the Romans sent an Arab spy. He carefully studied the condition of the Muslim camp for one day and one night and then reported: "They are RAHIBS (Saints or priests) in the night and horsemen in the day. In establishing and maintaining the Truth they are so firm that they cut off the hands of their monarch's son, if they find him guilty of theft and pelt him with stones till death if he is accused of adultery".

Following this victory and in order that the Romans might not be able to attack Arabia again from Palestine and Syria it was decided to occupy these two areas.

During October 636 A.D. the real siege of Jerusalem commenced with an army of Muslims under Khalid bin Walid. There were ten days of battles, with neither side giving ground even though the Muslims were badly outnumbered. On the eleventh day the Muslims were joined by the victorious Islamic armies under Abu Ubaidah who had completed the conquest of Syria.

The defenders of Jerusalem, although they were still outnumbering the Muslims ten to one lost heart and consulted Kumama, the high Priest of Jerusalem, as to what should be done He had with him some handwritten Scrolls from the "Evangel" regarding the surrender of Jerusalem. After consulting these he declared that Jesus had prophesied that no matter what anyone might do the defenders of Jerusalem would not be able to protect the city against one Omar, son of Khattab, who would be the head of the followers of Ahmad; the Promised Prophet. "The full, detailed description of this person is here. Take me to the walls so that I may see their leader; if he is the same then I shall surrender the city but if not then know for certain that even if anyone attacks this city for as long a period as 30 years with a superior number of forces and equipment yet they cannot succeed in storming this sacred city of King David".

Accordingly a temporary truce was called and the leader of the Muslims was asked to appear in front of him. Abu Ubaidah stepped forward, watched by Khalid bin Walid on one flank and Abdur Rahman bin Abu Bakr on the other. When Kumama saw Abu Ubaidah from the walls of Jerusalem, he proclaimed to the defenders that:

1. This is not the man whose description has been given by Jesus, therefore he would not be able to conquer Jerusalem!

2. The winter months are ahead when the attackers would not be able to keep warm and fight.

3. Oh defenders of Jerusalem! Take courage and fight. An easy and sure victory should be yours.

During the four winter months that followed a bitter battle was fought every day resulting in serious losses to the people of Jerusalem!

When spring set in all hope of victory for the defenders of Jerusalem vanished. Their casualties during the past five months had been staggering, yet the Muslims were unshaken in spite of their small numbers! Again they consulted Kumama, who was taken once more to the walls of Jerusalem. A truce was called for and again Abu Ubaidah stepped forward.

Then Kumama, through a Nazarene, who knew Arabic, said as follows:

"Know very well that this sacred city cannot fall even if attacked for thirty years according to the foretelling's of Jesus unless and until a particular person comes and you are not him".

Abu Ubaidah replied: "Then know very clearly that we shall stay here if necessary for thirty years until the city falls".

Kumama replied: "What do you want from us? If it is riches we are prepared to give you riches, but, do not trouble us any further".

Abu Ubaidah replied: "We are not interested in your riches and wealth".

Kumama asked: "Then what do you desire?"

Abu Ubaidah replied:

a. "Become Muslims and we accept you as our brothers; then there will be no barrier between you and us.

b. "If not then surrender and we shall leave you to follow your religion but you will have to pay a small tax for the maintenance of the army for your protection as we cannot allow the treacherous Christian Empire of Rome to stab us by deceit as they had done invariably for the past eight years.

c. "If not, and if you compel us against our will to take the city by force of arms with much loss of lives then know that we shall have no option left but to take compensation for our losses.

"Therefore think well on the various options before you and act in a manner to your best interest so that you cannot blame us later on".

Kumama replied: "Your first condition is not acceptable to us, the second is degrading and as far as the third is concerned we have no option left but to fight".

Abu Ubaidah thereupon asked: "Can you kindly give us the description of the man to whom this Holy city will fall?

Kumama replied:

"His name is Omar. His father's name is Khattab. He will be the follower of Ahmad, the Promised Prophet of the final period. He will be the second President of those who have surrendered themselves to the will of God".

Abu Ubaidah replied immediately:

"Omar bin Khattab, the follower of Muhammad the Promised Prophet is now the second Khalifa (in English: Caliph *i.e.* the viceroy or president of the Islamic State)". He asked if Kumama would recognise him if he called him from Madinah, his seat of Government.

Kumama replied that he would most certainly be able to recognise him as the fullest descriptions about him had been handed down generation after generation from Jesus. If the descriptions given were exact then only would he hand over the keys of Jerusalem and surrender this Holy city without any further fighting.

Abu Ubaidah, in consultation with his co-generals Khalid bin Walid; Yazid bin Abu Sufyan and Abdur Rahman bin Abu Bakr sent a full account to Khalifa Omar at Madinah and declared a truce pending his arrival.

The message was delivered in Madinah a few days later after morning prayers by the messenger to Omar at "Masjid-e-Nabavi" (The mosque where the Prophet's body has been laid to rest in Madinah). The message was read out instantly by Omar and public opinion was sought.

Osman opined that there was absolutely no necessity for Omar to leave Madinah and take the trouble to go to Jerusalem as its defenders would sooner or later have to surrender or suffer the consequences. That would be a complete humiliation for the Nazarenes.

Ali bin Abu Talib disagreed and said it would be a bad policy to crush the spirit of the vanquished. Instead, by acceding to such a simple request of the People of Jerusalem, it might open their hearts and win them over. Love was better than might. That was the repeated example set by the Holy Prophet Muhammad.

Omar accepted the opinion of Ali. In the next few days he made necessary arrangement of the Government, appointed Ali in his place as Khalifa (viceroy) during his absence and explained to him all affairs of the State. Then he set out from Madinah for Jerusalem in March 637 A.D. or Rajjab 16 A. H. taking with him:

1. A camel
2. A slave named Aslam bin Barkha
3. A large leather pouch for carrying water
4. A packet of dates
5. A packet of "*Sattu*" (*i.e.* barley or gram crushed into powder which could be eaten without further cooking but only after adding some water).
6. He tied a metal plate on his back.
7. He did not even take a tent on the journey or extra clothes for changing or wearing.

Some of the people of Madinah accompanied him on the first day's journey, a few on the second day also, whilst the rest returned to Madinah after the third day's journey. Omar and his slave pressed on unaccompanied towards Jerusalem, with the minimum stoppages enroute.

There is no difference whatsoever between the human rights of a Master and a slave under Islamic rule. Accordingly on the first day the President or Caliph Omar rode on the camel, whilst his slave led the camel walking on foot. Therefore on the next day Omar, President of Arabia, led the camel on foot, whilst his slave rested on the back of the camel. In this manner they continued their journey till they reached the Muslim camp outside Jerusalem.

Still, as soon as it was known that Omar, the Great, was marching from Madinah, everybody who was a disbeliever literally trembled with awe, even though his whole retinue comprised only his slave and his camel. There was no pomp or even bodyguards!

When news filtered in that Omar was coming some of the Muslim generals went to meet him. When Omar saw them wearing garments made of the finest silk, he remarked expressing his deep dissatisfaction: "So soon after the Holy Prophet's passing away have you fallen into the Persian habits of luxury and easy living? How can Islam progress with such leaders as you?"

The Muslim army were very much concerned at the thought of what the dwellers of Jerusalem would think of the Muslim Kingdom if they saw their great awe-inspiring chief and president in Omar's shabby attire, his tattered clothes with patches all over, leading a camel with his slave riding on the camel, as his entire retinue. Because by rotation it was the day on which by turn the slave was to ride the camel and Omar was to lead it on foot!

Therefore they quickly brought the finest Turkish charger and handsome dress of valuable materials and kept on pleading with him to put it on just once for only a few hours. Much against his wishes and with the greatest reluctance he put on the gorgeous robes over his own humble dress.

The Turkish horse started to prance as soon as Omar mounted on its back. He realised at once that what he had done would make him proud and arrogant and the unruly behaviour of the animal reminded him that he was acting contrary to the "*Sunnah*"—the teachings and examples of the Holy Prophet Muhammad. So he quickly jumped off the horse and threw off the beautiful silken garments exclaiming: "Miserable things to make one vain and haughty".

He then ordered his slave to get onto the back of the camel and taking its rope in his hand led it to the gates of Jerusalem without any further arguments!

Kumama, the high priest, stood on the top of the wall of Jerusalem examining from the scroll in his hands all the details given by Jesus about Omar, the second President of the followers of the Promised Prophet and after satisfying himself he asked: "*Who is the great Caliph Omar, the man leading the camel or the one sitting on its back and what is the relation between the two of them?*"

The reply was the man leading camel is Omar, the President of Islam, and the man riding it is his slave, Aslam.

Then Kumama enquired: "*Why is the master leading the camel and his slave riding it?*"

The Muslims replied that under Islam there was no distinction between a Master and his slave as far as human rights, equality, justice, prayers, penance, fasting, food or clothing are concerned. They are both alike. The Master is to treat his slave in the same way as he treats himself and his wife and children in all matters. Since, on the previous day, Omar had ridden on the back of the camel and his slave Aslam had led it on foot, so today it was

Aslam's turn to ride on the camel and Omar was to lead it on foot.

Then Kumama, after consulting the scroll in his hands, asked: *"Please count the number of patches on Omar's clothes and tell whether some of the patches are of leather?"* After the counting he was told that there were fourteen patches including several of leather.

The people of Jerusalem marvelled at the courage of this simple man, who had come alone all the way from Madinah through many a conquered town enroute without guards. They were all filled with awe and literally trembled at his sight.

Kumama publicly declared from the walls "Oh citizens of Jerusalem! Read, here is the original Aramaic Hebrew notings on this scroll recording the foretelling's of Jesus concerning the surrender of Jerusalem. Read it for yourselves and you will find that the man outside our gates is the leader of the followers of Ahmed, the Promised Prophet, and is the man to whom this city shall fall according to the foretelling's of Jesus. You may do what so ever you like, but you will not be able to defend Jerusalem against him according to the warning of Jesus. I have tested and checked everything from father's name, his position as head of the religion of the Promised Prophet Ahmad, the manner in which he will arrive leading a camel with his slave resting on the camel, the tattered clothes he would be wearing with more than a dozen patches even though he is the ruler of the Muslim Empire and details of his face, features, colour of skin and his principles of justice towards the weak i.e. his helpless slave, are all tallying with what Jesus had said and recorded in this hand written scroll in Hebrew in Aramaic Script.

"Under such circumstances there is no option but to surrender the city. *Tell me, Oh elders of the city, if you all agree to follow the advice of Jesus.* That seems to me to be the best and only course left open to us".

They all agreed. Then Kumama came down from the walls. The gates of Jerusalem were thrown open. Kumama personally handed over the keys of the city to Omar in token of surrender. (If anyone is interested in further details he may consult pages 308 to 316 of *"Tarik Waquedi Kamil"* in Urdu published by Nevalkisore Press, Lucknow).

First of all Omar, followed by the crowds of dwellers, went to the temple. On approaching the arch of David, he recited some verses from the Qur'an which speak of the Prophet King David as bowing down to God. He then prostrated himself in humble adoration to Allah.

Thereafter he called Kumama, the high priest, and asked him to show him where to pray in the temple of Jerusalem. Kumama pointed to the "Shakhrah", the sacred stone left by the ancient Prophets. The impressed crowds watched him pray there also. He visited reverentially the sites sacred to the Jews as also to followers of Jesus and also prayed there *because the Muslims believe in and respect all the earlier Prophets!*

As a large number of Military Officers and Provincial Governors had gathered there, Omar prolonged his sojourn in the Holy City of Jerusalem for many days and issued various necessary orders, which impressed the Nazarenes as they were full of justice, equality and forgiveness especially towards them and preserved their rights and privileges.

So great was the impact of the visit of Omar to Jerusalem on the advice of Ali and so great the opportunity to the believers of Jesus to study the teachings of Muhammad at close quarters in great detail, that very soon crowds of Nazarenes with their priests started converting to Islam, *realising that the mission of Jesus was to foretell of the coming of "Ahmad, Muhammad, the Comforter of the world, the Promised prophet".* Since the Promised Prophet had come so they had to abandon the previous teachings of the

Evangel, which had been burnt and destroyed by Emperor Constantine in 325 A.D., and follow this Promised Prophet if they desired their salvation.

Not only the Nazarenes spread over the Middle East, Iraq, Iran, Egypt and North Africa, but also the pagans living in nearby areas were so absorbed by the lofty ideals of Islam and the wonderful conduct of its President in tattered humble clothes giving equality to all including even slaves that it shook their conscience. They realised here was something which was undreamt of so far and was practised actually by Islam. It was universal brotherhood of love for all. This caused the inhabitants of these areas to participate in a storm of conversions to Islam. Thus Islam spread like wild-fire from mouth to mouth. Everyone hearing its wondrous principles and teachings realised it was incomparably better than any other religion on the face of the earth from the time of Adam.

Thus Islam spread to China and India in the East, to Morocco and Spain in the West and to Abyssinia, Somali, and East Africa in the South. A short period of about three decades saw people of all the known continents, of colours from black, brown, yellow, to fair and white, speaking a variety of tongues, having different manners and customs, bonded together in the common brotherhood of Islam for the first time in the history of mankind since the curse of God on Nimrod, which broke up the unity of the human race at the tower of Babel. Such a spread of love and goodwill between man and man, irrespective of caste or colour or nationality had never taken place before.

The last of the Heavenly books confirms the mission of Jesus as follows:

> "And when Jesus, son of Mary said: O Children of Israel! Lo! I am the messenger of Allah (come) unto you (*i.e.* the Jews), confirming that which was (revealed) before me in the Torah

and bring glad tidings of a messenger (*i.e.* the Holy Prophet Muhammad), who cometh after me, whose name is Ahmad (this is the other of the two popular names of the Holy Prophet Muhammad). Yet when he hath come unto them (*i.e.* the children of Israel and the followers of Jesus) with clear miracles, (many of them) they say: This is mere magic.

"He (Allah) it is who hath sent His messenger with the guidance and the religion of Truth, that He (Allah) may make it superior over all other religions, however much the disbelievers are averse" (Qur'an 61: 6 and 9).

It was on the basis of these passages of the Qur'an that the Nazarenes accepted Muhammad as the Promised Comforter of the world, who would be the spirit of truth and would perfect the religion which was left incomplete by Jesus.

L. Why the Jews hated Jesus

One day about the end of his tenure on earth, Jesus was in the temple of God at Jerusalem, when this incident took place.

"Jesus answered: 'As God liveth, I have not the devil at my back, but I seek to cast out the devil. Wherefore, for this cause the devil stirreth up the world against me, because I am not, of this world, but I seek that God may be glorified, who hath sent me into the world. Harken therefore to me, and I will tell you who hath the devil at his back.

"If I work iniquity, reprove me and God will love you, because ye shall be doing His will, but if none can reprove me of sin it is a sign that ye are not sons of Abraham as ye call yourselves, nor are ye incorporate with that head wherein Abraham was incorporate. As God liveth, so greatly did Abraham love God, that he not only brake in pieces the false idols and forsook his father and mother (see *Destruction or Peace*, Chapter 6: E and F), but was willing to slay his own son in obedience to God (see *Destruction or Peace*, Chapter 7: F)"

"The high priest answered: "This I ask thee, and I do not seek to slay thee, wherefore tell us: who was this son of Abraham?

"Jesus answered: The Zeal of thine honour, O God, enflameth me, and I cannot hold my peace. Verily I say, the son of Abraham was Ishmael, from whom must be descended the Messiah promised to Abraham, that in him should all the tribes of the earth be blessed'.

Then was the high priest wroth, hearing this and cried out: 'Let us stone this impious fellow, for he is an Ishmaelite and hath spoken blasphemy against Moses and against the law of God'.

"Whereupon every scribe and Pharisee, with the elders of the people, took up stones to stone Jesus, who vanished from their eyes and went out of the temple. And then, through the great desire that they had to slay Jesus, blinded with fury and hatred, they struck one another in such wise that there died a thousand men, and they polluted the holy temple. The disciples and believers, who saw Jesus go out of the temple (for from them he was not hidden), followed him to the house of Simon" (pages 457-459, *The Gospel of Barnabas*).

Hence the Jews hated Jesus, because he openly declared that the "Saviour" who will come will be from the children of Ishmael *i.e.* Muhammad.

Thus it will be clear the sacred mission of Jesus was not only to reveal the Evangel and correct the Mosaic Laws but also to announce to the world and to prepare the way for the coming of the Saviour *i.e.* Muhammad, the Splendour of God and His Messenger for whom the entire universe has been created. As such Jesus is the harbinger of the good tidings that the prophet after him is Muhammad, the Promised Prophet of the final period.

Chapter 11

The Fruits of Disobedience to Holy Jesus

It is well known that the curse of Allah fell upon King Nimrod at the tower of Babel, and broke up the unity of mankind by causing disputes, fights and separations. As long as this accursed religion continues to exist, *there must be disunity, and the destruction of man by man.*

If Christianity is the real religion of Jesus and not that of the cursed King Nimrod then the historical records of the past 2000 years should surely show that with the spread of Christianity has also developed unity which tends to make mankind into a single brotherhood of love and peace, irrespective of a person's birth, colour, status, culture or nationality.

A. Some of the consequences

Was St. Paul right in what he did? Could he have had any authority from Jesus? These are the questions posed in one's thoughts. The very last sentences of the Holy Bible give us the answers:

> "For I testify unto every man that heareth the words of the prophecy of this book, if any man shall add unto these things, God shall add unto him the plagues that are written in this book:
>
> "And if any man shall take away from the words of the book

of this prophecy, God shall take away his part out of the book of life, and out of the Holy city, and from the things which are written in this book" (Revelation 22: 18-19).

If this is correct then St. Paul and his followers must have suffered from the curse of Allah. Now let us refer to a very few instances out of many.

1. Disputes between the Nazarenes and the Brethren

There were very serious disputes around 61/62 A.D. between St. John and the 112 followers of Jesus (Acts 11: 2-3: 15: 1-2 and 24) now known as Nazarenes, as well as St. Paul and the dissidents including St. Peter and their "Brethren", who had increased to many thousands by about 60 A.D. This dispute took such a violent form that in 62 A.D., St. John, the 112 Nazarenes and their followers had to flee for their lives from Judea into Syria and other countries.

2. The Death of St. Paul in Rome

"The Encyclopaedia Americana", Edition of 1956 Vol. 24, page 160, shows that Paul was arrested, punished and beheaded in 64/65 A.D. at Rome, under orders of Nero. If St. John was in the wrong and not Paul, then surely St. John would have been arrested, punished and beheaded!

3. The cause for the Two Destruction of Jerusalem

When Jerusalem was filled with followers of Tammuz or Nimrod, what happened? Jerusalem was razed to the ground and obliterated in 607 B.C. by king Nebuchadnezzar. Now Jerusalem was once again full of the Brethren after the flight of St. John and the Nazarenes. The faith of the Brethren was the same Nimrodic faith for which Jerusalem was destroyed earlier. So God's curse again fell on the Brethren. Jerusalem was once again destroyed and razed to the ground in 70 A.D. by the Romans. Thus Jerusalem was destroyed twice for the same cause *i.e.* because its populace took to Nimrodism, once under the name of Baalism and then under the name of "Brethren". Does this not open one's eyes to the curse in the last sentences of Holy Bible quoted above?

Are any more examples still necessary?

4. The Last Warnings of St. John

Approximately twenty five years later St. John cautions the followers of Jesus to stay far away from the religion of Nimrod of Babylon and warns that this religion (which had been given a new shape by Paul and Peter and their Brethren) would not only delude the world, but eventually it would also lead to its annihilation after seven Empires have come and gone (Revelation Chapter 17 and 18).

5. The Disunity of the Church

If the Brethren faith was true then like the Nazarenes they would have remained united as one religion with Jesus as its author. But already in the second century, it was split up into three segments *viz*: The churches of Rome, Antioch and Alexandria.

6. The cause of Disunity

On page 44 of "*Islam and Christian Theology*" by J. Windrow Sweetman, part 1, vol. 1, published in 1945 by Lutterworth Press, London and Redhill one reads:

> "And someone had described the third century as one of the most unhappy of the beginnings of the controversy about the relation of the Son of God to the Father. The question of the divinity of Christ took first place in theological discussion ...

but the problem was raised as to how this recognition of Christ as Saviour and this worship of Him as Lord could be explained in relation to a religion which had asserted at the cost of its own blood a pure monotheism against the polytheism of the Roman world? Eusebius says that during the years of peace which preceded the Diocletian persecution, the Church fell on evil days and showed signs of degeneracy".

If the Church was adhering to the doctrines of Jesus during the third century then there could be no scope for disunity but if it was following the cursed religion of Nimrod of Babylon then there was no chance of unity. What do facts show? Which religion was the church following? The religion of Jesus of Nazareth or some other Jesus?

B. The Curses due to the Burning of the Evangel

At the Nicaean Council of 325 A.D., Emperor St. Constantine decided in favour of the "Trinity in unity" theory advocated by St. Athanasius. In spite of this, Arius persisted that God is Alone and Jesus is inferior because he is a created being, whilst God has never been created but is an everlasting identity from eternity to eternity. He proved this from the original manuscripts in his possession containing the Evangel in Hebrew Aramaic script recorded by Levi and St. John. Therefore Arius was exiled by Constantine at the suggestion of Athansius and all the original documents in the possession of Arius were seized and burnt.

If the real teachings of Jesus were burnt, then God's curse would fall positively. Did it so happen?

1. St. Athanasius

History shows that Allah's curse fell on St. Athanasius. He was exiled five times. At one time, with a price on his head, he had to spend seven years in the deserts of South Egypt, and this caused the loss of his eye-sight (page 27 of "*A popular History of the Catholic Church*" by Philip Hughes Universe Book Edition of 1958 published by Burn Oates and Washbourne Ltd, London). Thus St. Athanasius spent his life haunted by the curse of God because of the part he played in burning the *original Evangel of the Real Jesus.*

2. Emperor St. Constantine

Emperor Constantine, in spite of being raised to sainthood by the Church, did not escape from the curse of Allah either as will be clear from the fact that;

His death was that of a pagan Pontifex Maximus according to the *Cambridge Medieval History* Vol. IV-The Byzantine Empire, Part 1, Byzantium and its Neighbours—Edition 1966. On page 2 commencing from line 18 it states:

> "Nothing is more striking in the Eusebian account than the strongly pagan and traditional features of the ceremonial which attended the death of Constantine. The ritual which surrounded the "sacred" palace and the Emperor's DIVINE person can be traced back to the ruler-worship of the ancient East".

In other words he died the death of Nimrod the cursed! The Roman Senate even placed him among the pagan gods (page 479 of "*Babylon the Great has fallen!*" by The Watch Tower Bible & Tract Society).

3. The Destruction of the Roman Empire

Constantine had devoted his whole life and energy to mould the Roman Empire into a single united power. But the curse of Allah made him undo what he had achieved. He divided the Roman Empire, on his deathbed, between his three sons Constantine, Constantius and Constans.

This cursed action caused a continuous civil war between the Armies of the three rival *Emperors*. Thus, much of the old Roman world vanished permanently during the chaos and confusion that followed. This act of Constantine laid the very foundations for the total destruction of the Roman Empire. Famine and plagues followed. To maintain a strong army in these conditions meant inflation, devaluation, and heavy taxation.

The Governors of the distant provinces, owing to the weak Central Governments could act independently—thus causing a breakup of the Roman Empire.

Recruitment to the Roman forces became a permanent problem, which taxed all the resource of the Empire. This made necessary the recruitment of barbarians in the army. These Barbarian generals eventually took over the Western Empire and set themselves up as Kings. Thus started the Dark Ages of Europe!

4. The Dark Ages

As a curse for burning of the Original Evangel of Jesus, which was a light of Allah for the guidance of Mankind, the whole of Europe was severely punished and plunged into the Dark Ages—a thousand years of agony, of groping in the dark without any light or guidance!

5. The Church in Christendom

The following frank confession is found on page 188 of "*Life Everlasting in Freedom of the sons of God*" by the Watch Tower Bible and Tract Society (1966).

> "For the past sixteen centuries (since 325 A.D.), since the founding of what is called Christendom, there have been conflicts between the various religious organisations of Christendom and the political powers or authorities, between

the ecclesiastical powers and the secular powers. True, there have been marriage unions of Church and state, but even within such marriage of the religious clergy and the politicians there have been struggles to determine who is or should be on top, the Church or the State, as to whether the Church should bow to the will of the State or the State to the will of the Church. The Church-State difficulty is not yet settled altogether, the ways of keeping friendly relations varying from country to country, but with difficulties increasing due to the rise of powerful Communist Governments".

It is evident that the Christians have not yet shaken off the curse that fell upon them in 325 A.D. when they deliberately burnt the Original Evangel dictated by Jesus and recorded by Levi during his lifetime and by St. John a few years later.

C. The Cause of the downfall of Emperor Heraclius

The Western Roman Empire had long ago come under barbarian control owing to the curse of the burning of the Evangel. The Eastern Roman Empire was in a chaotic state around 610 A.D. The advent of Heraclius (610-641 A.D.) at the head of an army from North Africa did not end the tale of disasters which followed Constantine's decision to divide the Roman Empire among his three sons. The first ten years of Heraclius' reign witnessed sensational Persian triumphs, unequalled since the days of the Achaemedes. Antioch fell in 611, Jerusalem in 614, and the conquests of Syria and Palestine were followed shortly by that of Egypt. Heraclius at one point even contemplated a return to Carthage. In this condition of mind he had the treasures, taken by the Romans from the temple of Jerusalem in 70 A.D., opened. To his great surprise he discovered from these certain records, which said that these would be opened by him when he would be in his present desperate condition. They also contained the advice that he should become the follower of the Promised Prophet, who would be a descendant from the brethren tribe to the Jews and had already begun his preachings. If he obeyed this advice he would regain all his lost territories, but if he did not accept the Promised Prophet then he would lose them again. Also he would find description of this prophet in the last sheet in the golden casket, "*Sakina*".

This gave him renewed confidence. In a series of brilliant campaigns, based largely on the North-Eastern region of Asia-Minor, Heraclius shattered finally the military might of Persia around 629 A.D. and regained Syria, Palestine and Egypt.

His failure to convert to the religion of Islam as required by Jesus of Nazarene or true followers soon cost him his regained Empire, when the Muslims took over Syria, Palestine and even Egypt by 641/642 A.D. We have seen reports earlier of his attempt find the truth (see *Destruction or Peace*, Chapter 13: J). Does not all this speak for itself for one who thinks?

D. The Crusades

The Latin word "*Crux*" means "a cross". Hence Crusade stands for a Holy war of the Cross. There were at least six military and two children's Crusades by the Church.

1. The Causes leading to the Crusades

Fierce pagan Turanian nomads from Turkestan overran a large portion of the Muslim East during the eleventh century. These Seljuk Turks, as they were known, demolished beautiful cities, massacred their population by the millions and burnt down their Islamic libraries containing valuable books, records and literature, most of which have been lost to the world forever.

After causing unimaginable destruction and bloodshed, it dawned upon these barbarous Turks that they were ruining a culture far more advanced than their own. This realisation made them give up their pagan Nimrodic religion. They circumcised themselves and became devout Muslims, surrendering their lives to the Will of Allah.

These new rulers were shocked to find that in Jerusalem, the Christians were following their previous pagan faith of:

a. Trinity in Unity.

b. The blasphemy of calling a created being the only begotten son of God.

c. Idolatry.

d. Baptism instead of circumcision.

e. Instead of following the Mosaic Laws as taught by Jesus they were following the religion of Nimrod.

f. The sign of the Cross of Tammuz (Nimrod) to ward off evil.

Naturally they protested against these Nimrodic teachings. By presenting the Qur'an they, showed, what the real teachings of Jesus were! They also quoted therefrom that mischief-makers would corrupt the teachings of Jesus and blaspheme against God in his name. Further that Jesus would disown such idolaters on the Day of Judgment. That they as Muslims believed in Jesus as one of the great Prophets. They also accepted his miraculous birth and the other miracles performed by him as mentioned in the Qur'an (as read in *Destruction or Peace*, Chapter 10: A-O).

This protest of the Seljuk Turks simply frightened the Christian Churches. They knew that if this truth came out from Palestine through the Christian pilgrims visiting Jerusalem, then all would be lost for Christianity. It would be revealed that Emperor St. Constantine and St. Athanasius had burnt the Original Evangel together with the Gospel of St. John, and his other works, all in Hebrew Aramaic script, in 325 A.D. That all the books and records on Mithraism were burnt within the next 50/75 years with the backing of the Roman Emperors, so much so that except for excavations no other records were left in Europe or North Africa to show that Christianity was nothing but Mithraism. They were most apprehensive of the fact that Nazarenes, the true followers of Jesus had converted to Islam according to the advice and teachings of Jesus some 250 years earlier. The Christian Churches were very much afraid that if these truths became known to the Christians then they would also convert to Islam. That would be the death knell of Christianity!

Therefore these truths had to be suppressed and kept concealed from the Christian public. That was the sole reason for which the Church decided that Islam, the religion of Surrender to the will of Allah, must be removed in order to save their corrupted religion. Hence to prevent the truth from becoming known to the Christians a campaign of hate against Muslims was started even in spite of the fact that the Muslims are believers in Jesus. This hatred for Islam is still prevalent today. Why?

Accordingly crusades or holy wars of the Cross to perpetuate the sign and initial "*Tau*" or upright cross of Tammuz (Nimrod) were launched by the Church without any logical justification whatsoever except for the suppression and destruction of the truth!

2. The Primary Crusade

Peter, the Hermit of Amiens, Walter the Penniless, and other fanatics led an army of about 10,000 strong in 1096 A.D. They were deceived by the Church into believing that because their cause was right, God would give them an easy and convincing victory. They went through Hungary and Byzantium into Asia Minor. Here they were cut to pieces by a small force of Muslim frontier guards. Thus it became obvious that if their cause was divine or right, then they should have defeated easily the few Muslim Guards they had encountered.

3. The First Crusade

This shocking result, instead of opening the eyes of the Christians to the truth, made them still more fanatic. Accordingly a fully equipped, armed and trained army of 30,000 soldiers was prepared under French Generals in 1096 A.D.

"Man proposes, Allah disposes". The Christian clergy were out to hide the truth of Allah's religion of surrender to His will. But Allah wanted the Christians to know Islam from close quarters, so that on the Day of Judgment the Christians would not be able to deny their knowledge of the existence of the religion of "Surrender to His will". Therefore a period of about 88 years saw them in constant contact with Muslims.

This contact eventually became the cause of the end of the Dark Ages of Europe. It was indeed one of the best opportunities given to the Christian Crusaders by Allah.

This army fought their way through Asia Minor. They took Antioch in 1098 and finally captured Jerusalem in July 1099. The Crusaders celebrated this victory outside the walled sacred city by riding their horses through the blood and over the bodies of the slaughtered Muslims. Was this the way for a religious people to celebrate or were these Christian crusaders the worst type of pagan barbarians? Were these the teachings of Jesus or of Nimrod of Babylon?

Could such victory ever last? Can it not be compared to the recent forcible creation of Israel by Christians over the blood of the innocent Arabs? Something that they could not do through the numerous Crusades they are now trying to do through the

Jews. Can such victories bring about a permanent peace for any length of time in the Holy lands? Does one imagine for a moment that victory through bombs, guns and military strategy is greater than the might of Allah? Will not history repeat itself? Will not justice prevail eventually? Are these the ways to achieve International Peace and Goodwill? Do such questions require an answer? Will not Allah's will prevail ultimately? Has it not so happened in the past?

The Catholic kingdom of Palestine was set up with Jerusalem as its capital by the force of arms and bloodshed. Godfrey of Bouillon was made king under the title of "Defender of the Holy Sepulchre". Their main object seemed attained. The *"Tau"* for Tammuz (Nimrod) had displaced Islam, the religion of "Surrender to the Will of Allah" in the Holy land. For almost 88 years from 1098 A.D. to 1187 A.D. Jerusalem remained a captive city. in the hands of these barbarian horse-riders who celebrated their military victories by riding over the blood and bodies of the slaughtered Muslims. This is what Israel is also doing to-day with the backing of the Christian Nations!

To perpetuate their hold upon Palestine there now sprang up the most striking of all the institutions of medieval Catholicism— the religious orders whose members were not priests but soldiers, vowed to poverty, chastity and obedience. They were the defenders by the sword of the Holy Places for Christianity. The most famous of these were the Knight Hospitallers and the Knights of the Temple. Thus everything conceivable according to human intelligence and military strategy had been done. Yet what was the final outcome?

4. The Second Crusade

After about 48 years of Christian rule over Jerusalem came the news that Muslims were winning back the Holy Land. Bernard of

Clairvaus called for the second great Crusade. The call was answered by the Kings of Europe. Romans, Germans, and the French responded. The Holy Roman Emperor Conrad III decided to attack from one side with his German knights, whilst King Louis VII of France would do so from the other. This was in 1147-48 A.D. Their joint armies totalled over a million and a quarter soldiers. Against them were only 4000 Muslim slaves. The Muslim soldiers were on leave for the "Eid" Holidays when this surprise attack was made by the might and strength of entire Europe. So well did these personal slaves of the Muslim Ruler fight, that the Christians were routed, in spite of their numerical superiority of 300 Christians to every single Muslim. Does this not show on whom Allah's curse fell to make the second Crusade a complete fiasco in spite of the overwhelming odds in their favour! Does it require any imagination to realise that it was the curse of Allah which was still hounding the Christians?

Was this not the curse on Nimrodism from the Tower of Babel?

5. The Third Crusade

Saladin, an Armenian Kurd educated at Damascus, a devout Muslim, a cultured gentleman, an able statesman, and a brave warrior captured Jerusalem in 1187 A.D., along with nearly all the cities around it. He declared the city open to all Jewish and Christian Pilgrims from any part of the world who would be allowed to come freely and practise their faith in whatever manner they liked.

Christian Europe was roused from end to end. All the Kings of Europe including England joined in this Crusade. Armies several millions strong were collected, trained and equipped.

Emperor Frederick Barbarossa going overland with his army

through Asia Minor tasted Allah's curse by being drowned whilst crossing a river. His army was scattered!

King Philip Augustus of France and Richard I, "The Lion Heart", King of England went together by sea. But Allah's curse which caused disunity amongst mankind at the Tower of Babel fell upon them. The two kings quarrelled and Philip soon returned home from the Holy Land!

Saladin informed Richard that he had already declared Jerusalem open to Christian and Jewish pilgrims if they came unarmed. But armed Crusaders and their knights would not be permitted to enter Jerusalem. Richard remained and fought bravely but he failed to regain control of Jerusalem. Hence Richard had to return from the Holy land deeply disappointed without being able to visit the sacred places! Was this not a curse for King Richard of England?

The curse of the Lord continued to haunt Richard. When this brave Crusader King was returning from the Holy Land, instead of being revered and honoured by the Christians he was captured by the Christians and imprisoned! Can this ever be a reward for one who was pursuing a holy cause—an imprisonment by the Christians for 6 or 7 years? Eventually he had to be located and subsequently ransomed! He reached his kingdom after his Crusade in 1199 A.D. only to die shortly after, thus the curse of Allah haunted the Christians!

6. The Fourth Crusade

An extract on Pope Innocent III who was responsible for this Crusade is given hereunder from page 265 under Chapter 22 of "*A History of Europe*" by H. A. L. Fisher, Warden of New College, Oxford, published by Houghton Miffin Co., Boston (1939) by kind permission of Curtis Brown Ltd., London:

"The Pontificate of Innocent III"

"As we cross the threshold of the thirteenth century the dream of world dominion, which had died with an Emperor, springs to life again in the policy a Pope. We come to Innocent III, the proud Roman patrician and trained canonist, who, reaching the Papal chair at the early age of thirty-seven years and profiting by a temporary eclipse of the Empire, brought the Papacy to the summit of its power. This is the Pope under whose rule the Western Church was imposed upon Constantinople, who dared place England and France under interdict, who launched the most successful of the Spanish crusades, who exacted from the rulers of England, Aragon, and Portugal the surrender of their respective countries as fiefs to be held of the Holy See, and did not scruple first to excommunicate King John, and then when the culprit had made an abject submission, to set aside the *Magna Carta* and to excommunicate the barons by whom it was supported. It was this energetic ruler who cleared the Germans out of central Italy and Sicily, made himself master of Rome, preserved against dangerous opposition the Sicilian inheritance of his ward, the child, Frederick, fomented a terrible civil war in Germany, and then made and unmade emperors on terms most favourable to the Roman Church, and finally crushed out the formidable Albigensian heresy in Southern France, and with it the civilization of a brilliant people".

In 1201 Pope Innocent III called for a further Crusade. This mighty Catholic army with the Pope's blessings went to Venice en route to Jerusalem. From there they made a sudden unexpected attack upon Constantinople, the capital of the Eastern Catholic Roman Empire. These Crusaders sacked Constantinople in 1204 A.D. and massacred its Christian population for several days without even sparing the women and children. The Byzantian Catholics fled for their lives to Western Anatolia. From here these Christians recaptured their Capital in 1261 from the hands of the so-called Holy Crusaders of the Pope. Constantinople never recovered from its destruction by the Roman Catholics. This was the main cause of its fall into Muslim hands in 1453 A.D. Since then it has formed a part of Turkey.

Does this not show what happens as a result of disobeying Jesus and forsaking his religion for Nimrodism? How the curse at the Tower of Babel keeps on haunting Nimrodism or whatever name one may call it!

7. The Fifth Crusade

Frederick, King of Sicily, was elected Emperor in 1212 A.D. by the will of Pope Innocent III. One of the conditions was that he would lead a Crusade. Pope Innocent III died before this was fulfilled. Pope Honorius III (1216) got Frederick to renew his pledge every year. When Gregory IX became the Pope in 1227 he insisted that Frederick fulfil his pledge.

The statement of Frederick is recorded on page 279 of "*The Saracen Blade*" by Frank Yearby, published by Hamilton & Co. (Stafford) Ltd., London in 1963 as follows:

> "But I had one misfortune—gentle Honorius died two years ago" he said, "Since that time I've had to deal with Gregory IX, that same Cardinal Hugo of Asitia from whom I took the Cross. He is Innocent's image. He plagued me so much that in the summer of 1227 I assembled my hosts for the Crusade. But pestilence broke out amongst us—and more than half my forces died. I had put out to sea when I, too, was struck down. When I returned to port, and put myself under the care of my Saracen leeches, His Holiness branded me a liar, said I was not ill, that my preparations were a farce, and excommunicated me".

Does this not show how the curse of Allah again struck the forces of Christianity by reducing the army to half and causing disunity between the Emperor and the Church?

Next summer in 1228 Emperor Frederick went to Jerusalem with his forces. But instead of fighting, he made a pact with the Sultan that he would not cause any damage if he was permitted to go to Jerusalem and get himself crowned King of "Entire Christianity" in the Holy Sepulchre. This would raise his status in the eyes of the Catholics even higher than that claimed by the Pope.

Accordingly he was crowned Emperor of Christendom in the Holy Sepulchre in 1228 A.D.

On his return he found that Papal soldiers had taken over his kingdom! A short war drove them out. Gregory again excommunicated him and endeavoured to rouse Christendom against him but alas in vain!

Do not all these historical facts show how the curse of the Lord haunted the Christians? Could this ever have been possible if the Christians had followed the smallest part of the doctrines of the Real Jesus?

8. The Children's Crusades

The six above-mentioned military Crusades including the Primary one of ten thousand strong in 1096 A.D. proved to be miserable failures. The Holy Land continued to remain in the possession of the Muslims. It was thought by Christendom that what armed men could not accomplish might yet be achieved by innocent children. Two children's Crusades were organised in 1212 A.D. The result of these Holy Crusades was to send some 50,000 European children to their death or into slavery! Many were sold into slavery by those very Christian Ship-Owners, whose fleets were engaged and handsomely paid to carry them to the Holy Land. None of them ever reached their destination! An unparalleled disaster for children of such a magnitude in the history of mankind has never happened. Could such a calamity ever take place if these Christians were following the teachings Holy Jesus? No!

E. The Civilisation of Europe

The Almighty gave the Christians two wonderful opportunities — their 88 years of occupation of Jerusalem and their 800 years of contact in Spain with Muslims.

Thus the Christians were brought into close contact with Muslims. They could attain knowledge from Islam on the two main aspects of human life on earth:

1. Spiritual and religious

2. Material and worldly

As far as the former is concerned, they failed apparently to take advantage of it because of the brain-washing done by the Christian Church's preachings *of "Hate Islam*—the religion of Surrender to the Will of Allah". Any Church advocating hatred to the surrender of one's self to the will and pleasure of the Creator cannot by any stretch of the imagination be a divine religion of goodness. These were not certainly the teachings of the Real Jesus but of course, of Nimrod, the mighty hunter in rebellion against God (Genesis 10:9) *i.e.* Constantine's Christ!

As far as the latter is concerned, the Europeans learned from the Muslims about new plants, new fruits, new colours, new fashions in dress, new designs of houses, new architecture, the manufacture of sugar, spices, rice, lemons, apricots, melon, cotton, muslin, damask, lilac and purple. The manufacture and use of glass, glass mirrors, the mariner's compass, gun-powder, cotton-paper, writing paper, leather and iron goods, swords *etc.* The simple numerals (1, 2, 3, 4, 5, 6, 7, 8, 9 and 0) which we now call Arabic numerals, higher mathematics, Algebra, and many subjects of art and science have thus come into Europe from Muslim sources. Its universities taught culture and became the forerunners of the present European Civilisation.

Finally, the Crusaders' contacts with Muslims contributed to the breakdown of feudalism in Western Europe, to the growth of the middle class, to the strengthening of national monarchies.

Thus it was Islam's influence upon Europe that brought about the end of the "Dark Ages" and established the present civilisation in Europe.

If Islam's material values can bring about the present scientific progress for the European group of Nations from the U.S.S.R. to America as well as China, surely its spiritual and religious teachings of "Surrender to the Will of Almighty Allah" can also bring about "International Peace and goodwill amongst the Nations". Here indeed is food for thought!

F. The Warnings of Jesus

In addition to the few examples quoted, countless more could be cited to show how the Church in Europe has burnt fellow Christians who have died at the stake taking the name of Jesus and how Christianity was spread by the sword and fire. The most vivid example was of the Christian Spaniards when they made forcible conversions of the Central and South American Indians, who were following the Nimrodic religion with the very same principles as their own.

Now to conclude this section let us study only one of the several warnings of Jesus:

"Beware of false prophets, which come to you in sheep's clothing but inwardly they are ravening wolves.

"Ye shall know them by their fruits. Do men gather grapes of thorns or figs of thistles?

"Even so every good tree bringeth forth good fruit, but a corrupt tree bringeth forth evil fruit.

"A good tree cannot bring forth evil fruit, neither can a corrupt tree bring forth good fruit.

"Every tree that bringeth not forth good fruit is hewn down and cast into the fire.

"Wherefore by their fruits ye shall know them.

"Not every one that saith unto me, Lord, Lord, shall enter into the kingdom of heaven; but he that doeth the will of my Father which is in heaven.

"Many will say to me in that day, Lord, Lord, have we not prophesied in thy name? and in thy name have cast out devils? and in thy name done many wonderful works?

"And then will profess unto them, I never knew you: depart from me, ye that work iniquity.

"Therefore whosoever heareth these sayings of mine, and doeth them, I will liken him unto a wise man, which built his house upon a rock.

"And then rain descended, and the floods came, and the winds blew, and beat upon that house; and it fell not: for it was founded upon rock.

"And every one that heareth these sayings of mine, and doeth them not, shall be likened unto a foolish man, which built his house upon the sand:

"And the rain descended, and the floods came, and the winds blew, and beat upon that house: and it fell: and great was the fall of it (St. Matthew 7: 15-27).

If the teaching of St. Paul and the Brethren were correct, then the fruits of their tree would at least be as sweet as those of the

Nazarenes, who remained one united group until they accepted the teachings of the Promised Comforter according to the advice of Jesus and they accepted the religion of "Surrender to the Will of Allah". But if St. Paul, St. Peter and their Brethren were ravenous wolves in sheep-skin then their fruits or followers would break up into different groups and sects and there would be conflicts among them as happened at the Tower of Babel to the people of Nimrod, the cursed. *"In Babylon The Great Has Fallen! God's Kingdom Rules"* by Watch Tower Bible & Tract Society (1963) it is stated as follows on pages 496-498:

> "As the American nation grew and spread from coast to coast its separation of Church and State by the National Constitution resulted in its lands becoming the home of more than two hundred religious sects, all of which professed to be Christian.
>
> "Christendom as a whole became rent apart with religious sects, Roman Catholic, Eastern Orthodox and Protestant. In South Africa 1,400 religious sects have grown up among the Bantu people since 1910, when Christendom's missionaries poured in, according to an Associated Press dispatch from Johannesburg, South Africa, published August 12, 1957. Today the religious situation in Christendom is a mockery of the Christian unity that Christ taught his disciples.
>
> "The Reformation movement of the sixteenth century led to shameful religious persecution by both Protestants and Catholics, and to frightful religious wars.
>
> "The basic religious doctrines of the Roman Catholic Church as well as of the Eastern Orthodox Churches remained, such as the "Trinity", immortality of the human soul, punishment of wicked souls after death in an invisible spirit realm; the division of the religious worshippers into a professional priesthood or clergy and the profane masses or laity; the use of religion in the support of worldly politics, resulting in many Church-State unions, the celebrating of religious holidays

with pagan background; the lack of respect for blood of man and beast, as exemplified in the man who founded Babylon and built the first empire, 'Nimrod a mighty hunter in opposition to Jehovah'. Genesis 10: 8-12; 11: 1-6".

G. Love Thy Neighbour as Thyself

The basic teaching of Jesus has been one of "Love" and "Toleration" towards others. Just let us see how he showed his love even towards the non-Jews. Note how he cured the Centurion's Servant (St. Matthew 8: 5-13; Luke 7: 2-10) or the Syro-Phoenician's daughter (St. Matthew 15: 28; Mark 7: 25-30) and so many other instances. Jesus made no distinction between man and man, irrespective of his cast, colour, nationality, or belief. Hence his teaching "Love thy neighbour as thyself" implies toleration, love and equality to all others irrespective of their caste, colour or creed.

Was the bitter persecution of the Nazarenes by the Brethren in 62 A.D., which caused them to flee for their lives from Judea, according to these teachings of Jesus? Or was the burning of the Hebrew Evangel in 325 A.D. an act of love towards Jesus? Or were the unwarranted repeated attacks of the Crusaders for the destruction of Islam, "the Religion of Surrender to the will of Allah" resulting in the sacking of Constantinople in 1204 A.D. and the Holy Crusaders putting its Muslim population to the sword examples of "Love thy neighbour as thyself"? Or were the destruction of 50,000 innocent European crusading children to death or their enslavement by Christian ship-owners and their Christian ship masters acts of love? Were any of these actions conforming to the doctrines of the real Jesus or for that matter the burning of the French heroine St. Joan of Arc?

Is the apartheid of South Africa, and the denial of the rights to millions of blacks by the few whites of Rhodesia in any manner the teachings of Jesus of "Love Thy Neighbour As Thyself"? Can these Christians by any stretch of the imagination call themselves honestly and conscientiously the followers of *the Real Jesus?*

Does not all this prove beyond doubt that it is Constantine's Christ i.e. Nimrod's teachings of "I am the Infallible Pontifex Maxim" and whatever "I" say must go irrespective of its merits? Is it not "Egoism" of the worst type for each one to insist that whatever he thinks is right and everybody else is wrong, or if someone is correct but weaker then the weaker has no justification to his rights! Is not this "Egoism" responsible for so many unreasonable human calamities caused by Christians? A glance over the last hundred years shows clearly that all the major wars were the result of Christian intolerance and the deprivation of others of their rights owing to disobedience to the teachings of Jesus of "Love Thy Neighbour As Thyself". Just let us think of:

The Crimean War,	1854-1856
The American Civil War,	1861-1865
The Franco-German War, 1870-1871	
The Russo-Turkish War,	1877-1878
The Boer War,	1899-1902
The First Balkan War,	1912-1913
The First World War,	1914-1918
The Second Word War,	1939-1945

H. The Birth of Communism due to denial of "Love thy Neighbour as Thyself"

Was not this "Egoism" of the rich and the powerful Christians, the cause of the French Revolution?—the denial of the rights of the poorer Christians—the labourers and the peasants! As forecast by

Karl Marx—the denial of "Love thy Neighbour As Thyself", became the basis and the seed of the Russian Revolution. The rise and spread of Communism was most marked in those areas where the Nimrodic mentality of Christianity denied the rights of the masses of the poor and the weak.

It is but small wonder that they abhor the name of God, because they feel that it was Christianity that was the cause of their being held in serfdom and poverty! They little realised that Christ of Constantine was none other than Nimrod and as such had nothing whatsoever to do with *the Real Jesus,* who was not the son of a God, but the son of the Virgin Mary, a human being! And who was not Christ—The Trinity in Unity or Nimrod!

That Christianity had supported the rich to the prejudice of the poor and the helpless! Christ and Christianity meant to them the religion of God! Hence this spontaneous hatred for God and the denial of Him.

The anti-religious movement which has taken root in Russia and spread to other European and Eastern Countries is thus based on a misconception that any religion which is from God is unacceptable to them, because of their hatred for Christianity and because of Christianity's claim to be a religion from God. Their three chief objections to religion are:

i. Religion helps in the maintenance of the bourgeois capitalistic system with its consequent crushing of the aspirations of the poor people!

ii. It keeps the people enslaved to superstition and so hinders the advance of sciences and Progress!

iii. It teaches them to pray for their needs, instead of working for them and consequently it makes them indolent!

Unfortunately they did not know and still do not realise that

Christianity is nothing but the religion of Nimrod, who was cursed at the Tower of Babel. Christianity is not a religion from God and *has nothing to do with Jesus, son of Virgin Mary!* That as long as Christianity will prevail in large areas on the face of the Earth, there can be no lasting peace amongst the different groups of mankind. Hence it is their lack of knowledge of the truth that made them use "God" as the scapegoat of their hatred.

The following is an extract from *"Encyclopaedia of Religions"* by J.G.R. Forlong—University Books Vol. 1, page 421 under "Christianity":

> "No single real reform of morals", says Dr. Dollinger, "is due to the Popes; but to them were due the miseries and failures of the Crusades and the loss of Constantinople to the Eastern Church". "Though a sincere Romanist, he confesses that the priests were not only grossly ignorant ...; (to whom concubines were permitted) *but that they were responsible for papal forgeries, and for the violence which condemned whole towns and provinces to slavery.* Their faith he says was not only Tri-Theistic, but idolatrous. Europe has to thank the subjects of the great Arab Khalifs for preserving the ancient learning, and Greek philosophy, and for opposing Christian priests, interested only in childish legends and superstitions. They (the priests) corrupted all that they touched, and whatever truth reached them they converted into 'fabulous monstrosities'."

These historical proofs establish clearly that had Christianity anything to do with a religion from a Godly source then it would not and could not have driven millions of souls to "Communism" or a hatred for God!

I. Oh! What we have believed in is Good Enough!

If these scientifically advanced groups of European Nations from the U.S.S.R. to the U.S.A. to which China may now be added, do not take heed and decide upon changing their ideologies for the truth, nothing but the absolute truth—The Mission of Jesus according to which The Promised Prophet was to complete the religion left incomplete by Jesus—then they are heading for their own destruction! That is the only way to stop their groping in the dark led by their egoism of *"Oh! what we believe in is good enough!"* If Christianity had indeed been good enough, would there have been so many major disasters? Would the world then be faced with the threat of a Third great world war? Therefore, whatsoever the Europeans believe in is certainly not good enough by any means or standards! That this fact is well known to them will be evident from *Destruction or Peace*, Chapter 15: S of this treatise under the heading of "European indicates the Only Solution to bring Capitalism and Communism together" Let us for a moment look at some of the many advices given in the Holy Bible in this connection:

> "I (Jesus) beseech you therefore, (my) brethren, by the mercies of God, that ye present your bodies (including your intelligence and conduct as) a living sacrifice, (making it) holy, (by doing such good deeds as are) acceptable unto God, which is your (minimum) reasonable service, (expected of you towards your Creator).

> "And be not conformed to this (unholy) world (of lusts, iniquity, blasphemers by making a mockery of God's laws as taught by Jesus *i.e.* If anyone commits a sin as small as one jot or tittle and does not follow the Mosaic laws and whose good deeds does not exceed the good deeds of the scribes and Pharisees shall in no case enter into the kingdom of Heaven— St. Matt. 5: 17-19,—disobedient to God by becoming a despiser of those that do good deeds and taunting them with Nimrod's doctrines that those who follow the laws of God are those who hang themselves from a tree, scoffers walking after their own lust and believing in Nimrod's theories of sacramental food and drinks makes one into the pure sinless

son of God hence the boast of: What we are and what we shall be we know not? and that faith in Nimrod's teachings that the only begotten son of God has come on earth to save sinners by the sacrifice of his precious life *etc.*): but be ye transformed by the renewing of your mind (by getting out of your dream of vanity—Oh! what we have believed in for centuries is good enough), that ye may prove what is that good, and acceptable and perfect according to the) will of God.

"For I (Jesus) say through the grace given unto me, to every man that is among you, not to think of himself more highly than he ought to think (about others and their rights and that we are the superior *etc.*); but to think soberly, according as God hath dealt to every man the measure of faith.

"Let love be without dissimulation. Abhor that which is evil (and which we have been believing as good enough—the False Christ of Society who is none other than Nimrod, the accursed, who has been deified by Emperor St. Constantine in the Greek manuscript prepared under his orders when he destroyed the Original Hebrew Evangels at the Nicaean Council of 325 A.D.); cling to that which is good (the pure teaching of the real Jesus of Nazareth—the Jesus who was not the son of a god but the son of a human being *viz*: the Virgin Mary and his teachings referred to above from St. Matt. 5:17-19 that good deeds and following the laws of God are essential instead of sacramental food and drink and faith in Christ, the Saviour)" (Romans 12:1-3 and 9).

Jeane Dixon in her book *A Gift of Prophecy* writes on pages 178-181 :-

"Jeane describes the vision thus: Seated on a throne before fluted marble columns was a gorgeously arrayed Roman Emperor who, with great energy and strength, was hurling bits of food towards far-off throngs of ragged barbarians. The hordes gradually inched closer, seizing on the scattered titbits, while beauty radiated from the exquisite pavilion. Watching intently Jeane noticed that the emperor was beginning to cast the food more carelessly, with less vitality, so that some of it was falling near his feet; and at last the barbarians swept across the pavilion like a swarm of locusts, eradicating all traces of the culture and refinement which it reflected.

"As darkness enveloped the scene, Jeane felt that in a symbolic way she had not only witnessed the decline and fall of the Roman Empire, with the subsequent Dark Ages which obliterated the light of learning, but had also been given a subtle warning that America was similarly draining itself of needed strength by a careless disbursement of foreign aid.

"Jeane turned and stared again at the unspeakable litter covering the pavilion floor, and sensed that she belonged to this; that this was her America. Overwhelmed by a feeling of shame; she watched mutely while smoky gray clouds began to churn the debris about, like matchboxes caught in the funnel of a tornado. She lifted her eyes and noticed that above the murky clouds were even, blacker ones, rolling in angry billows as if sucked by a giant magnet.

"... Jeane interprets this vision as an advance warning that Americans must pay dearly for *the confusion, degradation, and immorality in our political, business, labor, family lives,* for our obsession with material things and our compromises with high principle...

"... This was the present time, and as the gray clouds began to churn I knew that they represented the struggle between the races—a struggle that will dominate the decades of the 1960s and 1970s. After that came the even blacker clouds, representing a horrible war in which many Asian and African nations whom we have helped with foreign aid will join with Red China (or will it be Russia?) to close in on us and, like the barbarians in the vision of ancient Rome, try to destroy our way of life. This will occur during the 1980s and because of a new kind of ... warfare many will die like ants".

Let the European Group of nations from America to U.S.S.R. comprising the so called Christians and ex-Christians realise well that what has not saved them in the past from wars, destruction and devastation cannot save them in the future either! History will surely repeat itself, unless they change their ideology from falsehood to the truth!

From:

The Christ of Constantine and of Society,
who is Nimrod of Babylon.

To

The Real Jesus of Nazareth, who has never claimed divinity.

The Jesus who taught: "In vain do they worship me" (St. Mathew 15: 9).

"The Jesus, who is not the son of a god as claimed by Nimrod but the son of a human being—the Virgin Mary!

The Jesus, who has warned that you cannot attain heaven unless you follow the Mosaic Laws, abstain from sins even as small as a jot or a tittle and unless your good deeds exceed the good deeds of the Scribes and Pharisees! (St. Matthew. 5: 18-21).

The Jesus, who is the harbinger of the glad tidings of the coming after him, of the Promised Comforter of the Universe, the messenger of God who would complete the divine message which was incomplete up till the time of the ascension of Jesus (St. John 16: 7, 12 and 13) .

This treatise is part of the book "Destruction or Peace" originally published in 1971 based on extracts from works of learned scholars, researchers, scientists and several rare manuscripts—among which some are the only copies known to be in existence.

Readers of this book may be surprised at the disclosures made herein and wonder why such vital facts have been suppressed and concealed!

Those of you who are interested in the full and complete book "Destruction or Peace" can obtain a personal copy from

DAR AL WAHI PUBLICATION
House of Revelation (Co. No. 001592307-T)
P.O. Box 12909, 50792 Kuala Lumpur, Malaysia
Email: daralwahi@yahoo.com ▪ Website: www.daralwahi.com

www.ingramcontent.com/pod-product-compliance
Lightning Source LLC
Chambersburg PA
CBHW031311160426
43196CB00007B/489